Introducing Anthropology

Laura:
To my own tribe, with love and thanks for all the support you have given me

Tomislav:
To Karmen, Iris, Lana and Shane with love

'When you do things from your soul, you feel a river moving in you, a joy.'
Rumi

LAURA POUNTNEY &
TOMISLAV MARIĆ

INTRODUCING

ANTHROPOLOGY

polity

First published in 2015 by Polity Press
Reprinted 2016, 2018, 2019 (twice)

Polity Press
65 Bridge Street
Cambridge CB2 1UR, UK

Polity Press
350 Main Street
Malden, MA 02148, USA

ISBN-13: 978-0-7456-9977-6
ISBN-13: 978-0-7456-9978-3 (pb)

A catalogue record for this book is available from the British Library.

Introducing Anthropology
Library of Congress Cataloging in Publication Control Number: 2014047152

Typeset in 9.5 on 13 pt Utopia
by Servis Filmsetting Ltd, Stockport, Cheshire
Printed in Italy by Rotolito S.p.A.

For further information on Polity, visit our website: ww.politybooks.com

Contents

Preface and Acknowledgements

There has been, and there continues to be, a huge effort to promote the subject of anthropology at pre-university level, coordinated in the United Kingdom mainly by the Education Committee of the Royal Anthropological Institute. This campaign goes beyond the UK – for example, to Germany and the United States. This book was possible because of those efforts, which resulted in the establishment of the A-level in anthropology in 2010. Since then, pioneering teachers have been working hard with existing anthropological material to make it accessible. Anthropology has also been successfully taught in access courses and in youth projects. So the subject is very much alive at this level. The current book is intended to present some of the material and activities that have been particularly fruitful.

Those who are already involved with anthropology know that it is a subject that could not be more relevant to contemporary society. At a time when differences between individuals and societies have become ever more significant, this book reflects the experience of many anthropologists and shows that, by understanding 'others' and reflecting on one's own cultural values, a more sensitive and compassionate view of the world can be achieved.

Anthropology is a subject that encourages a non-judgemental and respectful attitude towards others. Nowhere have the effects of this been felt more than in the classroom, where students of a pre-university age come into anthropology with a particular view of the world that may have been informed by all kinds of different opinions, only to leave having become aware of the complexity and value of all human cultures. Students of anthropology not only see the world differently, they also see themselves differently and begin a process of self-awareness that undoubtedly enriches their own lives.

Who is This Book For?

This book is an introduction to anthropology. It is important that readers recognize that it is not intended to cover every area of the subject; rather, it contains selected topics which may be of interest and explores them in an introductory way. Nor does it claim to reach the depth of many undergraduate textbooks. It was written to encourage people to begin to take an active interest in the subject, based on several successful and very enjoyable years of teaching anthropology at pre-university level. The book introduces information about what anthropologists do and explores some of the subject's subfields. It will accompany any introductory course in anthropology.

Many of the topics that have been included have been selected with A-level students and teachers in mind. However, the book will be an excellent guide for those studying the anthropology International Baccalaureate, as well as for first-year undergraduates and anyone wishing to know more about the subject generally. It is hoped that it will provide a starting point from which readers can explore areas of interest in greater depth.

What Makes Us Human?

This question lies at the heart of this book and, indeed, the subject of anthropology. We begin by taking a look at how early humans diverged from other primates, examining some of the important physical changes that occurred as well as some of the features of human cultural evolution. As human physical evolution has helped shape human culture, the role of human biology appears in various places throughout the text.

The rest of the book explores different aspects of human culture, from how people use the body to express their identity through to different ideas about what it means to be a person. There is a focus on contemporary anthropological research, as well as acknowledgements of the contribution of classical anthropological work. It is clear, for example, that new forms of technology are playing an ever greater role in people's lives, and this is reflected in anthropology, where studies are now being carried out in virtual worlds. Also, since globalization affects the vast majority of human societies, there are examples of ethnographic studies relating to the complex effects of this process.

Culture: Universality and Diversity

Given that the book is based predominantly upon cultural anthropology, it is worth thinking for a moment about what culture is. In the simplest terms, culture relates to everything that humans do that goes beyond their biological evolution. However, the degree to which biology shapes human behaviour is much disputed. It might be useful to see culture as the way of life of a particular group. Humans are social beings, and it is only through their relations with others that cultural characteristics become apparent. This book is concerned with cultural universals, things that all social groups do, while at the same time exploring the different ways in which such cultural practices are manifest.

Ethnographic Research

An important difference between anthropology and other disciplines is the centrality of ethnographic methodology. This in-depth, detailed research goes beyond many of the methods found in other disciplines in that it involves so much personal involvement and commitment from the researcher. Anthropologists often spend long periods of time with the people that they study, and this is often within the personal, private spaces of their lives. It is frequently through spending time with people, working, eating and laughing with them, that important anthropological findings occur, more often than not, unexpectedly. Examples of ethnographic research are central here, summarized throughout the book. These are not intended to substitute for the full ethnography; rather, they are simply an introduction to the main research.

How to Use This Book

Anthropologists need a range of skills, and the book is a starting point for these. Each chapter opens with a set of issues and debates about the specific topic followed by an introduction outlining the structure. Theories are not taught as a separate chapter; rather, the theories relating to each specific topic are highlighted in purple. There are key concepts which are also highlighted, and all the chapters offer suggestions for personal investigations.

In every chapter there are important relevant concepts with clear definitions. There are a range of questions throughout the book designed to stimulate anthropological ideas and ways of thinking. At the end of each chapter there is a suggestion for an end of topic essay, with guidance notes. There are also examples of how the topic can be linked to globalization.

The importance of ethnographic research in anthropology is reflected in the structure of the book, which includes many summaries of interesting ethnographic studies. The chapters do not (and could not) convey the sum total of studies and information on their topic; they simply provide examples and introductions to give the reader a starting point in their journey into anthropology.

Acknowledgements

We would particularly like to thank those without whom this book would not have been possible: Marzia Balzani for her time, patience, humour and thoughtful excellent comments; Brian Morris for his enthusiasm for our project, his advice and, most importantly, his belief that anthropology should be accessible to everyone; Thomas Hylland Eriksen, who always found the time to give valuable comments, encouragement and support; Katarina Fritzsche, who has been very supportive of the idea of the project of developing anthropology in pre-university settings; Andrew Canessa for so generously sharing his knowledge and experience and for his attention to detail. Many thanks to all who so generously gave their time to be interviewed and share their stories with us (too numerous to mention, but they appear throughout the book). Everyone who has contributed has surpassed our expectations. This is testament to the subject, which produces the kind of people who have become so much more than creators of new knowledge. Anthropologists have the shared qualities of an excellent sense of humour, life experience and an awareness of the richness of life. This was simply inspiring and motivating.

We are grateful to the following anthropologists and institutions who have been so helpful and supportive: David Shankland, the director of the Royal Anthropological Institute, the Education Committee at the RAI, Dr Edward Liebow, the executive director of the American Anthropological Association, Robin Dunbar, Daniel Miller, James Staples, Gary Marvin, Pat Caplin, Desirée Pangerc, Sarah Pink, Peggy Foerer, Liana Chua, Joy Hendry, Anabella Hendry, Hilary Callan, Theresa McCarthy, Angela Riviere, Emma Pountney, Ben Burt, Nicholas Badcott at the British Museum, the Horniman Museum, the Museum of Archaeology and Anthropology, the Pitt Rivers Museum, Heather Bonney at the Natural History Museum, and the Krapina Neanderthal Museum in Croatia. Thanks also go to the photographers whose pictures make this book so rich and interesting. We would like to thank the staff an Polity, particularly Amy Williams and Jonathan Skerrett, for their hard work and guidance during the editorial process. You have been amazing with your support and understanding.

We also, of course, owe special thanks to our students, who are without doubt the best critics and supporters of our book.

CHAPTER ONE

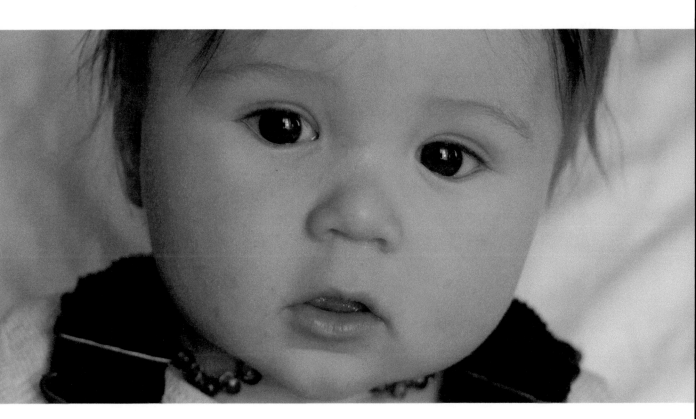

WHAT MAKES US HUMAN?

CONTENTS

What Makes Us Human?

KEY ISSUES AND DEBATES

- How and when did *Homo sapiens* evolve?
- How similar are humans to other animals and in what ways are they different?
- How do we know about early human life?
- What impact has humanity's specific biological evolution had in terms of shaping our cultural evolution: what is the relationship between human biology and culture?
- To what extent do humans vary?

Primate
A mammal of the order Primates, characterized, for example, by refined development of the hands and feet and a large brain

The question of what makes human beings different from all other species is central to anthropology. This chapter explores the particular characteristics that over the past 6 to 7 million years, since they shared a common ancestor with apes, have allowed *Homo sapiens* to become the most successful of the primates. Also, this chapter looks at the behavioural and physical traits that humans continue to share with other primates, such as chimpanzees and bonobos. The study of human origins and of the adaptations that make our species unique defines the field of evolutionary anthropology. The first evolutionary anthropologist was Charles Darwin himself, the creator of the theory of evolution. Evolutionary anthropology has since grown into a multifaceted discipline investigating the origins of humanity through fossils and ancient DNA, genetic analyses, ethnographic work with populations of hunter-gatherers, farmers and pastoralists across the globe, comparative studies of our closest relatives such as apes, and computer simulations. Together, these various approaches are providing an ever improving picture of what make humans unique. Among the many features that distinguish us from other species, perhaps the fundamental difference is the fact that humans have a highly developed culture. Simply put, culture is every aspect of life that goes beyond biology. Although there is evidence of culture in some other species, nowhere is it more complex, rich and evolved as within human societies. So, how did the specific physical evolution of *Homo sapiens* lead to the development of complex culture while that of other species did not? What is the relationship between biological evolution and cultural evolution? If all humans share the same biology, to what extent do they share the same culture? Are there such things as cultural universals?

Cultural evolution
The ways in which humans have evolved beyond their biology

The final section of this chapter explores the extent of biological variations between humans, making a clear distinction between biological differences and socially constructed ideas about race (which are widely criticized).

HOW DID HUMANS EVOLVE?

How do people explain human origins?
How do different groups explain the existence of dinosaurs and other extinct animals?

Explanations of Human Evolution

There have been a number of attempts to explain the origins of the human species. These explanations are of interest in themselves as they reflect the dominant ideas of the times from which they originate. They have also been highly contentious and have provoked a strong response that goes much further than anthropology, to religion, politics and economics.

CREATIONISM AND EVOLUTION

Until the eighteenth century, religion shaped the dominant explanations for the origins of human life. In Europe, these came largely from Genesis, the first book of the Bible. This explanation, known as creationism, was based upon the idea that God had created all life in six days, and that the characteristics of plants and animals were fixed and unchangeable.

That is not to say there was no interest in the great diversity of animal and plant life. Early scientists showed a strong desire to organize different species and locate human beings within classification systems. For example, the Swedish botanist Carl Linnaeus (1707–1778) was among the first to develop a scientific classification of animals and plants, or taxonomy. Linnaeus accepted the biblical explanation of creation, and his classification system is still influential today. This system is based on similarities and differences between species, which Linnaeus argued were part of God's plan.

Creationist ideas are not limited to Christianity. Muslim creationists, for example, base their thinking on similar scientific arguments and on passages such as this in the Qur'an: 'God has created every animal from water. Of them there are some that creep on their bellies, some that walk on two legs and some that walk on four. God creates what he wills for verily God has power over all things' (Sura 24:45). However, fossil discoveries during the eighteenth and nineteenth centuries challenged the ideas central to creationism by proving that different types of life had existed in the past. Creationists responded to these findings by arguing that various forms of catastrophe had occurred, which they claimed had destroyed other ancient species. This branch of creationists, known as catastrophists, argued that events such as the biblical flood involving Noah's Ark destroyed ancient species, after which God had created new species again, leading to contemporary species.

There has recently been a resurgence of creationism. For example, the Discovery Institute, an American non-profit public-policy think tank, has developed a theory known as **intelligent design** (or neo-creationism). This is defined as a belief that the universe could not have been created by chance and that some higher power must have had a hand in it. The effects of this theory have been felt within the public and the political sphere. For example, there has been a lot of debate over the teaching of the origins of human life in schools. Some creationists argue that teachers should explain the origins of human life through creationist ideas only.

Creationism
The belief that all life was created by the actions of God

Taxonomy
The classification of organisms in an ordered system that indicates natural relationships

Fossils
The preserved remains or traces of animals, plants and other organisms from the remote past

Catastrophism
The theory that the Earth has been affected in the past by sudden, short-lived, violent events, possibly worldwide in scope, which have led to the contemporary world with its current variety of animals and plants

SCIENTIFIC EXPLANATIONS OF HUMAN ORIGINS

The Enlightenment and Victorian naturalism

The Enlightenment, which occurred around the eighteenth century, prompted a major revolution in the way Europeans thought of the world in which they lived. Whereas previously the Bible had been relied upon to explain the world, during the Enlightenment people increasingly sought explanations based on science and rational thought. The period coincided with the expansion of Europeans across the world and the discovery of previously unknown people. This diversity of humanity needed explaining somehow, since there were clearly many more people in the world than were described in the Bible.

Later, through the work of nineteenth-century British naturalists influenced by Enlightenment ideals, an alternative explanation to creationism emerged: the idea that new species arose from existing ones through a long and gradual process of transformation, known as evolution. Charles Darwin (1809–1882) is best known for his theory of evolution by natural selection or, in other words, the view that competition for resources (the 'struggle for survival') is both unavoidable and ubiquitous in nature and is the force causing the continuous transformation of living forms.

> **Evolution**
> Any change across successive generations in the inherited characteristics of biological populations

Darwin's theory of natural selection was one of many emerging ideas of the time which attempted to explain the diversity of animals and species found in the world. Alfred Wallace (1823–1913), a naturalist working separately from Darwin at around the same time, had developed a very similar theory. Both Darwin and Wallace presented their ideas to the public in 1858, which caused great controversy because they directly challenged prevailing religious explanations.

What is natural selection?

Natural selection is a process whereby nature selects the forms most likely to survive and reproduce in a particular population. For natural selection to work, there needs to be inheritable (i.e., genetic) variation within populations – which there usually is – as well as competition for resources necessary for life, such as food and space. Those organisms that manage to get copies of their genes into future generations transmit characteristics that continue to evolve through the generations. Over time, the organisms that are less successful in passing on their genes and are less suited to their surroundings gradually die out, while the more successful organisms survive. This process changes according to the environment in which the species exist. Changes to the body that are acquired in the course of life, for example losing a limb, do not get passed on.

> **Natural selection**
> The process in nature by which, according to Darwin's theory of evolution, only the organisms best adapted to their environment tend to survive and transmit their genetic characteristics in increasing numbers to succeeding generations, while those less well adapted tend to be eliminated

Sexual selection

In order to leave descendants, individuals must not only survive but also reproduce. As a supplement to the principle of natural selection, Charles Darwin developed the idea of sexual selection to attempt to explain the presence of characteristics of male animals, such as the elaborate tails of peacocks or deep voices in men, claiming that these secondary sexual characteristics evolved not because they increase the survival prospects of individuals, but because females preferred to mate with individuals that had those features. If this is the case, then preferred mates are more likely to have those specific characteristics passed on to future generations.

In birds, for example, the first form of sexual selection occurs when males compete for particular territories. A bird that manages to get the best location is more likely to be chosen as a mate. Geoffrey Miller (2000) develops Darwin's ideas and argues that

The peacock's tail is an example of female preference driving the evolution of longer, more colourful tail feathers. (Amanda Grobe / Wikimedia Commons)

human culture arose through a process of sexual selection. He argues that there are many characteristics of human culture that are not necessary to survival yet play a strong role in sexual selection, for example humour. Miller believes that human culture arose through sexual selection for creative traits. In summary, since the main challenges faced by living beings are survival and reproduction, species are the outcome of both natural and sexual selection. Evolutionary anthropologists are still debating which features of humans were caused by natural selection and which were the result of sexual selection.

STOP & THINK

Can you think of other traits that humans might look for in each other that are not necessary for survival?

AFTER DARWIN

Following Darwin's contributions, the field of genetics emerged, which went into more detail in explaining biological variation. Gregor Mendel (1822–1884) was a naturalist and a monk who made a series of original discoveries in the field of genetics that eventually provided support to Darwin's theory of natural selection.

More recently, geologists have been able to date the history of the Earth into specific periods or epochs. It is now generally agreed by scientists, archaeologists and anthropologists that the group of primates to which humans belong, known as hominins, first appeared 6 to 7 million years ago, with modern humans (*Homo sapiens*) appearing around 200,000 years ago. Palaeoanthropology (the study of human fossil remains) and anthropological genetics (the comparative study of genes in humans and other species) have made significant progress in reconstructing the steps that led from our earliest ancestors to modern humans. Since the earliest forms of life date back to 4,000 million years ago, human beings are a relatively recent species in the history of life on planet Earth.

Early Humans

There were around twenty different species of early humans, including australopithecines (bipedal hominins that resembled chimpanzees in brain and body size and had a predominantly herbivorous diet), early *Homo* species (larger, larger-brained, meat-eating hominins such as *Homo erectus*), archaic humans (such as Neanderthals, with brain sizes almost similar to ours), and even Hobbit-like hominins (such as *Homo florensiensis*, miniature creatures living on the island of Flores in Indonesia until about 12,000 years ago). There are two examples that provide significant insights into the evolution of hominins.

AUSTRALOPITHECUS AFARENSIS: LUCY

Lucy was discovered in 1974 by anthropologist Professor Donald Johanson and his student Tom Gray, at Hadar in northern Ethiopia, and became one of the best documented of all early humans. Johanson and Gray named their fossil skeleton Lucy, after the Beatles song 'Lucy in the Sky with Diamonds', which was playing on the radio when Johanson and his team were celebrating their discovery back at camp. The significance of this discovery was that it confirmed that bipedalism, the ability to walk on two legs, not four, was a key to what makes humans distinctive.

Johanson immediately recognized the bones as belonging to a hominid, and his team eventually unearthed forty-seven bones of a single skeleton dating from 3.2 million years ago. Based on the small size and pelvis shape, they concluded that the skeleton was female. Like a chimpanzee, Lucy had a small brain, long dangly arms and short legs. However, the structure of her knee and pelvis show that she usually walked upright on two legs.

HOMO NEANDERTHALENSIS

The earliest discoveries of *Homo neanderthalensis* (who lived from 200,000 years ago to around 24,000 years ago) were in various parts of Europe, including at Forbes' Quarry, Gibraltar (1948), and at the Neander Valley near Düsseldorf (1856).

Reconstruction of a Neanderthal community based on archaeological excavations at Krapina, Croatia (© Krapina Museum, Croatia)

One of the largest collections of fossilized bones of *Homo neanderthalensis* in the world was found in Croatia, at a site in Krapina, Hušnjakovo, between 1899 and 1905. The most important finding there was a skull that belonged to a young, mature Neanderthal woman. This skull was particularly significant because of the forty-two thin cuts that were found on the frontal bone (the front part of the skull). The cuts were made shortly after the death of the young woman, which suggests possible ritual behaviour. This information provides important evidence that *Homo neanderthalensis* had a developed culture.

Recent studies confirm that *Homo neanderthalensis* were self-conscious beings who lived socially as part of a community. They understood how to treat some illnesses and how to care for children and vulnerable groups. They were also very good hunters. The large number of the various artefacts that they made from stone for different purposes, such as scrapers, reveals much information about their technological development.

Interestingly, genetic evidence has confirmed that there was contact between *Homo sapiens* and *Homo neanderthalensis*. Recent findings in Gorham's caves in Gibraltar suggest that *Homo neanderthalensis* survived until much later than previously suspected, up to 24,000 years ago, suggesting much more overlap with *Homo sapiens* than had been thought. However, the legacy of the relationship between *Homo sapiens* and *Homo neanderthalensis* is the subject of much debate.

Activity

What kinds of evidence prove that *Homo neanderthalensis* were social beings with specific cultural practices?

What are the implications of the recent findings that *Homo neanderthalensis* overlapped with *Homo sapiens*?

Climate Change and Human Evolution

Earlier hominins evolved and diversified in Africa, and the fact that they migrated into Asia and Europe (*Homo erectus* nearly 2 million years old have been found in Asia) shows that they managed to adapt successfully to diverse climatic conditions. One particularly important characteristic of humans is our ability to acclimatize to changes in the environment. The climate became more changeable around 6 million years ago. Some anthropologists argue that certain adaptations, such as upright walking or tool-making, coincided with periods of environmental change.

One example of this view is the Savannah Hypothesis, which claims that many important human adaptations arose in Africa as the savannah, an area of grassland between the rainforest and the desert, expanded. According to this idea, upright walking proved to be an energy-efficient and beneficial way of moving across an open landscape. Furthermore, walking upright had the additional advantage of freeing the hands.

Overall, evidence suggests that early hominins were able to adjust to changing environments in different parts of the world, giving them a huge advantage over other species. This adaptation included the ability to use resources from a vast variety of plants and animals and to employ many specialized tools. Human beings are social and also use communication skills to exchange resources and information to help them survive in a constantly changing world.

> **Activity**
>
> Go to your local natural history museum and investigate early human life. Think about the differences between humans today and early humans.

Where Did Modern Humans Originate From?

Despite the success and diversity of our ancestors, only one hominin species survived: modern *Homo sapiens*. Scientists do not all agree on the levels of contact or conflict that these early forms of humans had with each other, the extent of interbreeding that occurred, or the factors that influenced the evolution and extinction of other hominin species. What we do know is that *Homo sapiens* evolved in Africa at around 200,000 years ago and first migrated in small numbers into Asia, probably between 130,000 and 115,000 years ago, by travelling up the Nile to the Levant (more on the 'Out of Africa' thesis later, in chapter 11). However, the ancestors to all current humans migrated into Europe later, around 60,000 years ago, and it was not until much later still that modern humans populated other parts of the world. For instance, people probably first came to Australia within the past 50,000 years and to the Americas within the past 16,000 years or so. By 14,000 years ago our species had spread to every continent except Antarctica. The beginnings of farming and complex societies occurred within the past 12,000 years. Understanding the success of our species remains a fundamental question for evolutionary anthropologists. This problem brings us back to the question of what differentiates us both from our closest living relatives, the apes, and from extinct hominins.

Similarities and Differences between Humans and Non-Human Primates

So what characteristics do humans still share with other primates, and which are unique? Evolutionary anthropologists attempt to answer this question by comparing genes, morphology, physiology, behaviour and cognition in *Homo sapiens* and other primates. This section considers some of the main similarities and differences between them.

Humans and African apes share most of their DNA, but important functional differences have accumulated. Scientists have shown how humans continue to manifest striking similarities to the African apes both physically and genetically, especially to the chimpanzees and bonobos. For example, humans have forty-six chromosomes in their cells, while all of the great apes have forty-eight. Research on mapping the entire genome of common chimpanzees was completed in 2005 and shows that that 99 per cent of DNA sequences and 96 per cent of protein sequences of humans and chimpanzees are the same. This reflects the relatively recent split between the species since their last common ancestor 6 million years ago. However, it was discovered, unsurprisingly, that the genes that differ mostly control speech, smelling, hearing, digesting proteins, and the likelihood of catching certain diseases, as well as the growth and efficiency of the brain, reflecting the fact that humans have been evolving separately for the past 6 million years.

Activity

Go to your local zoo or watch video clips of chimpanzees.
What physical similarities are there between humans and chimpanzees?
How do chimpanzees move?
Make a list of the behaviours that are similar to those of humans and those that are different, thinking about language, tools, parenting, learning, ways of thinking and social relationships, for example.

- **All hominins and African apes lack external tails**
  Humans and the African apes all lack external tails. Monkeys, on the other hand, do have tails, which are useful for gripping trees and objects. Tails disappeared from apes 15 to 20 million years ago. Apes shin up and down trees rather than walking along branches as monkeys do. The earliest hominins climbed trees and walked on the ground. Fossil evidence shows how early humans made a gradual transition from climbing trees to walking upright on a regular basis.

- **All humans and African apes have opposable thumbs**
  Both humans and African apes have hands with a thumb that is sufficiently separate from the other fingers to allow them to be opposable for precision grip. Possession of an **opposable thumb** means that objects can be carried more easily and manipulated. There is considerable evidence which suggests that, by being able to throw and powerfully grip an object, early humans were better at protecting themselves from animals and other humans (Young 2003). The development of the opposable thumb, however, primarily helped humans to make tools, which was an essential advantage in human cultural evolution. However, the mere presence of opposable thumbs does not explain why humans make tools: if it did, then chimpanzees should make tools too (and they do not).

Hand of an African ape and of a human (Denise Morgan for the University of Utah / Wikimedia Commons)

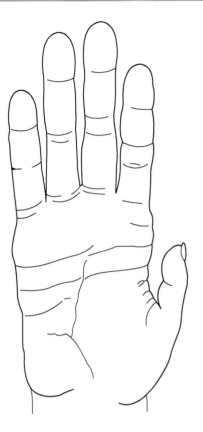
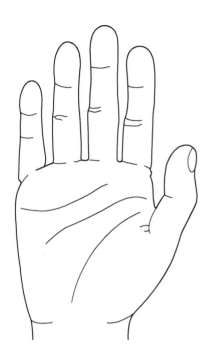

> **Activity**
>
> Take off your shoes and socks and sit on the floor. Try to open a banana skin with only your feet. What happens? What does this activity tell us about the advantages of having opposable thumbs? Make a list of all the things that early humans might have been able to do as a result of having opposable thumbs. How might these activities have helped humans survive?

● **Sexual dimorphism**

Sexual dimorphism refers to both the internal and the external differences between males and females found in a variety of animals and plants. The earliest fossil evidence to show sexual dimorphism in early primates demonstrates that canine teeth and body shapes were different in males and females (Krishtalka, Stucky and Beard 1990). Hominins have not shown dimorphism in canine size, but there was a significant level of body size dimorphism in early hominins such as australopithecines. However, sexual dimorphism was significantly reduced in the larger-brained *Homo erectus* and their descendants (including *Homo sapiens*). This suggests an important development in social organization, with a possible change from polygamy (frequently associated with larger males) to monogamy (often characterized by low sexual dimorphism). Modern humans are sexually dimorphic to some degree. It is estimated that males are 5 to 10 per cent larger on average and have greater upper body muscular development. This is small compared to over 100 per cent body size dimorphism in gorillas and at least 15 to 20 per cent in chimpanzees and bonobos.

> **STOP & THINK**
>
> Suggest some reasons for the gradual reduction in human sexual dimorphism.

Diet and internal organs

Like chimpanzees and bonobos, humans are **omnivorous**; this means that humans and chimpanzees kill other animals for food in addition to eating a wide variety of plants. Essentially, the human body is similar to that of the great apes; humans have the same arrangement of internal organs and bones, share several important blood types and suffer from many of the same diseases. However, there is a significant difference in the amount of meat that humans eat compared to chimpanzees. While chimpanzees extract at most 5 to 10 per cent of their calories from animals (including both small monkeys and termites extracted with tools), *Homo erectus* obtained most energy from meat (either from scavenging or from hunting). This heavy reliance on meat lasted until very recently, when agriculture appeared. There are only a handful of human populations (fewer than fifty across the globe) still able to survive without agriculture: they are known as **hunter-gatherers**.

> **STOP & THINK**
> What are the advantages of an omnivorous diet?

Competitiveness, hierarchy and aggression

One controversial characteristic that we may share with other primates is the potential for aggression. Field studies have shown differences among non-human primate species in the incidence and circumstances of actual intraspecific (within-species) violence. In anthropology, there has been much debate about the human capacity for violence and aggression. Sociobiology, for example, is an area of scientific research and thinking which claims that some social behaviour is a product of evolution (although not all sociobiologists agree on the extent of this). Some argue that certain behaviours (such as aggression and competitiveness) may have been advantageous to human survival. E. O. Wilson, one of the founders of modern sociobiology, described some behaviours thought to be human universals as genetically based, such as male–female bonds, male dominance over females and aggression. These claims have been disputed by many human scientists, who have shown that there is much more variation in patterns of social behaviour across human societies.

More recently, biological anthropologists such as Richard Wrangham and Dale Peterson (1997) have argued that violence played an important role in the evolution of humans and chimpanzees. However, such views have been heavily criticized for their lack of supporting evidence. An alternative view gaining strength in evolutionary anthropology is that our capacity for cooperation is what made humans behaviourally unique. While other species of primates mostly show alliances among closely related kin, studies of hunter-gatherers have shown that we frequently exhibit cooperative behaviours (such as food sharing) towards those who are unrelated. Some of us are even able to display cooperation and altruism towards unknown individuals (think about giving blood or about charity work). The reasons for the coexistence of extreme cooperation and aggression in human societies is one of the most debated issues in evolutionary anthropology.

Social relations

Humans and some non-human primates share some similarities in their behaviour towards each other. However, social behaviour varies from species to species. Two examples of non-human primate behaviour are explored here: that of bonobos and chimpanzees, our two closest evolutionary relatives.

Bonobos

(© LaggedOnUser / Flickr)

Bonobos, found living in the forests of the Democratic Republic of the Congo, have been noted for their sociability. Groups of bonobos range from about fifty to one hundred individuals; however, these groups do break up during the day to form foraging parties. Every night bonobos make a sleeping nest from branches and leaves, usually nesting with the smaller group they have travelled with.

Bonobo societies are female-centred in structure. Interestingly, like humans, bonobos have sex for purposes other than reproduction. They often manage and resolve social conflicts through sex, making aggression less common than with chimpanzees. In fact, sex is a very important part of the social relations of bonobos. They engage in both homosexual and heterosexual relations, although incest is generally avoided. Sexual interactions occur more often among bonobos than among other primates. Despite the frequency of sex, their rate of reproduction in the wild is about the same as that of the chimpanzee.

Bonobo communities have ranges that overlap with other groups. Males are protective of other members of their group and carry out any hunting. Males typically remain among their family group while females range further afield. While males show aggression towards each other, conflict rarely escalates into acts of physical violence. In spite of physical superiority, evidence suggests that males are not aggressive towards females.

Bonobos are social animals, and food sharing occurs between males and females, unlike the situation with chimpanzees. Also the female–female relationship is much stronger in this species than it is for chimpanzees.

Although they seem very lively, bonobos, like humans, control their emotions when expressing themselves in times of happiness, sorrow, excitement or anger. They are very animated and perform similar gestures to humans when communicating without using language. For example, they will beg by stretching out an open hand

Chimpanzees

(Matthew Hoelscher / Wikimedia Commons)

Common chimpanzees, living in tropical forests of Africa, live in small communities. These typically range from twenty to more than 150 members; however, chimpanzees spend most of their time travelling in small, temporary groups consisting of a few individuals that are made up of any combination of ages and sexes. Both males and females will sometimes travel alone. Chimpanzees, like humans, have complex social relationships and spend a large amount of time grooming each other. Grooming is an important way in which alliances are built.

Chimpanzee society shows considerable male dominance. Interestingly, male aggression has an important function in establishing a social hierarchy. However, aggression is often only displayed rather than followed through with violence. Males maintain and improve their social position by forming coalitions. These coalitions increase their influence, giving them power that they would not be able to gain alone. Social hierarchies among adult females tend to be weaker. Nevertheless, the status of an adult female may be important for her offspring.

Chimpanzees have been described as highly territorial and have been known to kill other chimps for territorial dominance, although there is some suggestion that highly aggressive behaviour by chimpanzees happens only when artificial feeding occurs.

A female may mate with several males, though a dominant male may stop other males gaining access to the female with whom they are consorting. Infanticide (the killing of babies) has been recorded among chimpanzees. This is often carried out by male coalitions that invade an existing group, expel their dominant males and kill their offspring: the new males do so in order to mate with the same females and have their own offspring. Care for the young is provided mostly by their mothers. As with humans, babies are dependent on care from an adult for a substantial period. Mothers provide their young with food, warmth and protection and teach them certain skills. In addition, a chimp's future rank may be dependent on its mother's status. For their first year, or foot and will make a whimpering sound if they fail at something.

Females become sexually mature after about twelve years of age and may give birth soon thereafter. They have babies at five- to six-year intervals, so population growth can never be rapid. As with humans, there is a relatively long period of socialization for the young. Females nurse and carry their babies for five years, and the offspring reach adolescence by the age of seven. Females have between five and six offspring in a lifetime.

chimpanzees cling to their mothers. By the time they are six, adolescents continue to spend time with their mothers. Like humans, chimpanzees use their highly expressive faces, postures and sounds to communicate with each other. There are many different sounds which signify specific meanings, such as danger, excitement and anger.

Activity

Make a list of the differences and similarities between humans, bonobos and chimpanzees. Are there more similarities or differences?

- **Tool use**

  Tool use was once thought to be one of the characteristics that set humans apart from other primates, and, indeed, if you look at the variety and complexity of the tools employed by humans, this would seem to be true. However, tool use has been seen in a number of primate and non-primate species, both in captivity and in the wild. The study of tool use provides important information concerning the evolution of human abilities.

  A tool can be defined as any object manipulated by an animal in order to perform a specific task. This tool usually has some beneficial effect, such as making a task easier. Therefore a tool can be very simple, such as a stick to scratch the animal's back. This sort of tool, which requires no alteration to be functional, is sometimes described as a 'naturefact'. Tools used by non-human primates include stones, which might be used to cut, grind or scrape.

  Chimpanzees, for example, often make use of tools. They will adapt sticks, rocks, grass and leaves and use them when foraging for honey, termites, ants, nuts and water. Despite the lack of complexity, there does seem to be planning and skill involved in using these tools. For example, when foraging, chimps will employ modified short sticks to scoop honey out of a hive – that is, if the bees are harmless. With the hives of the dangerous African honeybee, they use longer and thinner sticks to extract the honey. Modification of leaves and branches, and their use as simple tools, has also been observed in elephants, crows and dolphins. However, none of those species created or used more sophisticated tools, such as the stone tools that earlier hominins started to produce over 2 million years ago. Human tools of course became much more complex and diverse: hunting tools, tools to create and control fire, and much more.

- **Bipedalism**

  Modern chimpanzees occasionally walk upright, but their skeletons are not adapted for regular walking on two legs. The skeletons of early humans, on the other hand, evolved to support their bodies in an upright position. This means that modern humans have bodies adapted for walking and running long distances on two legs – that is, they are as bipedal. Walking upright undoubtedly helped early humans survive in the diverse habitats in which they lived, including forests and grasslands.

  Bipedalism
  Walking upright on two feet for the majority of the time

There are several physical changes which had to occur to make bipedalism possible, among them modifications in foot and knee structure, a curved spine (to absorb shock), broad-shaped hip bones, and a change in the point of attachment between the skull and the neck from a posterior position (as found in other primates) to an inferior position. Bipedalism was an adaptation to the open environments of the African savannah, where the earliest hominins evolved.

One disadvantage of bipedalism is that climbing is much harder, as the feet cannot grip trees. Another disadvantage is the back pain and other skeletal problems that occur as a result of walking upright. Placing all the body's weight on just two limbs can result in back pain and slipped discs. A further disadvantage of bipedalism was that it resulted in the narrowing of the hips and pelvis, resulting in greater risk in childbirth.

- **Human pelvis shape and size is different to that of other primates**
As we have seen, bipedalism and the long, slim bodies that go with it were advantageous for humans to be able to move quickly and efficiently in the savannah environment. However, these changes also resulted in changes in the shape, size and position of the female pelvis, which meant a narrower birth canal in females. As a consequence, giving birth became a more difficult and risky process for humans than for most other primate species. The result is that humans give birth to babies that have not achieved the stage of brain development that is typical at birth for apes, monkeys and most other **mammals**. This particular feature of our evolution appears to be quite recent; it was around 500,000 years ago that there was evidence of the large human brain.

During delivery, human babies must turn to be able to squeeze through the narrow birth canal in order to accommodate their comparatively large heads followed by their shoulders. The way that this is achieved is by babies having soft skulls which are not fully formed at birth. Birth, therefore, is usually a long, tiring and painful process for the mother as well as a risky one for the baby. Because of this, unlike other primates, human mothers generally need help in childbirth.

The consequence of this evolutionary adaptation is that newborn human babies are more vulnerable and undeveloped. The bones of the skull grow together during the first year of life, which means that human babies are extremely vulnerable during this time and in need of a lot of protection and nurturing.

> **Activity**
>
> Summarize the benefits and disadvantages of bipedalism for humans.

- **Hairless bodies and sweating**
Another way in which humans are different from other primates is in having a largely hairless body, along with a very efficient set of sweat glands that allow the regulation of body temperature, as opposed to panting, like many other mammals. Humans are the only primate species that has mostly naked skin. However, scientists are still trying to find out which hominins were the first to have lost their body hair. If the advantage of naked skin was the ability to regulate body temperature in the open environment of the savannah, in contrast to the more shaded forests where apes live, then our naked skin may have evolved million years ago.

- **The brain**

One of the most significant differences between humans and other primates is that humans have a much larger brain. The modern human brain is three times larger in volume than those of the great apes. But it is not just the size of the human brain that is significant; it is the complex functional and cognitive abilities the brain engenders. However, a larger brain is also a more expensive brain. The human brain to body size ratio is significantly greater than in other species, and as a result the human brain requires 20 per cent of the energy used by the body, which is more than any other organ. Therefore the evolution of a larger brain suggests that a higher energy diet had also to evolve as a condition. Although the hominin lineage is over 6 million years old, brain size shows significant increases only from the time of *Homo erectus*, less than 2 million years ago. It was also around that time that we find evidence of a dramatic change in diet towards increased meat eating, more extensive use and manufacture of stone tools, and reduction in jaw and tooth size.

Large, complex brains can process and store a lot of information. This was a big advantage to early humans in their social interactions and encounters with unfamiliar habitats. Having a larger brain enabled modern humans to have much more complex forms of verbal communication than any other primate species. Humans are the only animal to create and use symbols as a means of communication. Humans also have more varied and complex social organizations. The most distinctive feature of humans is our mental ability to create new ideas and complex technologies, which has proven invaluable in the competition for survival. Another striking capability that derives from a larger and more effective brain is the ability to know what others might be thinking. In psychology, this is known as having a 'theory of mind'.

Steven Mithen, an archaeologist, suggests that human forms of intelligence fall into four categories – social, technical, linguistic and natural history – which, once combined, led to the creation of consciousness. Having consciousness means having self-awareness, a sense of past and present.

However, the great apes are also surprisingly intelligent, having mental levels equivalent to a three- to four-year-old human child. This is sufficient to allow them to learn and use the sign language of deaf humans in at least a simplistic way, but, despite this, they do not have the capability of producing human speech and language.

- **Females live beyond the menopause**

There is one additional interesting difference between humans and all other primates that is worth noting. At around the age of fifty, human females go through the menopause and become sterile. Even in societies where life expectancy is low on account of the absence of medical care, such as those of hunter-gatherers, women often live for decades after ceasing to reproduce in their late forties or early fifties. In contrast, female chimpanzees, gorillas and other non-human primates usually remain capable of conception and giving birth even when they are older.

One explanation for this difference in humans is that years of life following menopause has proven to have natural selection value for our species. Having raised their own children, post-menopausal women around the world often take care of their grandchildren while their daughters are working. It is argued that this additional experienced and caring attention increases the chances that the grandchildren will survive to adulthood. The role of grandmothers in human societies is another example of cooperation in our species.

CULTURAL EVOLUTION

Cultural evolution
The ways in which humans have evolved beyond their biology

Despite the many physiological and behavioural features that differentiate humans from apes, it is culture that separates us from all other species. Since culture allowed humans to transform the environment around us, we have to a large extent ceased to evolve any further physically. While some other animals show evidence of some form of culture, no species other than humans has such a complex and well-developed culture.

- **Cooking**
  There is evidence that the brain became larger as a result of increased nutrition in human beings. One interesting argument put forward by Richard Wrangham (2009) is that cooking food – behaviour unique to humans – played a large role in our evolution. Around 800,000 years ago, early humans gathered around camp-fires that they made and controlled. There may have been lots of different reasons for this, including socialization, comfort and warmth, to share food and information, and to find safety from predators. Wrangham argued that the habit of eating cooked rather than raw meat permitted the digestive tract to shrink and the human brain to grow even further, since cooked meat is easier to digest and gives out more calories.

- **Language**
  Spoken language is essential to modern human cultures. We use language to communicate in a complex, ever changing world. It is very difficult to assess when language developed, as there is little fossil evidence which relates to language. Currently it is believed that language first appeared in the form of gestures around the time of *Homo erectus*, in association with our larger brains and the higher cognitive requirements of hunting in groups. Spoken language, on the other hand, may be a much more recent adaptation. There are various theories about why and how language developed (some will be discussed later in the book). However, anthropologists estimate that spoken language developed around 100,000 years ago. This is because objects began to be made which involved complex behaviours that probably required language. Being able to use a language undoubtedly contributed to and was a result of greater self-awareness in human beings.

- **Symbols**
  Language is only possible because humans are able to think symbolically. Malinowski (1939: 955) pointed out that 'symbolism must make its appearance with the earliest appearance of human culture'. The use of symbols (something which is used to represent an idea or object) changed the way that humans lived and provided new ways to communicate and cope with an unpredictable world. The ability to use symbols and communicate helped humans to pass on information, cooperate and ultimately become more efficient and survive.

  Symbol
  Something which is used to represent an idea or object

  Ultimately, words and symbols led to elaborated language and the complex human societies which now exist. With materials such as ochre, our human ancestors marked objects and possibly their own skin. Colours were probably used as symbols by which they identified themselves and their group. Symbols can be complex and mean several different things at the same time for humans. By 40,000 years ago, humans were creating two- and three-dimensional images of the world around them. By 17,000 years ago, they had developed complex artistic techniques.

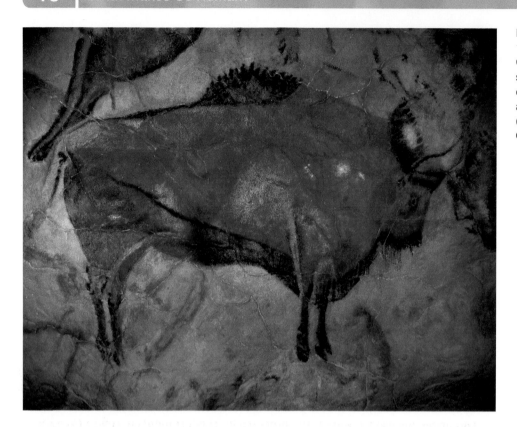

Picture of a bison from 16,500 years ago in Altamira Cave, Spain, showing sophisticated use of three dimensions to represent the animal's legs and stomach (Rameessos / Wikimedia Commons)

- **Recording information: the origins of written language**

Around 70,000 to 80,000 years ago, there is evidence of markings which indicate information was being recorded. Their meanings are not easy to understand, and anthropologists do not always agree over what this early recorded material signifies. However, it is generally agreed that, by around 8,000 years ago, humans were using symbols to represent words and concepts. Specific forms of writing developed over the next few thousand years. But it should be clear that written language is a purely cultural construct and that its origin required no changes in cognition. People living in pre-literate societies such as hunter-gatherer groups are as cognitively competent as the agriculturalists who invented written language.

- **Social life**

Another feature of human beings that distinguishes them from all other primates is their much more complex social lives. However, in the long evolution of human beings, it is only in the past 10,000 years that farming, herding, cities, trade and warfare emerged.

On a more basic level, sharing food, caring for infants, and building social networks helped early humans meet the daily challenges of survival. The concern for the well-being of others and a willingness to help them is key to what makes us humans; this is sometimes known as altruism. Over time, early humans began to gather near fires and shelters to eat and socialize. As human brains became larger and more complex, growing up took longer, requiring skilled care and attention and the protective environment of a home. Expanding social networks led, eventually, to the complex social lives of modern humans. Interestingly, another feature of humans is that they usually maintain lifelong ties with their children. The systems of kinship and marriage that preserve the links between parents and their offspring and across generations over time are also major differences between humans and other primates.

> **Altruism**
> The ability to put the needs of others before your own

- **Sharing resources, exchange**

There is evidence which indicates that, around 2.6 to 1.8 million years ago, some groups of early humans began collecting tools and food from a variety of places and bringing them to favoured resting and eating spots. Sharing vital resources with other members of the group led to stronger social bonds and enhanced the group's chances of survival. About 2 million years ago, early humans transported materials such as stone several miles, from which they made tools for killing animals. Evidence has shown that, around 40,000 years ago, materials such as shells were being transported a long way from their original location, which suggests that humans were sharing resources and communicating with others from a range of different places. This sharing of goods led to the development of exchange systems, which are fundamental to the success of the human species and are a universal feature of all human societies.

- **Rituals**

By 100,000 years ago, early modern humans buried the dead together with beads and other symbolic objects. Burial rituals heightened the group's memory of the deceased person. These **rituals** may imply that such groups shared the belief that a person's identity extends beyond death. By 24,000 years ago, there is evidence of child burials, with children being buried covered in ochre markings and with mammoth tusks.

- **Expressing identity**

Our ancestors used jewellery and other personal adornments to reflect their identity. These adornments may have represented membership in a particular group or someone's age, sex and social status.

> **Activity**
>
> List as many advantages you can of the specific ways in which humans evolved culturally.

Evolution in humans has selected for:

- ✳ VERY BIG BRAINS – we can deal with complex and abstract concepts
- ✳ LANGUAGE – we are able to store and transmit knowledge
- ✳ NARROW HIPS – we can run, but giving birth is difficult and our babies are immature
- ✳ SWEATY/HAIRLESS SKIN – to help regulate temperature, e.g., to keep cool when running
- ✳ LONGEVITY – humans are among the only primates that live beyond the menopause
- ✳ ALTRUISM – we have empathy for other humans.

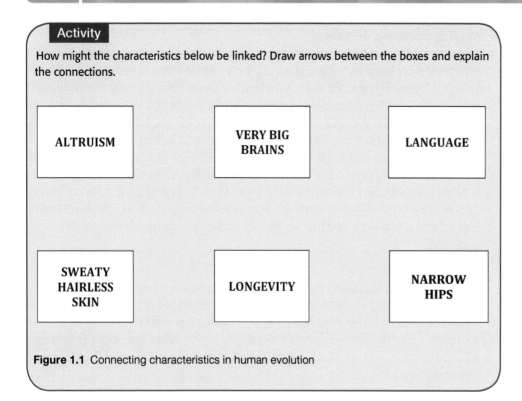

Activity

How might the characteristics below be linked? Draw arrows between the boxes and explain the connections.

ALTRUISM	VERY BIG BRAINS	LANGUAGE
SWEATY HAIRLESS SKIN	LONGEVITY	NARROW HIPS

Figure 1.1 Connecting characteristics in human evolution

HOW DO HUMANS VARY? THE CONCEPT OF RACE AND A CRITIQUE OF THE CONCEPT

Biological Differences between Humans

It is now agreed that *Homo sapiens* evolved from one of many types of early human and then spread around the world, interacting to some degree with other forms such as Neanderthals and gradually displacing these other types.

Among modern humans, there is stronger evidence for group intermingling, which tends to be more likely between neighbouring groups. There was little significant mixing of human social groups until much later with the rise of large complex societies. Using genetic information, it is now possible to investigate people's ancestry as well as trace their movements. For example, it has been found that 95 per cent of Icelandic men have Norse ancestry, whereas 85 per cent of Icelandic women have Celtic ancestry, which indicates that they had relations with Celtic men on their way to Iceland. This kind of information tells us a lot about the kinds of social relationships occurring between groups.

It is clear that there are some physical differences between human groups. These are based on minor genetic differences and the variations that have arisen further from these lineages. For example, we know that Inuit are different to Australians, and no one confuses the !Kung San hunter-gatherers from the Kalahari desert with the Bantu farmers. Therefore race, in biological terms, refers simply to specific genetic lineage.

In wider society, the concept of race has been interpreted in a number of ways. During the nineteenth century there were several attempts to create stratified categories of race along the lines of perceived (or given) physical and intellectual differences between various social groups. Often these categories were created to reflect power differences.

Some early attempts to understand the differences between humans resulted in taxonomies or classification systems that were often crude and based judgementally on superficial physical differences. For example, In 1757 Carl Linnaeus divided *Homo sapiens* into five categories, among which were 'wild man', who was apparently mute and hairy, and 'European', who was 'gentle'. Significantly, Linnaeus conflates physical characteristics such as hair type with cultural differences such as dress and political organization. This is a highly problematic assumption, one that is reflected in many ways by the widespread **racism** that has occurred in almost every single society in the world.

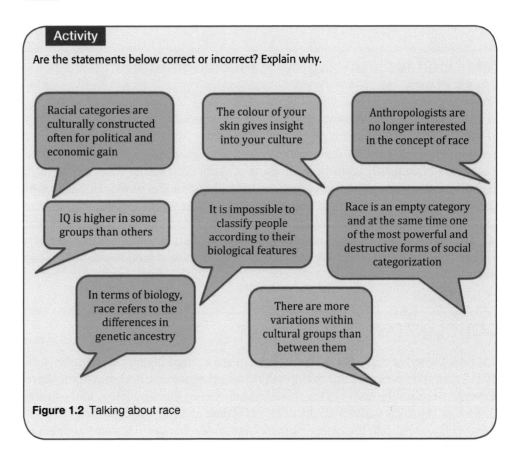

Figure 1.2 Talking about race

The speech bubbles in the activity read:

Activity

Are the statements below correct or incorrect? Explain why.

- Racial categories are culturally constructed often for political and economic gain
- The colour of your skin gives insight into your culture
- Anthropologists are no longer interested in the concept of race
- IQ is higher in some groups than others
- It is impossible to classify people according to their biological features
- Race is an empty category and at the same time one of the most powerful and destructive forms of social categorization
- In terms of biology, race refers to the differences in genetic ancestry
- There are more variations within cultural groups than between them

Culturally Constructed Concepts of Race

It is now widely accepted that there *are* minor biological variations between humans. However, it is the **social and political** interpretations of the real or imagined differences between people on which cultural anthropologists now focus: the culturally constructed concepts of race.

Varying skin colour provides a useful example for considering the differences between biological and socio-political approaches to the concept of race. Skin colour in humans correlates quite closely with the ancestral location of the people concerned because it has ultimately been determined by the radiation level in that particular

Culturally constructed
Something which is created by society

ancestral homeland. As such it is a reasonable indication of origin, although it does not take into account population movement. In contrast, cultural anthropologists are interested in the ways that skin colour has been assigned particular political and social status, in many cases, both historically and in contemporary society, as the basis of forms of discrimination. Anthropologists are interested in why and how the socially constructed concept of race becomes assigned with greater significance at certain times and in certain places.

A useful comparison is in the naming of groups. It is very unusual for people to use outsiders' terms of discrimination to describe themselves. One of the few examples in which they do is the term 'Welsh', which is a corruption of the Anglo-Saxon word for 'slave' (*Wealish*), as opposed to the word *Cymri*, which is the correct Welsh word. The word 'Welsh' has stuck and has even eventually been adopted by the Welsh themselves.

American Anthropological Association Statement on Race (1988)

In an attempt to ensure that anthropology was not associated with any discriminatory or colonial attitudes concerning race, and to provide a unified approach to the issue, a statement was issued by the American Anthropological Association condemning the misuse of culturally constructed notions of racial differences. What recent work in evolutionary anthropology has shown is that, although some genetic differences in skin colour, the predisposition to certain diseases, and the ability to digest lactose (the protein in milk) or alcohol do exist among human populations, there is no evidence that cognitive or behavioural traits (such as IQ) show any variation. For this reason, human evolutionary studies have actively contributed to the demise of pseudo-scientific racial classifications of intelligence.

CONCLUSION

It is possible to see that what makes us human are evolved biological characteristics that in many complex ways link to culturally evolved behaviours. Anthropologists have different views on the extent of the relationship between human biology and culture. One major key to the survival of human beings is their ability to adapt to their environment. This was crucially important, as there were major changes in the environment at critical stages in human evolution.

There are minor biological differences between human groups. Biological anthropologists are interested in these differences in terms of genetic ancestry. Cultural anthropologists, however, are interested in the ways that perceived differences between groups of people are misused by some for economic and political reasons.

The relationship between human biology and human culture is only one of the many problems addressed by evolutionary anthropology. Understanding the processes behind the origin of humankind and the evolution of our unique adaptations are among the most fundamental questions that we have posed to ourselves. The search for answers places the study of human evolution at the heart of anthropology.

END OF CHAPTER ASSESSMENT

Assess the view that humans continue to share many cultural and biological characteristics with their non-human primate cousins.

Teacher's guidance

This question is asking you to consider the extent to which humans and other primates are similar, which means you need to explore the characteristics humans have retained and those which make humans different and come to a conclusion confirming if, in your view, there are more differences or similarities. Remember that some claims about similarities are controversial and problematic, such as the view held by some sociobiologists that humans are biologically predisposed to aggression.

Begin by defining evolution, cultural and biological, and explain briefly the pathway that began 6 to 8 million years ago when our human ancestors became different to other primates. Assess a range of biological and cultural qualities shared by humans and other primates, using what you have learnt about bonobos and chimpanzees. Then discuss what makes humans different to other primates, the main features of human biological and cultural evolution – language, the use of symbols, complex social groups, altruism, consciousness (awareness of past and present), abstract thought. Discuss some of the suggested reasons why humans became so different to other primates. Point out that, while human biological evolution may have slowed or ceased, cultural evolution continues, including through the use of various forms of technology. Come to a clear conclusion explaining why you feel there are more similarities or differences between humans and other primates.

KEY TERMS

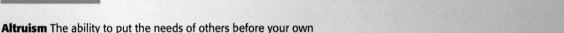

Altruism The ability to put the needs of others before your own

Bipedalism Walking upright on two feet for the majority of time

Catastrophism The theory that the Earth has been affected in the past by sudden, short-lived, violent events, possibly worldwide in scope, which have led to the contemporary world with its current variety of animals and plants

Creationism The belief that all life was created by the actions of God

Cultural evolution The ways in which humans have evolved beyond their biology

Culturally constructed Something which is created by society

Evolution Any change across successive generations in the inherited characteristics of biological populations

Fossils The preserved remains or traces of animals, plants and other organisms from the remote past

Intelligent design Also known as neo-creationism, the belief that the current state of life on Earth has come about through the actions of an intelligent designer; this designer need not be God, but most proponents of intelligent design seem to have God in mind

Mammal Any warm-blooded vertebrate animal, including humans, characterized by a covering of hair on the skin and, in the female, milk-producing mammary glands for feeding the young

Natural selection The process in nature by which, according to Darwin's theory of evolution, only the organisms best adapted to their environment tend to survive and transmit their genetic characteristics in increasing numbers to succeeding generations, while those less well adapted tend to be eliminated

Opposable thumb A thumb that is sufficiently separate from the other fingers of the hand to allow for precision grip

Primate A mammal of the order Primates, characterized, for example, by refined development of the hands and feet and a large brain

Racism Discrimination against an individual or group based on their perceived ethnicity and the idea that 'race' is a fixed and bounded reality

Ritual Behaviour prescribed by society in which individuals have little choice about their actions; sometimes having reference to beliefs in mystical powers or beings

Symbol Something which is used to represent an idea or object

Taxonomy The classification of organisms in an ordered system that indicates natural relationships

Personal investigation

Visit your local zoo, or the Internet, and investigate the bonobos and chimpanzees. Consider the ways in which humans share biological attributes and discuss the impact of this on the behaviour of the primates. Consider the ways in which the primates relate to one another and how they use their space and arrange social relations. Explore and investigate the extent to which captivity affects their behaviour. Make notes on any cultural characteristics you see – for example, in terms of hierarchy. Draw up a detailed report on your findings.

SUGGESTED FURTHER READING AND FILMS

Books

Barnard, A. (2011) *Social Anthropology and Human Origins*. Cambridge University Press.
Mithen, S. (2005) *The Singing Neanderthals: The Origins of Music, Language, Mind and Body*. Phoenix Press.
Wrangham, R. (2009) *Catching Fire: How Cooking Made Us Human*. Profile Books.

Ethnographical films

BBC, *The Incredible Human Journey* (2009), presented by Alice Roberts
BBC, *Origins of Us* (2009), presented by Alice Roberts
BBC, *Prehistoric Autopsy* (2012), presented by Alice Roberts
BBC, *Racism: A History* (2007)

Websites

American Anthropological Association, www.understandingrace.org [a great website for understanding the concept of race and all the problems associated with it]
American Anthropological Association, Statement on Race, www.aaanet.org/stmts/racepp.htm
Smithsonian Institution, http://humanorigins.si.edu [gives an excellent interactive overview of human evolution]

CHAPTER TWO

THE BODY

CONTENTS

Photo on p. 25 © Gregory Davies.

CHAPTER

2 The Body

> **KEY ISSUES AND DEBATES**
>
> - How do humans use bodies to communicate differences between one another?
> - What are the meanings of body modification and body image?
> - What are the different anthropological theories about bodies?
> - How does the body reflect the values and beliefs of the wider society to which it belongs?
> - How is tattooing used to express different meanings for individuals and the cultures in which they live?

The first chapter explored the ways in which human beings evolved physically and the ways their evolved bodies have shaped culture. Anthropologists are also interested in the meanings and values that are attached to the body in different cultural settings. The body plays an important role in how we classify (put into categories) the world around us. This chapter looks at different relationships between the body and society. The body is seen to communicate a range of statuses, ranks and relationships. Bodies can be perceived as things to be beautified, fixed and adorned and can be recognized, among other things, as male or female, black or white. They may convey national pride, as was the case during the Olympic Games in London in 2012. Bodies can also communicate the effect of racism, neglect and abuse. The anthropological literature and number of ethnographies on the body are vast. This chapter looks at some ways in which the body is studied in anthropology.

STOP & THINK

What should the human body look like? What exercise should bodies do? What is the shape of the perfect body? Is it the same for men and women? Where do ideas of the 'perfect body' come from? What do ideas about the body say about people's notions of health, culture and identity?

BODY MODIFICATIONS AND DECORATIONS

All cultures paint, pierce, tattoo, reshape or decorate their bodies. Humans do not go out naked; they dress or decorate some part of their body to present themselves to other humans. Body decorations can communicate a person's status in society, their identity, and the differences between them and others. Body decoration and modification form a visual language through which humans navigate the world in which they live. However, not all cultures share the same values and beliefs, and certain body modification practices are often misunderstood or misinterpreted, even within the same culture.

Body Modifications

Body modification
The deliberate altering of the human anatomy

In the past and present the body has been reshaped in many culturally relevant ways, from traditional foot binding in China to more recent cosmetic surgeries in Western society. Humans modify their bodies for many reasons. Some religious traditions believe that marking the body is a corruption of the perfect human form designed by God, while many others consider those who are undressed not fully human. For some, body decoration is something that distinguishes humans from the animal world or from other humans in different cultures.

The body can be either temporarily modified (for example, body painting, make-up, toiletries, hairstyles) or permanently modified (tattooing, scarification, reshaping and piercing). Below are three examples of body modification in different cultures and different times.

- **Foot binding**
  The foot binding of girls was practised only in China and became popular in the twelfth century among the elite. Its purpose was to restrict the growth of the foot as a sign of beauty, wealth and discipline. A woman with bound feet could not walk properly. She was also considered attractive as a marriage partner because her physical impairment indicated she was honourable and a virgin. Foot binding began at three to six years of age, when all the girl's toes apart from the big toe were folded down under the sole of the foot and bandaged tightly in that position. The bones of the toes broke and the instep was artificially curved and raised in an attempt to create the 'lotus foot', the perfect arch of the foot. Women with these modifications would need constant support to stand, and walking was very painful and problematic in terms of balance. Men found women with bound feet very attractive. Foot binding was officially banned in China in 1911.

- **Lip plates**
  Lip plates are worn in parts of Africa and South and Northwest America. The Kayapo men of Brazil still wear lip plates, though it is best known as a practice among the women of certain African cultures. A hole is sliced into the lower lip and a small object is inserted. After the hole heals around the object, it is removed and is replaced by a larger plate, gradually stretching the hole. The purpose and meaning of lip plates is different in different cultures. The Lobi women of the Ivory Coast and Ghana wear lip plates to protect against evil spirits that enter the body via the mouth. For others, lip plates are a status symbol; Terence Turner explains the meaning of lip plates for Kayapo men (see later in this chapter, p. 39).

- **Scarification**
  Scarification is a way of permanently marking the body through cutting the skin and is often carried out as part of a ritual. Scarification was and is still today practised most widely in Africa and among Australian Aboriginal people. The main point of African scarification is to beautify, although scars of a certain type, size and position on the body often indicate group identity or stages in a person's life. Among the Dinka of Sudan, facial scarification, usually around the temple area, is used

A Datoga woman with traditional facial scarification (Kathy Gerber / Wikimedia Commons)

for clan identification. In southern Sudan, Nuba girls traditionally receive marks on their forehead, chest and abdomen at the beginning of puberty. At first menstruation they receive a second set of cuts, this time under the breasts. These are enlarged by a final, extensive phase of scarring after the weaning of the first child, resulting in designs stretching across the sternum, back, buttocks, neck and legs. Nuba scarification is determined by social status and maturity and is perceived as a mark of beauty. In the context of the cultural traditions of the Dinka and Nuba, the individual has little choice in the matter of scarification.

In other parts of Africa, scarification is carried out for different reasons. Pain and blood can play a large part in the scarification process, determining a person's fitness, endurance and bravery. This is especially the case in puberty rites, since a child must prove readiness to face the responsibilities of adulthood, in particular the prospect of injury or death in battle for men and the trauma of childbirth for women. However, traditional scarification has declined in Africa, Australia and elsewhere as a result of health concerns and politico-cultural changes.

Body Modification in Western Societies

In different cultures there are different ideas about what is most important regarding the body; for example, in some cultures adult men must have beards, in others they may spend hours plucking every hair from their bodies (for the example of Kayapo culture, see below, pp. 37–9). One common form of body modification in Western society is through cosmetics, which are used to beautify the external body. A person decorated with make-up may be believed to be more beautiful than that person in their undecorated state. In the United Kingdom people spend hundreds of millions of pounds a year on personal hygiene and make-up. A survey was conducted in 2011 by the natural deodorant range Bionsen. It shows that, between the ages of sixteen and forty-five, women spend an average of nearly £40 a week on make-up. The national poll of 2,200 women

Cosmetics, hair dye and breast implants are some of the most visible ways of modifying the body to follow Western ideals of female beauty. (wwv / Wikimedia Commons)

found that, on average, women own fifty-four items of make-up from twelve countries, worth over £500. People in Western society spend a considerable portion of their time on their appearance. Ways of conforming to ideas of beauty and attractiveness vary through time and cross-culturally.

For example, historically defined body shapes and expectations change: at the moment in British and Western fashion, the ideal beautiful body is often very thin, but in the 1950s and early 1960s the ideal body shape was curvaceous and in 'good proportions', meaning measurements of 36″–24″–36″ around the bust, waist and hips.

A popular body modification in Western society for aesthetic reasons is plastic surgery. One example is breast enlargement. As one of the strongest identifiers of a woman's gender and sexuality, breasts have been the subjects of modification for many years. Silicone gel implants were developed in the 1960s, but breast enlargement surgery became more widespread only in the 1980s. Despite the considerable cost and health risks involved, breast enlargement is still the most popular cosmetic procedure performed on British women: more than 30,000 women receive breast implants every year (www.nhs.uk/conditions/breast-implants/Pages/Introduction.aspx).

Activity

Interview an elderly person and ask them to tell you what the ideal of beauty was during their youth (you can ask questions about the way they dressed, beauty routines, style icons, how they met their wife/husband, etc.).

> **Activity**
>
> Find examples of each technique of body modification (tattooing, scarification, plastic surgery, circumcision, body painting, etc.) mentioned in this chapter, in magazines, newspapers and books and on the Internet, and prepare a presentation for your class. The presentation should include the following:
> - a description of the body modifications
> - the significance of the modification for the people with the body modification
> - how each example reflects the notions of power, individuality or group identity, life transitions, or beauty
> - your thoughts, ideas and feelings about the body modification you chose before conducting your research. Have your ideas changed? If so, how and why?
>
> Use the concepts from this chapter in your explanations. Support your presentation with ethnographic study. Illustrate the presentation with images before presenting it to the rest of the class.
>
> Use the Pitt Rivers Museum virtual collections (http://web.prm.ox.ac.uk/bodyarts) in your research.

Body Image in Fiji (Becker 1995)

To be healthy, the body mass of the human body has to be within a certain range. If the body is anorexic or obese (too thin or too fat) then it will be unhealthy. It could be argued that certain body types are more likely to produce healthy children and, therefore, that there may be an evolutionary explanation for why one body type may appear more attractive to the opposite sex. However, within the range of body shapes there is a wide variety of possibilities. Becker conducted fieldwork in Fiji and examined the cultural context of the embodied self through her ethnography of bodily aesthetics, food exchange, care and social relationships. She contrasts the cultivation of the body/self in Fijian society with that in the USA, arguing that the fascination of Americans with, and motivation to work on, moulding (shaping) their body as a personal effort is permitted by their notion that the self is individuated and autonomous. On the other hand, because Fijians concern themselves with the cultivation of social relationships expressed largely through nurturing and food exchange, they have a vested interest in cultivating others' bodies rather than their own. So, while they pay careful attention to weight and appetite changes among community members, Fijians demonstrate a relative lack of interest in self-reflexive work on the body. Becker demonstrates how the individual body is communally observed, cared for, worked upon, and interpreted in Fiji, and how it is in many ways regarded and experienced as a manifestation of its community rather than of the self. Fijian embodied experience not only reflects and includes community processes but also at times overcomes the body's physical boundaries. Becker's study shows that other cultures may have very different ideas from those of Western culture of what the 'ideal' body should look like. The reasons for favouring one body type over another relate to social factors – for example, in Fiji, a woman who can work hard is valued, and strong calf muscles are an indication of that. In modern Western society, the mass media are very influential in forming ideals of body shape, as the body does not have the same importance in relation to work or reproduction.

Training the Body in Sport (Wacquant 2004)

Humans have a basic anatomy, and there are limits to what the body can do; for example, it cannot be trained to fly. Doing physical activities produces positive hormonal changes that result in feelings of wellbeing. In more competitive sports, the person can experience an adrenaline rush, which is a pleasurable feeling. However, within these limits the body can be trained to do many things that are beyond most people. Although a sociologist, Wacquant has used participant observation to study boxing culture in the deprived area of Woodlawn, on the South side of Chicago, USA. He spent three years as an amateur boxer and joined the gym himself. He also conducted research on racial and class inequality in the city. In Western cultures competitive sports are valued and so form a means for people to gain in self-esteem. Many people from all social classes use sport as a vehicle for gaining a respected place in society. In Wacquant's study, many young men from disadvantaged backgrounds in society saw boxing as a way of doing something with their lives. They experienced many problems of racism and discrimination, and Wacquant found that sport was seen as a way out of the ghetto.

Wheelchair basketball players must train their upper bodies and arms to become more adept at their sport. (Pierreselim / Wikimedia Commons)

Ideal Male Body Type, Size, and Symbolic Power (Strathern 1971)

The ethnographic record concerning body preferences in males is weak, yet preliminary research suggests a universal preference for a muscular physique and for tall or moderately tall stature. Men tend to aspire to a muscular shape characterized by well-developed upper-body muscles and a slim waist and hips. Efforts to achieve this ideal body generally centre around exercise rather than diet. Large body size may serve as an attribute of attractiveness in men because it symbolizes health, economic success, political power and social status. 'Big-Men', political leaders in Highland New Guinea, are described by their constituents in terms of their size and physical wellbeing: a leader is a man 'whose skin swells with "grease" (or fat) underneath' (Strathern 1971). The spiritual power (*mana*) and noble breeding of a Polynesian chief are also expected to be reflected in his large physical size.

Sexy Bodies (Yu and Shepard 1998)

A good example of the way people's ideas about body shape are socially conditioned comes from anthropological research on the Matsigenka people from a remote area of Southeastern Peru. People here were not bombarded with images and ideas about conventionally attractive female body shapes. Douglas Yu and Glenn Shepard showed pictures of females with different body shapes to male members from this culture. The Matsigenka men favoured more rounded female bodies, arguing that slim-waisted females looked skinny and pale and were perhaps recovering from a bout of diarrhoea! The researchers then tested the perception of men who used to live in the same area but had since moved to towns, where advertising and media was more common. They favoured the slimmer female forms.

Anthropological Theories of the Body

The following Box examines some key anthropological theories of the body.

BIOLOGICAL MODEL – NATURALISTIC APPROACH

Anthropological interest in the body began in the early eighteenth century through the 'naturalistic' view. The main naturalist writings at that time regarded the body as the biological base from which developed the superstructure of the society.

According to this perspective, human bodies are defined by their physical characteristics. The biological model looks at the body very much as a machine that can break down and so requires physical repair. This perspective is still dominant in the medical model in Western approaches to the body and is held by many doctors, surgeons and health practitioners. The main assumptions of the medical model are physical phenomena, such as illness is caused by bacteria; illness can be classified; medical specialists identify illness; illness can be treated and often cured. The medical model argues that the body is a biological organism.

Criticism: This theory was criticized as being reductionist, because the body is explained as a result of some aspect of physical or genetic constitution. In other words, biological explanations completely ignored social influences and the role of society or social processes and representations in the shaping of the body.

THE SOCIAL CONSTRUCTION OF THE BODY

In contrast to naturalistic views of the body, the **socially constructed** body is assumed to be the product of social processes, 'constructed' in terms of dominant social practices or cultural norms. This approach holds that the meanings attributed to the body, and the boundaries that exist between the bodies of different groups of people, are social products. Social constructionists consider that the way people view themselves and others is shaped not only by biology or nature but also by the social context in which they live. Foucault ([1973] 1994), for example, argues that the way humans view the body is influenced by dominant discourses (systems of thoughts composed of ideas, attitudes, courses of action, beliefs and practices that construct the subjects and the worlds of which they speak). Views of the body will vary from society to society depending on the dominant discourses used in that culture. For example, in contemporary Western societies, discourses about the body, especially for women, privilege thinness, so a thin body shape is likely to offer higher status and to be sought after. Such constructionist notions of what humans think is 'healthy' and what is 'illness' are shaped not by biology but by dominant ideas and discourses about the body. For Foucault, the body is a direct way for certain members of the society to implement control. Institutional power such as that found in prisons, hospitals, political regimes, schools and religious disciplines shapes both the appearance and the practices relating to the individual body.

The social constructionist approach has had a profound influence on anthropological theories of the body, many of which originate from notions put forth by one of the founding figures of both sociology and anthropology, Emile Durkheim – in particular, his notion of the person as a double being consisting of an individual biological self and a social self. In this duality, the body stands for the profane or 'natural' self, the mind for the sacred or social self. Anthropologists and others have long acknowledged that religious thought recognizes this duality in our nature through its opposition between body and soul, flesh and spirit, profane and sacred (see below, Robert Hertz on handedness, p. 35).

Criticism: Social constructionism is one-sided as a purely biological naturalistic approach. The body is not exclusively a social construction.

THE BODY AS SYMBOL

This perspective focuses on the representation or symbolic nature of the body as a way of giving it a social meaning. Mary Douglas ([1970] 2003) explored the symbolic significance of the body, arguing that it may be viewed metaphorically as a text that can be read as a symbol or signifier of the world that it inhabits. The general theme in her work is that the social body constrains how the physical body is perceived and experienced. Douglas writes about 'two bodies', the physical (natural body) and the social (cultural body). In her book *Natural Symbols*, the argument is that the human body is the most readily available image of a social system and that ideas about it relate closely to dominant ideas about society. According to Douglas, the more the social group exerts pressure on its individual members, the greater the demand for conformity expressed by the control of the body; bodily control is thus an expression of social control. The body, in other words, is above all a metaphor of society as a whole. An example of this theory may be seen in Terence Turner's 'The social skin' (see below, pp. 37–9).

FEMINISM AND THE BODY

Feminist anthropologists claim that gendered expectations and ideas about the body exist for both females and males. They point to the ways in which body ideals serve as mechanisms of social power and control. For most feminists, the rise of cosmetic surgery as a possible, and acceptable, means of self-modification represents the ongoing oppression of women by male concepts of beauty. They also claim that cultural institutions dominated by men, such as religion and medicine, also control ideas about women's bodies (see more on gender and feminism in chapter 9).

PHENOMENOLOGICAL APPROACHES

Although it may serve as a powerful symbolic medium, the body is also capable of participating in the creation of social meaning. Anthropologists have argued that the body is an active agent in the social world; it is not an object to be studied in relation to culture but is to be considered as the subject of culture.

In his analysis of perception (how we become aware of the sensory world around us), the philosopher Maurice Merleau-Ponty ([1962] 2014) rejects the notion of dualism and uses the concept of **embodiment**, which is the phenomenological way of knowing and experiencing the world around us through our own body. This perspective looks at how self-image and self-identity are affected by and help to shape notions of the normal body. Their perception of how they look may lead people to pursue real changes through dieting, exercise or even surgery to alter their body shape and change identity. Phenomenologically oriented anthropologists tend to focus on issues of individual identities, while social constructionists and feminists focus more on social meanings.

SYMBOLIC CLASSIFICATION AND THE BODY – THE BODY AND SOCIETY

Anthropologists look at the body as both an individual and a social entity which reflects the values and beliefs of the wider society to which it belongs. It is also seen as something that people continually 'create' or reproduce. Anthropologists have studied the relationship between the body and society – the body as a product of social and cultural forces. Robert Hertz and Terence Turner explored the body as a tool for thinking: how the human body is used to classify – that is, to place things into categories to make sense of the world around us. Although everyone has a body, not everyone speaks the same language or shares the same culture or religion. One way of understanding the body is to look at how it is used in symbols, myths, ritual, ethics and the definition of the sacred and the profane.

Handedness (Hertz [1909] 2008)

Hertz suggested that most societies encourage right-handedness through the process of socialization. He begins with the question of why the right hand should be associated almost universally with goodness, purity and auspiciousness and the left hand with evil, pollution and death. Hertz noticed that biological asymmetry was exaggerated by training, and that most societies encourage right-handedness at the expense of the left. Left-handed children may be discouraged from using their left hand or foot. They may be punished or ridiculed and have their hand bound or otherwise restricted. In many cultures it is common to eat and to greet someone with the right hand. The left hand may be associated with defecation and symbolize uncleanliness. The values and associations attributed to the right hand differ markedly from those of the left. The body gives societies a cue – left-handedness is everywhere less common than the dominance of the right. It is a convenient marker on which cultures have created symbolic associations that are as nearly universal as any symbol can be. When associations of left and right are compared cross-culturally, Hertz noticed that there is a striking uniformity. He also observed that, among the Maori, the right side is regarded as male and the left side as female and profane. For example he states that:

> Among the Maori, the right side is the sacred side, the seat of good and creative powers, the left is the profane side, possessing no virtue other than certain disturbing and suspect powers . . . the right side is the 'side of life' (and of strength) while the left is the 'side of death' (and of weakness). Fortunate and life giving influences enter us from the right and through our right side. Inversely, death and misery penetrate to the core of our being from the left. (Hertz [1909] 2008)

When asking himself why these polarities exist between left and right, Hertz suggests they derive from an attempt to link the human body to the natural world and to religion. The asymmetry between the right and left hand reflects the fundamental polarity of the spiritual world – that between the sacred and the profane – and this in turn reflects man's dual nature. 'It is because man is a double being – a natural/profane being and a social/sacred being.' With Hertz, the body is no longer seen as a mere biological given but is shown to carry the imprint of culture. What appears to be natural, the opposition between right and left, is in reality a social fact. (This is similar to Durkheim's understanding of the social world through social facts.) Bowie (2006) suggests that it is the human ability to use the body as a symbol, to think with and to impose meaning on the world that makes handedness so relevant. Therefore cultural rules can be made to appear natural. The symbolic weight given to right–left polarity is decreasing in Western societies, but this does not mean that categories associated with left- and right-handedness necessarily disappear. They may become attached to new meanings. This may reflect secularization or a reduction in gender role differentiation.

> **Handedness**
> A preference for using one hand as opposed to the other

Activity

What does handedness tell us about the power of culture as a means to control our bodies? Summarize the ways in which the 'left' and 'right' have been characterized in different societies.

Think about your own experiences of handedness. Were you encouraged to be right-handed? Think about others that you know. Are left-handers advantaged by being left-handed – say, in sport?

In your exercise book, try writing out your name and date of birth and the courses that you are taking in the opposite hand to the one you usually use. Can you read what you have written? How long did it take compared with writing with your usual hand? Do you think you could improve with practice?

What does this tell us about handedness?

Body Techniques (Mauss [1934] 2007)

Mauss describes 'techniques of the body' as the ways in which the body is trained within any culture. 'In every society, everyone knows and has to know and learn what they have to do in all conditions.' Every biological and physiological skill of which the human body is capable, such as eating, washing, sitting, swimming, running, climbing, child-rearing, and so on, has to be learnt. Mauss provides many examples of culturally varying body techniques, including the following observations:

- Polynesians do not swim as the British do.
- The French army does not march as the Germans do.
- Girls who have been raised in convents, unlike other girls, tend to walk with their fists closed.

These techniques can change within one person's lifetime. Mauss used the concept of 'habitus' (habit or custom, acquired ability) to describe these learnt techniques of the body. All humans have to eat in order to survive, but the way they eat, whether with a fork, chopsticks or with their fingers, is a cultural construction. Mauss extends the study of society to include physiological experience and emphasizes both the point that the body is symbolically constructed and that the way in which it is used is as much a product of culture as it is of nature. The body must therefore be studied in the context of wider symbolic systems, and the way in which it is used and represented provides us with a mirror of society. Each society has its own special habits. Humans are conditioned in using the body in different ways through the process of socialization. The body is a person's first and natural instrument, according to Mauss.

> **Habitus**
> The lifestyle, values, dispositions and expectations of particular social groups that are acquired through the activities and experiences of everyday life

Gregory Bateson studied the people of the Balinese village Bajoeng Gede (Bateson and Mead [1942] 1962). He explains how children's body positions are socially constructed. In order to separate themselves from animals that walk on all fours, the Balinese do not allow children to crawl. They separate themselves from animals and teach their children from the moment they are born how they should use their bodies.

> **Social construction**
> The view that the phenomena of the social and cultural world and their meanings are created in human social interaction

Every culture teaches young ones how to use their bodies. Here children are taking part in a school sports day in Sarawak, Malaysian Borneo. (© Liana Chua)

Babies grow up 'vertically' and are never allowed to crawl. From birth the body position is created by culture.

Habitus (Bourdieu 1977)

Bourdieu elaborates on the concept of habitus by explaining its dependency on history and human memory. For instance, a certain behaviour or belief becomes part of a society's structure when the original purpose of that behaviour or belief can no longer be recalled and becomes socialized into individuals of that culture. According to Bourdieu, the body is the most certain reflection of class taste, by the way that someone's hairstyle, clothing, diet, or even their manner of walking functions to signal social class position within the structure of society. Bourdieu places bodies within modern consumer culture, arguing that the body bears the imprint of social class based on **habitus** (an internalized framework or set of guidelines for social action, taste and social location). The body is a resource for, and can be converted into, economic, cultural and social capital. Bourdieu conducted fieldwork in Algeria and studied the culture of the Kabyle people. Their main habitus is based on honour, which underpins their basic schemes of thought and action. This provides them with a model of action even in new situations. The lifestyle, values and expectations of Kabyle people that are learnt through the activities and experiences of their everyday life are reflected in their body language. Bourdieu suggests that habitus can be changed throughout the lifetime of an individual.

'The social skin' (Turner 1995)

Terence Turner conducted his anthropological research on the Kayapo people of the grasslands of the Mato Grosso, south of the Amazon region, who live in scattered villages comprising several hundred people. He suggests that dress and bodily adornment is a cultural way to communicate personal and social identity. The Kayapo male, with his lip plate, penis sheath, large holes pierced through the ear lobes from which hang small strings of beads, overall body paint in red and black patterns, plucked eyebrows, eyelashes and facial hair, and head shaved to a point at the crown with the hair left long to the sides and back, has many cultural meanings to the tribe.

Turner shows how, for the Kayapo, the body is conceptualized as a 'social skin'. Turner's notion of the body as a social skin is connected to the idea that the body is in some ways a microcosm of society. He suggests that decorating, covering and uncovering the human body in accordance with social ideas of everyday expectations or sacred dress, beauty or status seems to have been a concern of every human society. Turner describes and discusses how the surface of the body becomes the symbolic stage upon which socialization is enacted. He argues that bodily adornment, which ranges from body painting to clothing, from headdresses to cosmetics, becomes the language through which socialization is expressed. Further, he argues that culture is not only the medium through which identities (social status, attitudes, our desires and beliefs) are communicated. Turner describes how the Kayapo possess a complex code of what could be called 'dress' or bodily adornment, but which does not actually involve the use of clothing: the bodily adornments listed above (lip plates, body paint, etc.) constitute what Westerners call 'clothing' in their society. Here are some of the meanings for Kayapo which turn the biological body into a social body.

- **Cleanliness**
  All Kayapo bathe at least once a day; to be dirty is to be antisocial and is even dangerous to the health of the unwashed individual. Health is perceived as a state of full and proper integration into the social world.

- **Hair**
  The removal of facial and bodily hair, including eyebrows and eyelashes, transforms the skin from a mere physical body part into a sort of social filter. The length of hair signifies an individual's bodily participation with others in reproductive processes. The wearing of long and short hair ties into Kayapo ideas about the nature of family relations. Different Kayapo groups have their own distinctive hairstyles, which stand as symbols of their own group culture.

  Certain types of people in Kayapo society are allowed to wear long hair, including women who have given birth to children and adult men who have been through initiation and received their penis sheaths. The cutting of the hair on the head represents a distinct social code that communicates information about the individual's stage of development. Those who must keep their hair short include children and adolescents of both sexes. The child's hair remains short as a sign of its biological separation from its parents.

- **Body painting as 'social skin'**
  The bodies of Kayapo of all ages and genders are painted according to a code comprising colours, design and style. The painting of the body marks stages and modes of socialization of the body's natural powers, symbolizing muscular strength and energy, sexuality and reproductivity. Two colours are used in the painting – red and black – and each serves to signify different things. The word for black also means dead, and the colour is associated with **taboo** and natural states incompatible with normal social existence. Red is associated with vitality and energy. The application

of these two paints on different parts of the body is also significant to the social meaning of bodily adornment for the Kayapo.

- **Pierced ears, ear plugs, lip plates**
Just as hair and body painting becomes a code that represents a whole system of ideas about the relationship between the individual and society, so the piercing of ears and ear and lip plugs comprise a similar set of complex meanings. The emphasis here is on socialization and self-expression. The Kayapo distinguish between passive and active modes of knowing. The most important aspect of passive understanding is the ability to 'hear' language. To be able to hear and understand speech is referred to in terms of having a hole in one's ear. The piercing of the ear lobes of babies represents this. The lip plate, which is most pronounced in older men, is also symbolic. Only males have their lips pierced, soon after birth, when their lower lips are fitted with a string of beads. The lip plug, and later the disc, is a physical expression of the oral assertiveness and power of the orator. It also embodies the social dominance of the senior males. In short, speaking and 'hearing' (or understanding and conforming) are complementary and interdependent functions that constitute Kayapo political and social life, and it is through the medium of bodily adornment that the body becomes a microcosm of the Kayapo body politic.

For the Kayapo, the various stages and types of bodily adornment as described above represent the human life cycle. The life cycle is biologically linked to others through social form and expression. Bodily adornments constitute a system of categories and meanings. Turner concludes by acknowledging that bodily adornment, considered as a symbolic medium, is not unique to Kayapo culture, but that every society has a number of such media and languages with which to communicate the relationship between the individual and social bodies.

STOP & THINK

How are body paintings in Kayapo culture used to classify status, age and gender?
What is the meaning of hair, ears, face painting and lip plates in Kayapo culture?

Tattooing

The skin is the body's largest organ. **Tattooing** involves the penetration of the skin with ink in order to stain it permanently with colour. The permanent modification of the human body through tattooing is culturally constructed. The word 'tattoo' derives from the Polynesian word *tatau*, meaning 'to strike' or 'to inflict wounds'. In the past, high-status men among the New Zealand Maori and in the Marquesas, in Polynesia, were completely tattooed. Considerable portions of the body were also tattooed in Samoa, Tahiti, Hawai'i, and other Pacific islands, while in the West tattoos were always associated with sailors, adventurers and prison inmates. In Japan, tattoos carried an association with gangsters known as Yakuza. Tattoos, in some societies, have been used throughout history to mark someone as an outcast or as someone else's property. Examples are the tattooing of slaves in ancient Rome, of gangsters in Japan and China, of convicts transported to Australia in the eighteenth and nineteenth centuries, and of Jews in Nazi concentration camps such as Auschwitz. Prostitutes in some parts of Eastern Europe are tattooed as an indication of ownership. All of these practices denied personhood to certain groups of people. This shows how some bodies were

In the West, tattoos have become seen as an art form, allowing an individual to express part of their personality or beliefs in a permanent way. (© GOLFX/Shutterstock.com)

controlled and labelled as less important and unequal to others. However, since the 1960s, tattooing has become increasingly popular in the West as a statement of individualism, independence, rebellion, and fashion or gang culture. Sports people and celebrities have made tattooing a fashion statement and increased its popularity. David Beckham, Chris Brown and Lil Wayne are some examples of high-profile celebrities who are heavily tattooed

Anthropologists have always been interested in studying tattooing and how the body is used to express different meanings for individuals and the cultures in which they live. Tattoos are a visible non-verbal way of expressing many things. They are an example of people using their bodies as a canvas. What is chosen as a **tattoo** is the result of both personal and cultural factors. A tattoo may be a personal symbol but it also has social meaning.

Tattoos can provide an effective way of communicating many things, such as personal, social or religious characteristics or cultural pride and identity. Tattoos can be linked to a transition from one stage of life to another. They can form part of an initiation that marks the passage from boyhood to manhood or from girlhood to womanhood. For some cultures, tattooing is necessary to establish humans as full social beings. The Roro people of Central Province, Papua New Guinea, describe a person who is not tattooed as 'raw', comparing him to uncooked meat. Maori warriors of New Zealand have facial tattoos (called *moko*) to intimidate and distract enemies. Throughout history in many different cultures tattooing has been a way of creating an

Tattoo
A permanent mark or design made on the skin by a process of pricking and ingraining an indelible pigment or by raising scars

identity. The following ethnographic case study is an example of how young people in Polynesia use tattoos as a way of establishing solidarity within their peer groups.

Tattoo: an Anthropology (Kuwahara 2005)

Kuwahara conducted fieldwork in Tahiti, Polynesia, from 1998 to 2000. During her fieldwork she spent many hours in participant observation of tattoo artists. This included visiting tattoo studios and festivals and conducting formal and informal interviews of tattooists, clients and friends. Kuwahara explains the meaning of tattooing in contemporary French Polynesian Society and argues that, as a permanent inscription, a tattoo makes a powerful statement about identity and culture. She examines the complex significance of this art in relation to gender, youth culture, ethnicity and prison life. There are many ways that Tahitians modify their bodies, but one very powerful modification is tattooing, which is highly visible and permanent.

HISTORY OF TATTOOING IN TAHITI

The Tahitian body has been treated differently across different periods of history. Before the arrival of the Europeans, Polynesian culture was highly structured by class, and tattooing was used as a powerful way to mark these class differences. It was abandoned in the 1830s due to suppression by Christian missionaries, who perceived it as uncivilized, and a law was introduced forbidding it. However, it was revived in 1980 as a part of a cultural revitalization movement. The contemporary practice is implicated in youth culture, prisons, modernity and gender relationships.

THE BODY AND IDENTITY

According to Kuwahara, the body is the basis for identifying ourselves as different to others and a medium through which we relate to others. We form personal and social identities and establish social relationships through the body. The manipulation of the body by tattooing can be considered as an active practice by which people engage in self-identification and positioning in their relationships with others. Kuwahara explores issues of identity, position and relationship by investigating the following questions:

- What is the meaning of the body when related to tattooing?
- Why do people mark the body?
- What are the consequences of marking?
- What is the relationship between the body, the self and the society?
- Do people get tattoos simply of their own free will?

She demonstrates that the body is socially and historically constructed; it remains physical but it is marked by ink. She considers that tattooing as an inscription or writing is significant in terms of identity formation.

AGE

Agency
The capacity for human beings to make choices, create their own world, have their own ideas, etc.

Adolescence is a period of life in which young people are integrated into the adult community, and those who have gone through this stage are socially recognized as being ready to take an adult role by marrying and having children. However, this approach obscures young people's **agency**. Through the processes of modernity and globalization, young people from Tahiti were involved in cultural transformation. Tattooing in Tahiti was practised in the past as a part of an initiation ceremony and indicated maturation and a person's availability for sexual relations. Tattoos on the arm were tokens to show that children had gone through the ceremony and were allowed to participate in adult social activities. The adolescents had tattoos on their buttocks, which were not only associated with rites of passage but also had the function of demonstrating availability for sexual access and fertility. In Tahiti today, tattooing no longer marks maturation. Those who are tattooed neither perform the ceremony nor get the tattoos on their arms or buttocks to prove maturity. Kuwahara argues that contemporary tattooing has been developed mainly by young people and has become a significant component of youth culture. Such body marking has an effective role in the formation of solidarity, as it shows that adolescents belong to the same group and also differentiates them from others. Tattooing is practised not to integrate young people into adult social networks but to form an extended network of friendship and identity of adolescents of similar age. Kuwahara analyses the reasons why young Tahitians mark their bodies when they are at this stage of their lives.

People from different cultures use tattoos to mark transitions from one stage of life to another. This photo was taken in Bali. (© Shane Tan)

IDEOLOGY AND THE BODY

The tattooed body is constructed and constrained within a system of social meaning. Kuwahara argues that there is an individual agency in this social construction and transformation. Body modification, including tattooing, is an active practice of individuals. To be masculine for Tahitian men is to be physically and mentally strong. Physical strength is expressed in the figure of the ancient warrior. Masculinity is established through adolescence – the period in which to enjoy liberty from the domestic and social obligations that will arrive with age. By embodying warrior masculinity, Tahitian men are emancipated from female-dominated households. The male is constructed through interrelations with different genders and ethnicities. The Tahitian world of tattooing is dominated by males from their late teens to early thirties, and tattooing encourages bonding between boys and solidarity during adolescence. Kuwahara shows how identity has been established locally, regionally and globally based on gender, ethnic and age differences and transformed through inclusion or exclusion and similarities or differences in various social interactions and relationships. During the period of gaining independence from the French, many Tahitian tattooists, dancers, artisans and musicians involved in leading the cultural revitalization movement freed tattooing from a colonial moral structure which disapproved of it and reconnected it to their ancestral significance as a body marking of cultural identity.

Globalization: Tattoos and Tattooing

In an increasingly global world, designs, motifs, even techniques of tattooing move across cultural boundaries, and in the process their original meanings are often lost or changed. Polynesian tattoo designs worn by Westerners are admired for the beauty of their graphic qualities, but their original cultural meanings are rarely understood. A tattoo in Tahiti was once worn to signify status and beliefs, but in London it becomes a sign of rebellion from conformist culture. Traditional body modifications are given new meanings as they move across cultural and social boundaries. In the past, tattoos in Tahiti showed the importance of an individual's social status. In contemporary global society, while drawing on traditions from around the world, a tattoo is more likely to indicate a person's individuality.

Tattooing is a physical personal experience which is also embedded in the historical and cultural context of each society. In Tahiti, being tattooed or not is no longer a question of social obligation but a matter of stating who you are and who you are living with and for. Thus, to be tattooed is to write one's relationships on the body. Kuwahara examines how people situate themselves in the world, physically and ideologically, through the process of tattooing. Tattooing allows the young people of Tahiti to reinvent themselves, to rebel, to follow fashion, or to play and experiment with new identities. People in everyday life use body art to cross boundaries of gender, national identity and cultural stereotypes.

Ways of Modifying the Body: Tattooing the Convict Body (DeMello 2000)

Another way of creating identity through tattooing, though in a different context, was explored by Margo DeMello, who spent three years doing fieldwork among the American tattoo community. She interviewed convicts and prison guards from the Folsom State Prison, California.

The body is a site on which gender, ethnicity and class are symbolically marked. Tattoos and the process of inscription create the cultural body; as well as erecting and maintaining specific social boundaries, they articulate body and psyche. If tattoos make the body culturally visible, then prison tattoos, and especially those on the face, neck and hands, are especially conspicuous. DeMello explores the significance of tattoos in prison and beyond and also looks at how tattooing is carried out. She argues that tattooing plays a crucial role in creating the convict's sense of identity and acts as a way of asserting cultural differences. Prison tattoos are not professional and are, therefore, particularly distinctive. They range from the crude to the relatively refined.

WHAT MAKES PRISONERS CHOOSE THEIR TATTOO?

The choice of tattoo can be based on where the prisoner came from or on his present situation in prison. One of the most popular tattoos is the *loca*, which gives the name of the convict's neighbourhood of origin or his gang affiliation. This is very important as it serves as a reminder of the community to which the displaced convict belongs and distinguishes him when he encounters other gang members from rival groups. Also having an ethnic affiliation – e.g., 'white power' – tattooed on one's body means identifying with another type of community. Other popular choices for tattoos are bars, the scales of justice, barbed wire, and other themes which echo the prisoner's experiences. Perhaps the most powerful prison tattoo is the tear, tattooed just below the corner of the eye. These can, for example, be for each person killed. The tear may alternatively symbolize the convict's suffering at the hands of justice. Christian symbols are also popular. Finally, tattoos of women, Harley Davidson imagery and fantasy images, as well as antisocial statements such as FTW (fuck the world), are also very popular.

HOW ARE PRISON TATTOOS DIFFERENT FROM NORMAL TATTOOS?

In prison, tattoos are paid for with drugs, money or canteen food. Because there is less money in prison than outside, the costs are relatively low. There is an important distinction between a convict and an inmate in prisons. An inmate has no respect. He is a model prisoner, one who bows to authority. Tattooing therefore is largely a convict activity, not for inmates. The average age for tattooing seems to be between twenty and thirty-five. There are no statistics, but DeMello guesses that over 50 per cent of all prisoners have tattoos, and of these most are whites and Chicanos (Mexican Americans). Tattooists tend only to tattoo someone of their own ethnic origin – it can be dangerous to tattoo someone from a different ethnic group. An 'honourable' prison tattooist doesn't want to be responsible for helping to ruin a young prisoner's life, and once someone has been tattooed it can make concrete his identity as a convict. Those who are in prison for some time tend to cover old tattoos and get new, better-looking ones. Convicts who leave prison either wait for their tattooist to get released or simply reoffend to have their tattoo completed.

Tattooing is illegal in the prison where DeMello interviewed prisoners, and the ramifications when caught include having equipment confiscated, privileges removed, and being locked up in solitary confinement. The work is carried out in secret, typically during the day, when other inmates are exercising or playing cards. The guards in this prison have mixed views on tattooing; some will turn a blind eye or even get tattoos themselves, whereas others are more strict in upholding the rules.

WHY IS TATTOOING IMPORTANT?

Tattoos are linked to fundamental patterns of social stratification among wearers. Different tattoos are associated with different classes, with prison tattoos being the lowest social position, as opposed to the fine art worn by elite members of the professional community. Tattoos therefore provide boundaries between low and high culture. Tattooing also creates the 'convict body', revealing the particular affiliations – gang, ethnic, personal – of the convict, and these have important ramifications for such individuals inside and outside of the prison. Convicts who try to get their tattoo designs published in magazines are generally rejected, and rarely are they employed in professional tattoo shops. Tattooing in prison is also about creating a shared culture. It enables groups within the prison to distinguish themselves from others and also helps produce meaning in the prisoner's life. A tattoo can act as an initiation into a new group. Moreover, tattoos represent an act of defiance, rejection of the rules and values of mainstream society.

> **Activity**
>
> Why is tattooing important?
> What is the difference between tattoos gained by convicts and inmates?
> Identify the functions of tattoos in prisons (there are at least five).
> What are the similarities and differences in creating identity through tattooing in prisons and Tahiti?
> Explain some of the reasons tattoos are used to modify the body.

Globalization: The Body

Body organ trafficking

As a result of consumerism, media, the tourist industry and global migration, in most societies people have changed the way they think about the body. The vulnerability of bodies is apparent within the context of globalization, illustrated by a rise in global organ trafficking in which the human body is viewed as a pure commodity. It is mostly the poorest and the most disadvantaged people of the Global South that sell their organs and other body tissues to affluent people in the First World countries. In the UK, tens of thousands of people are on the waiting list for organ transplantation. Organ procurement is based on a voluntary system, where individuals choose to donate organs. There is more demand for the organs than supply in this process, and many people never receive the organ they need to survive. This has led to an increase in transplant tourism, where buyers from the UK, the USA or Europe travel to developing countries in search of affordable kidneys and other body parts.

Virtual bodies

Cyber-culture and new media technologies have expanded and extended the way the body looks and functions in the boundary between the real and virtual, as the human and the machine overlap and merge (this is explored more fully in chapter 10). Since the Internet has become a common public sphere of social interaction, networking and recreation, the constitution and definition of the body has become even more fluid in cyberspace. Interaction in the virtual world does not require physical presence. Through the mediated image of the self, humans communicate and create versions of their own bodies in this cyberspace. Virtual places, such as Second Life, free the body from its physical limitations, as it can be rewritten through an avatar or a visual representation of the user. In real life humans encounter characteristics such as gender, race, ethnicity and age, but in the virtual world the avatars transcend biological and social status variables.

The global capitalist economy has also fuelled female sexual slavery, sexual tourism and the trafficking of women and children, especially from undeveloped countries. These exploited people provide examples of how bodies are shaped through technological, political, economic and cultural traditions in the modern global world.

CONCLUSION

Bodies are socially constructed in different ways across different cultures. Human bodies transmit complex information about themselves even within a single cultural context, and the message of the body is subject to change over time. The body is a form of communication, whether permanent – through tattoos, scarification, piercing or plastic surgery – or temporary – via make-up, clothing or hairstyles. All of these body modifications convey information about a person's identity. Many forms of body modification are associated with initiation or marriage, marking the transition from one status to another. There are many ways in which humans attempt to control and modify the body. These are universal, but they are also diverse. The body therefore is a symbol of culture in that it 'performs' or represents the culture of an individual. The ways that humans are able to place value on the body or control it are becoming ever more complex through technological advances.

END OF CHAPTER ASSESSMENT

Examine some of the ways in which humans attempt to control and modify the body.

Teacher's guidance

This is asking you to consider how human bodies are used to interpret the world around them. You should show your knowledge and understanding but be critical and analytical too. Begin by illustrating at least three ways in which humans attempt to control the body and at least two ways in which humans try to modify the body. Consider the following in your answer: Is there such a thing as the 'natural body'? How do culture and society impact on the body? And, in turn, how does the biological body influence how humans think, create language and culture, and engage with the environment?

Use ethnographies to support and illustrate your arguments. Are bodily gestures, expressions and postures genetically programmed and universal or learnt and culturally relative? How is body image related to society? How is the body socially constructed? Include some theoretical approaches to the body. Come to a clear conclusion about the ways in which humans attempt to control and modify the body.

KEY TERMS

Agency The capacity for human beings to make choices, create their own world, have their own ideas, etc.
Body modification The deliberate altering of the human anatomy
Embodiment A tangible or visible form of an idea, quality or feeling
Habitus The lifestyle, values, dispositions and expectations of particular social groups that are acquired through the activities and experiences of everyday life
Handedness A preference for using one hand as opposed to the other
Social construction The view that the phenomena of the social and cultural world and their meanings are created in human social interaction
Taboo A custom prohibiting or restricting a particular practice or forbidding association with a particular person, place or thing
Tattoo A permanent mark or design made on the skin by a process of pricking and ingraining an indelible pigment or by raising scars

> ### Personal investigation
>
> **Martial arts culture**
>
> Find and join a martial arts class – Judo, Karate, Kung Fu, Thai Chi, Taekwondo, etc. The following are issues to address in your research.
>
> **Social and cultural aspects of the body**
>
> Most martial arts originate from East Asia. Look into the historical background to your chosen martial art and explain how it offers an insight into how the cultures of China, Japan and Korea have developed the martial arts as a way of training and mastering the body.
>
> **Attitudes towards the body (what's important in society – e.g., gender, size)**
>
> The body is central to the martial arts. Martial artists develop their bodies to the extent that they can be used as a weapon. Strength and ability to do extraordinary tasks are respected by these cultures. However, the martial arts masters also emphasize that mental attitude is vital. There is an important relationship between the mind and body in becoming a martial arts expert.
>
> **The body as a symbol: expression of identity (individual or part of a group) and communication**
>
> The martial arts body is an important source of identity for those who practise martial arts. By performing and showing what they have been able to do with their bodies, they manage to achieve a certain status. The martial arts body can communicate strength and ability to defend itself against those who threaten it.
>
> **Controlling the body: self-control, discipline**
>
> Through years of hard work, the individual can do what may be considered almost 'superhuman' feats with the body. This is exemplified by Shaolin monks, who perform extraordinary body feats. Their bodies are able to endure pain through constant exposure to it – e.g., putting their hands in hot sand or banging them against hard surfaces. The work to become a martial artist requires incredible self-discipline. It shows how human beings are able to overcome many biological disadvantages through what are essentially cultural practices. There is no practical reason today to develop the body's ability to such an extent. The motivation is more to do with self-esteem and self-satisfaction and social status. It may also relate to economic motives – martial artists can earn money through their performances. The control of the body therefore comes from the individual and their own motivation, as well as cultural pressures.
>
> **Society's control of the body**
>
> The martial arts appear to be mainly about the individual's own identity. Martial arts training is not forced on anyone. However, aside from martial arts, many men and women may feel the pressure of society to gain respect by developing the body. This can be seen especially in concern over the shape of the muscular body.

SUGGESTED FURTHER READING AND FILMS

Books

Bowie, F. (2006) *The Anthropology of Religion: An Introduction*. 2nd edn, Blackwell.

Csordas, T. J. (1999) 'The body's career in anthropology', in H. L. Moore (ed.), *Anthropological Theory Today*. Polity.

DeMello, M. (2000) *Bodies of Inscription: A Cultural History of the Modern Tattoo Community*. Duke University Press.

Kuwahara, M. (2005) *Tattoo: An Anthropology*. Berg.

Lock, M., and J. Farquhar (2007) *Beyond the Body Proper: Reading the Anthropology of Material Life*. Duke University Press.

Rubin, A. (1988) *Marks of Civilization*. Los Angeles Museum of Cultural History.

Staples, J. (2010) 'Body', in A. Barnard and J. Spencer (eds), *Encyclopedia of Social and Cultural Anthropology*. 2nd edn, Routledge.

Turner, T. (1995) 'Social body and embodied subject: bodiliness, subjectivity, and sociality among the Kayapo', *Cultural Anthropology* 10(2): 143–70.

Wacquant, L. (2004) *Body & Soul: Notebooks of an Apprentice Boxer*. Oxford University Press.

Ethnographic films

Tighten the Drums: Self-Decoration among the Enga (1983), anthropologist: Chris Owen [a look into the art of body decoration as a visual language in the western highlands of Papua New Guinea]

Websites

The displays at the University of Oxford's Pitt Rivers Museum and the Body Arts, Virtual Collections website are designed to illustrate some of the many ways in which people around the world have modified their bodies and to offer some explanations for why they have done so: http://web.prm.ox.ac.uk/bodyarts.

CHAPTER THREE

WAYS OF
THINKING AND
COMMUNICATING

CONTENTS

Ways of Thinking and Communicating

> **KEY ISSUES AND DEBATES**
> - What is classification and why do humans classify?
> - How do people explain events beyond their control?
> - How do humans communicate and how is this different from other primates?
> - How did humans acquire language and why?
> - What is the relationship between culture and language?
> - How have new forms of technology affected communication?

As we saw in chapter 1, part of what makes humans unique is their ability to organize their thoughts and communicate. This chapter looks at the variety of ways in which humans make sense of their environment. Human beings also appear to need to explain events beyond their control: a number of different types of explanations will be explored, drawing on a number of cross-cultural examples. There is much debate among anthropologists about the relationship between the ways in which people understand and explain the world around them – for example, the extent to which their language reflects a particular world-view. The final section of the chapter examines the ways people communicate in a variety of verbal and non-verbal ways. This section will also consider the impact of new forms of technology on how people communicate.

> **Activity**
> How do we learn to put things into categories?
> What are the functions of classification?
> Why is it important for anthropologists to understand classification systems in other cultures?

Classification
A system of organization of people, places and things shared by all humans in different ways in different cultures

CLASSIFICATION

Classification seems to be one of the most basic aspects of human thinking and language. It helps people make sense of the complicated and potentially confusing world around them, and it also provides a shared system from which language can be developed. People divide up the world into categories which are specific to their place and context. It is necessary for these categories to be shared in order for people to communicate and share meaning. However, as we will see, learning the classification system of a specific culture is a complex process which goes beyond simply learning a language.

> **Activity**
>
> Look around the room that you are in and pick three objects. Use three words to describe the objects other than those most commonly used for each. Compare your results with those of someone else. What does this activity tell us about classification?

How Do We Learn our Classification Systems?

Humans learn their culturally specific forms of classification through **socialization**. Socialization is a process of internalizing the norms and values of a particular group. This is more than simply learning the name of something, as words take on specific cultural meanings, which may be implied or inferred. When babies learn their first words, they also learn a meaning connected to the word. They learn to label a word for each 'category' of meaning. For example, the word 'Daddy' in some cultures may be used initially for all adults or men until greater understanding has developed. Alternatively, in some cultures 'Daddy' applies to a person or a specific range of people throughout life. Later the child learns that there are variations in their classification systems in relation to a person's social status, for example. Early meanings and classifications become so ingrained that people do not usually question them or their meaning.

Anthropological Research and Classification

When studying a new culture, it is the anthropologist's job to make sense of alternative classification systems. Rodney Needham (1963) commented that a person's first impression of another culture is usually confusing, complex and hard to make sense of. The question is how can anthropologists make sense of another classification system, given that they are so steeped in their own?

It is important that anthropologists are aware of their own view of the world when studying other cultures. **Cultural relativism** is an important concept in this context: it means accepting that each culture has its own value and worth and that all beliefs, customs and ethics are bound by their culture. In other words, 'right' and 'wrong' are culture-specific; what is considered moral in one society may be considered immoral in another. Cultural relativism is somewhat controversial as a doctrine, but to some extent it is part of many anthropologists' methodological approach to understanding other cultures.

> **Cultural relativism**
> The idea that each culture has its own value and worth and that all beliefs, customs and ethics are bound by their culture

In the past, anthropologists tended to focus on understanding classification systems of so-called primitive people. Lucien Lévy-Bruhl ([1910] 1985) described the mentality of such people as 'pre-logical', while W. H. R. Rivers ([1926] 1999) questioned the idea that there was a difference between the so-called primitive and the observer in terms of their capacity for logical thought. He claimed that things were simply classified in different ways in other cultures. For example, in Melanesia, the word *mate* means dead, yet the word is also applied to the living. *Mate* can also mean 'very ill' or 'very old'. Therefore this reveals that, in Melanesia, life and death are less than clear-cut categories.

Primitive Classification: Mental Categories Originate in Society (Durkheim and Mauss [1903] 1963)

An early study of classification was carried out by the French scholars Emile Durkheim (1858–1917) and his nephew Marcel Mauss (1872–1950), who collected information gathered by anthropologists from various parts of the world and discussed the classification of space and time, as well as of people and animals.

Durkheim and Mauss both argued that classification systems are a product of society. They claimed that the way humans classify has a significant impact on many aspects of life. For example, classification may dictate whom a person might marry. Durkheim used Australian Aborigines as an example of alternative systems and argued that the classifications of family or **kinship** relations cannot necessarily be translated into other systems of classification (for more on kinship, see chapter 4).

Durkheim and Mauss also explore the issue of space and time. They point out that everyone on Earth sees the sun rise and set daily and the moon wax and wane monthly, and witnesses a variety of seasons coming and going on an annual basis. However, there are many way of classifying these events. It is quite common to have a system of directions that includes north, south, east and west, measured, of course, in reference to the movement of the sun. Some systems also include the directions of up and down and/or centre. Complications arise for an outsider when other aspects of the universe are classified with these divisions. For example, some Native Americans organize their clans in relation to each of the directions, which also have animals and plants associated with them, as well as aspects of colour, climate and character (more on this later).

Another topic that was discussed in some detail by Durkheim and Mauss was the classification of time. They used the example of the twelve Chinese signs, which mark each year as associated with a particular animal or bird. They also noted that each day, and even each hour, can be further classified as associated with one of the five elements – fire, water, wood, metal and earth – each an aspect of yin and yang. Such associations have interesting implications, thought to affect the character of a child born on a particular day, or to make a day good for doing business, or carrying out a baptism or a funeral. Such a system may affect the way that decisions are made in Chinese communities around the world. This system is different from, though comparable to, the Western astrological signs, which may have some of the same implications. Another parallel with the West is in the way days of the week have been given different associations, some according to religious ideas, set aside for worship, others related to work. In this way Durkheim and Mauss stress the **culturally constructed** nature of classification.

The structuralist Claude Lévi-Strauss (1966) argues that it is the physical brain structure that predisposes people to classify what we find in the world in a particular way, and thus that classification is a universal feature of the human mind.

> **Cultural construction**
> The creation of ideas by people in a specific social context which then take on their own perceived reality

Changes in Classification Systems: Gender

There have been significant changes in the role of women in the West over the past forty years. The ways that men and women are classified is continually being renegotiated and reformulated. For example, the role of women in Western societies in the recent past has been based largely around the view that women's specific biology determines their role as caregivers. The increase in the number of women choosing to remain childless in the UK, for example, demonstrates that **gender** roles are not linked to biology alone. There have also been significant changes in the ways that masculinity is constructed (see chapter 9 for more on gender).

Colour Classification

In the UK, Newton's classification of bands of colour into the seven 'colours of the rainbow' identified by scientific measurements is widely accepted. However, there are many different shades of blue. The Japanese word *aoi* may be applied to something described as 'blue' (light), as 'green' (pine tree colour), the 'go' traffic light colour, or a person feeling sick or pale. The Welsh language also has differences in colour classification; there is no Welsh equivalent for the colour brown in English. *Gwinau* is brown when referring to a horse or someone's hair colour, but the word cannot be applied to other objects, such as a car; talking about a *gwinau* car would be seen as quite ridiculous. This example alone demonstrates the complexity of classification systems.

> **STOP & THINK**
>
> Think about words used to classify colours that are also used to describe a mood or emotion. Provide three examples, and be ready to explain why these colours are linked to moods or emotions.

EXPLAINING EVENTS

Different Systems of Thought, the Rationality Debate and Ways of Explaining Events

The way that people think can be a challenging area to understand, as many thoughts are private and internally understood and are not always observable using the methods typically employed by anthropologists. On the other hand, thoughts are often expressed in social life, through actions, in rituals and other public performances, which are directly observable. One interesting area to explore is how different social groups explain events beyond their control, such as natural disasters, accidents, illness and death, and human wrongdoing.

THE RATIONALITY DEBATE

Studies of thought and reasoning have been central to anthropology since its beginnings. Early thinkers such as James Frazer ([1890] 1993) regarded non-Western people as 'savages' with a very limited ability to think rationally and logically, a view for which he was heavily criticized, primarily for his **ethnocentric** attitudes but also for his lack of empirical evidence.

The idea of 'rational thought' was a product of the **Enlightenment** (see chapter 1) and coincides with the development of the natural sciences and secularization. This world-view (which was found not only in Europe but also in other parts of the world, such as in medieval Islam) claims that events can be explained through rational principles. However, rational explanations are often used in combination with other ways of understanding the world. For example, if someone is hurt, it may be argued that this is because of an accident or bad luck, yet the person may also seek medical advice. Combining different beliefs or explanations is known as **syncretism**.

Ethnocentrism
Regarding one's own ethnicity as superior to others and/or viewing others only through one's own cultural categories; privileging one's own cultural world-view

SPIRITUAL POWERS

Many believe that misfortune is caused by spiritual powers. The violation of a taboo can lead to sickness, as the ancestral spirits of kin groups cause their members to become ill because of conflict or bad feelings within the group. Drowning, falls, snakebites, failure to succeed at some activity – such events may all be evidence of unfavourable supernatural intervention. The victim has offended a god or a spirit, who brings an 'accident' as punishment.

MAGIC AND SORCERY

Magic
The performance of rites and spells intended to cause supernatural effects on oneself or others

Sorcery
The performance of rites and spells for the purpose of controlling individuals (not always involving the supernatural)

Magic can be defined as the performance of rites and spells intended to cause supernatural effects positive or negative, on oneself or others. **Sorcery**, on the other hand, is a form of bad magic. Sometimes, people think illness or other misfortunes are caused by the action of some evil human using supernatural powers against an afflicted person. This belief that certain individuals, called sorcerers and witches, have powers to harm others by mystical means is enormously widespread. Sometimes, witches and sorcerers are thought to strike randomly and maliciously against innocent people who have done nothing wrong. More commonly, however, they direct their evil magic or thoughts towards those against whom they have a grudge.

The prehistoric monument of Stonehenge, located near Salisbury in the English county of Wiltshire, was built 5,000 years ago. There are no written records as to why it was built. Some suggest that it was a burial site, others that it was a place of healing. Alternative reasons include the idea that it was built for human sacrifice or astronomy.
(© Tomislav Marić)

WITCHCRAFT

Witchcraft
The use of psychic powers to produce a particular effect on others

Witchcraft can be defined as the use of psychic powers to produce a particular effect (often unwelcome) on others. Witchcraft varies enormously: for example, the Navajo of the American Southwest associate it with the worst imaginable sins, such as incest or cannibalism. In contrast, the Nyakyusa of Tanzania argue that witches are motivated mainly by their lust for food; accordingly they suck dry the udders of people's cattle and devour the internal organs of their human neighbours while they sleep. The Gebusi of Papua New Guinea have been known to blame illness on witchcraft. They killed so many individuals identified as witches that nearly one-third of all deaths among them resulted from revenge attacks.

E. E. Evans-Pritchard was among those who criticized Lévy-Bruhl for judging other societies as inferior. In the 1930s he carried out lengthy fieldwork in the Sudan among the Nuer people. However, one of his best-known works is the study he carried out several hundred miles south of the Nuer, on the Azande people. This research is much respected and provides detailed insight to a non-Western system of thought. The study of witchcraft among the Azande tells us about a way of explaining events that maintains social order. Evans-Pritchard's research was based on an ethnographic approach, which involved him living not only with but also in the manner of the people being studied. He was particularly interested in the problem of 'cultural translation'. This refers to the difficulty anthropologists face when trying to understand another culture based on a very different mental world and then trying to explain that world accurately to others without losing the essential aspects of that culture. His research, then, consisted of efforts to see a culture from the point of view of those living inside it.

Witchcraft, Oracles and Magic among the Azande (Evans-Pritchard 1937)

In order to understand Evans-Pritchard's study, it is important to appreciate some of the history of Sudan. Sudan is the largest African country and was colonized first by the French and Belgians in the late nineteenth century, then by the British in the early twentieth century. The Azande were crop growers. Azande traditional leaders were seriously undermined in their role and power by British colonizers.

When an untoward event occurs, according to Evans-Pritchard, Azande people were likely to explain it in terms of witchcraft. The next step was to consider who might wish to cause harm to the affected individual. Using witchcraft, the Azande question why it was that that a particular person had happened to sit underneath the granary at the specific time when it collapsed on top of him/her. Evans-Pritchard claimed that the Azande people maintain that witchcraft had to be involved in such an event. Death and disease among the Azande are also seen to be a result of witchcraft.

The Azande say that the soul of witchcraft travels through the night but that it cannot travel far. As a result, the Azande like to live some distance from their neighbours. In order to discover if an individual is a witch, an oracle is consulted. The Azande have a hierarchy of oracles, and not all of them are human. An oracle is someone or something acting as a medium for communicating with ancestors and finding out who might be responsible for committing witchcraft. By consulting an oracle, the Azande people hope to bring about some resolution to conflict and to restore peace and equilibrium.

There are different types of oracle, but the most expensive and well known is the poison oracle, which uses a strong poison and chickens. The poison is fed to a chicken, and then the poison is asked if a particular person is a witch or not; if the chicken dies, the answer is yes, if it survives, the person is not a witch. To determine an accurate answer, a range of different questions are asked of several chickens. If it is discovered that a person is a witch, the dead chicken has its wing cut off and it is placed on a stick and brought to the local deputy chief, who is given the name of the accused. The wing is presented to the accused, who then takes a mouthful of water and sprays it on the wing. In doing so, he or she asks the victim of the witchcraft to recover, and the deputy chief is informed. In the case of a 'murder' or the death of a person, the penalty could be higher: revenge was sought and sometimes led to the death of the person accused of witchcraft. In pre-colonial times, the accused person was required to swallow the poison. Evans-Pritchard argues that the Azande people's way of explaining events and acting is rational and logical given their cultural context. He showed how witchcraft functioned to maintain social order by managing conflict and explaining events that could cause problems within a social group. It was usually people of an equal social ranking who accused each other; men, for example, accused men and women accused women. Accusations were usually made among the politically weak, not the powerful, maintaining and reinforcing social hierarchies.

In these ways, witchcraft can act as a powerful sanction against socially disruptive behaviour and results in a good way of handling hostility between individuals. Also, by reducing competitiveness (since inequality in wealth means some people become jealous of others who have more) the balance of wealth is maintained in Azande society. Furthermore, the process of finding out who is responsible for witchcraft is a lengthy one that prevents hasty or emotional confrontations; the charges against the accused need group support and cannot be done carelessly.

Interestingly, witchcraft practices continue today among the Azande, with some modifications, despite the fact that the resettlement programmes carried out by the government have meant that they have been forced to accept living closer together.

Activity

How is the Azande way of explaining events different to your own? (How, for example, would you explain the collapsing granary store?)

Why might one way of explaining events be regarded as better than another?

Witchcraft is an effective means of social control. What major institutions and beliefs in your society function in a similar way? How are people encouraged to behave in a socially acceptable way?

UNDERSTANDING WITCHCRAFT TODAY

Although classic works such as Evans-Pritchard's study of the Azande are excellent for understanding how witchcraft is used to explain events, their relevance to today's societies may be limited. This section examines the role that witchcraft plays in the context of contemporary African society. To what extent is witchcraft used to explain events and how has it adapted to the changes brought about by modernity, globalization and the spread of Western ideas?

Todd Sanders (2003) argues that witchcraft, as a way of explaining events, remains important and central in many African societies. He claims that African notions of witchcraft are far from static and fixed and, in fact, are flexible and help individuals reflect on the complexity of modern life. Sanders explores one particular type of witchcraft – involving rain among the Ihanzu of Tanzania. In this case, a person is accused of witchcraft if they are seen as having stopped or sent away the rain, ultimately resulting in the failure of crops.

In a highly organized and regulated set of procedures, the person accused, who is often perceived to be either jealous or lazy, usually admits to the witchcraft and then apologizes to those affected. Witchcraft accusations are an important way of dealing with uncertainty and lack of resources. However, Sanders argues that the practice of witchcraft among the Ihanzu is about people understanding modernity and exploring and reaffirming what is meant by tradition. As Comaroff and Comaroff (1993) argue, notions of African witch-craft have proved surprisingly flexible and thus survive – indeed thrive – in Africa today. Witchcraft allows individuals to carry out traditional practices creatively and reinforces ethnic identity, so it is much more than simply a way of explaining events.

Sanders concludes that witchcraft remains highly important in many parts of Africa today and that using the terms 'the African witch' or 'African witchcraft' are problematic since witchcraft can mean such different things to different people.

> **Activity**
>
> How has witchcraft changed according to Sanders?
> What is the role of witchcraft among the Ihanzu of Tanzania?

LANGUAGE

So far we have seen that both classification of the world and the ways that humans clas-sify and explain events beyond their control reflect the world-view of the social group. However, many of these ideas are expressed through language, so the next section of the chapter explores the way in which language developed and how it relates to the way that different societies and individuals see and explain the world around them – in particular, to what extent language is shaped by culture.

> **Language**
> A set of symbols which are used to represent and communicate ideas

> **STOP & THINK**
>
> What makes human beings different from other animals in the way they communicate?
> How does human physiology contribute to the human ability to speak?
> Is language something that humans are born with or is it something that is learnt?
> Does language shape culture or vice versa?

All animals communicate. For example, bees signal the location of resources by danc-ing in their beehives, and gorillas stick out their tongues, grunt and beat their chests to intimidate intruders. Any action that conveys a message to another is communication. However, human communication is unique to our species in many ways.

Language forms the labels that arise as a result of classification. However, language can take on different meanings in practice. This can present a real challenge for anthropologists in terms of interpretation. It is important to be aware that it is not just language through which humans communicate – for instance, humans also communi-cate through objects (see chapter 12).

Language can be defined as a collection of **symbols** which are used in different ways according to the specific context. Human language is characterized by speed and accu-racy, and humans can speak to many people at once. Words, which are symbols, can have multiple meanings. There is a huge variety in the ways words are selected and put together. Human language is also always evolving; it has infinite potential for creat-ing new meanings. When the Société de Linguistique de Paris was founded in 1866, it banned any attempt to discover the origins of language. Over the past decades interest in this topic has grown significantly, as has the concern to protect minority languages

Road signs are objects which humans use to communicate across time and space. (Hoggarpiste1991 / Wikimedia Commons)

which are in danger of dying out or to revive those that have already become extinct. For example, the Cornish language was categorized as extinct in 2010, though efforts have since been made to revive it.

Shallow and Deep Symbolism

There are two forms of signals used by animals. Shallow signals are used by some primates and consist of short and simple sounds. These sounds are literal and have single meanings. This type of communication is rigid, unchanging and lacks innovation. For example, howler monkeys have a predator alarm screech.

The second form is deep symbolism, which is used by humans alone; it involves a wide and complex vocabulary with grammatical rules governing its usage. There are multiple meanings for single words, and words have the capacity to mean different things to different people and often do not have literal meanings. For instance, consider the proverb 'a leopard cannot change its spots': we know this to be true, but we also know the saying is about the idea that humans may not be able to change who they are in terms of personality. The way that individuals use language reflects their individual and group identity. There have been many studies, for example, on the ways that men and women use language differently.

Why Do Humans Need Language?

Language is essential to human survival, as it allows cultural knowledge to be transmitted from one generation to the next. This is important because our cultures are our primary means of survival. Language acquisition takes many years and, indeed, human language never stops evolving throughout an individual's life. Consider your own childhood: it is likely that you learnt your language through listening to other people speaking and demonstrating its use. In other words, your parents would not necessarily have sat you down and taught you. Some linguists argue that there is a critical period of learning from birth to around six months, when infants begin to understand sounds, that forms the basis of language development (Pallier 2007).

Figure 3.1 The development of human language

How Did Human Language Evolve?

There is no doubt that certain stages in human physical evolution led to the potential for speaking. The hyoid bone, which is essential to speech, is thought to have developed around 300,000 years ago, which is when language is thought to have developed significantly. The hyoid exists in other animals also, but humans are the only species where the location of the hyoid bone permits it to work together with the tongue and larynx to articulate a large variety of distinct sounds. Also the fact that human beings developed larger brains and, particularly, larger frontal lobes made possible abstract thought and the expression of complex ideas. A particular mouth shape and a muscular jaw and tongue also enabled complex sounds to be made.

Derek Bickerton (2000) claims that early humans such as our forerunners *Homo neanderthalensis* may have had a relatively large selection of words available to them which they could use with a reasonable degree of accuracy and coherence. Language at this stage was more likely to convey messages than complex meanings. As modern humans emerged from Africa and began to spread across the world, they developed their own dialects and languages. There is some debate as to why languages vary so much, but it is thought that different words and meanings emerged in different geographical surroundings. The following section explores a selection of different explanations of language evolution.

The Singing Neanderthals (Mithen 2005)

Mithen argues that it is impossible to understand language without understanding music, and he is highly critical of the way that researchers in the past have failed to pay attention to the role of music and emotion in general, arguing that the past has been depicted, wrongly, as 'silent'. For Mithen, language and singing were made possible through a complex set of physical and cultural evolutionary stages. For example, he argues that bipedalism may have initiated a musical revolution in human society through the rhythm and movement that became possible as a result of being able to walk and run on two legs.

Mithen contends that language and music did not emerge quickly, but that meaningful sounds gradually evolved, resulting in the 'Singing Neanderthal', who lived 250,000 years ago in Europe. Interestingly, he points out that language and music evolved alongside dance-like movements and gestures. There were many potential uses of music for early humans, such as being a means by which to express emotion or create group identities and as a form of entertainment.

Social Grooming Theory (Dunbar 2004)

Dunbar proposes that early humans evolved language essentially for 'small talk' or gossip, which at first may seem a little far-fetched. However, this interesting argument begins by pointing out that primates differ from other animals because of the intensity of their social relationships. Dunbar claims that social relations were partly constructed this way because of the amount of time early humans spent grooming one another. He explains that grooming is not just a matter of hygiene but also about creating and maintaining social bonds and a way of influencing others. Early humans, in their characteristic large groups of around 150 or so, would have spent almost half their time in mutual grooming. Dunbar argues that, over time, early humans evolved a more efficient mechanism of grooming, namely, language. By developing language, it is claimed that group cohesion is maintained, showing how important small talk is. Dunbar claims that language has evolved as a way of making social relationships in primate groups more developed and more complex.

The Origins of Ritual and Religion (Rappaport 1999)

Being able to use metaphors and deep symbols does so much to promote individuality that Rappaport (1926–1997) believed that ritual and religion emerged as a way of reducing the potential for disorder and disruption. He suggests that rituals and religion established rigidity, not fluidity, of thought. The use of clear rather than unclear definitions of things to channel thought in a particular direction further dampened individual thought. Rappaport was not criticizing religion, simply trying to explain why it came about, and showing how important language was in religion and ritual.

> **Activity**
>
> Evaluate each of the above explanations of the development of language. Which do you find the most plausible and why?

Languages Today

There are approximately 6,500 languages today. Many of these are spoken by minority groups, causing concerns over the loss of traditional languages worldwide. Most people on the planet speak one of the following nine languages: Mandarin, Spanish, English, Bengali, Hindi, Portuguese, Russian, Japanese and German. Languages are very much alive and in constant flux, and their extinction is not new; however, the pace at which they are disappearing today is alarming, and over 40 per cent are at risk. **UNESCO** estimates that 200 languages have become extinct around the world over the last three generations.

During the past several years linguists have become concerned about ethnolinguistic groups which are shifting from their original language to another that offers more power or opportunities, or whose population is becoming so reduced that there is little chance that their language will survive in the long term. With every language that dies there is a loss of cultural knowledge – the understanding of how humans relate to the world around them and their scientific, medical and botanical knowledge. If lost, this cultural information may be gone forever, particularly where the language is not recorded in writing. As discussed later, in chapter 10, language is political, and the right to speak a particular language can be a very important part of a person's identity. There are many cases where cultural groups have had their language marginalized, banned or stigmatized.

Political repression of languages means that some nation-states work to promote a single national culture, which limits the opportunities for using minority languages in the public sphere, schools, the media and elsewhere, sometimes even prohibiting them from use altogether. Sometimes ethnic groups are forcibly resettled, or children may be removed to be taught in the dominant language, perhaps away from home, or otherwise have their cultural and linguistic patterns disrupted. For example, many Native American languages and indigenous Australian languages were lost or diminished by this means.

Furthermore, cultural pressure may be imposed on certain groups, ensuring that their language becomes marginalized. This happens when political and economic power is closely tied to a particular language and culture, so that there is a strong incentive for individuals to abandon their language (on behalf of themselves and their children) in favour of another, more prestigious one. This frequently happens when indigenous populations, in order to achieve a higher social status, adopt the cultural and linguistic traits of a people who have come to dominate them through colonization, conquest or invasion; an example of this kind of endangerment is the loss of indigenous languages in South America that are less valued than Spanish or Portuguese. In some cases, these two causes are combined with poverty, disease and disasters that often affect marginalized minority groups disproportionately – perhaps resulting in the dispersal of the group and, as a consequence, the loss of their specific language.

Finally, **cultural hegemony** may often occur, not as a result of domination or conquest but from increasing contact with a larger and more influential language community through better communications in comparison with the relative isolation of past centuries. In conclusion, language transmits culture, which has definitely played an important role in human cultural evolution.

> **Cultural hegemony**
> Domination by the ideas of one particular social group

What is the Relationship between Language and Culture?

One conception of the relationship between language and culture that is widely studied in anthropology is the Sapir–Whorf hypothesis. The Sapir–Whorf hypothesis claims that culture and language are inseparable: in other words, language is culture and, as such, affects the way that people think. Benjamin Whorf, who was a pupil of Sapir at Yale University, studied the language of the Hopis of the American Southwest and discovered that Hopi grammar was completely different from that of any European language. In European languages, time and space are separate. Something can be far away but be going on right now. Time is divided into past, present and future. However, in Hopi grammar the world is very different: there is no time apart from space; if something took place long ago, that is the same as if it took place far away. There are no special words or forms of words for time considered by itself. However, there is nothing that goes on in the world that you cannot talk about in Hopi, just as in English. They are different ways of looking at the world, which works equally well. Whorf concluded that ideas about time and space come directly from language, which reflects the classification system of a social group.

Despite the fact that the Sapir–Whorf hypothesis has never been proved definitively, it remains an important idea today. Most anthropologists agree that language has some effect on thought; it is a question of how this occurs and to what extent.

NON-VERBAL COMMUNICATION

> **Activity**
>
> Pick three films or books and play charades with three people around you. Consider the ways in which you are communicating with the group.
> Next, in the same groups, list as many forms of human communication as you can.

Anthropologists do not rely on language alone to understand the culture of a specific group. For instance, it might be assumed that, to gain access to people's knowledge, anthropologists must listen and talk to people. Another assumption might be that, by learning a different language, an anthropologist can automatically understand how people think.

There is no inevitable connection between concepts or ideas and words; indeed, concepts can exist independently of language. Pre-verbal children, for example, may have understood the concept of 'house' before they can say the word. Therefore there is a significant proportion of knowledge that is non-linguistic. Concepts or ideas involve meanings that are formed through experience of, or practice in, the external world. In certain circumstances, it is possible to gain practical knowledge through non-linguistic communication. In fact, language actually plays a very small role in the learning of various types of knowledge. It is very unusual for people to need to have every single detail explained to them when they are learning something new. Certain kinds of everyday or practical knowledge are not passed on through spoken instruction, reading or writing. Examples may include bathing or washing clothes.

> **STOP & THINK**
>
> Think of four more examples of practical everyday tasks that you perform. How did you learn to do them? What role did language play in your learning?

The ways in which people exhibit their knowledge varies. Generally, learning practical tasks is non-linguistic. That is, people tend to demonstrate a skill rather than explain it. Everyday, practical knowledge is sometimes stored and transmitted non-linguistically.

Maurice Bloch (1998) refers to this kind of knowledge as '**schemas**', which are small networks or collections of understandings, ideas and practices that enable us to cope with everyday situations. Schemas are not lists of rules but general understandings that can be applied to a broad range of situations. A good example of a schema is making a cup of tea. Certain connected ideas or networks might be very difficult to explain through language. An example is playing a musical instrument: you can talk about it, but it is really only through actually playing the instrument that you really understand what is involved.

The type of knowledge expressed through practices is different from the knowledge expressed through verbalized language. Perhaps a more useful way of thinking about non-verbal knowledge is the idea of '**performative knowledge**' (Marchand and Kresse 2009), which is knowledge that can be gained only through *doing*. This approach suggests that anthropology must avoid relying too heavily on language-based information when trying to understand other cultures. Participant observation, and in

Schemas
Small networks or collections of understandings, ideas and practices that enable us to cope with everyday situations

Performative knowledge
Learning that occurs through practical actions

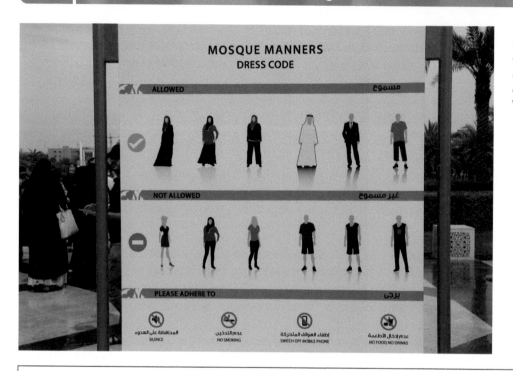

Dress codes are a form of non-verbal communication which are usually learnt by example within a culture or group. (FritzDaCat / Wikimedia Commons)

> **STOP & THINK**
> Can you think of any other examples of schemas?

particular participating in activities, may well reveal important information about a specific culture as much as, if not more than, words.

> **STOP & THINK**
> Is it helpful to distinguish between 'linguistic' (spoken) knowledge and 'performative' knowledge?
> Are there other ways of conveying knowledge (besides spoken or performative language)?
> What is the relationship between verbal and non-verbalized forms of knowledge?
> What role does language play in learning practical skills?
> Is it really possible to access people's practical knowledge by simply talking to them?

The next section will explore ethnographic studies that demonstrate the importance of non-verbal communication when trying to understand other cultures.

Singing Pictures, Women Painters (Lina Fruzzetti and Ákos Östör, 2005)

For generations the Patua (Chitrakara) communities of West Bengal have been painters and singers of stories depicted in scrolls. This film follows the daily lives of Muslim Patua women from Naya villages near Kolkata who have formed a scroll painters' cooperative and demonstrates the way in which objects can be used to communicate ideas.

'Not talking about sex in India' (Lambert 2001)

One of the biggest obstacles to reducing the spread of HIV in India is that talking about sex is strongly disfavoured; it is a taboo subject. So what happens if verbal accounts are not readily given? Most verbal references to sex in India are highly allusive. In Northern India, sexual intercourse is referred to through terms such as 'meeting' (*milna*), 'sitting' (*baithna*) or 'conversing' (*bacit*). Women are more reluctant than men to describe sexual encounters in direct terms. This suggests that girls and women might also lack the language with which to talk about sex directly. Discussing sexual issues may be seen by the women as jeopardizing their honour and is regarded as improper behaviour.

Sex in marriage is often referred to by North Indian women in terms of *bacit* (to converse) or *bat karna* (to speak). The metaphors of verbal speech are used in order to express physical intimacy. This fits in with the wider rules about women not speaking to other men. If talk implies intimacy, then not talking implies a lack of intimacy. This is consistent with the strong constraints on the discussion of explicit sex by women as a way of maintaining social order.

In the absence in North Indian languages of an appropriate vocabulary, mostly English words are used when discussing sex in the context of health. Silence therefore can be expressive; in this case, it is a very important part of women preserving their status. Silence can be just as interesting as what is said. The political silence around the AIDS epidemic for such a long time exemplifies this point.

One way in which people can and do talk about sex is through folk songs, seen as appropriate in particular contexts. These include references to sex that are acceptable, as they are sung when men and women are separate. Dress also acts as a code for expressing and communicating about sex. The veil, for instance, can be worn in many different ways and in different styles and colours, while hair and jewellery, among other things, communicate information relating to sex. Body language, such as hand-slapping by *hijras* (transsexuals), is a non-verbal way in which this group acknowledges other *hijras*. These examples of not speaking about sex show how anthropologists have to work hard to understand non-verbal communication.

Activity

Why is sex not discussed in India?

Why are women less likely to discuss sex than men?

What are some functions of folk songs?

What impact is this pattern of communications having on the spread of AIDS?

What does this example show about how anthropologists must look beyond verbal forms of communication?

Are there any similarities to your own culture in terms of not discussing sensitive subjects?

'Eating your words: communicating with food in the Ecuadorian Andes' (Bourque 2001)

In Sucre, a peasant community in the Central Ecuadorian Andes, the actions of preparing, distributing, accepting and eating food in particular social and spatial contexts are used to communicate, confirm, reject and transform notions of relatedness and difference; tradition and modernity; age; gender and ethnic identities; and economic, political and social status. This communication takes place in the context of, and is shaped by, changing economic circumstances at the micro and macro level, the introduction of new cooking techniques, and variations in the availability of foodstuffs.

STOP & THINK

Explain the meaning of the title above.

A range of messages in this particular culture are sent non-verbally, and most food carries particular meanings that are understood by all in the region. The importance of food has not been overlooked in structural anthropology. Among other discussions, Lévi-Strauss compared cuisine to language and claimed that an item of food takes on meaning only in opposition to another type of food. Roland Barthes (1974) claimed that all foods are a system of communication and that foods can translate as concepts such as masculinity and femininity. Mary Douglas ([1975] 1999) also treated food as a code about social relations and events as well as boundaries.

Bourque, however, utilizes an interpretivist approach: looking at how food and language are used by social actors. In her research, she became aware that where and with whom you eat is highly significant. For example, at the end of a working day, it is an obligation to feed everyone who has worked in the field, but the household members eat inside and the non-household workers eat outside the house. Overconsumption is a sign of generosity; it is seen as a way of pleasing supernatural beings. Overfeeding also acknowledges the ability to provide.

Festivals are a key time when communication occurs with food. Those with wheat fields give a bag of flour to their workers, who make bread, and then everyone can offer food for the souls of the dead relatives and friends to eat. The dead make a note of who offers what type and quantity of food. In return for the food, the dead are said to increase the fertility of the fields. Women manage food exchange and relations between households. Not all relatives are given food; women decide who will be a recipient. If the gift is not reciprocated, food will not be sent the following year. Sending food can be the start of a new relationship – for example, inviting a new person to be a worker. The giving process can be competitive: giving large amounts of food, for instance, can mean the gift is for someone considered very important. Also certain foods are not shared with workers, reinforcing status differences. Cooking is an important way of creating female identity. In Sucre, a woman must be able to cook before she is considered ready for marriage. Women also use food to exert control over their husbands.

> **Activity**
>
> How is food used to communicate in this society?
> How does this type of communication affect women?
> How does giving and sharing food specifically reinforce status and boundaries within this community?

HOW DID HUMANS COMMUNICATE BEFORE WRITING? ORAL TRADITIONS

Oral testimony can capture aspects of life which are informal and unwritten and which would otherwise disappear without trace. It can bring to light the experiences of groups of people who are often barely mentioned by the history books – the poor, women, ethnic minorities and disabled people. It can sometimes go back beyond the lifetime of the speaker. So, oral histories are part of the way we transmit culture. Native American oral histories involve what Vansina (1985) terms 'oral traditions', which may still continue today. These oral traditions, which include storytelling, teachings, and family and tribal history, as well as contemporary literature, lie at the heart of tribal culture. It is largely through such tradition that American Indian cultures have been preserved and transmitted through the generations.

Native American stories, teachings and oral histories are rich in cultural context and provide great insight into the world-view, values and lifestyle that are an integral part of the heritage of these peoples. For American Indians, the oral traditions must be treated with respect. Many of the stories are seasonal. Most often, the winter months form the season for stories.

> **STOP & THINK**
>
> What are oral traditions?
>
> Why are oral traditions important for anthropologists to understand?

How Are Modern Technologies Affecting Communication?

New forms of technology have without doubt increased the ways in which people can communicate. There has been increasing interest by anthropologists in the way that

Are mobile phones an inseparable part of people's lives? How does this affect social relationships? (Ed Yourdon / Wikimedia Commons)

the Internet, mobile phones and other new technologies are being used to create or negotiate social relationships.

New Forms of Communication through New Technologies: *Coming of Age in Second Life* (Boellstorff 2008)

Tom Boellstorff carried out ethnographic research on the virtually human world Second Life and explored the ways in which people communicate in online communities. Notably there are no voices used in Second Life, only ambient sounds and typed words. The lack of human voices is significant and may enable those who are usually silent or muted in society to communicate in alternative ways. This type of virtual world has challenged ideas about the way people communicate. Boellstorff's study is part of a growing body of research which suggests that new forms of communication emerge through technological advances and that these have a range of complex effects on people's non-digital worlds.

> **Activity**
>
> Pick two new forms of communication and write a report on each, using anthropological concepts and ideas about how new forms of communication have transformed communication.

Globalization: The Use of 'Voice' and the Internet

Globalization and technological advances go together, and nowhere is this clearer than in the development of new forms of communication as a result of the Internet and the idea of 'voice'. Voice, according to Jo Tacchi (in Horst and Miller 2012), can be defined as the ability to represent oneself and the right to express views. The right to a voice is central to modern democracy. Simply put, the Internet has led to a whole range of ways in which people can have voice or communicate their views. The Internet therefore is fast-changing, political, complex and of great interest to anthropologists. There is evidence of the positive effects of the development of certain technologies. For example, Faye Ginsberg (ibid.) argues that virtual reality computer programs enable people with disabilities to access digital media in a positive way, giving those who feel muted in other contexts voice and status and providing the opportunity for self-determination and equality.

Another recent area of interest for anthropologists is the impact that mobile phones are having particularly in Africa. Archimbault (in Horst and Miller 2012) studied rural Mozambique, where mobile phones have had complex effects, both providing and opening up economic opportunities and at the same time making personal information more secret.

However, modern technologies are not shared by everyone in the same ways. Different groups within and between societies communicate very differently through new technologies.

CONCLUSION

Human beings classify the world around them in culturally specific ways. It is very important for anthropologists to understand the classification system of the particular culture they are studying. All classification systems have their own logic and ways of explaining events beyond people's control, and they need to be studied in their total context. These ways of seeing the world vary enormously and shape the nature of language to some degree (how much language shapes culture and vice versa is an issue that remains disputed).

There is a lot of information to be uncovered in non-verbal communication and in new forms of communication. Communication is a fluid, dynamic aspect of human culture that not only reflects individual and group identity but also shapes the nature of social relationships, which are explored further in the next chapter.

END OF CHAPTER ASSESSMENT

Examine the relationship between culture and language.

Teacher's guidance

Start by explaining how language makes humans distinct from other animals. Explain how human language evolved and why. Giving examples, explore the diversity of languages around the world. Explain the difference between deep and shallow symbolism and how this supported human evolution. Consider the various explanations of how language developed. Link each one to culture and criticize each theory, explaining the cultural role of language. Conclude by stressing the importance of non-verbal communication. Highlight the fluid, dynamic nature of language.

KEY TERMS

Classification A system of organization of people, places and things shared by all humans in different ways in different cultures

Cultural construction The creation of ideas by people in a specific social context which then take on their own perceived reality

Cultural hegemony Domination by the ideas of one particular social group

Cultural relativism The idea that each culture has its own value and worth and that all beliefs, customs and ethics are bound by their culture

Ethnocentrism Regarding one's own ethnicity as superior to others and/or viewing others only through one's own cultural categories; privileging one's own cultural world-view

Gender Culturally constructed notions about what it means to be a man or a woman

Language A set of symbols which are used to represent and communicate ideas

Magic The performance of rites and spells intended to cause supernatural effects on other people

Performative knowledge Learning that occurs through practical actions

Schemas Small networks or collections of understandings, ideas and practices that enable us to cope with everyday situations

Socialization The process of internalizing norms and values that takes place throughout life

Sorcery The performance of rites and spells for the purpose of controlling individuals (not always involving the supernatural)

Symbol Something used to represent an idea or an object

Syncretism The combining of two or more belief systems or world-views

Witchcraft The use of psychic powers to produce a particular effect on others

---

Personal investigation

Research an endangered language and explore the reasons why it is under threat. Try to establish contact with an organization that seeks to protect the language and find out what is being done in their campaign. If possible, try to conduct a case study with someone who speaks a minority language and discuss with them the challenges that they face in maintaining their language and what using it means to them in terms of their identity. Consider political and cultural forces which may influence use of this particular language and explore the ways in which individuals may respond to such pressures.

SUGGESTED FURTHER READING AND FILMS

Books

Dunbar, R. (2004) *Grooming, Gossip and the Evolution of Language.* Faber & Faber.

Mithen, S. (2005) *The Singing Neanderthals: The Origins of Music, Language, Mind and Body.* Phoenix Press.

Rappaport, R. A. (1999) *Ritual and Religion in the Making of Humanity.* Cambridge University Press.

Ethnographic film

Strange Beliefs: Sir Edward Evans-Pritchard (1902–1973) (1985), directed by André Singer

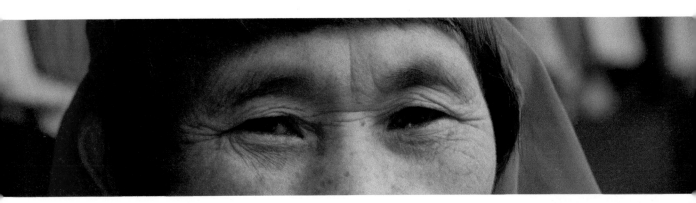

CHAPTER FOUR

ORGANIZING SOCIAL RELATIONS

CONTENTS

Organizing Social Relations

A notable universal feature of human culture consists of the complex social relationships that are found in every single social group on the planet; these can be based on biological relatedness, political alliances, marriage, social ties or, more often than not, a combination of these. Social relationships often reflect power differences between individuals and groups and, as such, are important in determining the way a society is organized. Power hierarchies are present in most social groups – based, for example, on social class, age grade or caste.

A substantial part of this chapter is devoted to exploring probably the most significant principle around which social relationships are organized, **kinship**. A range of different kinship practices will be explored – universal patterns as well as local differences. One recently emerging area in the anthropology of kinship is the exploration of the impact of technology – for instance, the effects of reproductive technologies and new social media on the ways that relationships with others are created, mediated, reformulated and challenged. The final part of the chapter examines the way in which objects are used to express a range of social relationships, including exchange and gift giving.

STOP & THINK

What differentiates human social relationships from those of other animals? Are there any similarities? What might be the reasons for having complex social relationships? What might be the benefits or problems? How important are biologically based relationships?

AGE, GENDER, CASTE AND CLASS

As well as examining kinship, it is important to consider other ways in which relationships are organized, such as through gender, caste and class, which can and do play a significant role in the social hierarchies of particular societies. A **hierarchy** is a form of social organization where some individuals or groups have greater power, social status or ranking than others.

Marx and Social Class

Karl Marx (1818–1883) argued that social hierarchies were decisive in historical change. His ideas were highly influential, and his opposition to **capitalism** (society based on the ownership of private property and individual rights) contributed to the development of communist societies, which at the turn of the twenty-first century accounted for over a third of the world's population. Marx claimed that social relationships and a person's position in society are defined by the individual's relationship to the **economy**. He saw capitalist society as comprising two **social classes**, the working class (the **proletariat**) and the capitalists (the **bourgeoisie**). The former do not own anything except their labour, which is a **commodity** (something that can be bought or sold) that they use to earn a wage. The bourgeoisie, in contrast, own the **means of production** (the factories, etc.) and use this to **exploit** the working class and take profit from production. According to Marx, the relations of production shape social relationships.

Marx argued that this system, capitalism, justifies itself through a particular **ideology** (a set of ideas supporting the interests of a particular group), which prevents the working class from criticizing the system or organizing a formal challenge against it. He acknowledged that, although people might question the system, they would not strive for an alternative to it – seeking solace in religion, for example. Marx predicted that the gap between the working class and the bourgeoisie would grow and that the working class would eventually become aware of the true extent of their exploitation, resulting in a revolution and the overthrow of capitalism, leading to a new form of economy and set of social relations, known as **communism**. In communist society, Marx claimed, that there would be no private ownership of property and, in theory, everyone would have their needs met.

Some have criticized Marx for assuming that individuals are passive, instead arguing that it *is* possible for an individual to change their class position. Although there are many interpretations of his ideas, some suggest that Marx places too much emphasis on the influence of the economy, ignoring the role of other institutions.

It is clear of course, that the revolution never happened universally as Marx predicted and that capitalism has continued to expand across the world. There have been places where an interpretation of Marxist ideas has been applied, as in the former USSR, but these were not communist in the way that Marx envisioned.

In some contemporary capitalist societies, there has been an increase in living standards for many, challenging Marx's idea that the gap between the ruling and the working class would grow. There has been much debate recently about the significance of class in determining social relationships: one argument is that the divisions between social classes in some societies are becoming blurred while they remain clear and are growing in others. For example, in America in the last few years, the rich have become richer while the economic situation of ordinary Americans has stagnated.

Hierarchy
A form of social organization where some individuals or groups have greater power, social status or ranking than others

Capitalism
Society based on the ownership of private property and individual rights

Commodity
Anything that can be bought or sold

Means of production
The factories, machines and other resources that help produce goods and services and result in profit for those who own them

Ideology
A set of ideas supporting the interests of a particular group

Caste

Endogamy
Marriage takes place only within a group

Caste refers to the differentiation of society in Hindu India and Hindu-influenced areas of South and Southeast Asia into **endogamous** social categories according to ritual purity and impurity. Castes are ranked from the sacred and pure down to the *Dalits* (the 'untouchables'), who perform the most polluting and menial duties. Caste played an important role in pre-colonial India, but in some respects it took on a more significant role under colonial rule. Dirks (1992) argues that colonialists adapted the pre-existing caste system to manage the complex new system they had put in place. By reinforcing caste differences, land and work rights as well as legal codes could be established. The caste system is central in determining the type of social relationships a person can have.

Marriage

Ascribed status
A position that is given, usually at birth

Reincarnation
The rebirth of a soul in a new body

A person's position in the caste structure is also based on their **ascribed** position from birth, depending on behaviour in past lives: the belief in **reincarnation** is essential. Although discrimination against lower caste groups is now formally illegal, the practice and beliefs are deeply ingrained. It is common to see adverts for spouses for the top caste families in Indian newspapers, and caste is still likely to determine the type of occupation a person has. The system also determines boundaries within this society, between individuals and other groups. It is clear that the caste system is interpreted differently according to the individual (who has varying degrees of agency within the system). The ways in which it is practised vary from place to place, so there is a danger of overgeneralizing the ways in which social relationships are organized.

> **Activity**
> Which belief system is caste society based on?
> Carry out some research into the type of influence that a person's caste might have on their life chances today. What are your findings?

Age Sets and Age Grades

Age set
A group of individuals of a similar age, often sharing special social links with one another

Age grades
Levels of seniority through which age sets pass collectively as they grow older

Age may determine the roles a person plays and to some extent their position in the social hierarchy; therefore it is often an important organizing principle. An **age set** is a group of individuals of similar age, often forming special links with one another. **Age grades** are levels of seniority through which age sets pass collectively as they grow older – such as those of boy, warrior, married man and elder. Examples of societies with age grades are found predominantly in Africa. The Karimojong, pastoralists of Uganda, who have a cattle-based economy, initiate their men, in young adulthood, into a named age set. Every five or six years the age set into which they are being initiated is closed and a new age set is formally opened. At any time there will be some six active age sets, spanning a range from young adulthood to old age, the senior groups enjoying a higher status.

Different stages of the life cycle also play a part in the construction of age. Grandmother, mother and baby cover a range of ages, yet each also implies a 'typical' age. (Azoreg / Wikimedia Commons)

In Western society, older people are often regarded as having less status and power, as their economic value is generally lower than that of younger age groups. Western society prizes youth and the middle aged, who are at the height of their earning power. Children and the elderly therefore may even be perceived as a burden to society. Consider the recent phenomenon of ageism: discrimination against old people. An example of this may be the lack of representation of the views and voices of the elderly in government. This attitude in many parts of Western society contrasts sharply with that in many non-Western societies, where old age is perceived as a time of wealth in experience and wisdom. Cultural constructions of age vary, and it is clear from these two examples alone how ideas about age can differ vastly.

STOP & THINK

Explain the difference in attitudes towards older people in Western and non-Western societies.
What are the possible functions of age grades?
What advantages might older people bring to a social group?

Gender

When men and women compare experiences or are confronted with statistical information about gender differences, it becomes clear that whether a person is born male or female profoundly affects their opportunities, life chances and view of the world. **Patriarchy** appears to be a widespread pattern.

Gender is a socially constructed, and increasingly fluid, category, and recent changes in Western societies alone indicate how complex, rich and varied gender differences can be. These are often expressed not just through the roles that men and women play but also through dress, sexual behaviour, language and symbols. In some cases, upon closer inspection gender relationships may in practice be more equal than assumed. Eleanor Leacock (1978) argues that, among hunter-gatherer populations, gender relations tend to be more equal.

> **Patriarchy**
> Male dominance over women in formal or public spheres

The idea of equality between men and women is worth considering carefully, as different gender roles do not necessarily imply gender inequality. For example, Andrew Canessa (2012) claims that gender roles among the Aymara of Bolivia are not necessarily framed in terms of inequality; rather, they are complementary – in other words, different but perhaps equal (for more detail, see chapter 9). In many societies, from Native Americans to Scandinavians, equality is seen as ideal. In practice it may be taken for granted that equality means that men and women should perform different tasks. In most societies it is a case of finding a balance between difference and complementarity.

In other cultures, such as the Fulani of Africa's Western Sahel, men and women are very strictly segregated (for more on gender, see chapter 8). Patriarchal ideology is itself complex, and women as well as men can uphold oppressive relationships. There can be tension within Western societies, where the majority regard gender equality as increasingly important while minority groups may see gender very differently. What is clear is that, in all societies, gender is a universally significant means by which social relationships are organized.

STOP & THINK

To what extent does your gender affect your life chances today? Has this changed? If so, why?

The !Kung: A Society with No Hierarchy?

The !Kung of South Africa and Botswana provide an example of a society which has less developed forms of power hierarchies and therefore might be considered close to egalitarian. Richard Lee (1979), who spent three years conducting ethnographic research on a !Kung group whose population was around one thousand people, suggests that, within this group of hunter-gatherers, property and produce are generally equally distributed and individuals work hard to prevent the distribution of wealth becoming a source of power and introducing inequality. It is notable that the way of the life of the !Kung is under threat, as they have been under considerable pressure from the state to move from their ancestral lands, and as a result many of their customs, ideas and ways of life are under threat.

STOP & THINK

Do you believe that true equality in society is possible? Give reasons for your answer.

Evaluation: *Siva and her Sisters* (Kapadia 1995)

It might be convenient to imagine that social hierarchies such as class, gender and caste are understood and accepted as part of a cultural consensus. However, this is not always the case. Many ethnographic studies highlight the ways in which different types of social hierarchies overlap with a variety of effects. Social hierarchies are also likely to be contested, challenged and possibly rejected or reinterpreted by the individual.

One good example of this is to be found in Karin Kapadia's ethnographic study carried out in a village in rural Tamil Nadu in India, which focuses primarily on women who belong at the bottom of the caste hierarchy, those formerly called 'untouchables'. Kapadia applies critical feminist theory to uncover the different ways in which caste, class and gender intersect and explores how women resist and reject upper-class representations of them. She explains how the women in this particular village not only contest their position within the caste system but also challenge their position as oppressed women in a highly patriarchal society. The female workers of the village have a much greater ability to assert their rights, as they carry out paid work, giving them a certain status which enables them partially to reject the patriarchal ideology that surrounds them. This study highlights the importance of individual agency; indeed, it may be possible for individuals to contest, interpret and reconstruct their position within a social hierarchy.

KINSHIP

What is Kinship?

> **Kinship**
> Sets of relationships considered primary in any society, in practice demonstrating huge variety in different societies

The nature of **kinship** is often discussed in anthropology; however, it is very difficult to define since the forms it takes can vary enormously. One possible definition is that it involves sets of relationships considered primary in any society, also called family and relations, but in practice demonstrating huge variety in different societies. It is an important principle of social organization as it may determine a person's livelihood, career and marriage – how alliances are created. It also embraces patterns of descent and inheritance. Kinship may appear to be governed by strict social rules, but in practice the reality of such relationships can be less clearly defined. In addition, persons do not always conform to their assigned or chosen kinship role; each individual may interpret their role differently.

STOP & THINK

What makes someone kin?

What factors (blood, marriage or social kin) are the most important in defining kinship ties?

Activity

How are kinship relations expressed?

Write a list of all the different ways in which your position within a family can affect your life. Consider the ways in which kinship practices vary and compare at least two cultures where kinship is organized differently.

To what extent is it possible for individuals to challenge or change their kinship position? Consider the role of the state in shaping and deciding the nature of kinship. Who gets to make rules about kinship and relationships?

Kinship in Anthropology

Given that there are so many different aspects of kinship to study, it is not surprising that there have been many different interpretations of the nature of kinship and how it is best understood. There are structuralist perspectives which chart the way in which kinship systems vary, and there are also studies which focus on the degree to which an individual has agency within kinship systems and can negotiate his or her role and position.

Early anthropological studies of kinship focused on evolutionary explanations as well as trying to understand the classification of kin. Lewis Henry Morgan (1818–1881), for example, carried out research on the Iroquois of North America and pointed out how

Kinship can be defined and understood in many different ways beyond the 'nuclear family' of parents and children. (oneVillage Initiative / Wikimedia Commons)

important kinship is in some traditional societies in terms of organizing political power, inheritance, roles and exchange. In fact, Morgan believed that kinship was the most important and earliest organizing institution.

In general terms the theoretical approaches to kinship in anthropology can be divided into the two groupings described in the box below.

Structural Functionalism

Kinship was central to anthropology during the height of structural functionalism in the first half of the twentieth century, particularly in the work of A. R. Radcliffe Brown (1881–1955) on understanding **small-scale societies** where no government exists and kinship was seen in terms of alliance and descent.

Structural functionalists stress the role of kinship institutions in promoting social stability, a central concern being to explore genealogy and examine varying patterns of relatedness. This view has since come to be regarded as problematic as, in practice, kinship relationships are considered far messier and rules are not always observed.

Genealogy
The study of kinship and descent patterns

Structuralism

Lévi-Strauss's work had major impact on the study of kinship by shifting away from relationships by descent to those of marriage, and to the topic of exchange more generally. He saw marriage as central to the foundation of the social order and thus essential in establishing and maintaining relations between groups. In fact, he claims that marriage is an elaborate, long-term exchange involving the transfer of goods, services and people that strengthens relationships between two groups of **affines** (or in-laws). Lévi-Strauss drew attention to affinal relationships, which are not based on biology but involve strong bonds of **reciprocity** (mutual exchange) that strengthen alliances between kinship groups.

Affine
Kin created through marriage

In the West, kinship is often seen as playing a less important role in organizing social relations, as the role of the state has expanded into many areas of kinship.

While some anthropologists continue to focus on the instrumental or functional aspects of kinship – for example, inheritance, property and economic exchange – others such as Trawick (1990) argue that emotions are very important in understanding kinship. Feminists and Marxists have also contributed to Western understandings, providing a critique of kinship systems as a means of maintaining patriarchy and class society respectively.

Activity

In your own words, describe the ways in which anthropological views on kinship have changed.
What explanation of kinship might Marxists and feminists give?
What are the problems with making generalizations about kinship?

Kinship among the Bolivian Aymara: My Grandfather the Mountain (Canessa 2012)

There may be a risk of assuming that, when describing kin, we are always talking about other humans or, at the very least, other living beings. However, in the Andes in Bolivia, there is a village where the indigenous Indians, the jaqii, have a different view of the nature of kinship relations. Andrew Canessa's findings are based on detailed ethnographic research which took place over twenty years in the village of Wila Kjarka (fictitiously named to protect the anonymity of its residents).

Canessa explains how the jaqii have a kinship system that includes their surrounding physical environment, specifically the mountain, which is known as a grandfather. Consequently, when the Wila Kjarkeños walk through the land, they feel emotionally close to every outcrop of rock, every distant peak and every area of flat land, all of which have names. The Jaqi explain that these names are given by the *achachilas* (the spiritual ancestors), who play an important role in jaqii life by bringing not only rain but also wisdom and guidance. This type of relationship with the land is important for several reasons, particularly because it makes clear the differences between what it means to be *jaqii* (Indian) and what it means to be *q'aras* (non-Indian) – the latter being concerned with alternative belief systems, such as Catholicism, which relate to Jesus and God. The Jaqi way of relating to inanimate objects as kin has not gone unnoticed by missionaries, who have rather cleverly used images of mountains at church altars as a means of (attempting) to convert the jaqii to Christianity, with varying degrees of success.

The relationship that jaqii people have with their land is at the very core of their sense of personhood (discussed in more detail in chapter 6). Canessa reminds us that this relationship is not to be confused with a desire to protect the environment. Rather, Wila Kjarkeños see life as a journey in which becoming a fully developed person is achieved gradually through the establishment of a series of relationships that involve giving and receiving. The ultimate aim of life is to become merged with the ancestral spirits. These spirits are often seen as part of the landscape, and thus this relationship is particularly important and must be maintained throughout life. Canessa explains that being jaqii is not about what one *is* but what one *does*, so relationships with kin (mountains included) are crucial to the maintenance of identity.

Canessa explains that Teodosio Condori, the **shaman** of the village until very recently, had a particularly important relationship with the mountain, as his healing powers were based on the world of the spirits. Canessa notes how Teodosio himself begins to recognize that kinship relationships with mountains, rocks and rivers are steadily becoming less important, as spiritual explanations of the world are being replaced with modern, secular explanations. This example is useful, as it demonstrates how kinship is not necessarily limited to human beings and can also be conferred upon inanimate objects.

Animals and Kin (Morris 2000)

Based on extensive fieldwork in Malawi, Brian Morris (2000) explores the ways in which humans engage socially with animals to the extent that they are considered kin. He argues that Malawian people have a particularly complex and close relationship with mammals that they regard as having various powers, energy and agency. Malawians tend not to make a clear distinction between humans and animals; rather, they consider both as sharing many qualities. Morris gives the example of the close friendships that some have with domestic animals such as cats and dogs, as well as a strong empathy expressed between humans and the animals they hunt, reflecting the fact that Malawians recognize that they share the world with animals and are often in competition with them.

> **STOP & THINK**
>
> How might the work of Canessa and Morris challenge some understandings of kinship?

Kinship Patterns

To understand kinship fully, it is important to look at the economic and political arrangements of which it is a part. Inheritance patterns are key; these refer to the rules for passing on assets, moveable wealth, titles, rights, status and spiritual qualities from

> **Activity**
>
> Write a list of examples of as many things as you can think of which can be passed from one generation to the next.

one generation to the next. These are often determined by legal systems.

PATRILINEAL FAMILIES

Inheritance through the male line is the most common pattern. Within this system it is generally considered important that a child is recognized by a father figure, even if biological paternity is not necessarily seen as essential. This pattern of inheritance has been dominant in the majority of societies, particularly in Europe, where, in places, this set of rules has only recently changed so that inheritance is shared between men and women.

MATRILINEAL FAMILIES

In matrilineal families, women take the significant role in inheritance patterns. This does not mean that women are more powerful or wealthy than men, although it is true that women tend to have a higher formal status within matrilineal societies. Quite often it is a woman's brother who becomes significant in terms of descent. For example, in the Trobriand Islands, women pass on inheritances to men. This system of descent is not to be confused with matriarchy, which is relatively uncommon. Interestingly, matrilineal practices can occur within patriarchal societies. For example, Traveller women pass wealth through the female line in the form of jewellery. It is worth noting that it is not just material objects that are passed down from generation to generation. In Judaism, only a child born to a Jewish mother can be Jewish, even though the Jewish religious text, the Torah, does not explicitly discuss the conferring of Jewish status matrilineally.

An ethnographic study of matrilineal society was carried out among the Na (Hua Cai, *A Society without Fathers or Husbands*, film 1995; text 2008). The Mosuo or Na, as they tend to be known, are an ethnic group in China living in villages where each household is composed of **consanguineous relatives** (blood relatives). Matrilineality may take many different forms, and in this particular society it is expressed partly through sexual relations which involve the Na men making nocturnal visits to women with whom they have formed a romantic attachment.

In matrilineal families the relationships a mother has with her children and her siblings determine how wealth and culture are passed on. (© Andreas Mieras)

In this society, genetic fathers have no recognized kinship with children and are not involved in their upbringing. Both men and women take multiple sexual partners. Men make secret nocturnal visits to women's homes and must return home before sunrise; they develop no economic and usually no public social bonds with their sexual partners. Hua claims that any attempt to monopolize one's partner is always considered shameful and foolish. This may seem strange, but Hua argues that this type of arrangement is most practical given the Na way of life. Children belong to the mother's side of the family, and the most important relationships in a household are mother–child and brother–sister. Siblings live and eat together all their lives and raise whatever children the women bear. All the males of a household are called 'uncle' by the children, and all children are treated equally no matter who their genetic father might be.

The Na regard a vow of fidelity as shameful because it involves a negotiation or exchange, which goes against their customs. Hua argues that sexuality is not commodified (like a service that can be bought or sold); rather, sex is considered to be a purely sentimental and amorous matter that implies no mutual constraints. The only time cohabitation of an unrelated couple occurs is when natural circumstances leave a household short of males or females and survival of the line is threatened.

STOP & THINK

How might the kinship patterns found in the Na be different from those of your own kinship system? How does the example of the Na challenge the emphasis often placed on biological paternity in the West?

MARRIAGE PATTERNS

Marriage in the West is now generally perceived as being built upon romance: we expect to love the person we marry. Perhaps this type of expectation is less common in some non-Western societies. Among the Maasai of East Africa, for example, it is seen as a disadvantage if romantic love between the spouses is too powerful. In Maasai society, marriage is viewed predominantly as a business relationship, to raise children and make the cattle herd grow, as well as to provide opportunities for creating alliances with other kinship groups. Marriage can therefore reduce potential conflict between different groups and can lead to the creation of new social and economic ties. If spouses fall in love, the result may be jealousy and passionate outbursts with adverse effects on the family economy. That said, it is only relatively recently that marriage in the West has centred around love and personal happiness. Marriage can occur for many reasons, practical, romantic, or both, depending upon the context.

Activity

Write a list of all the functions of marriage.
Which functions might be most important in your society? Why?

Marriage ensures that parental responsibility is organized (though not necessarily through the biological parents). There are different forms of marriage practices, and these are summarized next.

Monogamy refers to a relationship where a person is married to one partner at a time. This arrangement is found in many different forms but is common in a variety of societies. Friedrich Engels, in *The Origin of the Family, Private Property and the State* (1884), argued that monogamy became the dominant marital pattern in Europe due to the fact

Monogamy
A relationship where a person is married to one partner at a time

Western marriages are traditionally monogamous and seen as the joining of two families. (© Mike Pountney)

that it ensured that **primogeniture** (inheritance from father to eldest son) occurred, meaning that middle-class families maintained their wealth, which in turn supported and perpetuated capitalist society.

Every Good Marriage Begins with Tears (Simon Chambers, 2006)

There are many cross-cultural examples of monogamous marriage. In some cases, women have little or no say in whom they marry. Examples of the issues relating to an arranged monogamous marriage are seen in the ethnographic film *Every Good Marriage Begins with Tears*, which is set in East London. A Muslim girl, Shahanara, changes from pink hot pants into a sari to meet her husband at the airport. She has met him only once before, when she was married in a union arranged by her Bangladeshi family. Shahanara only agreed to the marriage in order to try and heal old wounds with her father, who had banished her from her family for her Western ways. Meanwhile her devout Muslim sister Hashnara is prepared for her own arranged marriage, something for which, at nineteen, she does not feel at all ready. Filmed by a close friend of the family, *Every Good Marriage Begins with Tears* explores universal themes of love and the conflicts between first and second generations of a British Bangladeshi family.

Polygyny is where one man is married to more than one woman at the same time. There are many different reasons for this arrangement – for example, having more than one wife and lots of children may be a way to gain a reputation for power.

Duka's Dilemma (Jean Lydall, 2001)

The anthropologist Jean Lydall has been making films with the Hamar community of southern Ethiopia since the 1970s. In 2001 she returned with her daughter and grandson to follow the continuing life story of Duka. Candid interviews reveal the complex polygynous family dynamics when Duka's husband, Sago, takes a second wife, Boro. The film provides an intimate and personal family portrait that captures Duka's ambivalence towards sharing her home and husband. The quiet suspense is only heightened when Duka's mother-in-law starts to stir up trouble. The high points of the film include the birth of the new wife's child and a heated dispute between the mother-in-law and her son, which leads to the building of a new house. This film highlights the importance of kinship relationships both in maintaining ties (or not!) within the family and between kinship groups and as a way of allocating gender roles.

Polyandry, which is much less common than polygyny, is where a wife has more than one husband simultaneously. In parts of Tibet, among the Nyinba, there are pockets of fraternal polyandry (one woman marries brothers), particularly among the higher social strata, who praise its material advantages and see it as a practical response to environmental constraints. According to Levine (1988), the Nyinba say that polyandry prevents the dispersion of household wealth, the fragmentation of land and the proliferation of households, thus restricting village growth and keeping wealth in the hands of the wealthy, as well as resulting in a higher standard of living.

As the Nyinba see it, the only way to juggle the multiple economic involvements of agriculture, herding and trade is through polyandry and the economic specialization of brothers. There is a strong relationship between fathers and sons, with fathers regarding specific children as belonging to them. This marital relationship also has an impact on the division of labour, as it allows men to engage in long-distance trade while the women trade within the village. There is a high percentage of unmarried women in this society, and, because of this, polyandry is linked to population decline.

DOWRY AND BRIDEWEALTH

In European and some Asian societies, the **dowry** has traditionally been an important institution. It means that the bride brings gifts from her family, such as utensils, linen, and other things for the home, into the marriage. The institution can be seen as a compensation for the man taking economic responsibility for the woman. It can also be seen as an advance on inheritance. The costs can be steep, so much so that they are a major cause of high levels of female infanticide (the murder of baby girls) in India.

Bridewealth (sometimes called bride price) is more common than dowry in some societies. Here the groom's kin is obliged to transfer resources to the bride's kin in return for his acquisition of rights to her labour and reproductive powers. The payment of bridewealth establishes the rights the man has over the woman and her children. If it is not paid, the marriage can be considered void, which can be the cause of feuds, whereas payment creates moral bonds of various types and strengthens solidarity within the paying group. It can promote mutual trust between families, especially where bridewealth is paid over a long period.

RESIDENTIAL ARRANGEMENTS

In some cases, such as (formerly) the Nayar of Southern India and the Na of China, sons and daughters continue to live with their mothers throughout their lives, liaising with their lovers or the parents of their children only on a visiting basis. This does not mean that the father of the child is not recognized: he may play a very special role in the lives of his children. However, the mother may have a number of men to choose from as a father.

Matrilocal/patrilocal residence

The classification of kin often dictates who belongs to the female and who to the male line of the family. As we saw earlier, the Na are a good example of a matrilocal society in which the women are the focus of the household and relatives live with their mother's side of the family.

Men and women often set up some kind of home when they marry, though they may live near the parents of one of the spouses. A matrilocal pattern is where residence is with or near the family of the wife or mother. Residence with or near the family of the husband or father is known as patrilocality.

Kinship Rules

All known human societies prohibit **incest** – that is, sexual relations between persons who are classified as close blood kin, which includes at least father–child, mother–child and sibling relationships. This does not mean that these relationships do not occur, but rather that there is a norm prohibiting it; incest is **taboo**. There are variations concerning who is included in the taboo. In some places, incest consists of sexual relationships with anyone in your clan, in other places it covers those to whom you are related within seven generations. Marriage between cousins may be common, encouraged even, in many societies – for example, within some Muslim communities.

There are various theories about the reasons for the incest taboo: some point out that incest leads to biological degradation. In fact, the actual chances of birth defects are lower than is often assumed (Bennett et al. 2002). In fact, the risk of serious birth defects in children varies according to how close the relationship is. The average risk of genetic defects is just over 2 per cent, while in children born from first cousins it is 2.6 per cent. In children born to siblings, the closest potential genetic match, the risk of defects is at its highest, between 7 and 9 per cent. This means that over 90 per cent of all children born from incestuous relationships between these categories of relatives have no serious birth defects. It is therefore the practical and social consequences of incest that are the main cause of concern and that help to maintain the taboo: one reason for this might be the way incest could lead to role confusion and instability.

Edward Westermarck ([1891] 1922) was among the first to argue that close relatives such as cousins and siblings who grow up together fail to develop mutual sexual attraction. However, there are societies which prescribe that their members should marry their relatives or those of a similar social group, though never the very closest kin. This is known as **endogamy**, practised, for example, among the Yanomamö of the Amazonian rainforest, who marry only within their group. Marrying outside the group is known as **exogamy** and is the more common pattern.

Kinship and Politics

Kinship can be an important organizing principle in politics and daily affairs. In many societies a man needs support from blood relatives as well as from affines (in-laws) in order to follow a political career, and where there is no state the kinship group usually forms the basis for political action and the promotion of political interests. The group is bound together through mutual bonds of loyalty – for example, in conflict or negotiations over (say) marriage payments or trade. In some societies, such as the Yanomamö, there can be a long-standing rivalry between strong kin groups. Women marrying between these groups create an important means of alliance and stop families from losing contact. Marriage in this case creates relationships between groups, not just between individuals.

Biology and Kinship

Some, such as E. O. Wilson (1978), take a sociobiological view and argue that men do their utmost to spread their genetic material, while women seek men who can offer their offspring security and protection. The emphasis on biology as the basis for kinship has been heavily criticized by Tim Ingold (1986) and Marshall Sahlins (1976), among others. The evidence for this criticism is that some of the strongest socially defined kinship ties are not based on biology. Holy (1996) uses the example of kinship in the New Guinea highlands, where people become kin by virtue of sharing food and an individual's relationship to their mother seems to be based on her role as someone who offers food rather than as the person who brought them into the world.

> **STOP & THINK**
> How do Holy's findings challenge some sociobiological views of kinship?

How Might Technological Advances Challenge Definitions of Kinship?

Ascribed status
A position that is given, usually at birth

In the past, kinship may have been viewed as ascribed – that is, given by birth and unchangeable – or perhaps as shaped by cultural practices. Anthropologists used to build their claims around the fact that kinship relations were based on biological or socially created relationships. This claim, however, has become less clear as technological developments and fertility expertise has raised new reproductive possibilities and created a new set of contexts within which ideas about kinship are shaped. These new **reproductive technologies** have also raised public concerns and have at times brought the state into direct conflict with families over how such forms of technology should be used. In some cases there has been a conflict between legislation, ethical guidelines regulating the use of technology, and individual rights.

In the 1970s and 1980s the study of kinship became less discussed in anthropology, but there was a resurgence of interest when techniques such as artificial insemination and IVF raised new questions both about the role of motherhood and fatherhood and about the connection between parents and their children. Janet Carsten (2004) uses the following two examples to highlight some of the issues raised.

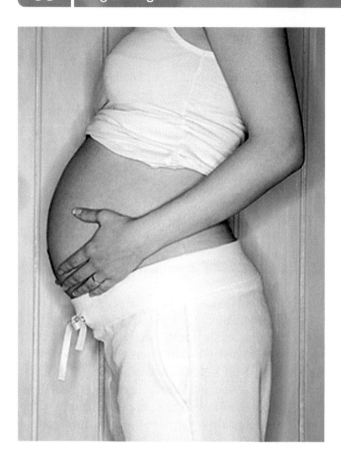

Assisted reproductive technologies, including donor eggs and sperm, IVF and surrogacy, are redefining how and what it means to be related to someone. (Swangerschaft / Wikimedia Commons)

Case Study 1

In 1995, in Nottinghamshire, Stephen Blood, critically ill with bacterial meningitis, lay in a coma on a life-support machine. His sperm were removed without his prior written consent. Within a few days he was dead. Although he and his wife, Diane, had been trying to have a baby before his death, the British Human Fertilization and Embryology Authority refused to grant permission for her to undergo artificial insemination using her husband's sperm. Diane Blood challenged the decision in High Court. In October 1996 the challenge was dismissed on the same grounds as the original ruling. Finally she took her case to the European High Court and was granted permission to transport her husband's sperm to Belgium to have treatment there. Diane Blood's case created widespread sympathy, but her predicament was a result of the new reproductive technology developments.

Case Study 2

In Israel in the 1990s there were a series of rabbinic debates on artificial insemination. The debate focused on two issues: Can sperm for artificial insemination be used by Jews, given that masturbation is prohibited under Halakha (Jewish religious law)? What is the relationship between the sperm donor and a child conceived using his sperm? Carsten raises the question of the status of the child conceived in this way. The Orthodox rabbinate reached some unexpected conclusions. In cases of male infertility, donor sperm must not be taken from non-Jewish men. In Israel, regulations governing fertility treatment and divorce law are grounded in and informed by Jewish law.

Globalization: Transnational Adoption and Kinning

Since the late 1960s, transnational adoption has emerged as a global phenomenon. Owing to a sharp decline in infants being made available for adoption locally, involuntarily childless couples in Western Europe and North America who wish to create a family have to look further afield.

Based on empirical research from Norway, Signe Howell (2006) identifies three main findings. First, by focusing on the perceived relationship between biology and social relations, she reveals how notions of the child, childhood and significant relatedness vary across time and space. She argues that, through a process of **kinning**, persons are made into kin. In the case of adoption, kinning overcomes a dominant cultural emphasis placed upon biological connectedness. Second, the study reveals the rise of 'expert knowledge' in the understanding of 'the best interest of the child' and reveals the ways that this affects national and international policy and practice of transnational adoption. Third, the study shows how transnational adoption both depends upon and helps to foster the globalization of Western rationality and morality.

This study draws on the personal experiences of parents in Norway and throws new light on the way in which children identify themselves as Norwegians despite the tendency of adults to associate with their birthplaces.

BIOLOGY OR SOCIAL TIES?

Because of the increasing awareness of the importance of social relations, the role of biology has come under question in recent years. **Fictive kinship** is a term used by anthropologists and ethnographers to describe forms of kinship or social ties that are based on neither consanguinal nor affinal ties. However, many anthropologists have abandoned a distinction between biological or affinal and fictive kin because – according to the **symbolic anthropologist** David Schneider (1984) – many cultures do not base their notion of kinship on biological relations.

Janet Carsten (2004) develops the notion of culturally constructed kinship through her concept of relatedness, drawing on her research in Malaysia, where she investigated which relations were based on social ties and which on biology. Carsten argues that relatedness should be described in terms of self-ascribed statements and practices, some of which fall outside what anthropologists have conventionally understood as kinship.

New Patterns of Technology-Based Social Relations: *Tales from Facebook* (Miller 2011)

Daniel Miller explores the effect that social media is having on relationships. In his study of Facebook in Trinidad and Tobago, he uses a number of individual narratives to examine the impact that it has on the lives of those who use it. Facebook is now used by a billion people throughout the world, many of whom spend several hours a day on the site. Miller argues that Facebook is not just used by the young and that it can be not only the means by which people find and cultivate relationships but also instrumental in breaking up relationships – or even, in some cases, marriages.

Miller describes how, in Trinidad, the word *friending* means to have sex with someone in a non-marital relationship. On Facebook, 'to friend' someone implies something rather different, but Miller points out that this linguistic difference in meaning leads some to become very suspicious of their partners' activities on the site. Promiscuous activities, which would previously have been frequent but private, suddenly become visible.

Miller concludes by saying that Facebook has contributed to the process of reconstructing people's kinship relationships as well as other close social relationships, with technology compensating for increasing distance and absence. In other words, he claims that Facebook allows individuals to continue to network socially in traditional ways, and that this works against the general tendency today towards less communication.

Globalization: The Internet and Relationships

In the film **The Internet Bride** (2004), Eleanor Ford explores Cali in Colombia, which is celebrated for salsa music and beautiful women. It is also the base of the Internet Bride agency Latin Best, which has 900 women on its files.

Accompanying the British and American men who arrive at the agency, the film-maker meets the potential brides and discovers their motivations for leaving the past behind and following the dream of a life elsewhere. The film raises issues of the impact of modern technologies on the construction of international relationships and the changing role of kinship, from locally based face-to-face meetings to virtual dating.

Activity

List the advantages and disadvantages of the impact of technology on kinship patterns.

USING OBJECTS TO EXPRESS SOCIAL RELATIONS

So far we have considered different ways in which humans organize their relationships. Next we consider the ways objects are used to express these relationships. There are two key areas to be explored: **exchange** – that is, the giving and receiving of objects or services – and **gift exchange**.

It is likely that early groups of humans cooperated by sharing resources, which helped them to survive, as well as enabling different groups to build relationships and alliances. Today many different patterns of exchange exist, both formal and informal. Exchange developed in many parts of the world into the use of currencies, including

Exchange
To give in return for something received

Gift exchange
The giving and receiving of objects, usually reciprocal

money, to buy or sell goods. Early forms were used for exchanging objects of a relative value, or barter. In parts of West Africa, and elsewhere, early forms of currency such as cowrie shells preceded money.

It is worth noting that the sale and purchase of land is often unthinkable in non-Western societies, where land is tied to kin, ancestors and spirits and labour cannot necessarily be measured. In **capitalism**, however, according to Marxists, almost anything can be bought or sold, making it a **commodity**. For Marxists, members of the working class became commodities, as their labour is bought or sold.

STOP & THINK

Can you think any other advantages of exchanging objects in early human groups?
Can you think of anything that is not a commodity (in other words, anything that cannot be bought or sold)?

Commodities and exchange patterns provide a lot of important information for anthropologists, as they demonstrate how people organize their social relations. Such patterns also reveal how the distribution of goods is organized, indicating power relations. Anthropologists have always been interested in the ways that the economy is an integrated part of culture. The drive for material goods is not natural but culturally constructed, and what is considered valuable varies from culture to culture. The desire to have more objects than are necessary for survival is known as **consumerism**. It is important that anthropologists take care not to make assumptions about non-Western societies where consumption patterns may differ: every human group has its own ideas of what and where to consume.

For the Yap people of the western Pacific, *rai* stones serve as currency; ownership is determined not necessarily by physically moving the stones (which can weigh up to 3 tons) but by recording the change of owner in Yapese oral history and songs. Owning a stone is highly prestigious. (Eric Guinther / Wikimedia Commons)

STOP & THINK

'Money, to the West, is like kinship is to the rest' (Sahlins 1972).
Explain the meaning of the above quotation.
How do exchange patterns inform anthropologists about the way social relationships are organized?

Gifts play an important role in establishing, confirming or even ending relationships. There are usually specific rules about gift giving which indicate the specific relationship between individuals or groups. Gifts can involve some form of obligation, though this is not always the case, and it does not mean immediate repayment has to be made.

In his essay *The Gift*, Marcel Mauss ([1954] 1970) explores gift exchange in Polynesian

Activity

Look at the following examples and consider what obligations might be felt by the person receiving the gift:
- pocket money
- a wedding ring
- having a meal cooked for you by friends.

society, where everyone in the local community has long-term obligations towards others that are a result of gift exchange. Mauss argues that gift giving does not simply have an economic function; it is a cultural act as well. He maintains that giving a gift leads to a bond being created between the person giving and the person receiving the gift. Raymond Firth (1981, 1988) challenged Mauss's interpretation and his idea of the spirit of the gift itself. According to Firth, Mauss was reporting his own intellectual interpretation of gift giving rather than understanding it from the perspective of the group being studied.

Activity

How, according to Mauss, is gift exchange an important part of a social system?
What is the meaning of the gift?
Why was Mauss criticized?

Potlatch, Reciprocity and Power

Research by Franz Boas (1897) and Ruth Benedict (1970) indicated the importance of the specific form of gift exchange known as potlatch as part of the economy of some of the indigenous peoples of the Pacific Northwest coast of Canada and the USA. Ceremonial gift giving is practised by specific groups and their neighbours. Those who are considered powerful and wealthy try to maintain and defend their position by giving spectacular gifts to each other in a form of competitive gift exchange. For some time this ceremony was rigorously banned by both the Canadian and the United States governments, before being reinstated in the 1950s. This was because **missionaries** and government representatives argued that it was wasteful, unproductive and contrary to 'civilized' values. In the past, when one chief received a gift from another, he would have to surpass the latter in his return gift. This competition could in some cases result in the destruction of considerable material wealth, as many gifts were often thrown onto a fire at the end of the ceremony. For example, participants destroyed valuables, throwing away salt fish or setting fire to tents and carpets. To reciprocate, another chief would try to increase the value of the gifts (and their destruction). The chief who showed that he could afford to destroy more would be regarded as having more power or higher status.

In some ways this example is similar to Mauss's ([1954] 1970) explanation of the competitive gift exchange he claims exists in the West. For example, in France people compete to give the most lavish gifts at weddings. Mauss regarded gift giving as essential to social relations.

Activity

Consider your own culture – can you think of an example of competitive gift exchange?
Why do you think the potlatch ritual was banned?
What effect might this ban have had on those cultures that practised potlatch?

The Kula Ring

Another example of the significance of gift giving is to be found in a ring of small islands in Papua New Guinea, where one chief makes a gift to another chief often hundreds of miles away across the open sea. The gifts (arm bands and shell necklaces) are essentially of a ritual nature and have very little value in themselves other than the cultural significance placed upon them. Nevertheless, these are treasured and handed on every year, until eventually they are handed back to the same chief, and so it goes on. At its simplest, there is gift and counter-gift, but these gifts play an important role in the economic exchange and bartering system that operates between the islands. The giving and receiving maintains important relationships between these geographically dispersed islands. The journey between the islands can be dangerous, so taking a gift is also symbolic of the distance involved.

The gift exchange in the Kula is different to many other forms in that a person intends to give away something of greater value than the item they receive. This is quite the opposite of Western market trading, where individual profit is pursued. The practice of giving a gift with a greater value than you receive is quite typical of non-Western economic systems.

> **Activity**
>
> In your own words, explain the Kula exchange system.
> How does this system reinforce social relations?
> How is this system similar and also different from the Western economic system?

Day of the Dead

In some cases gifts are given to the dead – for example, on *el dia de los muertos* (the day of the dead). This is a complex celebration, very deep with meaning, that takes place in

An elaborate *ofrenda* for the deceased: this is in a public square, though *ofrendas* are also constructed in libraries, offices and municipal buildings as well as in private homes and cemeteries. (Luisroj96 / Wikimedia Commons)

Mexico and in other parts of the world. People provide an *ofrenda* (an offering in the form of an altar), consisting of specially prepared food and drink, and sometimes cigarettes, dedicated to relatives and also loved friends who have died. At home, *ofrendas* may be decorated with photographs of the people honoured and, as on graves, with objects they liked and used when they were alive – for instance, toys for dead children. Sometimes, the ritual is celebrated with music.

STOP & THINK

What do you think are the possible functions of the day of the dead?

Stone Age Economics (Sahlins 1972): Three types of Reciprocity

It is already apparent that informal exchange is as important as formal systems. Informal exchange is sometimes referred to as **reciprocity**. Since virtually all humans live in some kind of society and have at least a few possessions, reciprocity is common to every culture. Sahlins (1972) identified three main types of reciprocity:

1 *Generalized reciprocity* refers to altruistic giving, where there are very vague or weak ideas about what is expected in return and when it is expected. This results in the recipient feeling as if they are not in debt to the person giving the gift, and so is sometimes referred to as a 'true gift'. In this type of reciprocity, the social part of giving may be considered more significant than the gift itself.
2 *Balanced or symmetrical reciprocity* occurs when someone gives to someone else, expecting a fair and tangible return there and then. Exchange is based less on social factors and is dominated by the material exchange and individual interests of the gift giver and the recipient.
3 *Negative reciprocity* is the least social form of gift exchange, and can include theft. In this form of reciprocity, a person expects to maximize their gains or, in other words, profit as much as they can.

Activity

In your own words, explain Sahlins's types of reciprocity.
Provide an example of each type.

Over the past three centuries, economic patterns in many parts of the world have become increasingly dominated by a specific system of economic exchange – capitalism – which is based on individual gain and wage labour. The spread of the capitalist economic system has had profound impacts not just on local economic practices but also on attitudes, on cultural practices and, as a result, on how social relationships are formed and maintained. The following example demonstrates how local practices are lost because of the transition to wage labour and capitalist attitudes.

Economic Spheres among the Tiv (Bohannan and Bohannan 1968)

The Tiv are traditional farmers who live in the savannah belt of central eastern Nigeria. They are **patrilineal** and transfer rights among the patrilineage. As in many societies where kinship plays a central role in organizing social relations, it was not possible for the Tiv to buy or sell land, since the land ultimately belonged to the ancestors. Personal identity was intimately tied to the lineage land. The Tiv grew cereals, fruit and vegetables and kept livestock. They produced food for subsistence, and the surplus was either redistributed or sold in the market. Until the Second World War, the Tiv had three economic spheres or centres in their economy, which were ranked according to a particular morality.

- **The lowest, the subsistence sphere** included cereals and other foodstuffs, kitchen utensils, spices and tools. These were considered as being of a similar value.
- **The prestige sphere** included the highly valued cattle, brass rods and magical paraphernalia. Brass rods functioned as a means of payment.
- **The third and highest sphere was where women and children were exchanged**. Generally, a person could be paid for with another person. Payment did not have to take place immediately.

Within each sphere, exchange was seen as morally neutral. Problems arose only in exchange between spheres – for example, exchanging brass rods for grain – which was considered wrong or foolish. **Colonization** had a huge impact on this economy; colonialists extended trading networks, which gave the Tiv access to previously unknown imported goods. Many Tiv left their way of life altogether and became small capitalist farmers producing specialized crops such as sesame seeds, which they sold for money to spend on food and other necessities.

The introduction of money had important consequences for Tiv society; money and the traditional system could not work alongside each other. In a matter of years after the introduction of money, brass rods, white cloth and grain could not be measured on a common scale. Eventually **bridewealth** was paid in cash; many felt this was a devaluation of women, as the new practice indicated that women were a commodity of the same kind as pots and chickens.

It is too simplistic to draw the conclusion from the example of the Tiv that money is inevitably 'morally bad'. The spread of capitalism and the cash economy has brought different consequences for different cultures for a number of situational reasons. While the collapse of the economic spheres or the moral economy of the Tiv shows how a cash economy can become detached from cultural values, they were able to communicate and trade on a much larger scale than before.

Activity

Describe the economy of the Tiv before the Second World War.
How is the cash economy different from the earlier economy based on moral spheres?
In your view, was the transformation of economies a positive one?

CONCLUSION

Many societies have clear hierarchies based on many different social systems. Kinship continues to be an important organizing principle in most societies, though significantly more so in non-Western societies. Kinship may not have the same influence on individuals or groups given the increasing individualism found in some Western societies. However, people's closest relationships affect their lives in profound and multiple ways.

In some societies where there is a less developed state, kinship remains crucially important, and for this reason emotional attachments are less likely to be developed, for example, between married couples – marriage having other important functions to play. Kinship patterns continue to be complex and to vary from place to place. Kinship definitions may, for instance, include inanimate objects or animals. It is clear that technological developments are challenging anthropological understandings of kinship in a variety of complex and interesting ways, alongside the complicated effects of globalization, opening new possibilities while simultaneously re-creating some very old problems.

Objects are used to express different social relationships as well as being used to initiate or maintain social relations. Exchange systems reveal a great deal of information about a social group and can reflect the various hierarchies and social relationships that exist.

END OF CHAPTER ASSESSMENT

Kinship remains the primary institution around which human social groups organize themselves. Assess this view.

Teacher's guidance

Begin by defining kinship, exploring problems and the role of biology in its definition. Explain different anthropological approaches to the study of kinship. Using a range of ethnographic evidence, look at the main kinship patterns, descent and marriage systems and demonstrate the ways in which kinship continues to play a key role in organizing social relations. Analyse the extent to which kinship remains an important institution within contemporary societies. Discuss alternative important ways of organizing social relationships, through class, caste, gender and age, and suggest how interlinked these may or may not be with kinship relations. Consider the spread of capitalism and globalization and the impact this may be having on the importance of kinship in different societies.

KEY TERMS

Achieved status A position that is earned

Affine Kin created through marriage

Age grades Levels of seniority through which age sets pass collectively as they grow older

Age set A group of individuals of a similar age, often sharing special social links with one another

Bridewealth Payment by a groom's kin to a bride's kin in return for his rights to her labour and reproductive powers

Commodity Anything that can be bought or sold

Consanguineous relatives Kin related by blood

Consumerism The desire to have more material objects than is necessary for survival

Dowry Gifts that a bride brings from her family into the marriage

Endogamy Marriage is practised only within a group

Exchange To give in return for something received

Exogamy Marriage is practised only with people outside a group

Fictive kinship Forms of kinship or social ties that are based on neither consanguinal (blood) nor affinal ('by marriage') ties

Gender Culturally constructed notions of what it means to be male or female, depending on the social context

Genealogy The study of kinship and descent patterns

Hierarchy A form of social organization where some individuals or groups have greater power, social status or ranking than others

Ideology A set of ideas supporting the interests of a particular group

Kinning The social process where adopted/non-biologically related children become kin

Kinship Sets of relationships considered primary in any society, in practice demonstrating huge variety in different societies

Matrilineal Descent through the female

Matrilocal Where a married couple lives near or with the family of the wife or mother

Means of production The factories, machines and other resources that help produce goods and services and result in profit for those who own them

Monogamy A relationship where a person is married to one partner at a time

Patrilineal Descent through the male

Patrilocal Where a married couple lives near or with the family of the husband or father

Potlatch An important ritual practised by some Native Americans involving competitive gift giving, which plays an important part of the economy

Reciprocity Informal systems of exchange

Reincarnation The rebirth of a soul in a new body

Reproductive technologies New forms of technology, including IVF and other forms of fertility treatment, that create new forms of kinship relations

Social class A socio-economic group found within capitalist society, usually based on the occupation and attitudes of the individual

Social kinship Relationships created through social interaction rather than biologically based relations

---

Personal investigation

Establish contact or use an existing contact with a family from a culture other than your own. Spend time with the family members and explore the relative importance of class, caste (if applicable), age, gender and kinship in their particular context. Investigate the meaning of biological relations and socially based relationships for the family you are studying and consider how ideas about relationships may or may not have changed through the generations by speaking to people of a range of ages. Consider the ways in which a person's position in the family might affect their life in terms of status, role, job and rituals. In particular, focus on who is considered to be significant in terms of relationships and why this might be. Try to understand the nature of marriage and consider the functions that the family performs.

Try to understand the role of technology in creating, maintaining or even damaging social relationships and consider the nature of interactions mediated through technology. Be sure to take into account people's ideas about their relationships with others and contrast these with your own observations.

SUGGESTED FURTHER READING AND FILMS

Books

Carsten, J. (2004) *After Kinship.* Cambridge University Press.

Hua, C. (2008) *A Society without Fathers or Husbands: The Na of China.* MIT Press.

Kapadia, K. (1995) *Siva and her Sisters: Gender, Caste, and Class in Rural South India.* Perseus.

Miller, D. (2011) *Tales from Facebook.* Polity.

Sahlins, M. (1972) *Stone Age Economics.* Aldine-Atherton.

Ethnographic films

Duka's Dilemma (2001), directed by Jean Lydall
The Internet Bride (2004), directed by Eleanor Ford
Without Fathers or Husbands (1995), directed by Hua Cai

CHAPTER FIVE

ENGAGING WITH NATURE

CONTENTS

CHAPTER 5

Engaging with Nature

KEY ISSUES AND DEBATES

- What are different subsistence patterns?
- What is the meaning of nature – as a theoretical perspective, methodological approach and way of describing nature?
- To what extent is human culture shaped by nature?
- How can relationships with animals show different ways in which humans engage with nature?
- What are the main ways in which different people live on the land?

This chapter explores some of the ways in which people interact with the natural environment and the cultural consequences of these interactions. There are many ways that people from different cultures formulate and answer the following questions: What is nature? What is human nature? What is the place of humans in nature? What should be the place of humans in nature?

Many anthropologists consider how people interact with nature as a primary cause of cultural differences and similarities. One important way people interact with the environment is by productive activities, which require labour, technology and natural resources, discussed below. The second part of this chapter examines different ways in which humans relate to animals.

CULTURAL PRACTICES IN RELATION TO THE ENVIRONMENT

Humans interact with their environments not only biologically; they do so through culture as well. Over the last half million years, hominids and modern humans invented tools that have enabled them to populate new environments without needing to evolve biologically. Houses, clothing and fire have permitted people to live in a very wide range of climates. All animals must meet the basic requirements for survival: they must obtain food and water, and to fulfil these requirements all human societies have developed forms of subsistence.

Leslie White (1943)

White suggests that one of the most important ways people interact with nature is by harnessing energy (e.g., food, fuel) and raw materials (e.g., minerals for tools, wood and stones for shelter). Acquiring energy and materials from the environment is part of production – the patterned, organized activities by which people transform natural resources into things that satisfy their material needs and wants. Productive activities involve the use of labour and technology to harness natural resources.

101

Economic anthropology often classifies the economies of groups of people into different categories according to their subsistence patterns or modes of production and makes a distinction between subsistence economic systems and those based on the market and (since the nineteenth century) on industrial production. A **subsistence economy** is non-monetary, where people produce food and products mainly for their own use and rely on primary resources for meeting their needs. Barter and the exchange of goods may often be involved in subsistence economies, but they contrast with market systems. In the latter, the exchange of goods for money is based on profit and its maximization for those engaged in the exchange.

Although subsistence economies rely on only the resources around them, this does not mean that these societies have always been poor or impoverished. Marshal Sahlins (1972) thought that the hunter-gatherer !Kung (San Bushmen) were the 'original affluent society': enviably, they worked long enough each day only to provide for their needs, spending the rest of the time relaxing and enjoying themselves. These days, subsistence economies rarely exist in isolation from other modes of production and have often been confined to marginalized areas.

The main subsistence modes of production identified by anthropologists are foraging (hunters and gatherers), pastoralism and horticulturalism/non-intensive crop production.

> **Subsistence patterns**
> The sources and methods a society uses to obtain its food and other necessities

> **Mode of production**
> The dominant way in which people make a living in a particular culture

---

STOP & THINK

Getting food is the most important way in which people interact with their environment. How do you get your food? Where does it come from? Where is it produced? How connected are you to your environment?

Foraging (Hunters and Gatherers)

Foragers, or hunter-gatherers, get their food from collecting (gathering) wild plants and hunting or fishing the animals that live in their regions. Foraging for wild plants and hunting wild animals – acquiring food by collecting what is available in nature – is the oldest of human subsistence patterns. Foragers do not plant crops, and the only domesticated animals that they usually own are dogs. These useful animals often have many functions for foraging peoples. They serve as pets, hunting aids, watch-animals and camp waste scavengers (see the Hill Pandaram hunters and gatherers in chapter 13, pp. 284–6).

Hunters and gatherers used to (and some groups still do) live exclusively from the wild plants and animals available in their habitats, making little change to their environments, relying mainly on their own muscle power in carrying out their subsistence tasks. Most labour is done individually or in small groups of relatives and friends. Every man is primarily a hunter of animals and every woman is mainly a gatherer of plants, although examples of women hunters of large game have been recorded, and even in societies where women are described as 'gatherers' they may 'gather' small game too. Most foraging societies have relatively temporary encampments with tents or other easily constructed dwellings. The length of time that they stay in any one location is determined largely by the availability of food and water. Their migrations are limited by the fact that most foraging societies travel on foot. The majority of humans today rely on intensive agriculture for food, but small communities of foragers still exist. Many of them live in tropical forests and arid regions in the developing world that are considered undesirable for agriculture. Over the centuries, they have been pushed to these marginal lands. Small groups of scattered true hunter-gatherer groups live in the Amazon, the Arctic, Papua New Guinea, Australia, the Andaman Islands and Africa. Robert Kelly (1995) has identified ninety-two hunter-gatherer groups around the world, some of whom are only partially reliant on this mode for their subsistence.

Pastoralism

Pastoralism is a subsistence pattern in which people make their living by tending animals. The species of animals vary with the region of the world, but they are all domesticated herbivores that normally live in herds and eat grasses or other abundant plant foods. Cattle, camels, sheep, goats, reindeer, horses, llamas, alpacas and yaks are the most common animals kept by herders. There are essentially two forms of pastoralism: nomadic and transhumant. **Pastoral nomads** follow a seasonal migratory pattern that can vary from year to year. The timing and destinations of migrations are determined above all by the needs of the herd animals for water and food. These nomadic societies do not create permanent settlements but, rather, live in temporary dwellings such as tents. **Transhumant pastoralists** follow a cyclical pattern of migration that usually takes them to cool highland valleys in the summer and warmer lowland valleys in the winter. This is seasonal migration between the same two locations in which they have regular encampments or stable villages, often with permanent houses. Transhumant pastoralists usually depend somewhat less on their animals for food than do nomadic ones. They often undertake small-scale vegetable farming at their summer encampments. They are also more likely to trade their animals in town markets for grain and other things that they do not produce themselves. Pastoralism is often an adaptation to semi-arid open country in which farming cannot be easily sustained without importing irrigation water from great distances. When there is a drought, pastoralists disperse their herds or move them to new areas.

Most pastoralists also get food from their animals without killing them. Horses, goats, sheep, cattle and camels are milked. Pastoralist societies most often have patrilineal

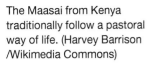

The Maasai from Kenya traditionally follow a pastoral way of life. (Harvey Barrison /Wikimedia Commons)

descent patterns and are male dominated. Men usually make the important decisions and own the animals, while women primarily care for children and perform domestic chores.

Horticulture

Horticulture in the anthropological context is small-scale, low-intensity farming. This subsistence pattern involves part-time planting and tending of domesticated food plants. Pigs, chickens, or other small domesticated animals are often raised for food and prestige. Many horticultural societies supplement their farming subsistence base with occasional hunting and gathering of wild plants and animals. The population that can be supported by horticulture is higher than those of most foragers and pastoralists. Some horticulturalists are not only subsistence farmers but also produce a small surplus to sell or exchange in local markets for things that they cannot produce themselves. Horticulture is currently practised by many thousands of people, mainly in sub-Saharan Africa, South and Southeast Asia, the Pacific islands of Papua New Guinea, Central and South America, and some Caribbean islands. It was a common subsistence base elsewhere in the world until populations rose to high levels and people were forced to develop more intensive farming methods.

Intensive Agriculture

At the present time the world population has reached 7 billion and is still growing. The majority of people worldwide are living in cities. The emergence of urban society introduced a new set of human and environmental interactions. In large-scale societies today, agriculture has become highly efficient, requiring many fewer people to produce the food. Intensive agriculture is the primary subsistence pattern of large-scale societies and results in much more food being produced per acre than is the case with subsistence patterns. Beginning about 10,000 years ago, the development of intensive farming methods became necessary as the human population grew in some major river valleys to levels beyond the carrying capacity of the environment. Many of the plantations now are large, labour-intensive farms that mostly produce fruit, sugar, fibre or vegetable oil products for the international market. People who work on these farms often labour for very low wages that keep them in poverty. Transnational companies own many of the plantations of the Global South. The effect of this form of agriculture generally has been the flow of wealth from poor nations in the Global South to rich ones in the Global North. (See http://anthro.palomar.edu/subsistence/default.htm.)

Activity

Why is the future of hunters and gatherers uncertain? What is the biggest danger to their way of life? What is their relationship to nature?

What is the difference between pastoral nomads and transhumant pastoralists? What kinds of animals do pastoral nomads and transhumant pastoralist use? Are pastoralists self-sufficient? What are some differences between ranchers and pastoralists?

What is large-scale intensive farming? What changes in the environment has this type of subsistence produced? What is the relationship between people in large urban areas and their environment?

Activity

Ways of Engaging with Nature

How do others engage with nature?	How does this compare to your culture?
The **Nuer** people of South Sudan depend on cattle for their very existence in terms of meat and milk. Evans-Pritchard ([1940] 1987) found that cattle were at the core of Nuer culture, as rules regarding marriage exchange, ritual and settlement of disputes could be understood only through the cattle and terms surrounding them.	
The **Tsembaga** of New Guinea are horticulturalists who also keep pigs. About once every ten years, to show respect for their ancestors, they slaughter nearly all the pigs and after a huge party go to war against their enemies and then build a new village in a fresh location. Rappaport (1968) claimed this is actually because, when the pig population increases, the cost of keeping them starts mounting, as they destroy crops. Coupled with the soil becoming impoverished from years of cultivation, this is the underlying ecological cause of the move. (For a longer discussion of this, see the section on **Ecological anthropology** below, p.110.	
Mauss ([1979] 2013) found seasonal differences in the activities among the **Inuit** in the Arctic region. Winter was devoted to group activities, with fishing as the main economic pursuit and rituals concerning human relations; whereas summer was spent more on individual activities, hunting, and rituals of human/animal communication. The people's ideas of the seasons corresponded with their social organization.	
Rankoana (2001) found that the **Dikgale** people of South Africa used plants extensively for medicinal purposes.	

The **Hadza** people live in the lands of northern Tanzania around Lake Eyasi in the Great Rift Valley. Like most hunter-gatherers, they are nomadic, having no fixed residence and move from place to place in search of food and water according to the seasons. About a thousand Hadza live in their traditional homeland. Some have moved close to villages and taken jobs as farmhands or tour guides. But approximately one-quarter of all Hadza remain true hunter-gatherers. They have no crops, no livestock, and no permanent shelters. The things they own (a cooking pot, a water container, an axe) can be wrapped in a blanket and carried over their shoulder. Hadza women gather berries and baobab fruit and dig edible plant roots. Men collect honey and hunt. They will eat almost anything they can kill, from birds to wildebeest, zebra and buffalo.

Nowak and Laird (2010) studied the **Basseri** people – a pastoral nomadic society in southern Iran. Their territory is diverse, ranging from deserts to mountain. Being nomadic, the Basseri have traditional migration routes which they follow annually. Domesticated animals are of vital importance: sheep and goats are the most significant because they provide the bulk of the subsistence products. Milk and milk products are the staples of the Basseri diet. In addition to milk products and hides, the animals also provide wool, both for sale and for the people's own use. Donkeys are used as pack animals and are ridden by women and children. Men ride horses that carry no other load. Camels are burdened with the heaviest items to transport. The Basseri do not herd cattle because their trek is long and difficult and the terrain is too rocky for the animals to navigate.

> **Activity**
>
> Find examples in magazines, newspapers, books, and on the Internet of the economic systems mentioned in this chapter – foraging, horticulturalist, pastoralist and intensive agriculture – and prepare a presentation for your class. The presentation should include the following:
> - a description of the culture and their modes of subsistence
> - how these people understand their environments
> - how they interact with their environments
> - how this culture is influenced by their ecological surroundings.

THE NATURE VERSUS CULTURE DEBATE IN ANTHROPOLOGY

The nature versus culture distinction is one of the most evident oppositions in Western society. What shapes us, both as individuals and as members of a culture? Is it inherited genetic predisposition (nature) or what we learn as we grow up (nurture) that predominantly shapes us, and our differences, as individuals? Similarly, anthropologists ask how much of our behaviour as a group is predetermined by geography, culture or history. The differences between individuals and those between groups can be explained not by a single factor but, rather, by the complex interaction between a number of factors. Some differences between people are related to ethnicity, genetics, environment, religion, economy, technology and development. Some of these factors are biological and some are cultural.

Concepts of Nature in Anthropology

Anthropologists explore external nature (the ecosystem) and inner nature (human nature). Culture is always something other than nature and always implies a transformation of nature. Every cultural project seems to imply a transformation of both external and human nature.

There are two approaches to the nature–culture relationship.

- How is nature and the nature–culture relationship conceptualized in different societies?
- How does nature (the environment or inborn characteristics of humans) affect society and culture?

Nature thus exists as a representation of something outside culture and society, yet influencing the ways in which people live. As a biological species, people take part in ecosystems and modify them and, as cultural beings, develop concepts about their environment and their place within it.

HUMAN NATURE

The traditional view of human nature is as a set of capacities universal to the species. Some of these are language, bipedalism, the ability to make and use tools, self-consciousness, and the capacity to represent the world symbolically through art, design and ritual (see chapter 1). It is said these capacities evolved gradually from ancient times. Human nature is common to all people and underwrites everything they do. Human beings vary from one another, both at an individual level and at that of different populations. However, this is not because of variations in their nature but because of the particular circumstances they encounter in their lifetimes, including both the cultural tradition and the physical environment in which they were brought up. Great differences, as well as similarities, can be seen when comparing world cultures. These are cultural differences. Culture is not something added on to human organisms but a measure of difference between them. There is no standard or universal form of human being. Humans of today are different not only from one another but also from their prehistoric predecessors. Since humans acquire culture through learning, people living in different places or different circumstances develop different cultures.

STOP & THINK

What is human nature?

CASE STUDIES ENGAGING WITH NATURE: ETHNOGRAPHIC FILMS

Anthropologists have used visual methods to portray how different people engage with nature. The following three examples show how different views of nature can lead to conflict.

The Kayapo (Michael Beckham and Terence Turner, 1987)

This film focuses on the conflicts and determination of a group of people trying to survive and to maintain their ethnic identity in the face of almost overpowering odds. It contrasts the reactions of two groups of Kayapo to outside influence. The Kapot have opposed contact and resisted both non-indigenous Brazilian settlers and gold miners. The Gorotire, by contrast, were invaded by gold miners who strip-mined their land and polluted their rivers. The miners paid the Gorotire very little for the destruction until 1985, when 200 warriors seized the airstrip and the miners were forced to increase the commission by 5 per cent. This commission amounts to $2 million per year for the Gorotire, and the tribe is learning to cope with the money, both with the problems it brings and the power it gives. They have trained several of their members to deal effectively with the outside world on behalf of the rest of the tribe and now run a plane (and hire a pilot) to patrol their land against intruders. The Kapot, in their own way, are also trying to assert their identity and independence, and the film shows them in the traditional activities of building and dismantling a hunting camp. The sight of the hunters returning with the tortoises they have caught is particularly impressive. The now famous Chief Rao-ni is featured as a leader of the Kapot, and he states eloquently his opposition to the Gorotire's acceptance of the gold miners. Despite their adherence to tradition, however, the Kapot use modern technology – video, radios, etc. – to protect their interests and record their rituals.

Chief Ra-oni Metuktire with another Kayapo leader during the Conferência Nacional Indígena in Brasília, Brazil. The Kapot use modern technology and engage with the dominant culture in Brazil to attain their goals. (José Cruz/Abr / Wikimedia Commons)

Since the Company Came (Russell Hawkins, 2001)

Set in the South Pacific, in a remote Solomon Islands village, *Since the Company Came* is the story of a community coming to terms with social, cultural and ecological disintegration. When village leaders invite a Malaysian company to log their tribal land, the Haporai people of Rendova Island find themselves at a difficult crossroads. Most of the men embrace the chance to earn money and participate in the modern economy; many of the women are more concerned with preserving the forests and traditions that sustain their families. At a village meeting, Chief Mark Lamberi calls into question the tribe's finances, only to find himself the target of furious accusations from the new 'big man' of the community and chairman of the logging project, Timothy Zama. The community is embroiled in conflicts over land ownership and logging royalties, conflicts that threaten the very core of their traditional social values.

The Land on which We Stand (Rebecca Payne, 2007)

This film is a glimpse into the life of the Landmatters Cooperative, a community of eleven adults and four children living in benders (simple shelters made using flexible branches of hazel or willow) and yurts (tents) in rural Devon as they develop a permaculture project. The 42 acres of land was originally designated for agriculture, which means the community does not have planning permission for residential use. The film follows the group as they fight for permission to live on the land in order to create a self-reliant way of life for a future that doesn't depend on fossil fuels. It also explores concerns of some local residents in the nearby hamlet who object to the 'hippies' living next door.

Activity

How can ethnographic film portray human life experience?
What are the similarities and differences between the Kayapo, the Haporai and the Landmatters Cooperative community in their relationship with nature?

Anthropological Environmental Theories

CULTURAL ECOLOGY

Cultural ecology takes the position that cultures interact with their environmental settings via a process of adaptation. The basic idea of this theory is that cultural features evolve as an adaptation to the local environment. The aim of cultural ecologists is to study human activity as an ecological adaptation. They use quantitative methods, and the topics investigated have often included energy exploitation and resource dynamics. Julian Steward ([1955] 1972) was the main thinker behind this theory. His basic argument is that, with a given technology, the local environment presents a series of problems and opportunities that bring out adaptive cultural responses. Steward recognized that there were multiple pathways for adapting to the same climatic conditions over time, a process he called **multilinear evolution**. The investigation of multilinear evolution was based on a comparison of the cultural ecology of societies at the same level of socio-cultural integration (bands, tribes, chiefdoms, states) in the same biome (deserts, savannas, tropical rainforests). This was based on detailed ethnographic investigations of the cultural ecology of several societies, concentrating on identifying the natural resources on which they depend for their subsistence, the technology and organization of labour used to extract and process the resources, and how these factors in turn influence other aspects of culture. So, rather than the crude idea that environment shapes culture, the approach states that specific environmental factors shape particular cultural features.

Criticisms: It has been argued that studies conducted within cultural ecology were limited to egalitarian societies. Furthermore, it is a theory and methodology used to explain how things stay the same, as opposed to how things can change. The focus of cultural ecologists on subsistence overlooks other adaptive domains (health/disease, reproduction, politics). What is adaptation, and what roles does it play in biological ecology and ecological anthropology?

ECOLOGICAL ANTHROPOLOGY

By the 1960s, many anthropologists had turned away from Steward's views and adopted the new idea that cultures could be involved in reciprocal relationships with the environment. The term 'ecological anthropology' was coined to label this new approach, accomplished by applying a systems approach to studying the role of a human population in the processes of energy flow and nutrient cycling within its ecosystem. Methodologically there was also far greater emphasis on the collection of quantitative data than in previous work.

Pigs for the Ancestors: Ritual in the Ecology of a New Guinea People (Rappaport 1968)

Rappaport studied the Tsembaga Maring people from New Guinea. Since ecological anthropologists use quantitative data collection, this meant that Rappaport had to conduct hard labour mapping gardens, weighing crop yields, sampling soil, recording rainfall, recording food consumption, counting pigs, and collecting botanical data and many other measurements of the ecosystem. He discusses the relationship between ecology and culture. Like many other highland peoples, the Tsembaga are horticulturalists who also keep pigs. About once every ten years they slaughter nearly all their pigs and, after a huge party, they go to war against their neighbours and then move location to build a new village. This, they claim, is something they do to show respect to their ancestors. Using his quantitative data, Rappaport shows that, when the crop-destroying pig population increases, the Tsembaga run into problems keeping the animals under control: the cost of looking after them comes to outweigh the benefit. At the same time, the soil is depleted, as usually happens after a few years of slash and burn cultivation. Thus, Rappaport argues, quite apart from pleasing the ancestors, these decennial rituals and movements can be explained **ecologically**, as an efficient cultural adaptation to the environment.

The Tsembaga gain access to new land and can begin raising pigs in modest numbers again. What this study might tell us is not only how ecology affects people but also about specific cultural ways of managing ecological surroundings.

CULTURAL MATERIALISM

Cultural materialism is an anthropological school of thought that says that the best way to understand human culture is to examine material conditions – climate, food supply, geography, etc. According to Marvin Harris (1998), cultural materialism is the way to understand the causes of differences and similarities among societies and cultures. It is based on the simple idea that human social life is a response to the practical problems of earthly existence. As a research method, cultural materialism emphasizes scientific method and objective analysis. Its goal is to explain politics, economics, ideology and symbolic aspects of a culture in relation to the needs of that society. From a cultural materialist point of view, society is certainly shaped by the factors of production and reproduction. All of the customs, however irrational they might appear to outsiders, emerge as a way of regulating resources, acquiring protein, controlling population, or otherwise adapting to material and biological existence. (For more on material objects, see chapter 12.)

'The cultural ecology of India's sacred cattle' (Harris 1992)

This is an example of the application of cultural materialism, specifically to the Hindu taboo against eating beef. Harris demonstrates that this taboo makes sense in terms of the local environment, because cattle are important in several ways. Thus, the religious taboo is rational, in a materialist sense, because it ensures the conservation of resources provided by the cattle. Harris argues that the cow is sacred in India because it is far more valuable alive for its milk, its dung, for cooking fuel and fertilizer, and for ploughing than dead for its meat and hide. The milk is used for nourishment, the excrement is used for anything from fertilizer to house building, and when the cow dies its hide is turned into leather, and even the meat is eaten by the (formerly designated) untouchables, the lowest caste of the society, as this food prohibition does not apply to them. In other words, Harris concludes that the cows are sacred because it is economically and ecologically sensible to keep it that way, and the religious notion about the sacred status of the cow is there because it supports the functional social use of cows.

Criticisms: If the sacred cow serves such a necessary functional role in India, then why do sacred animals of similar kinds not exist elsewhere? Most food prohibitions do not appear to be ecologically rational. This theory does not explain why pork is prohibited to Jews and Muslims but not to others who live in similarly hot or humid environments.

CULTURAL RELATIVISM

Theories of cultural relativism suggest that cultures can be fully understood only in their own terms. All cultures are equally valid interpretations of reality. There are many ways of interacting with the environment; there are multiple and complex perspectives on it. These different types of relationships can coexist within one society. For example, there can be high levels of cultivation or intervention from farming techniques, such as through mono crops, while in the same society individuals can enjoy less intensive forms of farming, such as in allotments.

THE NEW ECOLOGICAL ANTHROPOLOGY

The key environmental questions of the twenty-first century are population growth, economic development and underdevelopment, biodiversity loss, environmental management, the future of indigenous groups, and the link between consumption and globalization. People throughout the world face environmental crises. However, people of distinct genders, social classes and cultural orientations perceive environmental issues differently. Many anthropologists have witnessed a threat to the people they study, such as commercial logging, environmental pollution, radioactivity, **ecocide**, and imposition of intensive external management systems on local ecosystems that native populations have managed for centuries. The new environmental anthropology attempts not only to understand but also to devise culturally informed and appropriate solutions to such problems and issues as environmental degradation and the role of media, non-governmental organizations (NGOs) and various kinds of hazards in triggering ecological awareness, action and sustainability. The focus is no longer on a single ecosystem. Ecological anthropologists have to pay attention to the external organization and forces (for example, governments, NGOs, businesses) now laying claim to local and regional ecosystems throughout the world. Even in remote places, ecosystem management today involves multiple levels of intervention.

THE RELATIONSHIP BETWEEN HUMANS AND ANIMALS

The multiple ways in which people relate to animals provide a useful way through which to examine the relationships humans have with nature. As we have seen in the first chapter, humans are one species of animal. However, through their physical and mental abilities, humans change and transform their lives using other living organisms. From the food we eat and the clothes we wear to the medicines which sustain us, our lives are intertwined in complex relationships with other animals. Humans share their social and cultural environments with a wide variety of animals and for a wide variety of purposes. Animals are domesticated and used for food, clothing and transport. Animals are hunted for survival and sport, worshipped, sacrificed, represented in art, literature and film, used as pets, used by scientists for experiments, put on display in zoos and natural history museums, and also made to entertain us.

Anthropologists recognize the cultural significance of animals. Claude Lévi-Strauss (1964) explained the ways in which animals provide humans with an important means of defining themselves. Animals, he argued, are 'good to think with'. He suggested that animals are used by humans in order to classify who they are and to make clear the differences between themselves and animals. Other anthropologists have argued that animals serve as sources of power, wealth and inequality. However, today more and more animal studies are becoming the focus of anthropological research. Anthropologists claim that there are two contrasting views that humans tend to have towards animals – **anthropocentric** and **biocentric**.

> **Anthropocentric**
> The tendency for human beings to regard themselves as the central and most significant entities in the universe, or the assessment of reality through an exclusively human perspective

> **Biocentric**
> A view that nature does not exist simply to be used or consumed by humans, but that humans are simply one species among many

Luxury stores and services flourish in Roppongi Hills, Tokyo. It is no surprise that pets in this part of town should have their own outposts for high-end plush toys, leashes, collars and clothing, as well as healthcare consultations and 'beauty treatments', which range from grooming to massage and mud packs. Pets can get 'tattoos' with custom dye jobs or board at the store's hotel suite. Stores even offer dog birthday parties on site. For owners, there's a selection of large handbags for transporting small breeds in the Parisian style. (© Stèfan / Flickr)

The Anthropocentric View of Animals

ANIMALS AND PERFORMANCE

Many different animals are made to perform, in a variety of ways, for human entertainment. They are made to race and fight against each other. Some are ridden in a variety of performances and sports, challenged by humans in events such as bullfights and rodeos or judged in their relations with other animals in events such as herding trials and hunting. Anthropologists study these practices and try to understand the meanings expressed in such performances and what we can learn from examining humans watching animals, and participating with animals, in these practices. The following are clear examples of how animals are used to reinforce humans' anthropocentric views and the natural world around them.

Bullfight (Marvin 1994)

Garry Marvin conducted fieldwork in Seville, Andalusia, Spain, and his ethnography is entitled *Bullfight: A Study of Human and Animal Nature in Andalusia.* He spent more than two years living with people who were involved in rearing bulls, and with matadors, spectators and fans of bullfighting, traditionally Spain's national sport. Marvin explains why men risk their lives to perform the act of killing a bull and why it is a national celebration in Spain. The toreador (bullfighter) is a heroic figure in Spanish society and has celebrity status. Marvin explores the relationship between humans and animals in this specific setting, the main theme of his study being the masculinity associated with the practice. He explores how Spanish men manage their sexual identities. The toreador is at the centre of attention, and his skills and bravery are considered to be the ultimate expression of male power. The image of true masculinity and its symbolism are celebrated on national holidays when bullfighting is performed for the entertainment of the public (see Garry Marvin's testimony in chapter 13, pp. 286–8).

The biocentric view of animals (Morris 1982)

Not all cultures perceive animals in an anthropocentric way. Brian Morris conducted fieldwork in South India with the Malapantāram people, a foraging community of hunters and gatherers. They live in small groups of no more than twenty and have no

Bullfighting in Spain
(© Garry Marvin)

domestic animals other than dogs. These nomads do not see themselves as different from the environment in which they live as a forest people. They usually hunt for small animals such as bats, squirrels and tortoises. This group believes that animals, similar to themselves, are using their environment to gather food; it is unimportant to them that humans hunt and animals gather. This egalitarian attitude towards animals is reflected in many hunter-gatherer societies. Animals are seen as social and spiritual equals with thoughts and feelings just like humans. This is a clear example of the biocentric view of animals (see Brian Morris's interview in chapter 13, pp. 284–6).

> **Activity**
>
> Choose one of the major religions – Jewish, Christian, Muslim, Buddhist, Sikh. Find out what taboos they have regarding their food and consider the following questions. Explain the main food restrictions in the religion that you have researched.
> Why do they observe these rules? Who decides what is acceptable and what is not?
> What are the differences and similarities between different religions regarding food taboos?
> Why do they have these rules?
> What happens when any of the food taboos are broken?

Animal–Human Relations in the Industrial and Modern West

Relations between humans and animals in Western society are often dictated through science. Over the last three centuries, the emotional relationship to animals has undergone massive change. Industrialization and technological advancements have redefined the boundaries between humans and animals. Animals are considered mainly as a resource for human use. The continual destruction of their habitats restricts certain species' natural environments, and so their movement, and many animals are subjects for scientific research and objects of mass-scale husbandry for food production for the greater good of humans. Livestock and meat industries are becoming larger and more intensive. There are no longer many wilderness areas which are not under the control and management of humans. Most of those remaining are heavily managed for the express purpose of human enjoyment. In Western societies there is an increase in endowing domestic animals with human characteristics, meaning that pets are increasingly treated like people. For example, today you can find grooming saloons for pets, pet health products, and shops providing goods for pets.

Animals do not represent themselves in any way to human societies. Cultural meanings are bestowed upon them. The following is an example of the cultural representation and exhibition of animals, particularly of wild animals, which can be interpreted as a story which people tell about themselves through the medium of animals. It is a clear example of an anthropocentric view towards animals.

Stuffed animals in the Pitt Rivers museum, Oxford (© Laura Pountney)

'Monkey mountain as a megazoo' (Knight 2006)

In Japan, 'wild monkey parks' are popular visitor attractions that show free-ranging monkeys to the paying public. Unlike zoos, which display non-human animals through confinement, monkey parks control the animals' movements through provisioning (providing food). The parks claim to be a more **authentic** form of display. Knight's article challenges the claims of the monkey park that it shows monkeys 'in the wild', arguing that provisioning changes their behaviour. It is causing monkeys to **sedentarize** (move around less) instead of being **nomadic** (gathering, roaming), creating a **megazoo**. One major criticism of zoos involves the **denaturing** effect on their inhabitants, arising from animals being removed from their natural habitats. This implies that the habitat of an animal (which is integral to that animal) is insignificant. Knight argues that the new 'wild monkey park' may serve simply to disguise the confinement which is the primary fact of a zoo.

Visitors are charged an admission fee to observe the monkey troop gathered in this observation site. Such parks are often located near holiday destinations and can attract hundreds of thousands of visitors each year. They are essentially artificial feeding grounds or provisioning sites known as the *esaba*, where regular food handouts (wheat, soya beans and potatoes) are used to lure the monkeys to come and feed where they can be viewed. The park is therefore a human–animal relationship centred on food: the monkey park uses food to secure its catch, but the result is not capture but temporary immobilization so the animals can be observed. Therefore Knight argues that it is a zoo without cages. Some visitors experience the park as a place of authentically wild animal life and unspoiled nature, a notion that serves to provide a romantic anticipation and excitement about the place. Knight contends that the monkey mountain itself is a place where monkeys are subject to human control and where their behaviour is profoundly modified.

The provision of food and aggression

Used elsewhere elk, wild bird, tiger and dolphin watching, providing food enables direct observation without seeming to denature the animals in the way that zoos do. However, evidence from primates shows that provisioning intensifies feeding competition and is a source of 'social stress' as well as increased aggression, largely as a result of overcrowding in the feeding area. Furthermore this arrangement intensifies dominance and rank behaviour among monkeys.

Provisioning and sedentarization

According to the representation of the monkey park as a natural zoo, the *esaba* is just one (artificial) feeding ground among a multiplicity of (natural) others, suggesting that it has little control over the monkeys. In reality the parks have much more control over the monkeys than this implies. Food handouts are a powerful tool; for the most part this succeeds in installing the monkeys in their display space on a regular basis. For the park to be commercially viable as a visitor attraction, they need to be present for most of the daylight hours. To achieve this, a large amount of high quality food is dispensed.

However, this control comes at a price: the nomadic character of the monkeys is lost. Greater control requires that more and better food be given out. This increases the importance of the *esaba*, since, although the monkeys spend most of their lives in the forest, for most of the daylight hours they are in the *esaba* clearing, which therefore becomes the supreme feeding ground. There is evidence that provisioning leads to a contraction in the monkey troops' home range (e.g., one troop had a nomadic range of 8 square kilometres which contracted to 0.3 kilometres over twenty years). Their rest place has steadily come closer and is now often in the forest just above the *esaba*, requiring them to travel just the shortest of journeys each day to reach the food. So the monkeys are no longer mobile feeders in the way they used to be. In fact they are more like commuters, shuttling from the forest at night to the feeding site during the day. Some even claim this makes them like salaried workers.

Other pressures

There has been increasing human pressure on the monkey parks to contract so the land can be used for development; this has intensified greatly over recent years, meaning that the monkey parks may now be overlooked by buildings. Another factor affecting the natural habitat is the increasing size of provisioned monkey troops. This places greater pressure on the vegetation in and around the *esaba*, which cannot support the increased numbers, and also makes the monkeys increasingly dependent on the provisioning.

Although wildlife parks present themselves as superior alternatives to zoos, there is a definite trend for such places to become enclosed. According to Younghusband and Myers (1986), Kruger National Park in South Africa, for example, has become a 'huge island in a sea of people and farms' and 'the most intensively managed wildlife reserve in the world'. This enclosure trend means that the wildlife park can no longer define itself in clear contrast to the zoo.

In conclusion, it is clear that wildlife parks affect the behaviour of the animals and, despite representing themselves as natural zoos, might better be described as megazoos.

Activity

Explain the difference between a zoo and a wildlife park.

How does the representation of the wildlife park lead visitors to expect a more authentic experience?

Identify and explain the effects of the introduction of the *esaba* on the behaviour of monkeys.

What other pressures affect the wildlife park?

Do you agree with Knight's assertion that wildlife parks are simply megazoos?

Globalization: The Culture of the Guinea Pig as a Resistance to Development

The process of globalization can create tensions between the views of Western societies and indigenous conceptions of human relationships with animals. Animals in this particular example have been given religious significance with symbolic and spiritual power. Eduardo Archetti (1997) studied an Andean region in Ecuador in South America. Guinea pigs have been reared and eaten by indigenous people in the Ecuadorian Andes for a long time. Driven by the Western emphasis on the increase of capital, the government wanted to develop and modernize the production of guinea pigs and so help the people of this region to prosper. Development projects were set up in several villages in the region. When these did not work out, a team of anthropologists were invited to examine the reasons for the lack of success. They studied six different villages in the Andes and found that guinea pigs have a meaning in the social and ritual life of Ecuadorian peasants. Guinea pigs are a true festive meal for people in the Andes – in Ecuador and Bolivia as well as in Peru – and are eaten particularly at special occasions such as carnival, Mothers' Day, All Saints' Day and Christmas. The result was that the indigenous villagers rejected the attempts to increase the production of guinea pigs. They wanted to retain the festive life of the Andean community, which involves a quest for protein. This study shows how relations with animals can highlight not only cultural practices and views but also the impact of and resistance to globalization.

Western environmentalism

In Western industrialized societies there have been attempts from an environmentalist perspective to create policies and strategies to protect the environment. In the 'developed' world, nature was long seen as something to be overcome, to be harnessed, used and conquered. Early anthropologists saw their culture, at that time, as the pinnacle of the 'developed' world. It was as if they formed the last stage in a long process of evolution. But, today, the 'natural' environment is seen as under threat from too much development, as people are worried about deforestation, extinction and global warming. The very people who were once seen as 'primitive' are admired for their care of the environment and techniques of conservation. Kay Milton (1996) claimed that conservation and concern about the preservation of the environment are not new in small-scale societies. Environmental safeguarding and conservation of scarce resources are important goals from global, national and even local perspectives. Local people, their landscapes, their ideas, their values and their traditional management systems are being attacked from all sides.

The first encounter that many Muslims across the world have with animals often comes during the celebration of a religious holiday, Eid al-Adha. In many Muslim countries, families purchase a goat, cow or other domesticated animal weeks before the holiday. In some cultures, family members affectionately decorate the animal with flower necklaces, paint and colourful beads. Children often become attached to the creature, stemming from the natural affinity that children have for animals. However, when the day of Eid al-Adha comes, the animal is slaughtered with a sharp knife while it is fully conscious, and in many cases the slaughtering takes place on the actual grounds of the family's home. The meat is then typically distributed three ways: one-third for the family, one-third for friends and one-third for the poor. (© US Embassy Pakistan / Flickr)

ANIMAL RIGHTS AND ETHICS

In recent decades the issue of animal rights has engaged the attention, emotions and thoughts of the public. In many Western societies animals have come to be regarded as an oppressed minority, and various organizations have set about arguing for, and fighting for, a change in this status. This animal liberation movement, sometimes called the animal rights movement, is a social movement which in one of its forms seeks an end to the moral and legal distinction drawn between humans and animals. Many supporters of this movement also seek an end to the use of animals in research, food, clothing and the entertainment industries. A good example of these views is to be found in an ethnographic study by Hoon Song. This is also an excellent example of opposing views towards animals held within the same culture.

> **Animal rights**
> The argument that animals should be treated in the same way as humans, and not as property humans control

Pigeon Trouble (Song 2010)

Despite personally having a phobia of birds, Song conducted fieldwork in the small town of Hegins in Pennsylvania, America, where every year local people gather to shoot over 5,000 pigeons on Labor Day (the first Monday in September) to celebrate the economic and social contributions of workers. The organizers of the shoot raise tens of thousands of dollars for the local charities.

The local people in this mining community take live pigeons and put them into small boxes, with the gunmen lined up. Children pull strings on the boxes to launch the pigeons into the air, and then the birds are shot. Some die immediately; many die within the next couple of minutes. There is also another group of birds that will be wounded but can fly away, only to die over the next days. Very few birds manage to escape and survive. One shoot can result in the death of thousands of birds. The gunmen are mainly miners and working-class white Americans from the town and surrounding area. At the same time as the shooting takes place, animal rights protesters occupy the boundaries of the area and try everything possible to save some of the pigeons. Animal rights campaigners, who had been protesting since 1991 and had even created a human chain in order to prevent the shooting, succeeded in outlawing this practice in 2011. While this led to the end of the Hegins Labor Day Pigeon Shoot, such events still take place in private clubs. Song explores these opposing views towards animals existing within the same American society.

Alternative Views of Animals

Barbara Noske (1997), a philosopher and a cultural anthropologist from the Netherlands, challenges the social construction of contemporary human–animal relationships. She argues that animals should be portrayed as independent beings with special traits and behaviours that contribute to their interactions with people and explains that to define animals as human-like is wrong. Instead of increasing their importance, it reduces them to the status of sub-human. Noske proposes an interdisciplinary approach to evaluating animals and wants to break down the socially constructed boundaries that exist between humans and animals. A feminist, she argues that women, like animals, are assigned a lower status and that this is problematic and needs resolving through new culturally constructed ideas.

Activity

Choose one of the following topics and prepare a ten-minute presentation using anthropological concepts and theories from this chapter and your own research. You have to use ethnographic examples to support your arguments

- Animal rights
- Vegetarianism
- Animals in advertisements
- The uses of animals
- A particular animal and its relations with human society
- Animal symbolism
- Experimenting with animals
- Animals in sports
- Animal representations in a particular piece of literature
- Animals in human language
- Animal conservation projects

Woodland and Village in Malawi (Morris 1995)

Brian Morris has conducted extensive fieldwork in rural Malawi. He has researched people's relationship to the environment, especially to mammals, and studied social attitudes towards the woodlands. According to Morris, Malawian attitudes towards mammals – and more generally towards the natural world – are diverse, complex and multidimensional. On the one hand, in terms of the village community and agriculture, wildlife from the woodlands is seen as fundamentally hostile and opposed to human needs and wants; on the other hand, the woodland domain is seen as the external source of life-generating powers. Western cultures tend to view animals either as pets or as food and often overlook the vast number of roles that they may play within a culture and in social life more generally – their use in medicine, folk traditions and rituals.

Morris's study focuses on Malawi people and their rich and varied relationship with animals – from hunting through to their use as medicine. He provides insights which show how the people's relationship with their world manifests itself not exclusively in human social relations but also, and just as tellingly, in their relationships with animals – that, in fact, animals have a vital role in social relations. The mammals of the woodland are regarded as the embodiment of 'power' and fierceness and, as wild beasts, are seen as essentially opposed to humans, though they are also viewed as the source of meat and of activating medicines. Being closely identified with the spirits of the dead and the essential source of fertility, they ensure the continuity of the kin group and village. Wild mammals form a crucial part of the ongoing cycle of life and of social reproduction. These relationships are expressed in different ways: between the woodland and the village, between hunting and agriculture, between the relative by marriage and the matrifocal kin group focused around a core of matrilineally related women, and between spirits and wild animals, which are closely identified with one another, and living humans.

In this Malawian culture, society is not interacting with nature in just one way. Although the division between the woodland and the village environment is evident, the association of the woodland with the spirits of the dead suggests that the two domains are essentially connected so as to constitute a cycle that is fundamentally concerned with life and its renewal. By seeing social life as a cycle which includes the natural world, in this case the woodland, we can see how the latter is so important for the wellbeing of the humans in the village.

> **STOP & THINK**
>
> Explain how people in rural Malawi have both an anthropocentric and a biocentric view of the environment in which they live.

CONCLUSION

The environment is interpreted in different ways by different societies, who categorize it and organize it in their own way. Whereas the Western **anthropocentric** view was often to control the environment, other societies see themselves more as part of the environment, and so have a more **biocentric** view. For example, in the Ayurvedic system of thought, found in India, the components of nature and the components of humans are the same. Human populations have ongoing contact with and impact upon the land, climate, and the plant and animal species in their vicinity, and these elements of their environment have reciprocal impacts on humans. Cultural diversity has been the key to the adaptation and adaptability of the human species. Anthropological studies of nature show how the culture of various people is influenced by and interacts with their ecological surroundings. Individuals have an infinite ability to adapt to varying environmental conditions.

END OF CHAPTER ASSESSMENT

Examine some of the ways in which human culture is shaped by nature.

Teacher's guidance

In your introduction, outline the key views in the debate: explain the difference between biocentric and anthropocentric views on humans' relationship with nature. Show the roles of universality and diversity in dscussions on this topic: while every human society has a specific relationship with nature, this can vary on an individual and a societal level. Using contrasting cultural groups, examine differences between Western and non-Western relationships with nature. Add a point on Western environmentalism. Explain how the commodification of nature (for example, the spread of capitalism, nature parks, dam building, mining) affects local populations. Include anthropological theories of nature; make links with your previous paragraphs and support them with case studies such as Marvin Harris's cultural materialist case study of sacred cows in India. Examine what environmentalism is and give examples of the political debates about it. In conclusion, explain how all humans have a relationship with nature. Using Morris's example of a Malawi village's relationship, mention that this cannot be reduced simply to 'West is bad and small-scale society is good'. Class, power, gender and globalization all have impacts on this relationship.

KEY TERMS

Animal rights The argument that animals should be treated in the same way as humans and not as property humans control

Animism A belief that natural phenomena such as rocks, trees, thunder, or celestial bodies have life or divinity

Anthropocentric The tendency for human beings to regard themselves as the central and most significant entities in the universe, or the assessment of reality through an exclusively human perspective

Anthropomorphism To attribute human characteristics to animals

Biocentric A view that nature does not exist simply to be used or consumed by humans, but that humans are simply one species among many.

Cultural ecology The study of the adaptation of human societies or populations to their environments: the emphasis is on the arrangements of technique, economy and social organization through which cultures mediate the experience of the natural world

Cultural materialism A view that says that the best way to understand human culture is to examine material conditions – climate, food supply, geography, etc.

Ecocide The extensive damage to or destruction or loss of ecosystem(s) of a given territory, whether by human agency or by other causes, to such an extent that peaceful enjoyment by the inhabitants of that territory has been or will be severely diminished

Ecology The study of the interaction between living and non-living components of the environment

Environmental determinism An approach based on the assumption that cultural and natural areas are interconnected, because culture represents an adaptation to the particular environment

Environmentalism A social movement seeking to protect the natural environment

Ethno ecology Any society's traditional set of environmental perceptions – i.e., a cultural model of the environment and its relation to people and society

Greenpeace An international organization that works for environmental conservation and the preservation of endangered species

Market economy An impersonal but highly efficient system of production, distribution and exchange characterized mainly by the use of money as a means of exchange, having the ability to accumulate vast amounts of capital, and having highly complex economic interactions

Mode of production The dominant way in which people make a living in a particular culture

Sociobiology The study of the biological determinants of social behaviour

Subsistence economy Involves the production of food for a group's immediate needs, rather than, e.g., cash crops

Subsistence patterns The sources and methods a society uses to obtain its food and other necessities

UNESCO The United Nations Educational, Scientific and Cultural Organization works to create the conditions for dialogue among civilizations, cultures and peoples, based upon respect for commonly shared values: it is through this dialogue that the world can achieve global visions of sustainable development encompassing observance of human rights, mutual respect and the alleviation of poverty, all of which are at the heart of UNESCO'S mission and activities

Personal investigation: animals in enclosed spaces

One of the ways to investigate the relationship between humans and animals is through the study of zoos. Some of the things to think about are as follows.

Background research

Research and find the relevant ethnographies and anthropologists who have studied human and animal relationship – for example, Bob Mullan and Garry Marvin's book *Zoo Culture*. This will help you to use anthropological concepts and theories in your analysis.

Mapping

Draw a map of the zoo and mark all of the different areas and buildings within it. Indicate clearly the different species in the animal enclosures. How many animals and species are there? If it is a big zoo, you may focus on only one group of animals, such as primates.

Meanings

What is the meaning of the zoo? Why do humans keep wild animals in cages and restricted areas? Who are the visitors and what is the purpose of their visits? Why do humans get pleasure from watching the animals in enclosures? What are the rules of behaviour in zoos? Can humans interact with animals? Which ones? What is the difference between wild and domesticated animals? Who runs the zoo? How do they feed the animals? Where do they get the animals? Who decides on, and what are the rules for, obtaining animals for the zoo? Who are the zoo keepers and other humans who work there? What are their roles and what do they do? What is the official reason behind keeping animals in this zoo? Why do visitors have to pay for entrance to the zoo? Are animals commodities? Is the role of the zoo to entertain or to educate? What are the programmes and promotions that are run by the zoo?

Once you gain access, follow the ethical guidelines of anthropological fieldwork. At all times observe and follow the rules of behaviour at the zoo. In order to answer the above questions you will have to attend the zoo for longer periods of time. As part of your observation you can conduct unstructured interviews with zoo keepers, management, zoo vets, visitors. You want to find as much information as possible about all of the activities of humans within this environment.

Record your observations in a field notebook. The more you jot down the easier it will be for you to prepare and write your investigation report, which should be about 3,000 words. Take photographs and include them in your report.

SUGGESTED FURTHER READING AND FILMS

Books

Dove, R. M., and C. Carpenter (2007) *Environmental Anthropology: A Historical Reader*. Wiley-Blackwell.

Haenn, N., and R. R. Wilk (eds) (2006) *The Environment in Anthropology: A Reader in Ecology, Culture and Sustainable Living*. York University Press.

Knight, J. (2006) 'Monkey mountain as a megazoo: analyzing the naturalistic claim of wild monkey parks in Japan', *Society and Animals* 14(3): 245–64.

Milton, K. (1996) *Environmentalism: The View from Anthropology*. Routledge.

Morris, B. (2000) *The Power of Animals: An Ethnography*. Berg.

Ethnographic films

The following ethnographic films can be found at the RAI film library, www.therai.org.uk/film/film-library-a-archive/.

Disappearing World series (Granada TV): *The Kayapo* (1987), directed by Michael Beckham, anthropologist Terence Turner

The Land on which We Stand (2007), directed by Rebecca Payne

Raised by Humans (2010), directed by Karlia Campbell

Since the Company Came (2001), directed by Russell Hawkins, Icarus Films

Websites

Anthropological and ethnomusicological fieldwork among hunters and gatherers (Pygmies) and other peoples of Central Africa: www.luisdevin.com/home.php

Cultural Survival (2013) A non-governmental organization which partners with indigenous communities around the world to defend their lands, languages, and cultures: www.culturalsurvival.org

Patterns of Subsistence (2011) Classification of cultures based on the sources and techniques of acquiring food and other necessities: http://anthro.palomar.edu/subsistence/default.htm

CHAPTER SIX

PERSONHOOD

CONTENTS

CHAPTER

6 Personhood

KEY ISSUES AND DEBATES

- What does it mean to be a person?
- When does someone begin and cease to be a person? (Are there times when someone is a 'partial' person?)
- How do concepts of personhood vary in different cultures?
- What is the relationship of an individual person with wider society?
- To what extent did modernity lead to the development of the Western concept of personhood?
- Who has the power to decide who is a person?
- How might concepts of personhood result in tension between the state and individuals or families?
- How do specific concepts of personhood shape the relationships of people with animals, cyborgs and other entities?
- How are concepts of personhood challenged by technological developments?

Every individual in the world has culturally specific views on what it means to be a person, when one becomes a person and when one ceases to be a person. Indeed, the process of deciding what it means to be a 'normal' person makes very clear what a non-person or an abnormal person is. The way that personhood is understood by a group can also affect the way that people define themselves as individuals or as part of a wider social group. The concepts of personhood held by an individual or a group determine the way that individuals relate to animals, spirits and other entities such as cyborgs (short for 'cybernetic organisms': beings whose original human bodies have been more or less mechanized, sometimes featured in science fiction films. The term 'cyborg' is also relevant to medicinal advances in relation to transplants and artificial limbs).

In this chapter we explore personhood from a number of perspectives, describing different concepts. In practice, these concepts are not necessarily clear or distinct. According to Melford Spiro (1993), there has been a tendency in anthropology to exaggerate the differences between different concepts of personhood when, in fact, according to the situation a person is in, they may overlap or even change.

Furthermore, Beth Conklin and Lynn Morgan (1996) suggest that there may be differences *within* cultures in understandings of what it means to be a person. Therefore, in reality, concepts of personhood are far messier and more negotiable than the neat types that are often cited in academic discussions. It is also worth remembering that no single concept of personhood is more correct than another.

Concepts of personhood are not fixed in time: rather, they are continually being challenged and renegotiated. Interestingly, new forms of technologies have led to a whole new set of debates over the boundaries of personhood, raising many issues about who should decide when someone begins and ceases to be a person.

Activity

Write a definition of what is meant by 'person'.
List as many characteristics as you can of what it means to be a person.
When does somebody begin and when do they cease to be a person?
What factors may influence the way people view personhood?
Are any individuals seen by others as less or more of a person?

THE DEVELOPMENT OF THE WESTERN PHILOSOPHICAL CONCEPT OF PERSONHOOD

Personhood
A social status granted in various ways to those who meet certain criteria; all societies have criteria concerning who can become a person

John Dupré (1998) discusses the different ways in which **personhood** has been explored and explained. He claims that there are two main views in the West, the first being biological, developed by evolutionary psychologists and geneticists, who see personhood as rooted in empirically based biological evidence. The alternative view is the philosophical approach, which points to the socially constructed nature of the concept of personhood. It is the latter, philosophical view on which the following discussion is based.

When and How Did the Western Philosophical Concept of Personhood Begin?

Western concepts of personhood are by no means fixed, and there is no agreement on a single philosophical model. However, Western views of personhood generally share the idea that what defines this concept are individualism, egocentrism, self-containment and autonomy. Personal wellbeing is generally perceived as more important than social obligations. The body is also seen as a material entity, a biological organism that is controlled largely by 'natural' forces. It is assumed that a person's body is separate from every other person's body, and to suggest otherwise is considered strange. The body also reflects social characteristics such as self-discipline and control. These ideas were the product of a specific set of social, cultural and political ideas about the body, mind and soul called the **Enlightenment** that developed during the eighteenth century.

THE ENLIGHTENMENT

The modern idea of a person as an individual is closely linked to the **Enlightenment** (which is discussed in more detail in chapter 1). During this period in Europe there were many scientific discoveries which contradicted the accepted teachings of those in authority, notably the Church. These discoveries encouraged philosophers to question the knowledge that had previously been accepted as 'true'. The Enlightenment resulted in a group of writers, philosophers and scientists discussing ideas and thoughts on what being a person actually meant.

In philosophy, having a mind or consciousness was a key criterion for being a person. There is much debate about the characteristics of the mind, but many philosophers consider rational thought and the ability to reason as key aspects; others would argue that it is a sense of morality and language acquisition that are important.

During the Enlightenment period key philosophers began to see personhood as associated with 'individualism'. The philosopher who originated this view was **René Descartes** (1596–1650), who proposed in his **Cartesian dualist theory** that the mind is separate from the body. By replacing religious and spiritual explanations of personhood with rational, scientific explanations, it was possible to regard each person as a separate entity. Another characteristic of Western personhood was the idea that individuals should take responsibility for their own actions and have fewer obligations to others, implying that persons are **autonomous individuals**. Within this view of personhood, the individual came to see him- or herself as centrally important, a position that can be described as egocentric.

Anthropological Explanations of Concepts of Personhood

> The person is a rational substance, indivisible and individual. (Mauss [1954] 1970)

Considered the father of modern French anthropology, Marcel Mauss (1872–1950), who was the nephew and student of the French sociologist Durkheim (1858–1917), was one of the first to begin anthropological debates about the nature of personhood. Mauss ([1954] 1970) based his ideas on the ethnographic findings of others as well his own examination of objects found in museum collections. He claimed that all cultures have an awareness of individualism, both physically and spiritually. However, he argued that the **concept** of the 'self' or 'person' changes according to local legal systems, religion, customs, social structures and ways of thinking, and he was particularly interested in showing how the concept of a person assumed by Western people – that of a rational individual – differs from the concept of person in non-Western societies.

Mauss traced the development of the Western notion of selfhood to the Latin term of *persona*, which means 'mask', and argued that masks were originally used to make people seem the same, on the surface. However, they eventually came to represent the essence of the individual. Mauss claimed that personhood as we know it today is a relatively recent development. In earlier societies, he suggested, people had an essentially **sociocentric** conception of the person; this is where individualism is not fully marked and identity is more closely linked to the group, meaning that people see themselves more as part of the group than as acting individually.

For example, Mauss noted that, among Zuni Pueblo Indian societies, there exist only a limited number of first names, as individuals are expected to adopt the clan mentality. Therefore naming practices can give real insight into the way in which a culture understands personhood. Pueblo Indian concepts of personhood were explored by Frank Hamilton Cushing (1857–1900), who showed how masks are used to confer sociocentric concepts of personhood, unlike the use of masks described by Mauss. Cushing ([1901] 2007) explained that, in Pueblo society, rituals are acted out by individuals who take on distinct roles. They wear particular masks as part of their role. A person wears a mask

Clothing can outwardly show and reinforce group identity. This photo shows Hmong people in northern Vietnam. (© Maria Salak)

and thus assumes a role, a role that does not belong to him or her individually but is taken on as a result of the social position into which she or he was born. An individual wears a particular mask because it is the mask that his or her ancestor wore and who now lives again in the body of the person who bears that name and is entitled to wear that particular mask.

> Thus, in short, you will understand that with the Pueblo we already see a notion of the 'person' or individual, absorbed in his clan, but already detached from it in the ceremonial by the mask, his title, his rank, his role, his survival and his reappearance on earth in one of his descendants endowed with the same status, forenames, titles, rights and functions. (Du Gay et al. 2000: 331)

In other words, there is no individual mind with its own status, rights and responsibilities, free to direct its own life; the 'person' for the Pueblo is a 'role' in society that passes from one generation to another.

STOP & THINK

How would you feel if you were given the same name as another family member?
Why would you react in that way?
Apart from naming, what other processes make people aware of their individuality?

Mauss argued that Christianity also contributed to the emergence of the notion of an autonomous individual concept of personhood. Philosophers **Immanuel Kant** (1724–1804) and **Johann Gottlieb Fichte** (1762–1814) considered that the emergence of Western individualism became complete when a 'person' became a distinct psychological category. Therefore the individual self is not innate or biologically inevitable but **socially constructed**. This also explains why personhood varies in different places and over time. So, culture and person cannot be separated; concepts of personhood are a product of specific cultural and historical contexts.

In Western society, the person is usually perceived as a unique individual, whole and indivisible. During the life course, the single individual makes a number of personal decisions or choices and has to take responsibility for their consequences. When someone dies, he or she ceases to exist as an individual. However, in Western societies there is no general agreement as to what happens after death. Some argue that death is the end of the individual, whereas others maintain that deceased persons somehow continue to exist as spiritual beings in an invisible world.

Geertz: An Interpretive Approach

Clifford Geertz uses an interpretive approach which focuses on meanings, arguing that humans are symbolic creatures and that it is therefore the job of the anthropologist to map out the symbols that people use in different cultures. One such important set of symbols is related to the way personhood is constructed.

Geertz makes a clear distinction between a person and an individual: an individual is 'a living biological being that is living, born and grows to maturity, grows old and dies, the person is a vehicle of meaning, a representation of a kind of individual' (in Kippenberg et al.1990). In one important respect Geertz's view is similar to that of Mauss, in that he argues that personhood is historically constructed.

Geertz was particularly interested in establishing the differences in concepts of personhood in various cultures, drawing attention to how unique and different the Western concept of personhood is. To understand other people, he argued that it is important to set aside Western concepts of personhood and interpret the experiences of the world from within the concept of selfhood held by non-Western societies. In other words, concepts of personhood shape the way people see the world around them.

Activity

Use the following characteristics to write a summary of the Western individualist concept of personhood:
- individual, indivisible
- not agreed upon or fixed
- egocentric
- materialistic (being a person means you need a body)
- rationalistic (being a person means you are logical and can think in a rational way)
- reflects Western culture, which has lost its sense of the mystical (being a person does not have to be linked to spiritual/religious ideas)
- bounded (personhood is contained within the physical body)
- self-sufficient/narcissistic (being self-interested)
- dualistic: mind and body are separate
- being a person is linked with being physically alive.

Contested Boundaries of Personhood in Western Society

Personhood, then, is a socially constructed concept, and there are usually values that are associated with being a 'normal' person (Dupré 1998). However, there are some people who do not meet the full criteria for being considered a 'complete' person. For example, slaves in the past were considered as *property*, not persons with full rights and an individual identity. This shows how specific ideas about what it means to be a person may be used as a way of classifying humans and therefore how they are laden with values.

STOP & THINK

Can you think of an example of someone who might not be considered a full 'person' in today's society in your country?
Why might this be?

Death, Illness and the Person

Western philosophical concepts of personhood are linked to the biological body and its ability to carry out certain functions. The body reflects social characteristics that are considered signs of strength. The person is seen to be wholly contained within the physical body – in other words, **bounded**. The production of bodily fluids such as semen, sweat, urine, menstrual blood and breast milk may be seen as necessary at times but also often as polluting. Bodily functions are frequently kept private.

When a person becomes older or ill and there may be physical problems – for example, the loss of urinary function – a society or group may not tolerate the individual and may separate them from the wider society by placing them into an institution which is sanitized and impersonal, such as a hospital or old people's home. There is a danger that, as a result of being removed from society, an individual may potentially be considered a non-person or a partial person. By contrast, in non-Western societies, where the self is not necessarily restricted to the individual body, there may be different issues to do with the boundaries of personhood. Malfunctions within the body may not be seen as quite so problematic.

STOP & THINK

Can you think of how people may lose their individuality in hospital? Give examples.

Furthermore, Western ideas about personhood may also make clear particular boundaries concerning death. Death when it occurs is based on a **binary** (two-part) division between life and death. So, typically, we feel someone is a person when they are physically alive and not a person when they are dead.

However, due to medical technological developments, there are times where it can be very difficult to define someone as clearly alive or dead. For example, when relatives are asked to consider donating the organs of kin who have died, they may not unreasonably experience confusion when confronted with a body that appears to be living, breathing and warm to the touch, but which the medical personnel declare to be clinically dead.

Technological advances in medicine have therefore presented challenges to our

Most people in the West see death as a singular event which marks the end of the person's life and makes the individual no longer a person. (Monster4711 / Wikimedia Commons)

pre-existing or earlier understanding of the boundaries of personhood. This shows how concepts of personhood, rather than being fixed, are continually negotiated and renegotiated as an ongoing process. The next section explores examples of concepts of personhood beyond Western philosophical ideas.

Globalization: The Spread of Western Philosophical Concepts of Personhood

From the discussion above, it might be possible to suggest that the Western philosophical concept of personhood was a product of modernity. In the context of an increasingly global postmodern world, it might also be possible to argue that Western ideas about personhood threaten to engulf alternative concepts. Isak Niehaus (2002) challenges the extent to which modernity did in fact lead to the shift from the '**dividual**' (where a person is incomplete and forever involved in the process of being made up of and through the relations with others that define them) to the 'individual' concept of personhood. He claims that modernity brought with it increasing commodification and argues that persons were no longer involved in social networks of reciprocal exchange; instead, they acquired a sense of individual autonomy and began to see the body as bounded and separate from external influences.

Niehaus claims that, in the Bushbuckridge area of South Africa, people continue to see the body as permeable and **partible**. In this particular case, this means that the body transmits substances to and incorporates substances from other bodies, and that the conjunction of breath, aura, blood and flesh gives rise to a dangerous condition of heat. The locals believe that, by observing various taboos associated with sex, pregnancy and death, it is possible to avoid contamination.

In this case, personhood is not necessarily contained just inside the physical body. One's aura and sweat contaminates one's clothes, and sometimes that sweat can be substituted for the person. For example, if for some reason a person was unable to attend a ritual, that ritual could be performed on their clothes instead. The importance of sweat as a part of a person is demonstrated by the fact that there is much concern over clothes falling into the wrong hands and that witches might put a spell on the clothes and, through them, the person who owns the clothes. Because of their concerns, men allow only their mothers or wives to wash their clothes and bedding.

Ojibwa Indians

The Ojibwa Indians have an understanding of personhood which is very different to Western classifications. The Ojibwa were traditionally nomadic hunters and fishers living in North America who communicated with their ancestors through dreams. Spirits are also considered to be very important as a guide through life. Parts of the natural environment, such as winds, are categorized as persons, as are also the sun and moon, animals and spirits. This idea that animals might be considered as persons is called **animism.** The idea that personhood can be extended to non-humans and objects may seem very strange to people from a Western society.

> **Animism**
> A belief that natural phenomena such as rocks, trees, thunder, or celestial bodies have life or divinity

Therefore, as Alfred Hallowell ([1955] 2009) points out, Western categorizations of personhood challenge the Ojibwa classification system. The Western distinction between what is myth and what is reality is not made by the Ojibwa, or not made in the same way as in other societies. This example demonstrates some of the potential challenges faced by (Western) anthropologists researching other groups: they have to be careful not to try to impose their own world-view, including their concept of what it means to be a person, on other cultures.

Hindu Sociocentric Personhood

Louis Dumont (1980) argues that, within Hindu culture, the concept of the individual is subordinated to the group as an organic whole. Although Hindu culture varies enormously, most Indian Hindus believe in reincarnation, which means that every newborn is a reborn person and not entirely new. One is born a member of a particular caste, already attached to that social group (strata). Furthermore, life is very much dictated by one's karma (fate) and dharma (destiny) as one begins to make decisions.

Life in Hindu culture is regarded as a journey; the destination a person is aiming to reach is **self-realization**, which means a very important spiritual awakening, where the individual feels complete and content. When someone dies, the cycle of birth, death and rebirth begins anew. The caste into which one is born depends on one's acts (good and bad) in previous lives. This concept of personhood in Hindu society is therefore **sociocentric**, which means that it is the society or the wider community, not the individual, that is central to understanding the concept of the person. However, as with all concepts of personhood, there is much scope for variation.

> **Sociocentric concept of personhood**
> Where a person is defined by the relationships he or she has with others

African Concepts of Personhood

Traditional forms of religion are often practised in African villages. Persons might have individual freedom and accountability, but at the same time ancestral spirits are present and play a role in defining what it means to be a person. These ancestors may be asked for advice, and a person may risk punishment by them. Those who die may themselves become ancestral spirits, and in many cases living spiritual mediums, who are able to communicate with the ancestral spirits, can have a lot of power. This type of personhood avoids having to create oppositions between the material and the spiritual.

> ### STOP & THINK
> Imagine how a person's view of themselves would change if they thought they did not have their own soul but were an embodied spirit of an ancestor. List the ways in which it might affect their life.

Being Human Does Not Make You a Person: Animals, Humans and Personhood in Malawi (Morris 1999)

A good example of an African concept of personhood is found in the work of Brian Morris, who uses ethnographic material from his extensive research in Malawi to illustrate the culturally constructed nature of the concept of a person outlined by Mauss. The people he studied are made up of a number of different ethnic communities but share a common cultural heritage and demonstrate a certain sense of cultural unity. Morris acknowledges, however, that such communities are always changing.

Hanuman, a Hindu god and devotee of Rama: many religions revere species of animals or worship deities in animal forms, blurring the boundaries between humans, gods and animals. (© Gregory Davis)

Morris claims that Malawians recognize that humans are a discrete form of living entity. Humans are distinct from animals because they each have their own species characteristics. However, Malawians do not make a radical distinction between humans and animals; rather, they see both as sharing many attributes. Therefore humans, like animals, are physical, social and moral, embedded in a specific context. Humans differ from animals not so much because they have the attributes of subjective agency, consciousness and sociality, but because they have these attributes to a greater degree. Malawians see humans and animals as kin.

In their day-to-day lives, Malawians will refer to animals in an anthropomorphic way, as happens in a number of cultures. So, like many other cultures, they make a distinction between humans and animals. However, the distinction does not produce a clear-cut boundary, with humans having minds and animals not having minds, but may be based on other attributes. Morris tells the following story to illustrate his understanding of the Malawian view of animals. He wanted to know what the difference was between baboons and humans, since baboons were referred to as if they were human. When he asked the question he was told, 'Father, you have a grey beard and know a lot about our culture, but sometimes you speak as a child; baboons have tails' (Morris 1999). In other words, Malawians acknowledge that there *are* differences between humans and baboons physically, but baboons may enjoy certain aspects of personhood, even if these are not as complete as those of humans.

Another interesting feature of Malawian culture is the way that humans themselves are classified as persons and included in the community. Humans are animals that are particularly adept at reason and language, but a very important aspect of personhood is that humans are part of a social community. There are certain individuals who are excluded from personhood because of their moral characteristics and become, for example, labelled as witches. Interestingly, as they are not considered full persons, children who die do not turn into proper ancestral spirits.

Activity

How does the Malawian understanding of being a person vary from your own concept of being a person?

How does your own culture distinguish between humans and animals?

Melanesian Relational Concepts of Personhood

According to Strathern (1988), the Melanesian concept of the self is more correct than the Western concept of personhood. In the highland societies of New Guinea, human beings are not perceived as complete until they have acquired the basic categories of local culture. Personhood therefore is gradually acquired from birth as the child becomes more familiar with the shared customs and values of the culture in which he or she lives.

Also, a person is not considered to be dead until all debts are repaid and the inheritance has been distributed. Therefore, it is only when all the social relationships of the dead person have been formally ended that he or she can be considered properly dead. Strathern argues that Melanesians see people in a similar way to social scientists, in terms of their relationships with others, unlike the British, who tend to see persons as isolated individuals.

STOP & THINK

Why might the Melanesian understanding of personhood be seen as more correct than the Western concept of personhood?

The Buddhist Concept of Personhood

Buddhism is a religion that focuses on personal spiritual development. It rejects the idea of self. The historical Buddha, who lived in India 2,500 years ago, achieved enlightenment after long meditation under a tree. He taught that people suffer because of ignorance and especially because they cling onto a false notion of self. The way out of suffering is to eliminate all of the desires and attachments that keep re-creating the self. Therefore, central to the Buddha's teaching is the idea of no self. The idea of self does not exist; the self is just a conventional name given to a set of elements. Buddhists believe in reincarnation; however, their goal is to educate themselves to break the cycle of rebirth and enter Nirvana.

> **STOP & THINK**
> How does Buddhism challenge the other examples of personhood we have looked at?

PERSONHOOD AND BOUNDARIES

Animals, Machines and Concepts of Personhood

Philosophers not only question what it means to be a person, they also explore the relationship people have with animals, spirits and other entities. In philosophy, having a mind or consciousness is the criterion for being a person. There is a debate about what constitutes the essential features of consciousness, but many philosophers consider key aspects of the mind to be rationality and the ability to reason. Others would consider language and a sense of morality. So if you can demonstrate that animals or machines have these qualities, then they have minds and could be included in the category of a person.

Philosophers have much to offer anthropology in this area, and vice versa. For example, anthropologists highlight the ways that the characteristics of mind or consciousness are defined, stressing that the historical and cultural context always permeates who (or what) is assigned a full mind and personhood, with its particular status, rights and responsibilities.

Descartes insisted that animals could not be persons because they did not have a soul, a perspective undoubtedly related to his Christian beliefs. Aristotle believed that only aristocratic males could be persons, reflecting his culture's prejudice against women and slaves.

If the category of a person is a cultural category and not a scientific fact, then the boundaries between animal, human and machine become more fluid and open to alternative interpretations. It is important therefore to consider why animals and machines *could* be considered persons were there to be a change in culture, causing a renegotiation of how we define consciousness and who has the power to define personhood.

> **STOP & THINK**
> If there is no definition of a person that remains fixed throughout time, what implications does this hold for the question of whether animals or machines could be persons?

Breeding Cells (2009)

The documentary film *Breeding Cells* (2009), directed by Anna Straube, Gregor Gaida, Miren Artola and Saskia Warzecha, explores the ways in which technology is challenging what it means to be a person. It was made in the ward of reproductive medicine in a Berlin hospital. In this context, fertilization is made visible and manipulable on a cellular level, while the couples themselves seem to become marginal participants in a process that involves a large number of different professionalized agents and technologies. This highlights the way that decisions about what it means to be a person are in some circumstances controlled and managed by the state.

The film approaches a scientific environment with an experimental ethnographic gaze. The 'fertility team' involved consider themselves to be simply assistants of nature, but 'nature' here is a hospital environment that is highly regulated by procedural methods, doctors' conventions and conservative laws. Closely describing the routines and moral concerns of the medical staff, *Breeding Cells* portrays a transition period in which biotechnological science fiction is turning into everyday life.

'Babies, bodies, and the production of personhood in North America and a native Amazonian society' (Conklin and Morgan 1996)

Beth Conklin and Lynn Morgan examine the social processes involved in turning foetuses and infants into social beings in two societies: the United States and the Wari Indians, who number around 1,500 and live in the rainforest of western Brazil in the state of Rondônia, near the Bolivian border. The beginnings of life are a particularly interesting point at which to understand concepts of personhood: life and death at the boundaries are frequently disputed, and this is often where ideas of personhood are shaped and negotiated.

In North America, which has been seen as the very epitome of individualism, the concept of personhood revolves largely around medical definitions of when the foetal organism develops certain capabilities, such as consciousness and the ability to survive outside of the womb. The Wari, by contrast, apply the concept of blood relations much more broadly. The sharing of body substances (blood, breast milk, semen and sweat) defines kin and other social relations. The Wari see personhood as based on social ties and consider the body as being made up of interpersonal exchanges of bodily fluids and foods. This exchange takes place through the skin, sexual intercourse, and oral and nasal ingestion. As a result of these exchanges, Wari personhood is fluid and changeable: it may be lost or gained under certain circumstances. It is also important to understand that this exchange of substances is an important part of Wari ethnic identity; sharing bodily fluids means an individual can become a Wari person, while not doing so means a person is not Wari and becomes an outsider, an enemy.

Interestingly, Conklin and Morgan argue that the 'negotiation of the boundaries of personhood also supports particular arrangements of power in society' (1996: 658). For example, who is designated to authorize personhood or to sanction foetal life or death? According to Conklin and Morgan, in this respect, personhood is inherently dynamic. Individuals use the negotiation of definitions of personhood to legitimize their actions and positions.

Conklin and Morgan point out that there is a tendency to regard personhood in a binary or structural way; there is a need for clear boundaries between being and not being a person. In the USA, for example, once a foetus is regarded as a person, it is given rights and status, whereas, with the Wari, becoming a person is much more of a process. The giving and receiving of nurturance is at the centre of definitions of personhood. Similarly, the Wari concept of personhood emphasizes the notion of shared substance. Therefore the body becomes a place where relationships are developed.

In many countries personhood is acquired when an infant is born; however, this is not true across all cultures. (Andréas Nieto Porras / Wikimedia Commons)

Like many other native Amazonian peoples, the Wari believe that conception occurs when a quantity of semen accumulates after multiple acts of sexual intercourse. This means that pregnancy cannot be seen as accidental; rather, it is the result of a relationship between a man and a woman. The foetus thus produced is viewed as a representative of the relationship between the mother and father. The Wari consider the production of a baby to be an ongoing process. For example, sex is encouraged during pregnancy to nourish the foetus; not to do so is seen as endangering the unborn baby. If the father of the baby is no longer present, the woman is expected to have sex with other men or risk the baby being sickly or underweight. Wari babies can have multiple fathers; any man who has sex with a pregnant woman can claim paternity. The Wari argue that the foetus is conscious and can recognize his or her kin from conception, as they believe that the head and the eyes develop first. The foetus is claimed already to know and love its parents while it is still in the womb. Its development also affects the identity of the mother, who takes the name of her youngest child. Mother and baby are treated as a unit; for six months they remain together inside their house, separated from the rest of society. During this period, the baby is forming its personhood through feeding on breast milk, and babies do not take a name of their own until they are about six weeks old. Instead they are known during this period as *arawe'*, which literally means 'still being made'. The naming occurs as the woman and her child leave seclusion and become social beings once again. Nor is the social construction of the body complete at birth. Wari personhood is acquired gradually with the sharing of bodily fluids as an individual goes through life.

The father continues to contribute to this process by ensuring that he provides food for the mother and baby. There are clearly important reasons for the sharing of bodily fluids beyond reproduction and the survival of infants – for example, creating alliances between two kinship groups (those of the mother and the father). As children may have more than two parents, this can be used to widen kinship networks in times of need or to provide social support.

The Wari argue that sex, or the exchange of fluids through sexual intercourse, causes menstruation at puberty. In fact, they claim that only sexually active women menstruate. In private, Wari women confess that their bodies do not always conform to this logic, but they dismiss vaginal bleeding when not having sex and claim that it is not real menstruation. There is a traditional belief that the ritual killing of a non-Wari was a key rite of passage in becoming a man: when an enemy is killed, the enemy's spirit blood enters the bodies of everyone who witnesses the killing. For both men and women, personhood is maintained by active participation in social life. A woman who does not have sexual relations is said to lose her fertility, and men who do not engage in warfare are believed to have weak blood that makes them vulnerable to illness.

Interestingly, a non-Wari woman can become Wari if she has a baby with a Wari man. This is possible as the blood of the pregnant woman merges with the blood of the foetus in the womb and takes on qualities of the child's blood. The process also works in the opposite way: for example, when a woman became pregnant to a Brazilian outsider (*Wijam*) she was seen as no longer truly Wari, as she was seen to have lost Wari blood.

In contrast, in the United States, the physical birth is viewed as truly an infant's doorway to personhood. The biological birth is coupled with the social birth. Miscarriage and abortion happen before foetal personhood has been acknowledged, and aborted or miscarried foetuses are commonly incinerated along with other hospital waste rather than having funerals. Stillbirths and infant deaths, by contrast, are much more publicly mourned.

Contested Boundaries of Personhood and the State

Conklin and Morgan (1996) argue that the tension between individualism and other concepts of personhood, such as relationality, are usually found in debates over the appropriate extent of state power. The state or government claims to have the final say in making clear the boundaries and definition of personhood. However, this often comes into conflict with families, who argue that life and death decisions should be left to them. There is also tension between the state and hospitals in the West, as members of the medical profession prefer to treat the body solely as a physical entity. The concept of personhood is therefore continually being renegotiated and adapted.

There are many public debates involving personhood in the West, including euthanasia, assisted suicide, organ transplantation, foetal tissue research, abortion and assisted **reproductive technology**. Conklin and Morgan focus on the way in which personhood is conferred on newborn babies. This is a very complex site for discussions of the boundaries of personhood, since there is a huge array of decisions to be made: for example, in cases where babies are diagnosed as having genetic defects or where a mother is in a coma and kept on life support until the baby is viable.

In conclusion, each society's view of the person contains significant tensions. It is clear that the boundaries between persons and non-persons are continually being tested, negotiated and renegotiated. For the Wari, the sociocentric concept of personhood does not mean that individualism is completely ignored; in fact, individualism is significant in particular circumstances. The qualities of individual autonomy and social interdependence are recognized and valued to varying degrees both in the United States and among the Wari. For example, the Wari acknowledge that the individual acts based on his or her interior beliefs that are known only to him- or herself. Equally, elements of sociocentric and relational concepts of personhood can be found in the United States.

Tensions in the United States between individualism and relationality are usually found in debates over the role of the state. These debates show how dynamic and political personhood concepts are. The state and hospitals would prefer to base decisions about life and death on uniform biological criteria, whereas families tend to take a more relational approach. Conklin and Morgan therefore suggest that there is often room for individualist and relational concepts of personhood to coexist.

CONCLUSION

There are ideas in every society about what it means to be a person. These ideas can be categorized into varying degrees of individualism or sociocentrism, but there can be elements of both within one culture. Equally there can be more variation within a society than between societies in terms of what constitutes a person. The boundaries of personhood are in an ongoing process of tension and negotiation. The tension between what constitutes a person and a partial or non-person is often expressed through a broader tension between the powerful (the state) and the families of those concerned. Concepts of personhood are also linked to the production of identity (this is explored further in chapter 7). Finally, ideas about what constitutes a person can change according to the particular social situation and therefore are far from fixed.

END OF CHAPTER ASSESSMENT

Examine concepts of personhood in different societies.

Teacher's guidance

Here you are being asked to examine the way personhood may be constructed in different societies. Define personhood. Explain that concepts of personhood are not necessarily distinct. In fact, they change and may overlap, they are negotiated, and there may be greater variation in concepts of personhood within a society than between societies. Outline the main concepts of personhood (Western philosophical and sociocentric/relational concepts). Explore the ethnographic and theoretical material on personhood and explain the different concepts. Discuss the contested nature of concepts, considering the role of technology and anthropomorphism. Investigate who decides what it means to be a person: the tension between the state and families, and possible tensions between the state and hospitals in the West, as well as in societies where there is no developed state. Come to a clear conclusion about the socially constructed nature of personhood –that drawing differences between different concepts of personhood may be overdrawing the differences between different societies. Stress the dynamic nature of personhood and the likely challenges to concepts of personhood with increasing technological advances.

KEY TERMS

Animism A belief that natural phenomena such as rocks, trees, thunder, or celestial bodies have life or divinity

Anthropomorphism To attribute human characteristics to animals

Bounded The idea that a person is restricted to his or her physical body and that personhood is not permeable or transferable to others

Dividual A being who is incomplete and continuously involved in the process of being made up of the relations that define him or her

Partible The idea that persons are permeable and that personhood can be transferred, in part, to others through the exchange of bodily fluids or auras

Personhood A social status granted in various ways to those who meet certain criteria: all societies have criteria concerning who can become a person

Sociocentric concept of personhood Where a person is defined by the relationships he or she has with others

Western philosophical individualism The idea that a person is a distinct entity, based on the view that personhood is derived from the biological separation of one person from another, each possessing individual autonomy

Personal investigation

Explore a range of people's ideas about what it means to be a person. Try to make sure that your selection includes people from different cultures. Consider how each individual feels about when someone becomes a person and when they cease to be a person and examine the idea of what it means to be a partial person – do such concepts exist? It is important that you use non-anthropological language to operationalize your concepts. Once you have gathered your information compare your results and consider how each example relates to the different concepts of personhood that you have learnt about.

SUGGESTED FURTHER READING AND FILMS

Books

Carsten, J. (2004) *After Kinship*. Cambridge University Press.

Morris, B. (1995) *Anthropology of the Self: The Individual in Cultural Perspective*. Pluto Press.

Morris, B. (1999) *Being Human Does Not Make You a Person: Animals, Humans and Personhood in Malawi*. Goldsmiths, University of London.

Ethnographic film

Breeding Cells (2009), directed by Anna Straube, Gregor Gaida, Miren Artola and Saskia Warzecha, Royal Anthropological Institute

CHAPTER SEVEN

IDENTITY

CONTENTS

CHAPTER
7 Identity

KEY ISSUES AND DEBATES

- What is identity?
- Which parts of a person's identity are chosen and which are given?
- How is group identity interpreted and negotiated by the individual?
- What resources are used to shape identity?
- How is identity changing as a result of globalization?

Chapter 6 explored what it means to be a person, which is closely linked to the concept of identity. Identity can be defined as the process that informs the way in which people see themselves and the groups they belong to and also how other people categorize a person. Some parts of a person's identity are unique to them and other parts are shared. Identity is a very widely used and important concept in many different academic fields, including psychology, politics, society and culture. In fact, identity has become a key topic in wider society today and is at the centre of many contemporary issues – wars, individual rights, ethnic conflict, gendered identity and much more.

This chapter takes a closer look at anthropological interpretations of identity. It discusses the ways in which certain resources may be used by individuals and groups in forming, negotiating and maintaining identity. Some of these resources, among them symbols, language, place, space and dance, are explored using a range of ethnographic examples, including a detailed summary of the work of Gaston Gordillo (2002). Gordillo's research on the Toba of Argentina explores how group identity in this context has been reinforced and maintained through a series of historical and economic changes.

One interesting aspect of the subject for anthropologists is the extent to which individuals themselves can shape their own identity. There are, however, aspects of a person's identity which may be impossible to shape or change.

STOP & THINK

Why do you think that some anthropologists claim that the word 'identification' is a more appropriate term than 'identity'?

HOW DO ANTHROPOLOGISTS UNDERSTAND IDENTIFICATION?

Identification
The ongoing process that describes the way in which individuals and groups see themselves and the way that others see them

In anthropology, identification usually refers to the way people develop their cultural identity. This is understood on an individual level as well as that of the group to which a person belongs or with whom he or she identifies. Anthropologists are interested in the ways that group identity provides individuals with a sense of shared characteristics. There are many social characteristics that may give people a sense of belonging: language, locality, kinship and family, nationality, ethnic membership, age, social class, political views, sexual orientation, religion and gender, for example.

> **Activity**
>
> Which of the above examples of social characteristics are ascribed and which are **achieved**? Which of the above examples are impossible to change? Why?

Until the 1960s, it was argued that ethnic identity was clearly definable, with obvious cultural differences between different ethnic groups. Fredrik Barth and his colleagues were among the first to acknowledge just how complex ethnic identity can be. It became increasingly clear that boundaries between groups were not as observable as once thought. There was also the issue of cultural variation within ethnic groups themselves. Barth ([1969] 1998) concluded that identity was not so much about the actual differences between people; rather, it was the *perceived* differences that become socially relevant because people highlight them and act upon them as if they are real.

Furthermore identity is relational: it is based upon contrasts. It is primarily through people's relationships with others that it is possible to identify who they are. For example, men might understand their gender identity by contrasting themselves with women. Kathleen Hall (2002) supports the idea that identity is relational, situational and multiple, arguing that it is better to understand identification as a process of continual negotiation and renegotiation.

Identity may be dependent upon the particular social context in which a person finds themselves. Individuals and groups may select which aspects of identity to bring to the fore or emphasize, according to the context. If this is the case, then it is possible to argue that certain aspects of identities are selected and negotiated.

> **Activity**
>
> Imagine you are an anthropologist giving a lecture to a group of secondary-school students on identity. You are working with the quotations below from some anthropologists about identity. However, you know the students will not be able to understand these. Summarize what each quotation is saying in some student-friendly language.
>
> 'In [today's] increasingly multicultural contexts identity obtains its meaning primarily from the identity of the other with whom self is contrasted.' (Van Meijl 2008)
>
> Identification is 'a continuous process, not a thing people either possess or don't'. (Eriksen 2001)

People use a number of different resources to create their identity; more often than not, many resources are used at the same time:

- symbols and totems
- place and space
- history
- social memory
- language and myth
- music.

Activity

Have a look at the following list of some of the things that might shape your identity. Pick the ones which are most relevant to your identity and explain why this is so:

Age	Gender
Class	Ethnicity (including religion)
Sexual orientation	Location
Language	Dress
Nationality	A particular team or group which you support

Food preferences – e.g., veganism

Which of the above aspects of identity are given by society (ascribed) and which are chosen (achieved)? Explain why.

With which groups do you share a sense of identity and why?

Symbols and Totems

INDIVIDUAL SYMBOLS

Chapter 2 explored how the body, or more particularly the surface of the skin, is used symbolically. The body can therefore be instrumental in expressing individual and group identity. DeMello's (2000) study reveals how tattoos are used by prisoners to symbolize status and identity. Equally, hair can be seen as symbolic; for example, among the Maasai, men shave their hair on completion of initiation rites (after formerly letting it grow wild) as a symbol of their new status. In other contexts, hairstyles, according to Firth (1973), can represent or reverse the ideas and preferences of previous generations – for instance, through youth subcultures. Hairstyles can also symbolize the influence of wider social changes such as colonialism. Mageo (1994) explores the ways in which hairstyles change over a period of time as a result of colonial influences in Samoa and suggests that this example shows how there can be significant overlap between public and private symbols.

STOP & THINK

Consider the symbols that you use as an individual and suggest how these might be related to wider societal issues.

Hairstyle or colouring, body art and clothing can act as individual symbols in addition to representing inclusion in a wider group or subculture. (Martin SoulStealer / Wikimedia Commons)

GROUP SYMBOLS

Symbols can play a significant role in conflict, as they may act as a form of social solidarity (a way of bringing people together) for a whole social group. Flags and banners, for instance, can represent a nation, and battle dress may be a powerful symbolic tool in raising morale. Police uniform is an example of a symbol of authority and order. According to Anthony Cohen (1985), group symbols are often malleable and can be made to 'fit' circumstances. They therefore enable individuals and groups to experience and express their attachment to a society without compromising their individuality. This also suggests that individuals can engage with group symbols in different ways.

Symbolic Anthropology

A symbol is something which represents something else. Prominent symbolic anthropologists Clifford Geertz, David Schneider, Victor Turner and Mary Douglas all argue that symbols are a very important resource in the creation of identity.

Clifford Geertz (1926–2006) is best known for his work on symbols within an interpretative approach. He claims that any analysis of culture should 'not be an experimental science in search of law but an interpretive one in search of meaning' (Geertz 1973: 5) and argues that culture is expressed mainly by the external symbols that a society uses rather than being limited to the individual mind alone. For Geertz, symbols are 'vehicles of culture', meaning that they should not be studied in and of themselves but for what they can reveal about culture. Geertz's main interest was the way in which symbols shape the ways that social actors see, feel, and think about the world (in Ortner 1984:129). Therefore, symbols can be seen as a major resource for understanding identity.

Victor Turner (1920–1983) is another major figure in symbolic anthropology. In his early career, Turner was influenced by the structural-functionalist approach. Upon embarking on a study of the Ndembu in Africa (1967), his focus shifted from economics and demography to ritual symbolism. Turner's approach to symbols was very different from that of Geertz. He was not interested in symbols as vehicles of culture, as Geertz suggests, but instead investigated symbols as part of a process, believing that the symbolic expression of shared meanings, rather than the value of objects, is central to human relationships and how individuals and groups understand themselves.

TOTEMS

Totemism is a system of belief in which each human is thought to have a spiritual connection or a kinship with another being, such as an animal or plant, or even a spirit. In some cases it is thought that a totem interacts with a given kin group or an individual and can serve as their emblem or symbol. As Durkheim famously commented, totemism can be a way in which people worship their society. Totems may or may not be inherited.

Group **totems** are often associated with myths or rituals. There are many reasons why a particular animal, plant or spirit is chosen to represent the group. These are not usually economic but generally relate to important historical or mythical events in a people's past. Group totems were common among peoples in Africa, India, Oceania (especially in Melanesia), North America, and parts of South America.

Totemism is expressed on an individual as well a group level. This entails an intimate relationship of friendship and protection between the individual and a particular animal or natural object; the natural object can grant special power to its owner. It is found not only among tribes of hunters and harvesters but also among farmers and herdsmen. Individual totemism is especially emphasized among Australian Aborigines and Native Americans.

> **Totem**
> A natural object, plant or animal that is believed by a particular society or group to have spiritual significance and that is adopted as a symbol of the characteristics of that group

Functionalist Perspective

One of the early founders of sociology, **Émile Durkheim** (1858–1917), explored totemism from a sociological and theological perspective. He hoped to discover a 'pure' form of religion in very ancient forms and claimed to have found its origin in totemism. For Durkheim, the sphere of the sacred is a reflection of the feelings, world-view and attitudes that underlie social activities, and the totem was, in his view, a reflection of group consciousness. This is an idea he went on to apply to the role of modern religions. Durkheim held that this type of religion reflects the collective consciousness that is made clear through the identification of the individuals of the group with an animal or plant species. He claimed that this identification with the wider group is also expressed through taboos, symbols and rituals.

Activity

Explain how totems are used to express identity for both the individual and the group.
Can you think of any symbols that you use to show you have a sense of belonging to a particular group?

Place and Space

Some anthropologists argue that a person's environment, whether physical or imagined, is important in shaping their identity. The concept of the nation-state emerged in an age in which the Enlightenment and revolution were destroying the legitimacy of the divinely ordained, hierarchical realm. The sense of nationhood that people feel with other members of their community occurs, for example, when their 'imagined country' participates in a larger event such as the Olympic Games. Even though we may never meet anyone in our imagined community, we still know they are there. A nation is a powerful form of imagined community because, regardless of any inequality and exploitation that may exist, it is usually regarded as a providing a strong sense of shared identity.

The idea of imagined communities comes from the work of Benedict Anderson ([1983] 2006), who explores the idea that sometimes place does not refer to a physical location but instead takes the form of a socially constructed, imagined community. This imaginary place is shared in the minds of people who perceive themselves to be part of that group. An imagined community is different to a physical community because it is not necessarily based on face-to-face interaction among its members. Instead, members hold in their minds a mental image of a particular place that is often defined as a nation or a spiritual home.

The Kaaba in Mecca is considered the holiest site in Islam; all Muslims should face in the direction (Qibla) of the Kaaba during prayers wherever they are in the world, which symbolizes the unity of Muslims under God's law. (Tab59 / Wikimedia Commons)

Place can also affect which aspects of identity individuals choose to bring to the fore. Ethnic identity is a good example, as there are very complex and important reasons for it to be revitalized or remain dormant at different times. It is worth considering how people may emphasize different aspects of their identity according to their location.

> **STOP & THINK**
>
> How might you imagine your own nation?
> Do you belong to any form of an imagined community? Can you think of any other examples of people who do?

History

A shared history can be a source of identity creation, especially when a particular historical event has had a profound impact on a group of people. When people have experienced a major event or have moved from their ancestral home as a result of conflict or instability, they often turn to this shared history in order to retain a sense of their ethnic or national identity.

DIASPORA

A **diaspora** (from Greek διασπορά – which means scattering, dispersion) is the movement, migration or scattering of people away from their established or ancestral homeland or people dispersed, by whatever cause, to more than one location. There are a number of causes of diaspora, among others war, conflict, natural disaster, colonialism and slavery. Moving from their place of belonging can have a variety of effects on individual and group identity. Consider the Jewish diaspora and the way in which a shared history of persecution has led to the strengthening of Jewish identity.

In her research on displaced peoples following the ethnic conflict in Rwanda in the early 1990s, Liisa Malkki (1995) explores the extent to which the conflict reinforced Hutu and Tutsi identity. In this case, as with many others, individuals can respond very differently, with some seeking **assimilation** and identification into their new social group and others retaining and strengthening their original identity.

Diaspora
The movement, migration or scattering of people away from their established or ancestral homeland, or people dispersed, by whatever cause, to more than one location

Social Memory: 'Folk' Memory-Making

There is general agreement today that ethnographic research should acknowledge the specific historical context of the group, and there is a growing appreciation of the anthropological histories of past societies. Archaeologists today suggest that material objects can also have biographies – that is, objects can have life stories similar to those of people. There is a strong relationship between past experiences and identity in the present. The collective retellings of past events which may shape identity in the present are known as social memories. One important and curious point to be aware of is that what people remember is not necessarily an accurate version of events; it is the way the past is reconstructed that is significant and revealing. In fact, the retelling of past events may highlight key areas of interest for anthropologists. So the events or occurrences that are left out of reconstructions may be as important as those that are included.

It is also interesting to attempt to explore the methods by which social memories are

Social memories
The collective retelling of past events which may shape identity in the present

perceived, shared and enacted. Social histories are the product of individuals or groups, and it is worth considering who or what influences these memories. Social memories, therefore, provide a platform on which understandings of personal identities, history and knowledge are contested, even if they are reinvented, rejected or accepted. Anthropologists are often interested in the process of developing social memories in specific contexts. As mentioned earlier, Malkki (1995), through her field research in Tanzania, explored the ways in which political violence and exile can lead to changes in historical consciousness and national identity among displaced peoples. Through extensive fieldwork in two refugee communities, she finds that the refugees' current circumstances significantly influence the way that they feel about their home land (for more on Malkki's work, see chapter 10).

Andrew Canessa (2012) describes how historical events such as conflict are remembered in the Bolivian highlands. For example, the Bolivian Revolution of 1952 is remembered differently by each local community, and there are also significant differences in the way that events are remembered by men and women: women, for instance, remember homes being destroyed in some detail, recalling specific domestic items that were burnt, whereas men simply recall homes being burnt down.

These memories of violence play an important role in shaping people's understanding of the present. It is also significant to consider what is remembered and what is forgotten (Canessa 2012: 92). The memories held by the villagers in the Bolivian highlands are very different from what appears in official documentation, in that they selectively displace certain events. One specific event is remembered by everyone in the village of Wila Kjarka, albeit in different ways, and that is the cannibalism of some of the inhabitants. Canessa argues that the actual events are not necessarily as significant as the way in which they are remembered. These memories serve a number of functions; the younger generation, who did not witness these events and heard about them only second-hand, describe the cannibalism in greatest detail. The effect of this is to ensure that those seeking to threaten Wila Kjarka are seen as 'other' and to reinforce the differences between themselves and outsiders, thus maintaining group and individual identity.

> **Activity**
> What is the difference between actual events and social memories?
> List some of the functions of social memories.

Myth and Folk Memory

Myth
A story which is not necessarily accurate, often told about a people and their origins, sometimes involving supernatural beings

Mythology is a term used by anthropologists to describe the study of myths, which are stories told by a people about themselves and their origins. Myths can form an important part of identification as they shape the individual's view of themselves and their cultural group. The functionalist Malinowski (1939) saw myths as important and as playing a specific role in society – 'a codification of belief' which acted as a 'charter for ritual', justifying rites, ceremonies and social and moral rules. So, for example, myths about the point of origin of local groups he explained as justification for clan hierarchies, and myths concerned with death as a kind of screen between man and the 'vast emotional void', which would otherwise 'gape beyond death'. Functional explanations work rather well with life-threatening problems, offering answers to otherwise unanswerable questions. **Lévi-Strauss** commented on the **mythographic** work of

Franz Boas (1958–1942) and argued that myths are a good way to gain a description of the life, including social organization, religious ideas and practices of a people. Lévi-Strauss maintains that it is possible to analyse myths only in relation to other myths. In other words, they need to be placed in some form of context in order for their meaning and role to be truly understood. He then went on to explore this further in his work *Mythologiques* (1983), a comprehensive study of Native American mythology. Lévi-Strauss argues that music and myth have the power to convey messages that ordinary language cannot, and these messages influence the way that people see themselves and others.

Gregory Bateson studied the Iatmul of coastal New Guinea and their myth of origin (Charlton 2008). In their past, according to the myth, on the shore there was an enormous crocodile, which flapped its tail continuously so that mud and water were constantly mixed. Then along came a great hero, named Kevembuangga, who killed the crocodile with a spear. The mud sank and the distinction between the water and the mud became clear. Bateson argues that this story represents the way societal boundaries became evident for the first time, and the myth ensures that these bounda-

Dancing, music and song are important ways in which cultural memories are preserved and identity is expressed. This image shows Legong, a form of dance from Bali. (Crisco1492 / Wikimedia Commons)

ries are maintained. This example shows how myths are very much part of the social production of ideas connected with identity.

In a similar way, folk memories, or the practice of telling stories or sharing memories as part of an oral history, provide rich data about the past and may also reveal why things are the way they are today.

> **Activity**
>
> Name three things myths can help the anthropologist to understand.
> What is meant by 'mythographic' work?
> What are 'folk memories'?

Language

Language is a resource that can be very important in establishing, maintaining and changing identity. The seventy-three languages that are spoken in Zambia are hierarchically organized. Seven of these are dominant ethnic-group languages, which are used in the media and are positioned above the other languages; at the same time, English, the official state language, is considered to be the most prestigious (Spitulnik 1998). Unlike the seven ethnic-group languages, English is placed in an unquestioned position of privilege. Mary Bucholtz and Kira Hall (2005) argue that this hierarchy results in any form of deviation from the ascribed and accepted languages being seen as deviation from the norm. Deviation then becomes the basis of inequality and discrimination, and ultimately individuals risk becoming marginalized as a result of the language they use. However, this argument does not take into account the possibility of people having agency and thus the ability to challenge, change and adapt language (Ahearn 2001).

When a speaker is fluent in two languages they may choose to bring to the fore one part of their identity over another, depending upon the situation. Alternatively, some use what linguists refer to as **code-switching**, which refers to swapping between two or more languages within a conversation. So choosing which language to use in a particular situation can be a way of emphasizing different aspects of a person's identity. In her study of Sikh youth in the UK, Kathleen Hall (2002) explains how Punjabi is spoken at home and the religious place of worship, the *Gurdwara*, but nowhere else. So language is important in understanding identity formation and maintenance (for more on Hall's study of ethnic identity, see chapter 10).

Music

Music has long been known as a key resource in the creation, maintenance and expression of identity. In the film *Temporary Sanity: The Skerrit Bwoy Story* (2006), Dan Bruun explores the cultural meanings of the gendered performances and political expressions that form part of Jamaican Dancehall in New York. By following 'Skerrit Bwoy', a Bronx-based performer and promoter of Dancehall music, the film gives an insider's view into the dancing, history and social roles of Dancehall clubs in the lives of the Jamaican and Caribbean diaspora in the United States. It demonstrates how important music and dance are in maintaining identity, as well as in mediating or transforming violence in a creative way.

Globalization: *Hip-Hop Japan: Rap and the Paths of Cultural Globalization* (Condry 2006)

Globalization has had interesting and complex effects on the way people create and maintain their identity. In some cases identities are protected and strengthened, and in others they are transformed by new influences. More often than not, both of these processes occur simultaneously. Ian Condry (2006) argues that, just as companies sell products that inform identities, individuals are locally producing new forms of music based on a mixture of different cultural influences. Where two aspects of a culture are combined, resulting in something new and unique, it is described as a hybrid identity. Condry calls this production of identity in globalization a bottom-up or 'genba' model. A genba is a site of cultural production. The genba on which Condry focuses are the darkened, bass-thumping hip-hop clubs of Japan. He asserts that the genba provides us with an alternative view of globalization that is much more personal and local. It is also suggestive of a far more active role for individuals in selecting resources to shape their identity.

In his ethnography, Condry interprets Japan's vibrant hip-hop scene, explaining how a music and culture that originated on the other side of the world is appropriated and remade in Tokyo clubs and recording studios. Illuminating different aspects of Japanese hip-hop, he chronicles how self-described 'yellow B-Boys' express their devotion to 'black culture', how they combine the figure of the samurai with American rapping techniques and gangsta imagery, and how underground artists compete with pop icons to define 'real' Japanese hip-hop. He discusses how rappers manipulate the Japanese language to achieve rhyme and rhythmic flow and how Japan's female rappers struggle to find a place in a male-dominated genre. Condry pays particular attention to the messages of the DJs or emcees, considering how their raps take on subjects such as Japan's education system, its sex industry, teenage bullying victims turned schoolyard murderers, and even America's handling of the war on terror.

Hybrid identity
The mixture of two different identities leading to the emergence of a new form of identity that is different from its constituent parts

The Teriyaki Boyz are a well-known Japanese hip-hip group who have collaborated with American rap artists such as Kanye West, Pharrell Williams and Jay-Z. (Sry85 / Wikimedia Commons)

Activity

Explain how globalization affects group identification.
Think about your own taste in music. What might your choices reflect about your identity?

The following ethnographic study shows both how group identity can be shaped by a number of different resources, including shared experiences, and how important memories of experiences may shape the identity of later generations.

'The breath of devils: memories and places of an experience of terror' (Gordillo 2002)

Gaston Gordillo (2002) examines an indigenous group of the Argentine Chaco, the Toba, whose experiences of exploitation and terror have been remembered as devil images that shape how they see the bush (their home) and their time spent on sugar plantations. In essence, the plantations, where some of the Toba worked for part of the year, became a place of terror, disease and death, which reinforced the idea that the bush is a place of healing and relative freedom and **autonomy**.

The sugar plantation

The Toba are a group of about 1,500 people living in a dozen hamlets located near the border between Argentina and Paraguay. In the mid-1900s many of the Toba took seasonal work 300 kilometres west of their settlement on the sugar plantations. Those who worked on these plantations had a great influence on the social memories of the rest of the group in future generations. Even those who never went to the plantations could give detailed descriptions of their parents' and grandparents' lives there. Many years after the Toba stopped this work, narratives of devils related to the terror are a key feature of their culture.

The Toba began to work on the plantations because of a complex military assault on their region, which resulted in restrictions on their hunter-gathering as they were unable to access certain parts of the land. This meant that, to survive without access to their usual natural resources, they began to rely on new forms of commodity – tools, instruments, guns and clothing – which they had not necessarily needed in the bush. Half to three-quarters of the population, men, women and children, worked at some point on the plantations for eight to ten months a year.

On the plantations there was a strict hierarchy along ethnic lines. The Toba were assigned a level of pay, tasks and living standards according to their ethnicity. Unfortunately for them, they were seen as the lowest ranking and therefore had the worst wages, jobs and working and living conditions. They lived in straw huts and were given virtually no medical attention. The Toba interestingly associate their diseases with the devils that they believe reside in the mountains. They describe the plantations as places of excess, material wealth and commodities, which made them return year after year, despite the harsh working conditions, disease, terror and deaths.

Evil spirits or devils living in the mountains causing death

The question is how do collective (shared) experiences of terror inform the production of devil images? The Toba did not experience the type of terror that others have suffered – torture or mass murder, for example; rather, it was the fear of death intertwined with appalling working conditions and high mortality rates linked to rampant diseases, as well as political repression. Its routine nature means that it is at least equal to more violent forms of terror. If terror is a form of domination based on horror and intense fear of death, the Toba experience of the sugar plantations was one of terror. According to Marx, this type of fear is part of an experience shared, in different ways, by groups of workers around the world.

Anthropologists have argued that devils are usually linked to particular places. In other words, the devil is present because of something wrong with a particular place, kept alive by a collective social memory. The Toba's memories of fear, death and illness are produced through the contrast to their own, generally positive, experiences in the bush. For example, when asked about the devils, a man in his seventies, Segundo, answered: 'There were many devils. Plenty of devils. All the diseases. That's why the kids died: the grownups, women, girls, everybody.' When asked why there were so many devils, he replied: 'We lived close to a mountain, that's why' (Gordillo 2002: 37).

Devils are called *payák* or *diablos* by the Toba. In their current memory, the diseases and death unleashed by the *payák* became part of the embodiment of the social strains embedded in the plantation. The death of children is a particularly painful theme in current memories. In 1996, Daniela, a woman in her late fifties, remembers that 'Almost all the children died there [the plantation] and when they were back in the bush, all the women cried for the children.' This memory shows that the loss of life also threatened the reproduction of the group, both socially and physically.

Despite the high mortality rate and the permanent threat of devils, the Toba did not stop going to the plantations every year. The desire for commodities, alongside their inability to hunt and gather at home, seems to have been stronger that the threat of death in the cane fields. On the plantations, the Toba counted (unsuccessfully) on the healing power of their shamans.

A view of the countryside surrounding the sugar plantations where the Toba worked. (Laurent / Wikimedia Commons)

The KiyaGaikpi – cannibal people

Local rumour had it that there were a group of cannibals, the KiyaGaikpi, who inhabited the surroundings of the plantations. This memory was passed on through the generations of the Toba so that, even though the younger members of the group had not seen the KiyaGaikpi, they knew very well who they were. Current memories of the KiyaGaikpi condense many aspects of the experience at the plantations. They came from the mountains, according to the Toba, the place they feared most. Some old people have a vivid memory of their appearance. Many claimed that the KiyaGaikpi were hungry for human flesh and that they were rich and 'very full of money'. Mariano, a man in his late fifties, claimed that they were fearless because of their wealth: 'They looked as if they were the owners of everything. They came down with trucks, for they were many, they have trucks and they are very rich. They have everything, they have airplanes . . . they have money. They have plenty money. That's why they are not scared' (Gordillo 2002: 40).

The KiyaGaikpi were believed to 'purchase' flesh. So the people hired for their labour believed that they themselves were being bought and sold as a commodity. Therefore the workers saw themselves as reduced to consumable and disposable objects. Most Toba remember the fear of encountering the KiyaGaikpi, which restricted their mobility on the plantations: men and women always had their children with them and avoided going off the campsite alone or at night. Therefore the KiyaGaikpi seem to represent the fear that the Toba had of losing the one thing they still owned while working on the plantation – their own bodies, which were permanently exhausted by work, mistreatment, disease and death. The connection between cannibalism and capitalist exploitation is not restricted to the Toba; narratives about people being 'consumed' or 'eaten up' are common around the world.

The Toba see the cannibals as having similar characteristics to their *patron* or boss: they were 'rich' and 'white' and 'didn't work'. The attributing of whiteness to devil creatures is widespread in Latin America.

The familiar: a devil inhabiting the sugar-processing factory

The manager of the plantation, Patrón Costa, was seen as a cannibal, though his cannibalism was concentrated in a particularly symbolic place: the sugar-processing factory. The factory was the place that the Toba feared the most because they saw it as the refuge of a diabolical creature known as *el familiar*, meaning relative. This is another form of devil, a non-human evil, a powerful creature that lived in a confined space – the basement of the factory. The Toba agree that after midnight this familiar acquired human and animal shapes. Many say that when the familiar appeared as a human he usually turned into a white man. This white man had a clear socio-economic class: he was well dressed and educated. Many Toba therefore see their *patrón*'s power as being closely linked to his relationship with the familiar. They argue that the familiar has provided their *patrón* with riches, looked after the factory and made sure that the sugar canes are always green. They also remember the familiar as a devil so powerful that any type of resistance was futile, an idea supported by those who ran the plantations.

Gordillo commented that in his research he was surprised to hear both positive and negative views of the plantations and the *patrón*: he therefore argues that the devil imageries represent power rather than capitalism that is inscribed in a particular place.

The return to the bush

The Toba's return to the bush reaffirmed it as a place that is everything opposed to the plantation. It emerged as a place of health and healing. In the bush there are devils, but these *payák* differ sharply from their counterparts on the plantations. The bush devils engage in forms of reciprocity with humans unthinkable on the plantations. They provide shamans with their healing power and regularly help foragers find food (fish, fruits, wild honey and meat). Therefore the food and life in general in the bush is much healthier. This does not mean that the bush is free from hardships. Many people continue to associate it with poverty and being constrained by local forms of domination.

Gordillo's study illustrates how narratives of devils are specific to particular places which become part of the social memory of the Toba. In this social memory of the plantation, the Toba's devils imply a critique of capitalism because they attribute unnatural, evil connotations to capitalist forms of accumulation of wealth. These memories inform the consciousness of the group and help them come to terms with the terrifying system at work in the cane fields.

A Summary of Anthropological Theories of Identity

Theory/theorist	Argument	Example
Barth ([1969] 1998)	Identity is negotiable and dynamic	Ethnicity, where people may decide which aspects of their ethnic identity to foreground
Kathleen Hall (1996, 2002)	Identity is chosen and situational	Sikh youths in the UK – 'There's a time to be Indian and time to be British'
Feminism (Gellner and Stockett 2006)	Gender makes up a large part of every individual's identity	A person's gendered identity is linked to power, age, ethnicity and other characteristics
Marxism and Identity (Gordillo 2002)	Capitalism results in class identity being imposed	The Toba of Argentina were disempowered as a result of colonialist segregation in the plantations

CONCLUSION

The formation and maintenance of identity is a complex process which involves a number of different resources. Identification takes place on both an individual and a group level, and there can be some interesting interpretations that are made of group identity. Some aspects of identity are given while others are achieved. Identity today can be highly political, contested and complex, particularly within the context of globalization.

END OF CHAPTER ASSESSMENT

Examine some of the ways in which different resources might be used to create and maintain individual and group identification.

Teacher's guidance

Begin by defining individual and group identity and explain that it is a process, not a fixed concept. Examine a range of resources that are used to create and maintain individual and group identity, including symbols, place and space, history, social memory, language and myth, dance and music, using named ethnographic studies. Use the work of Hall and also Gordillo to explain how different resources may be used simultaneously to maintain identity, and how certain aspects of an individual or group identity may become more relevant depending upon the context. Discuss the extent to which the individual creates their own identity or the degree to which it is imposed by structural forces. Perhaps mention the complex ways in which globalization is affecting identity.

KEY TERMS

Achieved identity Parts of a person's identity which are chosen

Autonomy Freedom and independence, the right to self-governance

Code-switching Where a person uses two or more different languages within one conversation

Diaspora The movement, migration or scattering of people away from their established or ancestral homeland, or people dispersed, by whatever cause, to more than one location

Hybrid identity The mixture of two different identities leading to the emergence of a new form of identity that is different from its constituent parts

Identification The ongoing process that describes the way in which individuals and groups see themselves and the way that others see them

Myth A story, which is not necessarily accurate, often told about a people and their origins, sometimes involving supernatural beings

Social memories The collective retelling of past events which may shape identity in the present

Totem A natural object, plant or animal that is believed by a particular society or group to have spiritual significance and that is adopted as a symbol of the characteristics of that group

Personal investigation

Investigate people who moved to your community from another location and note the ways in which they have retained the identity of their country of origin or the extent to which they have chosen to assimilate to their new culture. Talk to them about how they see their imagined community of origin. Consider what other markers they use to express their identity and what resources they use. Examine the extent to which the individual accepts the identity of the wider group, or adapts and negotiates their own personal interpretation of the group identity, and how they may or may not express this.

SUGGESTED FURTHER READING AND FILMS

Books

Gordillo, G. (2002) 'The breath of the devils: memories and places of an experience of terror', *American Ethnologist* 29(1): 33–57.

Hall, K. (2002) *Lives in Translation: Sikh Youth as British Citizens*. University of Pennsylvania Press.

Malkki, L. (1995) *Purity and Exile: Violence, Memory, and National Cosmology among Hutu Refugees in Tanzania*. University of Chicago Press.

Ethnographic film

Temporary Sanity: The Skerrit Bwoy Story (2006), directed by Dan Bruun, Royal Anthropological Institute

CHAPTER EIGHT

RITUAL

CONTENTS

CHAPTER

8 Ritual

KEY ISSUES AND DEBATES

- How can we define ritual?
- How do different anthropological approaches explain the role of rituals?
- How might rituals express power relationships?
- What is the nature of rites of passage?
- What role might rituals play in terms of reinforcing gender roles and status?

Rituals can be found in all cultures around the world. People have performed ceremonies observing birth, initiation, marriage, death or religion for tens of thousands of years. Rituals have many functions for individuals and society. Fiona Bowie (2006) suggests that they speak to people's core emotions and reveal values that a society holds most important. It is hard to define ritual, and in anthropology there are several definitions. One, suggested by Dennis O'Neil (2009), is that rituals are stylized and usually repetitive acts that take place at a set time and location. They almost always involve the use of symbolic objects, words and actions. Ritual is also defined as a highly structured social event which promotes a sense of community. Some definitions are limited to a religious meaning – and in fact rituals have been defined as the social aspect of religion. However, most anthropologists prefer a broader definition, which can include secular activities such as the way we greet people. Anthropologists do not look for a single definition, as rituals are complex and dynamic.

WHAT ARE RITUALS?

Joy Hendry (2008) suggests that, to test a form of behaviour to see if it can be called a ritual, one should try to change or omit it, and see how others react. For example, how would you react if someone failed to greet you after you knocked on their door? Rituals are intended to express belief and to bring about certain ends. They often deal with human concerns such as health, fertility and general welfare, but the purposes may vary among the participants. **Ritual** is widely regarded as the most fundamental unit of religious expression and is based on a set of principles. These principles express a people's relationship to an idealized social world – it may be with other people and often includes the supernatural. It is hard to define ritual as it comes in many forms and encompasses a wide variety of human activities.

Ritual
Behaviour prescribed by society in which individuals have little choice about their actions, sometimes having reference to beliefs in mystical powers or beings

Types of Rituals

Critical rituals often happen at such important times of life as birth, puberty, marriage or death. In these rituals there is often a change of status that involves a shifting of roles. Jean La Fontaine (1972) divides them into life crisis rituals (transition from one stage of life to another) and initiation rituals (gaining membership to a particular group). For example, at puberty, children become adults and responsible members of a community or religious group; they may become warriors or workers or, indeed, they may be eligible to marry.

Calendrical rituals care for the whole society; they take place at certain times of the year and reaffirm and maintain the cycle of life.

STOP & THINK

Give two examples of both critical and calendrical rituals from your own culture.

Rituals in Religion

Secular
Relating to worldly matters

Sacred
Pertaining to or connected with religious or spiritual matters

The performance of rituals is an essential part of all religions. Most religious rituals take place in special places and under special conditions, such as in a dedicated temple or at a sacred spot. There is an intentional separation between the secular and the sacred. By being removed from the ordinary world, the sacred acts are enhanced for the believers and the rituals are made more effective. Only allowing initiated people to participate in religious rituals can also have the same effect.

For example, before performing certain rituals, most importantly before prayers, Muslims are expected to perform a form of purification, known as ablution. This involves washing the hands, face, arms and feet with water. The Muslim prayer is a combination of physical actions, verbal sayings and internal feelings. Once the prayer is started, a series of sayings and actions are performed. The sayings include reciting parts of the Qur'an, the holy book of Islam, as well as other statements glorifying God. Muslims are required to pray five times every day at specific times – dawn, noon, mid-afternoon, sunset and night.

Religious ritual reinforces the basic system of belief. The feelings people experience during rituals provide positive support for continuing them and strengthen their belief that their religion is the correct one.

STOP & THINK

Can you think of some examples of rituals involved when entering a religious place? Do you remember having to adapt your behaviour when, as a tourist, you have entered a different sacred place?

Non-Religious Rituals

Rituals are symbolic actions that help people physically express their beliefs and values. Simple actions such as a handshake, a wave, or the sign of the cross can be considered as a ritual. However, non-religious rituals can be as complex as a presidential inauguration or the opening of the Olympic Games. The opening ceremony of the 2012 Olympic Games in London included welcoming speeches, the parading of national flags and the procession of athletes, together with artistic performances of the host nation's culture.

The Sema ritual, practised by Islamic Sufis of dervish fraternities, began with the inspiration of Mevlâna Jalâluddîn Rumi (1207–1273) and was influenced by Turkish customs and culture. An important characteristic of this 700-year-old ritual is that it unites the three fundamental components of human nature: the mind (as knowledge and thought), the heart (through the expression of feelings, poetry and music) and the body (by activating life, by the turning).The Sema ceremony represents the human being's spiritual journey, an ascent by means of intelligence and love to Truth. Turning towards the Truth, the dervish grows through love, transcends the ego, meets the Truth, and arrives at Perfection. He then returns from this spiritual journey as one who has reached maturity and completion, able to love and serve the whole of creation without discriminating in regard to belief, class or race. (Tomas Maltby / Wikimedia Commons)

This ritual was a special act which led people out of their everyday concerns into a special way of being together with others.

RITUAL OR ROUTINE?

The difference between a ritual and a routine is very similar to the difference between a sign and a symbol (see chapter 7 for more on symbols). Routines are one-dimensional in meaning, whereas rituals have deeper multi-level meanings. For example, brushing your teeth, washing your hands, eating and going to sleep at night are routines. However, the same actions can became ritual if certain symbolic actions are involved.

STOP & THINK
Give three examples of ritual and three of routine from your life.

Political ideologies and movements often involve rituals that can be profoundly important for people, especially when they become the focus of nationalism. Extreme nationalist movements over the last century essentially became secular religions in some countries. They had their rituals, created new sacred objects, and fostered beliefs that provided meaning and order for millions of people.

Activity

Think of a religious and a non-religious ritual in which you have taken part.
What characteristics did they share?
In what ways were they different?
How would you differentiate ritual from routine?

Common Features of Rituals

Rituals are always associated with action and formality. The forms of action involved in ritual are different from those of everyday life and have different purposes. Rituals are also associated with symbols and symbolic action. S. J. Tambiah (1990) suggests that ritual is a culturally constructed system of symbolic communication. Clifford Geertz argues that rituals have expressive value (see Geertz's interpretation of the Balinese cock-fight below, pp. 169–70). In Balinese culture, cockfighting is associated with the sexual and social status of the cock's male owner and also reflects social hierarchy and group rivalry. According to Audrey Richards (1956), rituals commonly involve participants in

- physical movement or action
- passive or active modes of communication, verbal or non-verbal
- **esoteric** (understood by the initiated) and **exoteric** (available to the public/anyone) knowledge in the context of heightened emotional states.

STOP & THINK
How is water used in rituals?
Why is cleanliness, and even the very act of cleaning, important in religious ritual?

Functions of Rituals

Anthropologists have long debated the functions of rituals. Early functionalist anthropologists suggested that rituals represented the worship of society itself, highlighting **integrating** functions (see Anthropological Approaches to Ritual, p. 167). More recently, increasingly complex explanations of rituals have been developed. For example, some argue that they function to **legitimate** (to make seem fair) power and have an **ideological** function (shaping ideas and values), as well as providing participants with strong emotional experiences. Others claim that rituals function to allow people to reflect on their culture and to consider what role they play within it. Victor Turner (1969) argues that rituals are ambiguous – their role is unclear and not straightforward.

An offering to the Ganges (ekabhishek / Wikimedia Commons)

Rituals have many functions, both at the individual level and for groups or societies, notably to

- channel and express emotions
- guide and reinforce behaviour
- support or subvert (challenge) the status quo
- bring about change
- restore balance and harmony
- play an important role in healing
- maintain life forces and the fertility of the earth
- ensure relationships with the unseen world (spirits/ancestors or other supernatural forces)
- pass on a culture's values from one generation to the next.

Activity

Think of a range of activities or behaviours that you consider to be rituals.

Identify if they are secular or religious.

Then think what the consequences would be if the ritual were not carried out.

Think of three secular and three religious rituals.

ANTHROPOLOGICAL APPROACHES TO RITUAL

Functionalism and Ritual

Most functional approaches attempt to explain ritual in relation to the needs and maintenance of a society.

DURKHEIM – RITUALS AS MEANS OF SOCIAL INTEGRATION

According to Durkheim (Farace et al. 1982), every society makes a distinction between the sacred and the profane. Religion belongs to the sacred. The function of religion is creating solidarity and integration through rituals which reinforce collective representations (shared ideas of seeing the world). Durkheim suggests that a ritual is a means of creating emotional bonds that maintain social order. It both reflects and supports a society's moral framework (sense of right and wrong) and underlying social arrangements. Rituals use symbolism to reinforce social statuses, norms and values, and they increase group solidarity by promoting empathy. Individuals who undergo a rite of passage together, such as members of the same **age set**, often develop strong personal bonds and form a community of equals within the larger society. Ritual functions as a means of social integration. It therefore tells us about society, as it is a direct representation of society itself.

ANXIETY – RITUAL THEORY

Bronislaw Malinowski ([1922] 2014) studied the Trobrianders of New Guinea between 1914 and 1918. One of the rituals performed by the Trobrianders was the Kula Ring, a recurrent exchange of valuable gifts between the different people of the various islands. Exchanging these gifts involved members of the society making dangerous voyages across the sea in canoes. There were many rituals that were performed before the canoes departed on their journey, and these served to control various emotions and to meet various psychological needs, such as anxiety, which the islanders faced before setting off. Such rituals served to bring about a sense of security and power and, in doing so, helped to overcome feelings of powerlessness and tension.

Malinowski also explained the popularity of rites of passage by pointing to their psychotherapeutic quality. Such rituals give individuals social support in confronting the anxiety they may feel facing new social roles or major life changes, such as parenthood or the death of loved ones. Funeral rites, for instance, help those who are grieving by ritually introducing the deceased into the world of the afterlife. Mourning rituals, in particular, provide the bereaved with structure at a time when their most fundamental social relations have changed. This structure helps them to face the loss of the deceased.

RADCLIFFE-BROWN

Alfred Radcliffe-Brown was one of the main anthropologists of the **structural functionalist** school. He viewed anthropology as a natural science, similar in essence to the physical and biological sciences. The object of natural science was to investigate the structure of the universe. Social phenomena constitute a distinct class of natural phenomena, and social structures are just as real as are individual organisms. Radcliffe-Brown suggested that there are five functions of ritual (Kuper [1977] 2010):

- expression of emotions and feelings; every ceremony is an expression of emotions and feelings between two or more people.
- awareness of duty and expectations; ceremonies are not random expressions. Obligations are attached to the rituals, and it is the duty of everyone in a community to participate in a ceremony. A ritual therefore expresses feelings of social cohesion and solidarity.
- connecting with laws; each ceremony may be explained by laws regulating the life of the community.
- redefining social sentiments; this function is performed for the people taking part in the ritual – for example, a peace-making ceremony is a method by which feelings of coldness or hostility are turned into feelings of friendship.
- fulfilment of social needs; ritual keeps balance and order in society so that things do not get out of hand.

RITUAL AS SYMBOLIC ACTION

The use of symbols is central to rituals. Rituals can be understood as symbolic action. Victor Turner looked at ritual among the Ndembu (see rites of passage below, pp. 173–4) and how it could be understood as symbolic action. He argued that the fluid produced by the *mudyi* tree could represent breast milk and the bond between mother and child, as well as women's solidarity against men's oppression as they sang and danced round the tree. It therefore relates to the body as well as having social meaning. According to Turner, ritual symbols are ambiguous. He suggests that symbols are **multivocal** (they are saying several different things at the same time), and that they need to be so in order to create social solidarity. People are different, and there needs to be some way of unifying them.

RITUAL AS SOCIAL CONTROL

Roy Rappaport (1968) looked at how ritual could help to regulate relations with the environment (see more on this ritual in chapter 5). He examined the way gift exchanges of pigs between tribal groups in Papua New Guinea maintained an environmental balance between humans, the available food (with pigs sharing the same foodstuffs as humans) and the resource base. Rappaport concluded that ritual helps to maintain a healthy environment, limits fighting so that it does not endanger the existence of the population, adjusts human to land ratios, helps the economy, and distributes surpluses of pigs throughout the region. According to his ethnography, the ritual acted as the regulator of the society and was done by tribal members to rid themselves of debts to the supernatural. Herds of pigs were looked after and fattened until the required workload pushed the limits of what the tribe could do, and then they were slaughtered.

RITUALS OF REBELLION

Max Gluckman (1955), who studied a number of rituals from South Africa, found that the participants were in fact taking normal expectations and reversing them. Gluckman suggests that maintaining social balance is difficult because of the conflicting views of different groups in this culture. In his approach, ritual is the space in which social conflicts are worked out. Through the ritualization of conflicts, existing tensions are exaggerated, and this has a positive functional value, eliminating the threat of disunity. For instance, among the Swazi, when a new king was crowned, every citizen was expected to criticize him in public, making a huge mockery of his weaknesses. This brings an almost theatrical character to rituals. Gluckman concludes that rituals show us how to behave appropriately by allowing us occasionally to do the opposite.

Another function of these rituals is to channel conflict in a harmless direction. By allowing people the opportunity to act out their problems in a made-up way, they provide more stability in their real culture. In these rituals the accepted social order was symbolically overturned. Gluckman observed how this symbolically inverted the normal social order, so that the king was publicly insulted, women asserted their domination over men, and the established authority of elders over the young was turned upside down. He argued that the ritual was an expression of underlying social tensions and that it functioned as an institutional pressure valve, allowing those tensions to be expressed without leading to actual rebellion. Annual carnivals are viewed in the same light. According to Gluckman, **rituals of rebellion** are common in loosely integrated state systems with strong tensions but no official controlling institutions.

Activity

Think about how we learn about the function of rituals. How might we interpret rituals in other countries?

Could there be any problems with our interpretations of the rituals of other cultures? If so, why?

What is necessary for an anthropologist to understand a ritual fully?

Can you think of any other 'periods of uncertainty' or times when people feel vulnerable and may be helped by religious rituals? Where can rituals bring hope in people's lives? How can religion/rituals help bring control to people's lives at these times?

Political Rituals

Some anthropologists argue that ritual is an indirect way of making complex statements with a strong ideological dimension about society. The following examples show some of the ways in which rituals are used as a political tool in different cultural contexts.

'Deep play: notes on the Balinese cockfight' (Geertz 1973)

Clifford Geertz conducted fieldwork in Bali and studied the ritual of cockfighting, the meaning of which is discussed in this article. Despite being illegal, cockfighting is a widespread and highly popular phenomenon in Bali. Geertz reports that the Balinese people hate animals and, more specifically, expressions of animal-like behaviour. However, they have a deep identification with their cocks and, in identifying with his cock, the Balinese man is identifying with his ideal male self. Geertz says that the Balinese word for 'cock' has the same dual meaning as the English one.

Although gambling is a major part of the Balinese cockfight, Geertz argues that what is at stake is much more fundamental than just money – it is prestige and status. He distinguishes 'deep fights', with high wagers, from 'shallow fights', usually with low wagers of both gambling and prestige. A deep fight is one in which results are unpredictable, the odds are more even and the bets are more balanced.

Cockfighting is a fight for status, with bets serving only to symbolize the risk. Participants in the deep fights are usually dominant members of society. However, according to Geertz, the fight is not between individuals but, rather, is an imitation of the social structure of kinship and social groups. People never bet against a cock from their own kin group. Fighting always takes place between people (and cocks) from opposing social groups (family, clan, village) and is therefore the most open expression of social rivalry and a way of addressing those rivalries. Social tensions are represented through the cockfight. The 'deep play' of the Balinese cockfight, according to Geertz, is a symbolically manufactured representation of something very real in social life. This is a ritual about social hierarchy, economic exchange, group solidarity and rivalry. Geertz concludes that such rituals are a form of text which can be read, as the fighting cock is a symbol of social and sexual status. The social meanings are more important than any material or financial gain.

According to Geertz, deciding which pairs of cocks should fight is an expression of social rivalry and determination of status. (© Anne-Mette Jensen / Flickr)

Ritual and Social Instability (Leach 1954)

Leach studied the Kachin people of North Burma and found that their rituals and myths reflected the instability of the social structure of their society. He argues that ritual is a form of communication. Kachin people worship their own gods and spirits. They also use them to justify who has power – for instance, their *Manau* festivals involve chiefs and high aristocrats proclaiming the ancestral (and therefore justified) sources of their authority and power. According to Leach, Kachin society is not stable, either socially or ideologically. He suggests that the spiritual world is a reflection of reality. Rituals tend to involve sacrifice, which provides a way of talking about society. However, whatever the type of ritual, it often seeks to legitimate those who have power in a culture.

Rituals for Redistributive Exchanges: *Ongka's Big Moka* (Charlie Nairn and Andrew Strathern, 1974)

Andrew Strathern studied the Kawelka people, who live scattered in the western highlands north of Mount Hagen in New Guinea. In this ethnographic film he follows Ongka, who is a charismatic Big-Man (highly influential person) of the Kawelka. The film focuses on the motivations and efforts involved in organizing a big ceremonial gift exchange, or Moka, planned to take place sometime in 1974. Ongka spent five years using all of his skills as an orator and negotiator to amass the 600 pigs and assorted other valuables, including a motorbike, which he will give away in a festive ritual, a Moka. In highland society, status is earned by giving things away rather than acquiring them, and a Moka is one of the most important rituals. For this, the Kawelka decorate themselves with painted faces, oiled bodies, bones stuck through holes in their noses, and bird-of-paradise feather head-dresses. These Moka rituals are one of the ways a Big-Man retains his authority. The best way for Ongka to maintain his status as a Big-Man is by showing off his generosity by giving away all of his wealth and leading by example. His motives in planning his big Moka are to gain influence over rivals and to win a sort of immortality for himself and his tribe. When a Big-Man such as Ongka receives an invitation from another Big-Man to a ceremony in order to receive large numbers of pigs, money and other goods, he becomes less superior. So he starts his own Moka and replies by giving many more pigs and money than he received.

The Moka ritual has the effect of distributing a society's wealth. It is a complex system of competitive feasting, speech-making, and gift giving intended in part to increase the status of the giver.

> **Activity**
>
> What are the functions of the above rituals?
> What are the similarities between these rituals?
> Are there any state rituals where you live that are similar to a big Moka ritual?

RITES OF PASSAGE

Rites of passage
A series of rites that mark the transformation from one stage of life, season or event to another

Rites of passage mark the transition from one stage of life, season or event to another. Everyone participates in rites of passage, and all societies mark them in various ways. The term 'rite of passage' is often used to refer to 'life cycle' or 'life crisis' rituals concerned with a change of status in the lives of individuals and groups. Rituals surrounding birth, initiation, marriage and death would be examples of such rituals.

> **STOP & THINK**
>
> There are many celebrations following birth. Some baptisms, for example, involve the baby being taken from the mother and being handed to the minister, and possibly a godparent.
> What does the baptism symbolize?

A key text on rituals is a book written by **Arnold Van Gennep**, first published in 1909, translated from French into English in 1960 and called *The Rites of Passage*. Van Gennep, like many early anthropologists, refers to the people under discussion as 'primitive'. He talks mainly about small-scale societies, but his theories have been shown to apply to societies in any part of the world. The life of any individual in any society is a series of passages from one age to another. The crossing of a threshold, real or symbolic, is the key element in all rites of passage. Van Gennep noticed, as he worked among different people in Africa, that birth, puberty, marriage and death are focused upon in every culture. The actual ceremonies may differ, but their meaning is universal; the celebration of the transition from one phase of life to another.

Van Gennep argues that all rites of passage share similar features:

- a period of segregation from the previous way of life – from a previous state, time, place or status (the **preliminal** stage). This first stage is concerned with **separation** from the previous situation and is marked by rituals that symbolize cutting or separating in some way (rites of separation or purification rites, e.g.. the removal of hair or scarification).
- the state of transition from one status to another, when initiates are neither one thing nor another. A person is symbolically placed outside of society, and there is a suspension of normal rules and the application of taboos and restrictions (the liminal stage). This second stage applies to rites of **transition**, **marginality** or **liminality**. Rituals characteristically mark this sense of ambiguity and confusion. Normal rules of behaviour may be suspended or exaggerated. Initiates may be required to wear a uniform, be stripped of clothing, be painted, or in some other way be marked out as different, special. Certain rules on speech and movement may be imposed. Symbols are frequently used instructively to reinforce any verbal teachings.
- the stage of **incorporation**, marked by **postliminal rites**, when the individual, in a life-cycle ritual, for instance, is reintegrated into society, but in a transformed state. This is a process of introduction to the new social status and the new way of life – reintegration in a transformed state, involving rites of incorporation, a transit to a new status and the lifting of restrictions.

> **Liminal**
> Relating to a transitional stage between states or categories

The concept of **liminality** was introduced by Van Gennep to describe the quality of the second stage of a ritual, especially a rite of passage that involves some change to the person, especially their social status. He used the term liminal to highlight the performative, active element of a rite of passage. The crossing of a threshold, real or symbolic, temporal or physical, is a key element in all rites of passage, which open the way to something new.

Van Gennep also identified two types of rite of passage:

- rites that mark the transition of a person from one social status to another during his or her lifetime
- rites that mark some important points in the calendar (such as a new moon, a solstice, the new year).

Van Gennep regarded rites of passage as the most important thing for the normal and healthy running of society. He believed that they preserve social stability by releasing the pressure built up in individuals and giving them a new social status and new roles.

The *annaprashana* is a Hindu rite of passage which celebrates an infant's first meal, usually a bowl of *kheer* (boiled rice, milk and sugar). (Nauzer /Wikimedia Commons)

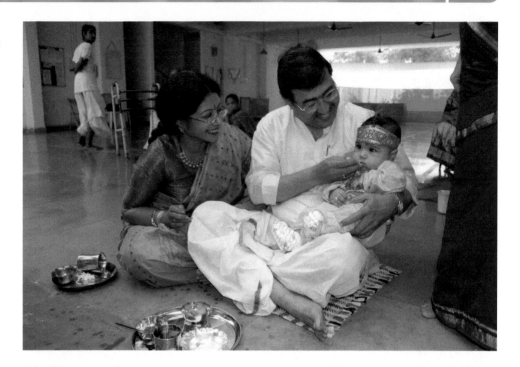

Activity

Choose two of the following rites of passage: birth, baptism, initiation, bar mitzvah, marriage, death, change of job or house, going away, coming back, anniversaries, graduation ceremonies.

Using Van Gennep's tripartite structure, explain each stage, including details about dress, food, place, people, behaviour, music, gifts, change of status, different expectations of behaviour after the ritual.

Victor Turner (1969)

Turner regarded ritual as a drama in which the participants are the actors. As a result of their actions they are transformed, and through their experiences they have the power to change society itself. Turner is concerned mainly with ritual symbols – a small number of objects which have generally shared meanings within a community.

Turner developed Van Gennep's theory further by studying rites of passage among the Ndembu people of Zambia during his fieldwork between 1950 and 1954. A main point in his findings is that the rites of passage simultaneously permit integration into society and give the participants a mystical experience of oneness with the spiritual world and the social group. According to Turner, social life is full of social dramas in transitional places.

Turner studied the liminal stage of rites of passage in great depth. Liminality shows up in some form in every society. During the liminal stage the rules and structures and normative patterns of behaviour relate to periods of heightened emotion and experience. Real or symbolic thresholds are very important components of ritual and symbolic experience. At these points the ritual subject is between fixed points of classification, in an unclear situation, structurally invisible in terms of society's categorization systems.

Liminal symbols are dense, rich and evocative and help the group to experience the liminal state in a language of shared meaning and experience. Multiple arrangements of liminal symbols produce complex meanings (**multivocality**).

According to Turner, the rules, norms, statuses and behaviours which comprise everyday life make up the structured portion of human existence. During the liminal stage he sees anti-structure, a place that all societies create to drop temporarily the normative ways of life and a place of possibilities, where people can express themselves without the usual constraints. Liminality describes a state of being outside of normal space and time. Such individuals are betwixt and between the normal roles, behaviours and positions assigned by law, custom and convention.

Liminality is revitalizing, according to Turner, and is essential because no society can function adequately without it. It is a way for societies to adapt, change and renew their fundamental qualities. Liminality is the condition of being midpoint between statuses. In liminal spaces a person can stand outside of their normal social roles and accept alternative social arrangements and values. It is a dangerous place where structure loosens its grip, as is illustrated by the many taboos surrounding these periods.

Characteristics of ritual participants in the liminal period

Initiates in the liminal stage are at once no longer classified and not yet classified. The symbols that represent them may be related to death and dying. They are very commonly secluded, partially or completely, from the rest of society. Such novices are sometimes treated, or symbolically represented, as being neither male nor female. They have nothing – no status, property, secular clothing, rank or kinship position.

Communitas

Turner argued that, during the liminal stage, a special bond is formed between initiates which he called *communitas*. Among participants, there is often complete equality. This friendship goes beyond differences of rank, age, kinship position, and even sex. All participants in the ritual are supposed to be linked by special ties that continue after the rites are over, even into old age.

> *Communitas*
> Group solidarity

Activity

What are the necessary steps to be taken when passing from one nation to another? (What do you need/need to do?)
Which part of this process involves becoming liminal (the transition phase)?
If the departure is for a long period, what rituals might occur, say with the friends and family of the person leaving/arriving?
Give an example of *communitas* during the liminal stage of rites of passage.

Case Studies of Rites of Passage

Masai Women (Chris Curling and Melissa Llewelyn-Davies, 1974)

The Maasai are pastoral nomads living in the East African rift valley: they grow no crops and are proud of being a non-agricultural people. Cattle are the all-important source of wealth and social status, and Maasai love their cattle, even composing poems to them. However, it is the men who have exclusive rights to the animals, and women are dependent, throughout their lives, on a man – father, husband or son – for rights of access to property. A woman's status as 'daughter', 'wife' or 'mother' is therefore crucial, and this film examines with depth and sensitivity the social construction of womanhood in Maasai society, concentrating upon women's attitudes to their own lives. It details a series of events in women's lives, from the circumcision ceremonies which mark their transition from girlhood to womanhood to the moment when they proudly watch their sons make the transition to elderhood in the *eunoto* (initiation) ceremony.

Masai Manhood (Chris Curling and Melissa Llewelyn-Davies, 1975)

This film was made after *Maasai Women* and in the same area. Together the two films provide a vivid view of Maasai men and women and their places in society. The Maasai have a social system which differentiates sharply between men and women and between age sets. A particularly crucial distinction is made between men who are *moran* ('warriors') and more senior men classed as elders. After circumcision men live in the forest on the fringes of Maasai society as *moran* and are barred from marriage and excluded from crucial decision-making procedures. The film focuses on the life of the *moran* and on the dramatic *eunoto* ceremony which marks the important transition from warriorhood to full social maturity and the responsibilities of elderhood. The *moran* are given an opportunity to talk about warriorhood, and they strive sensitively to explain their ideals to the anthropologist. Their words are effectively translated in subtitles. There is much valuable information in the film on the events leading up to the *eunoto* ceremony – including a fascinating sequence of a lighthearted verbal attack directed by the *moran* at their mothers – and on the ritual procedures involved in the rite of passage itself.

Tiempo de Vals (Rebecca Savage, 2006)

In Mexico, and much of Latin America, until recently the fifteenth birthday of girls has been marked by the 'Quinceañera' celebration, in which they dress in elaborate ball gowns and are made up to mark their transition from childhood to adulthood. This extravagant fiesta is a lived illusion in which the reality of daily life is shrugged aside. The *quinceañera* herself spends the day as a princess, but the party is a daydream shared by the whole community. In Tetlanohcan, a rapidly urbanizing agricultural town in Tlaxcala, Central Mexico, we are invited to join in the daydream of the Quinceañera. *Tiempo de Vals* combines observational footage of the preparations and the party itself with oral testimony from three generations of women to explore the meaning of this new tradition in the context of a globalizing economy. The scenes of fantasy and illusion are juxtaposed with images of the social and economic reality of the town. The dream is shared even by those living and working in the USA.

The birthday girl (known as the *quinceañera*) is expected to wear a formal ball gown during the celebrations, which include a Mass (if the *quinceañera* is Catholic), a dance and a formal reception. (© Prayinto / Flickr)

STOP & THINK

Give three examples of rites of passage in your own society.

'Rituals of first menstruation in Sri Lanka' (Winslow 1980)

Two-thirds of Sri Lanka's people are Buddhists while the remaining one-third consists of Hindus, Muslims and Christians. Deborah Winslow focuses on two religions in her study, Hinduism and Buddhism, though she did find huge similarities with Catholic ritual on menstruation, which was almost identical to that of Buddhism. These studies took place over three periods across the 1980s for around a year at a time, when the author observed these rituals in six villages within a 150-mile radius.

According to Winslow, almost all Sri Lankan women follow some form of first menstruation ritual. She suggests that the basic events are the same for all groups: the girl is isolated for some days, is bathed ritually, and then, with some recognition of specialness, is returned to normal life, yet with higher status, as a woman, not a girl. This process seems to be based upon two things: first, menstruation (particularly its first occurrence) marks the transition from childhood to adulthood and, second, menstruation itself is a transition in which the dirty female body is cleansed, thus becoming good enough for the men. When the first period starts, there is a physical segregation from society: the men cannot see the girl; she is hidden in a menstrual hut. Then the girl – now a woman – is made pure again; this is done through ritual bathing. Both rituals conclude with the return to normal life for the girl.

Separation

Separation from society is an important part of the menstruation ritual. It is there to protect both the woman and her community from her physical and spiritual impurities. Menstrual blood is perceived as dirty for some, dangerous or harmful for others, and a matter of shame for women. Separation happens during each menstruation to help keep the village running smoothly. As soon as signs of menstruation are clear, the female is carefully segregated from all male company, as the very sight of her is dangerous to society. She is given a separate plate, mug and mat, and there is a strong taboo against her presence at religious ceremonies. Winslow also describes this period of transition as a form of social conditioning, describing how the girl is led carefully through the details of the required behaviour of women. She must change from being at ease with men to being careful and modest.

Ritual bathing

A Sri Lankan woman's ritual bath is yet another part of her introduction to life as an adult woman in the society. The ritual bathing begins with the destruction of childhood clothing, which symbolizes the end of her childhood and beginning of adulthood. As a menstruating woman, she will not be able to bathe until her blood flow has ceased. During this time of impurity, she will also be unable to prepare food, make offerings, participate in family feasts, or go to the temple, into the kitchen, or to the well. When the period finishes, the woman pours water over herself and makes herself pure again.

STOP & THINK

How has a woman's first menstruation become ritualized in Sri Lanka?
How can this ritual be seen to be a form of social control based on the Sri Lankan social structure?

Women's Rituals (Lincoln 1991)

Bruce Lincoln's work *Emerging from the Chrysalis* shows the importance of recognizing the difference between women's and men's processes of initiation. He discusses the women's threefold scheme, which consists of enclosure, metamorphosis and emergence. Women are enclosed during initiation, often in homes with family members – mothers, sisters, and the like. The metamorphosis is that of menstruation or pregnancy or other important changes in a woman's lifetime. This is often linked with some physical change which is visible to the public, such as the wearing of elaborate jewellery or clothing. Women then emerge outside in the presence of others to conclude the initiation process, as can be seen from Winslow's study in Sri Lanka. If rituals are one way in which society can renew and reproduce itself, then disrupting rituals can become a strong way of creating change. However, for most women and disadvantaged groups, resistance may be limited and have high costs. For example, Sudanese women may insist on having their daughters circumcised even when living in Western cultures where it is illegal. This could be seen as a rational choice, in view of the loss of status within the community from which uncircumcised women would suffer. The alternative would be giving up male economic support or community membership, which may be impossible for a woman if she is to survive.

Rituals, therefore, involve the construction and categorization of persons and hierarchies. They are not neutral and often have victims. Lincoln regards Van Gennep's and Turner's models of rites of passage as essentially masculine, claiming that therefore they cannot be applied to women. According to Lincoln, most rites of passage, including male and female initiation rituals, 'transform people, replacing old roles, statuses and identities with new ones'. However, he claims that women's rituals do something more. They also involve varying degrees of **coercion** and **control** over women. Women's initiation therefore is about producing productive workers, docile, faithful wives and nurturing mothers. Society as a whole makes it difficult for women to struggle against this form of initiation.

Lincoln's Characteristics of Initiation Rituals for Men and Women

Women's initiation	Men's initiation
Emphasis on territorial passage is absent/much reduced	Associated with territorial passage
Women usually remain in or near their domestic dwelling	Men do not remain in or near their domestic dwelling
Rituals often involve dressing and decoration	Nudity is common, humbling, getting participants ready for their new status
No practical knowledge gained; married women must learn how to do such (boring!) mundane tasks as cooking and caring for children willingly	New skills or information learnt, and there are new areas of public or political life to become involved in
Women are usually initiated singly; there is no opportunity for bonding or shared initiation	Men are usually initiated together, which encourages bonding and solidarity

Activity

What does this information tell us about rituals and how they maintain cultures?

How are male and female rituals similar?

How are male and female rituals different?

The Sambia of Papua New Guinea (Herdt 1982)

The social recognition of the physical stages of becoming an adult (puberty) provides a large number of rites of passage. The initiation into adulthood can involve substantial periods of separation and/or special treatment. A modern classic of ethnography is Herdt's (1982) description of male initiation practices among the Sambia of the Papua New Guinea highlands. The first European to observe these rites, Herdt found that Sambian males must undergo a long, demanding ritual process through which to transcend feminized boyhood and achieve masculinity.

More than 1,000 different culture groups exist in the small country of Papua New Guinea. Among them is the Sambia tribe, a mountain people who live in isolated river valleys of the remote eastern highlands. They comprise around 2,000 people living over a wide region. Men hunt and both men and women work in the gardens. Women in this culture are perceived as polluting and inferior, and men should keep their distance from them. Men are in full charge of public affairs while women undertake heavy-duty gardening and engage in the polluting business of childbirth. In order for men to become adult warriors, and not to be polluted by women, they need to go through six stages of initiation.

The initiation begins at age seven with the separation of the boy from the mother. The boy will spend the rest of his young life only in the presence of men in an all-male hut. The gender separation is taken to such extremes that boys and women use different walking paths around the village. After being separated from the women, the young boy is subjected to several brutal hazing rituals. The first involves ceremonial bloodletting from the nose. This demonstrates how the men rid themselves of female pollution. The boy is held against a tree and sharp grasses and sticks are shoved up his nose until the blood starts flowing freely. Once the elders see blood, they let out a collective war cry. After the bloodletting, the boys undergo severe beatings and lashings. The purpose here is to make them into warriors (tough and aggressive fighters).

What sets the Sambia apart from other groups, according to Herdt, is the second part of the male rite of passage: semen drinking. The Sambia believe that both men and women are born with a *tingu*, a body part that allows for procreation. A woman's *tingu* is ready for reproduction when she first menstruates. A man's *tingu* is born shrivelled and dried, and the only way to fill it, and become strong and fertile, is to drink the 'man milk', or semen, of other sexually mature men. In the privacy of the forest, a boy will perform fellatio on young, usually unmarried men between the ages of thirteen and twenty-one; he is encouraged to drink the male essence as much as possible in order to become strong. At around the age of thirteen, a young man has started puberty and another stage in the ritual begins: a ritual nosebleeding takes place along with some beatings to purify him, after which he is considered a bachelor and can now provide the 'man milk' to young boys just starting down the path of manhood.

Around the age of twenty, a Sambian man is ready to marry, but before the wedding takes place the tribal elders teach him the secrets to protect himself from the impurities of women. For example, when having intercourse, a man should stuff mint leaves in his nostril and chew on bark in order to mask the smell of his wife's genitals. Moreover, when a man has sex with his wife, penetration should not be too deep, as this will only increase the chances of his becoming polluted. Finally, after intercourse, the man must go and bathe in mud in order to wash away any impurities he may have contracted from his wife. Even after marriage, a young man doesn't spend very much time with his wife but instead continues passing the time with the other men.

Herdt suggests that the primary focus of these initiation rituals is to transform boys, who are considered feminine persons polluted by women and their houses, into fierce, strong male warriors. In short, during the boys' collective initiation, ritual aggression is used to instil fear and obedience of male authorities, courage for fighting, and the avoidance of women.

> **Activity**
>
> What are the similarities and differences between the male initiation ritual of the Sambia and the female initiation ritual in Sri Lanka?

This is a photograph of the River Ganges, taken in the early morning hours in Varanasi, India. The Ganges is considered the holiest river in India and it is often called 'the river of life'. Each drop of her holy waters has the power to purify the living and liberate the dead. Cremation by her banks and immersion of the ashes in her waters gives the ultimate salvation from the cycle of births and deaths. Funeral rites and cremation in pyres are very common sights here. A ceremony in Varanasi begins with the covered corpse being carried through the streets followed by a procession of family and friends, all chanting and praying for the deceased. When it reaches one of the 'burning ghats', the body is placed on the 'eternal flames' within the ghat; these pyres are never extinguished thanks to the keepers of sacred fires. During the final stage of the immolation process, the ashes are released into the sacred Ganga River and float on their journey to heaven. (Antoine Taverneaux /Wikimedia Commons)

Death Ritual: *Ngat is Dead* (Christian Suhr Nielsen and Ton Otto, 2007)

This is an ethnographic film about how anthropological knowledge is developed through active participation in traditional exchange ceremonies on the small island of Baluan in the South Pacific. The film follows the Dutch anthropologist Ton Otto, who was adopted by a family on the island, negotiating his way through kin relations and family conflicts in order to study but also to find out which ceremonies should be carried out after the death of his adoptive father, Ngat. It deals with the dilemmas of a participating researcher, who is both social actor and anthropological observer, and gives the viewer a close look at the way Baluan people contest and negotiate their social reality: their kin relations, mortuary traditions, and also the participating anthropologists. Owing to the death of his adoptive father, Ton Otto has to take part in mortuary ceremonies whose form and content are forcefully contested by different groups of relatives. Through the ensuing negotiations, he learns how Baluan people perform and develop their traditions through the death ritual.

Activity

Using the ethnographic examples above, unpack and note what functions the rituals play in the societies.

How do the rituals mark transitions? How do they show or signify the changes metaphorically or physically?

How can rituals be seen to be an important part of maintaining social cohesion?

Define liminality and multivocality.

Most rituals demonstrate a transition, often between different statuses. Are these statuses symbolic of an overarching power relation enforced by ritual?

Globalization: Football and Rituals of Modernity

Sports represent one of the most significant rituals in a modern society. According to data compiled by KantarSport on behalf of FIFA, almost half the world tuned in at home to watch the 2010 FIFA World Cup in South Africa. Eduardo Archetti (1999) regards football as a celebration of masculinity, and the star players have status akin to religious icons. Archetti suggests that football is at once a ritual and a game and, as such, is a cultural construction that makes symbolic communication among its participants possible. The arrival in the 1900s of millions of European immigrants to Argentina, especially Buenos Aires, made possible the rapid expansion of football. According to Archetti, football is associated with the working class. But it also has an important role in expressing national identity. It bridges generation gaps when sons support the same teams as their fathers. Football can also be used to express political views. Classic confrontations between national teams such as England and Germany always produce national pride, and sometimes conflict, between the opposing fans. Football is a global phenomenon. Chelsea Football Club is virtually the home team for many Asians and has 135 million fans around the world. According to Christian Bromberger (1995), modern football contains all of the characteristics of ritual. Stadiums are special places where fans follow their team. Players and fans wear the same colours to identify with their club. The games are ritualized through rules which are observed by all of the teams. All of the supporters sing and chant during the game in support of their team. The sections of the stadium are divided among different supporters, who are very loyal and provide emotional support during the match.

CONCLUSION

Rituals are complex cultural practices. Ritual behaviour is a mechanism of non-verbal communication and meaning, which are fundamental to human cultures. Rituals have many functions, both for an individual and for cultures or societies. They have the potential to transform people and situations. The purposes of rituals are formed out of tradition, history and myth. Anthropologists' studies of ritual can provide a key to an understanding and interpretation of culture.

END OF CHAPTER ASSESSMETNT

Examine some of the ways in which rituals are used in different cultures.

Teacher's guidance

Give a definition of ritual, list its main characteristics, and explain its functions, drawing on anthropological theories. Include key concepts and definitions of rites of passage (Van Gennep's three stages of separation, liminality and reintegration). Provide a range of cross-cultural examples and use theoretical knowledge and understanding.

KEY TERMS

Age set A group of individuals of a similar age, often sharing special social links with one another
Communitas Group solidarity
Liminal Relating to a transitional stage between states or categories
Rites of passage A series of rites that mark the transformation from one stage of life, season or event to another
Ritual Behaviour prescribed by society in which individuals have little choice about their actions, sometimes having reference to beliefs in mystical powers or beings
Sacred Pertaining to or connected with religious or spiritual matters
Secular Relating to worldly matters.

Personal investigation: rituals

Find a ritual occasion to attend, one with which you are unfamiliar. You may need to attend an occasion more than once. Possibilities include:

● religious ceremonies (in a church, synagogue, mosque or temple) – services, worship or other activities
● rites of passage, such as weddings, funerals, birthdays, bar mitzvahs, baptisms
● secular rituals, such as graduations, inaugurations, opening ceremonies, awards presentations
● festivals, holiday or special day rituals (such as Halloween)
● organizational activities that are ritualized, such as those of political parties, town halls, the courts, etc.

Having followed ethical practice, write a detailed and accurate report of everything you learnt. Describe the sequence of events, the appearance of things, any specific speeches, symbolism, the use of objects, and routines. Include the following: setting (colour, lighting, symbols), sounds, people (ethnicity, age, gender mix), behaviours (gestures, other). Explain if there is any evidence of hierarchy. What are the similarities with and differences from other types of ritual?

SUGGESTED FURTHER READINGS AND FILMS

Books

Bell, C. (2010) *Ritual Theory, Ritual Practice*. 2nd edn, Oxford University Press.
Bowie, F. (2006) *The Anthropology of Religion: An Introduction*. 2nd edn, Blackwell.
Bromberger, C. (1995) 'Football as world-view and as ritual', *French Cultural Studies* 6(3): 293–311.
Eriksen, T. H. (2010) *Small Places, Large Issues: An Introduction to Social and Cultural Anthropology*. 3rd edn, Pluto Press.
Hendry, J. (2008) *An Introduction to Social Anthropology: Sharing our Worlds*. 2nd edn, Palgrave Macmillan.
Herdt, G. H. (1982) *Rituals of Manhood: Male Initiation in Papua New Guinea*. University of California Press.
Lincoln, B. (1991) *Emerging from the Chrysalis: Rituals of Women's Initiation*. Oxford University Press.
Morris, B. (1987) *Anthropological Studies of Religion*. Cambridge University Press.
Turner, V. (1967) 'Betwixt and between: the liminal period in *rites de passage*', in Turner, *The Forest of Symbols: Aspects of Ndembu Ritual*. Cornell University Press.
Winslow, D. (1980) 'Rituals of first menstruation in Sri Lanka', *Man: The Journal of the Royal Anthropological Institute* 15(4): 603–25.

Ethnographic films

Disappearing World series: *Ongka's Big Moka: The Kawelka of Papua New Guinea* (1974), directed by Charlie Nairn, anthropologist: Andrew Strathern

Disappearing World series: *Maasai Manhood* (1975), directed by Chris Curling, anthropologist: Melissa Llewelyn-Davies.

Disappearing World series: *Maasai Women* (1974), directed by Chris Curling, anthropologist: Melissa Llewelyn-Davies.

Ngat is Dead – Studying Mortuary Traditions (2007), directed by Christian Suhr Nielsen, anthropologist: Ton Otto, Royal Anthropological Institute

Tiempo de Vals (2006), directed by Rebecca Savage, Granada Centre for Visual Anthropology series

CHAPTER NINE

GENDER

CONTENTS

CHAPTER

9 Gender

KEY ISSUES AND DEBATES

- What does it mean to be a gendered person?
- How does a person's gender influence their roles, relationships, status and behaviour?
- To what extent can biological differences between men and women account for cultural differences?
- How do various concepts of gender challenge Western binary interpretations?
- What is the impact of technology on sex, gender and sexuality?

Gender
The socially constructed idea about what it means to be a man or a woman in a specific time and place

According to the feminist Simone de Beauvoir ([1952] 1989) 'one is not born a woman, but becomes one'. The same can be said of men. This chapter explores the process of becoming a gendered person, as well as what it means to be one. **Gender** is arguably the most universal and significant marker of identity and should therefore be of central importance to anthropologists.

Gender, as we are now aware, refers to **culturally constructed** ideas about what it means to be a man or a woman in a specific place or time. There are a number of processes involved in reinforcing ideas about gender identity, including **socialization**, **rituals** and **rites of passage**. One question which interests many anthropologists (particularly **feminists**) is why **patriarchy** (male-dominated society) appears to be almost universal. Furthermore, to what extent do biological differences between men and women shape the roles they play? **Alternative gender identities** will also be discussed in this chapter; becoming a gendered person does not necessarily mean becoming a man or a woman as inscribed in dominant Western ideas.

STOP & THINK

Do men always have more power than women? If so, why?
How might women uphold practices that oppress women? Can you think of any examples?
How might men and women's different biological make-up lead to gender differences?
Can you think of any examples of alternative gender categories?

GENDER AND BIOLOGY

This section explores the extent to which cultural differences between men and women are based on biological differences. There are three types of biological difference between males and females: the outwardly visible variations, such as genitals, breasts and body shape; differences in internal organs; and genetic and chromosomal differences. Some of these differences between men and women are shaped throughout life, depending on the diet, environment, socialization, personal preferences and life experiences of the individual.

Sexual Dimorphism

As discussed in chapter 1, evidence suggests that sexual dimorphism (the differences between men and women in size, shape and behaviour following puberty) became pronounced around 3 million years ago, when there were around four species of hominids. *Australopithecus afarensis* males, for example, were significantly larger than females. It is now thought that *Homo erectus* and *Homo neanderthalensis* demonstrated greater sexual dimorphism than any other hominid at the time.

It has been suggested that superior physical strength makes men more effective in hunting and fighting. However, there is evidence which indicates that, in hunter-gatherer societies, women also hunt small animals, even though they are often classified as gatherers by anthropologists. For example, Colin Turnbull ([1961] 1987) points out how Mbuti women help men to hunt animals using nets. There is some doubt over the significance of sexual dimorphism today. For example, in many societies, women are as strong as men and perform the same physically demanding tasks. Interestingly, David

Women carrying grass to feed water buffalos, Netala Uttar Kannand, India (© Karmen Mur)

Frayer and Milford Wolpoff (1985) argue that, as their roles have become more similar, men and women have become increasingly similar in size throughout evolution.

REPRODUCTIVE ORGANS

Only females can become pregnant and give birth. Men's contribution to the process of reproduction is limited; a teaspoonful of sperm is where biological fatherhood finishes. Men can have many children with different women and can reproduce until old age, while women have a limited number of eggs that are released throughout their reproductive years, from their first period until the menopause. It is notable that women can live far beyond their fertile years. As seen in chapter 1, the significance of having non-reproductive women in a society is great and is partly what defines human beings as distinctive. This highlights that non-reproductive women have an important cultural role in society. Despite the fact that women do not always have children, their biology still shapes the roles that they play. It is clear that the roles of both father and mother are both culturally constructed.

BIOLOGY AND LIFE CHANCES

The degree to which human biology shapes life chances and opportunities is very controversial: some feminists, for example, argue that women's reproductive capacity places them in a disadvantaged position in society. Others, however, claim that biology does not determine a person's life chances.

STOP & THINK

To what extent have biological differences influenced the cultural construction of ideas about men and women?

Activity

Answer the following questions individually, thinking about the construction of gender in your own culture.

How do you learn to behave like a girl or boy in your society?

What are considered to be desirable characteristics of men and women? Why is this?

How does gender identity change throughout the life cycle?

Are rituals different for men and women? If so, how?

Are tasks divided equally between men and women at home?

What type of jobs do men and women do for a living?

Do men and women spend their leisure time in the same way? Give reasons.

Do men or women have more authority, rights and privileges (for example, at home, at work, in public places, in terms of laws and policies)?

Do men and women have the same access to important resources and do they control what they earn?

What are the different expectations of men and women in terms of sexual behaviour?

How have gender roles changed over the past forty years in Western society?

Is equality between men and women a) desirable and b) possible?

Using your answers, write a summary of the impact of gender on different areas of life.

Geisha in Kyoto, Japan: a geisha is a traditional entertainer who dances, sings and chats to high-paying guests, usually men. They are trained in various traditional Japanese arts, such as dance and music, as well as in the art of communication. Their role is to make guests feel at ease with conversation, drinking games and dance performances. In Kyoto, young girls start training to become geisha at the age of fifteen. After an introductory training and examination, the talented and determined will go on to become geisha. (© Tomislav Marić)

FEMINISM IN ANTHROPOLOGY

Women in Anthropology

Feminists argue that the representation of women in some ethnographic accounts has been problematic (Moore 1988). Even where studies were made by other women, their training in ethnographic research had often been carried out by men, and this led them to overlook important aspects of women's experiences.

Margaret Mead ([1949] 2001) played an important role in questioning traditional anthropological understandings of gender. Her work in a range of societies helped break down prejudices based on concepts of what is 'natural' to women and men into an understanding of the importance of culture in people's development. Authors from outside anthropology also influenced feminist anthropology. Simone de Beauvoir ([1952] 1989), a French feminist existentialist philosopher, argued that women are all too often defined by men. She explained that men had made women the 'other' in society by putting a false air of mystery around them, and she claimed that men use this as an excuse not to understand or help them.

More recently, the post-structuralist philosopher Judith Butler (1990) challenged the distinction between sex and gender and claimed that both gender and sex are performative. This means that gender is expressed through action – in other words, your behaviour creates your gender. Butler suggests that, because of this, sex and gender have the potential to be altered and re-created. These ideas have given anthropologists much to consider in their own approach to theorizing and researching gender.

Critical Feminist Anthropology in the 1970s

The main criticism of existing work on gender was that it reflected a male bias – that of male anthropologists who bring their own assumptions and expectations about the relationships between men and women into their ethnographic research and writings. Ardener (1975) suggests that men and women have different ways of seeing the world around them (which he called different world-views) and that the answer to this problem is not to 'add women in' to existing anthropological models but to develop new ways of accessing women's distinctive life experiences ethnographically.

GENDER, SEX AND CULTURE

In 1974 the feminist Sherry Ortner asked the controversial question 'Is female to male as nature is to culture?' She asserts that we find women subordinated to men in every known society and suggests a cultural reason for this, arguing that all societies make a distinction between 'nature' and the operation of 'culture' (human consciousness and its products) upon nature. Every culture asserts itself to be not only distinct from but also superior to nature, through its ability to transform 'nature' into 'culture' (through tools and technology, as well as through being able to 'think' nature via symbolism, etc.). Ortner maintains that women's physiology gives them a bad start in the gender superiority stakes – women menstruate, give birth and lactate – all very 'natural' processes. Females are also assigned tasks and social roles that involve mediating the basic conversions of 'nature to 'culture', such as through the early socialization of babies into becoming infants and through cooking – the transformation of raw ('natural') into the ('cultural') cooked. These activities place them somehow 'in between' 'nature' (inferior) and 'culture' (superior). Meanwhile, men are free get on with the more creative and serious aspects of maintaining and developing 'culture' – from initiating youths into manhood and leading rituals to laying down the principles of haute cuisine (i.e., not just cooking!). This difference, between men and women, and the position of women 'in between' nature and culture, has left men feeling entitled to a position of superiority and control over women. Ortner's article caused a stir: much of the criticism and debate among anthropologists and the questions it raised are still relevant today. Ortner later challenged her own ideas, suggesting that her claim that male dominance was universal was perhaps overstated.

Marilyn Strathern (1988), a key feminist anthropologist, has written extensively about gender, based on her fieldwork in the UK and Papua New Guinea. She argues that there are different definitions of gender according to specific places and times. Anthropologists today acknowledge these important differences, and indeed there are now a number of branches of feminism. Among these are feminists from non-Western traditions, whose perspectives and experiences can differ from those of white European and American feminists. Specific forms of feminism in Latin America, for example, have been in existence for some time.

CRITICISMS OF FEMINIST ANTHROPOLOGY

Rosaldo (1974) is critical of the tendency of feminists to treat other contemporary cultures as if they have developed in the same ways as those in the West, even going as far as assuming that non-Western societies take a more traditional, patriarchal approach because of their lack of Western concepts of feminism.

Marilyn Strathern (1988) highlights the sometimes difficult relationship between feminism and anthropology. Feminism constantly tries to challenge the patriarchal ideology from which anthropology emerges; anthropology points out how narrow Western feminism is in its world-view.

More recently, feminist anthropologists have emphasized the differences between women as a way of understanding and researching them more effectively. There have also been attempts by anthropologists to explore men in terms of gender, and there is a greater tendency now to talk about the anthropology of gender.

> **Activity**
>
> How might the experiences of women differ from culture to culture?
> In your experience, do women somehow mediate between 'nature' and 'culture'?
> Should it be the case that only women should study women in anthropology? Give reasons.
> Is the spread of Western feminism a good thing? If so, why?

GENDER, RELATIONSHIPS AND POWER

Gender is based on difference; male is male because it is not female, and vice versa. This section explores the nature of the differences between men and women in relation to power using a range of cross-cultural examples. The differences in power between men and women may be expressed in many ways – for example, through decision-making, political roles, domestic roles, sexual relations and rituals. Agreed conventions and expectations about gender roles may not necessarily be carried out by individuals in practice. Furthermore, gender is not a fixed marker of identity; ideas about gender are subject to change.

Gendering the Body in Western Europe

In the past, ideas about gender were shaped largely by religious and doctrinal ideas which reinforced the idea of women's inferiority. The Enlightenment, a philosophical movement of the eighteenth century, challenged many of these ideas about women in Western society. It stressed human reasoning over blind faith or obedience, challenging the religious and political ideas of the time, while also encouraging 'scientific' thinking (for more detail on the Enlightenment, see chapter 1).

Historical scholarship shows how the Cartesian dualism of the seventeenth century was accompanied by the emergence of other dualisms (oppositions) which strengthened ideas about men and women being different. These ideas were reinforced through medicine, science and law. Following the Enlightenment, the importance placed upon science led people to see women's inferiority as a product of an inferior body. Women's bodies became depicted as weaker or subordinate and designed for the purpose of reproduction alone. Despite a significant shift in attitudes more recently towards equality, gender inequalities in Western Europe remain common.

This 'myth of equality' in Western societies disguises the extent to which sex and gender remain central organizing social principles. When men and women

Differences between gendered bodies in the West are reinforced by gender norms in clothing and personal style. Drag queen Conchita Wurst flaunts almost exaggerated 'feminine' traits (long, groomed hair, visible make-up and a glamorous dress) and tops all this with a beard. Her companion shows male gender norms in his clothing, hairstyle and lack of visible make-up. (Manfred Werner/Tsui / Wikimedia Commons)

compare social experiences, it becomes clear that whether we are born male or female profoundly affects the life chances, choices, opportunities, and view of the world we will have throughout life. The following section explores ethnographic evidence of the nature of gendered relationships from a range of different cultures.

GENDER, ROLES AND RELATIONSHIPS

The Chewong of Malaysia: Negotiable and Interchangeable Gender Roles (Howell 1989)

During Howell's first fieldwork in the 1980s, this traditional hunter-gatherer group was still living isolated from the outside world in the rainforest. Gender roles were organized along egalitarian principles. The Chewong recognized that men may be physically more adept at tasks requiring greater strength and that women have the biological task of childbearing and nursing. However, they ascribed no special status to any of the distinct male or female roles. Hunting carried no more prestige or value than cooking, planting, gathering or childcare. The married couple cooperated closely in their economic activities. If a woman was incapacitated, the man would do all of her chores. Likewise, women would help with hunting and went fishing with their husbands. Therefore the roles of men and women could be seen as negotiable and interchangeable.

In her later research on the Chewong, Howell found that the increasing influence of capitalism had led to changes in attitudes towards gender roles. As a result, the Chewong had also moved from the rainforest and their earlier traditional wooden huts to cement houses located outside the forest. Howell observed that buying and selling, along with a desire for material goods such as motorbikes, had become an essential part of their lives, causing inequalities within the group, as men became the main wage earners, changing the previously egalitarian principles. This suggests that capitalist ideology may foster patriarchal gender roles.

STOP & THINK

To what extent are gender roles interchangeable in your own culture?

The Mundurucŭ: Patriarchal Myths (Murphy and Murphy 1985)

Mundurucŭ society is politically dominated by men. Like men in many male-dominated societies, they tell stories of an original **matriarchal** social order where 'everything went wrong' before all was eventually transformed by a (male) mythical cultural hero. Such myths must be considered an important part of the **patriarchal ideology**: together with the emphasis put on hunting as a means of livelihood, they contribute to legitimating (justifying) male power. Although women seemed unlikely to take more power at the time of the study, the stories told are warnings that the women may rise again unless the men are vigilant.

STOP & THINK

Can you think of any similar 'myths' that are perpetuated about women in your own culture?

The San: Hunting, Men and Power (Lee 1979)

Richard Lee (1979) studied a !Kung group (one of many hunter-gathering societies in Botswana and South Africa at the time) and found that their diet was based on what could be found in the local environment. Yet there was a very clear division of labour between the men and women. Typically, food gathering was carried out by the women and children of the village. Consisting of food from the over 200 varieties of plants that grew in the region, these resources accounted for about 80 per cent of the !Kung diet. In addition, the women hunted for small game, such as lizards, snakes, the eggs of tortoises and birds, insects, and some small mammals.

Generally, the role of the men was to bring in the bigger game, and they went off for days at a time to find meat to bring back to the village. Because bringing meat into the community was highly celebrated, men acquired greater influence and power. According to Lee, men saw their society as a traditional hunting society, with little importance being placed on women's work.

In the early 1980s, diamonds were discovered in the area where the !Kung live. Government ministers told the Bushmen living there that they would have to leave because of the diamond finds. As a result, the majority of !Kung are no longer able to access their ancestral lands to hunt and gather.

STOP & THINK

Why do men get more recognition for their contribution of meat than women get for their larger contribution of food?

The Hopi: Female Power Linked to Childbearing (Schlegel 1977)

Hopi Native Americans are members of a tribe indigenous to the southwestern United States. This society is similar to many others: men hunt, and women prepare the food. However, the **ideology** of gender gives women a similar value to men. According to Schlegel (1977), this is due to the fact that women have the power to reproduce, and so the society revolves around the women and their role in sustaining and nourishing the clan. The men are seen as 'messengers to the gods' who help to raise the crops, which are given life from Mother Earth.

Birth and Death in the Sudan (Boddy 1998)

Despite progress being made in some areas, women in many societies today continue to experience oppression and societal control of their bodies and sexuality. Often this is supported and carried out by other women. Janice Boddy explores the suffering which women experience in both Canadian and Sudanese society during childbirth. In Sudan, female circumcision is common, and as a consequence women often have very difficult pregnancies, as was the case with one eighteen-year-old Sudanese bride:

> Amal was pregnant and understandably apprehensive. She had been ill with malaria, anemia, and a bladder infection. . . . From the moment she knew she was expecting, Amal wore her wedding gold to thwart capricious spirits that might seize her womb and loosen

its captive seed. Amal's body had become a protected domestic space, a figurative house wherein mingle the male and female contributions that shape and sustain human life. (Boddy 1998: 28–9)

In Sudan, maternal mortality is high and, while she successfully gave birth to a baby girl, Nura, Amal herself did not survive childbirth. Boddy suggests that medical intervention could have saved her life and highlights the distress caused to women by circumcision. Where female circumcision has occurred, a midwife is essential to cut a woman open to allow a baby to pass through the sewn genitalia, and the procedure is high risk even then. There is no such thing as a 'natural' birth. The situation Boddy describes for women is grim. Boddy compares narratives of pregnancy and birth in Sudan and Canada. On the surface these seem very different.

In Canada pregnant women can expect to survive pregnancy and to deliver a healthy child. Mortality rates for both mother and child are low and have declined as medical intervention has increased. There is evidence that it is increased nutrition and the elimination of poverty, rather than medicalization and the ready resort to Caesarean deliveries, that accounts for this trend. However, despite the fewer health risks associated with giving birth, many women feel angry, deprived of control, and turned into objects of a (male) medical gaze through the medicalization of childbirth (adapted from Bowie 2006).

Vanatinai: Gender Equality in New Guinea (Lepowsky 1994)

Maria Lepowsky, a feminist anthropologist, carried out research in Vanatinai, which is a small, remote island in the southeast of New Guinea that claims to be an egalitarian society. Lepowski maintains that, unlike other Melanesian islands, Vanatinai has no ideology of male superiority and female inferiority. While there is not perfect, total equality, it comes close. Men have no formal authority or powers of coercion over women except for physical violence, which is extremely rare.

The rules of social life stress respect for the autonomy of each adult, male or female. There are no chiefs, and there is nobody with the formal authority to tell another adult what to do. Vanatinai women participate and contribute to the economy and play a visible part in important rituals, which gives them influence over others. They have equal access to material resources, and they also practise a **matrilineal** kinship system (where inheritance is passed down through the female).

STOP & THINK

In your view, is equality between men and women possible?

The Saloio district in Portugal: Official and Unofficial Gender Roles (Riegelhaupt 1967)

In an interesting study of a Portuguese local community outside Lisbon, Joyce Riegelhaupt explores the relationship between male and female power in a society where male power is officially dominant. At the time of her fieldwork, the subordination of women was established by law, in the domestic as well as the **public sphere**. Nearly all important political offices were held by men. However, Riegelhaupt discovered that, in practice, all women were sometimes more powerful than men.

The reason for the strong position of women in this community seems to lie in the **division of labour**, which allows women a more public role than their husbands. The men carry out agricultural work, while female members of their household divide their time between housework, childcare, some agricultural work, marketing and shopping. Since the men work in the fields, only the women stay in the village during the day. They then meet in the shops, where they may exchange new information and develop important networks. They may also travel to Lisbon to sell commodities, and in this way they are able to develop social networks outside the village. The men have much less contact with one other, since they work in isolation on their separate plots.

As the women market the family's produce, they are central to the domestic finances. They are also important in politics, despite the fact they are publicly considered to have less power. As a result of their wide-ranging networks, the women frequently succeed in persuading the wives of local politicians to make them take the 'right' decisions. In other words, there is a great discrepancy between the social rules and practices in this case. The law and official ideology state that men ought to be in charge of politics and the domestic economy. In practice, the women seem to exert more power than their spouses in both respects. The Saloio example indicates that the subordination of women cannot be assumed to be a true reflection of gender relations.

STOP & THINK

Can you think of any examples in your own culture of where publicly agreed gender roles are not upheld in practice.

Aymara women in traditional dress (Aapaza14 / Wikimedia Commons)

The Bolivian Aymara: Complementary Gender Roles (Canessa 2005)

Andrew Canessa argues that gender roles among the Aymara are judged to be not patriarchal but **complementary**. This means that, although men and women do different tasks, their roles complement each other: they work together. Women are strong and carry out many heavy duties, but they remain responsible for domestic work. Men farm and hunt. In this society you are considered to be a full person only when you have a partner. This interesting example shows that gender roles can be different but more or less equal.

> **Activity**
>
> Summarize each study, showing how gender roles vary.
> To what extent are gender roles negotiable in different societies? Use examples.

Gender roles are complex, although it appears that patriarchy remains widespread. However, this assertion depends very much on how equality is understood. As we have seen in the Saloio district of Portugal, social rules do not always reflect reality, showing that both men and women have a degree of agency and that it is possible for people to negotiate their gender roles. Finally, it is worth considering that it is not certain that men and women regard power in the same ways. It is possible, for example, that men and women's priorities and aspirations may simply be different.

ALTERNATIVE GENDERS

In many societies it is a social norm to take a **binary view of gender** – that is, to regard male and female as the only possible gender patterns. In the following section we will be examining a range of alternatives to these male and female categories. There are a number of frequently found characteristics of alternative genders:

- knowledge about recruitment to the role: gender variants show an awareness and interest in the opposite sex, learning about their role, dress and status;
- special language and ritual roles: each variant group has particular roles and language as well as **cosmology**;
- transvestism: women might wear men's clothes to hunt in. Among the Mohave and the Navajo, the male variant role adopt almost all the aspects of woman's dress and behaviour;
- cross-gender occupation: interest in tools of the opposite sex – for example, cooking utensils or work tools – usually indicates gender variance. Variants are often considered as particularly skilled or capable. Female gender variants have often been known as highly esteemed hunters and warriors. These women often opted out of motherhood;
- association with spiritual power: variants may have powerful visions or dreams.

Interestingly, sexual behaviour varies enormously within gender variants. Some practise homosexuality, some are bisexual, and others have no sex at all. The sexual partners of the gender variant may not be considered gender variants themselves. For example, among the Navajo, a sexual relationship between a variant and a non-variant was

In Thailand, *kathoey* is a transgendered woman, an effeminate man or a person who identifies as a third gender. (© Fairtex from Thailand / Flickr)

acceptable but a relationship between two non-variant men or two women was considered taboo or incestuous. Sexual relationships, in this case, were a result of the variance, not a cause of it. Similarly there can be very specific ideas about who the sexual partner should be. Despite this, rules about sexual behaviour are not always upheld in practice.

Sex and Gender Diversity in the West

The contemporary Euro-American view is that there are only two sexes and two genders, and that the distinctions between male and female, man and woman, are natural, unchangeable, universal and desirable.

In the mid-1800s, Victorian culture ensured that the definition of 'normal' sexuality was confined to the attraction of opposites. Homosexuality was seen as a female soul enclosed within a male body. Although European culture focused on male gender variance, examples of female variants appeared throughout Europe, often defined by their rejection of sexuality.

> **STOP & THINK**
>
> In your own words, explain why Western cultures often have a binary view of gender.

Multiple Genders among North American Indians (Roscoe 1991)

According to Will Roscoe (1991) the history of two-spirits among indigenous American cultures dates back hundreds if not thousands of years and has been documented in over 100 North American societies. Throughout history, a person who was recognized as two-spirit was someone who identified with both male and female gender roles, and so two-spirit is essentially a third gender recognized in these cultures. Native Americans took the view that having this third gender was positive and something that could benefit their society. Interestingly, in Zuni culture, gender was not given at birth; rather, it was something you grew into around the age of three or four.

Perhaps the most famous two-spirit individual was from the Zuni tribe of New Mexico during the late 1800s. We'wha died in 1896, but not before befriending anthropologists who were able to document her story, giving us insight into the historical role of two-spirits in indigenous American culture. One of the female anthropologists who was close to her described We'wha as 'the strongest character and the most intelligent of the Zuni tribe' (Roscoe 1991: 29). We'wha's family referred to her as he or she, as it was believed that two-spirits embody characteristics of both males and females.

Two-spirits were seen as valuable members of society who made important contributions to their communities. White Europeans did not feel the same, however, and did not know where to place such individuals, since their own values meant that homosexuality was something to be repressed. To white Europeans, two-spirits were seen as 'freaks of nature, demons, deviants, perverts, sinners, and corrupters' (Roscoe 1991: 4).

By the late nineteenth and early twentieth century, this example of gender variation had begun to be incorporated into anthropological studies from a structural perspective. Such accounts were slightly less negative, regarding the role as 'institutionalized homosexuality' or as a way out for 'cowardly' or 'failed' men. More attention was gradually paid to the connection of gender variation with shamanism and spiritual powers. The homo/heterosexual dichotomy is not culturally relevant in Native American society. As with nearly all non-Western societies, sex is not central to alternative gender roles.

In the past twenty-five years there have been important shifts in perspective which have emphasized the importance of **occupation** rather than sexuality. There has also been a change in terminology – 'berdache' was often used by Europeans as a way to describe the Zuni alternative gender negatively as effeminate. However, this term is seen as offensive by the Zuni and has been rejected in favour of the widely accepted **'two-spirit'**.

> **Activity**
>
> Explain what is meant by 'two-spirit'.
> How did Europeans regard two-spirit people? Why might this be?

The Alyha: A Male Gender Variant Role among the Mohave (Devereux [1937], in Nanda 2000)

The Mohave, who lived in the southwestern desert area on the Nevada–California border, had a male role called *alyha* and a female role called *hwame*. In this society, pregnant women had dreams forecasting the anatomic sex of their children. Mothers of a future *alyha* dreamt male characteristics, but with hints of their child's gender variant status. A boy indicated that he might become an *alyha* by acting strangely at around the age of ten or eleven, before he had participated in the male puberty ceremonies.

The future *alyha* avoided masculine activities, instead imitating the domestic work of women, demanding to wear the female bark skirt instead of male clothing.

At first parents would try to dissuade a child from becoming *alyha*, but they soon became resigned and prepared for the transgendering ceremony. After this ceremony, the *alyha* assumed a female name and would resent being called by his previous, male name. He would also insist that his genitals were given female genital names. *Alyha* were considered to be highly industrious and much better housewives than young girls. It is partly for this reason that they had no problems finding husbands. In courting such 'wives', men treated *alyha* like a divorcee. Sex followed particular rules, with the *alyha* taking the female role. When an *alyha* found a husband, (s)he would begin to imitate menstruation by scratching herself between the legs with a stick until blood appeared. The *alyha* then submitted herself to female initiation as a girl would.

The *alyha* also imitated pregnancy, stuffing rags up her skirt and drinking potions to bring on constipation. After a day or two of stomach pains, she would go to a designated space and defecate in the position of childbirth. The faeces would be treated as a stillborn and buried, and the *alyha* would weep as a mother of a stillborn would. The *alyha* and the husband would then clip their hair in mourning. In general, the *alyha* were not teased, as it was felt it was not their fault for being inclined thus. Despite being so clearly female in dress and role, *alyha* were perceived as different from women. They did not take lineage names. As is the case with many alternative gender categories, the *alyha* were also considered to have special powers, for instance to cure people of illness.

Occupation was one of the main indicators of women changing to men. While their tendencies were often displayed in childhood, female variants often transgendered later in life than male variants.

> **STOP & THINK**
> How do the Mohave people see *alyhas*?

Hindu Ascetism: Hijras and Sadhin (Nanda [1989] 1999)

As with Native Americans, gender diversity among Hindu Indians is mainly connected to religious beliefs. However, gender diversity in India is set within a society that is hierarchical and patriarchal rather than one that is egalitarian.

In India, sexual variants are acknowledged, although they are often marginalized. *Hijras* are born as males and through a ritual surgical transformation become an alternative, third sex/gender category; culturally they are defined as neither man nor woman. Their traditional employment is to perform at marriages and after a child has been born, when they sing and in return receive traditional payments of money, sweets and cloth. *Hijras* are seen as different, but inferior to homosexual men and women. They have usually been rejected by their families and occupy lower caste positions.

In Hindu mythology, ritual and art, the power of the combined man–woman is a frequent and significant theme. All *hijra* households contain a shrine to the goddess that is used in daily prayer. *Hijras* also identify with Shiva, a central, sexually ambivalent figure in Hinduism. The census of India does not count *hijras* separately, so 50,000 is an estimate of their numbers. They live predominantly in the cities of the North, where they find their greatest opportunity to perform their ritual roles. *Hijras* are highly motivated and organized and participate in a special subculture that extends throughout

In Bangladesh *hijras* are legally recognized as a third gender. (USAID Bangladesh / Wikimedia Commons)

the nation, with some regional variations. They usually live in a household containing between five and twenty members with one elder as 'manager'.

Although mentioned in ancient Hindu texts, *sadhin* are not as widespread, visible or prominent as the *hijras*. Marriage and reproduction are essential to recognize someone as a social person in Hindu India; spinsters rarely exist in rural areas. The *sadhin*, however, renounce marriage and avoid wearing women's clothing, instead wearing everyday men's clothing, and keep their hair short. A girl voluntarily becomes a *sadhin*, usually making her decision around puberty. This decision is irreversible. To be a *sadhin*, a girl must be a virgin and comes to be regarded as asexual. This transition is not marked by a ritual. Women may take men's work but can also continue with women's work. On gender-segregated ceremonial occasions, adult *sadhin* may continue to sit with the men as well as smoke water pipes and cigarettes – definitely considered to be masculine behaviours.

Secular performance in contemporary Thailand and the Philippines

According to Nanda (2000), gender diversity in the Philippines and Thailand applies mainly to transgendered males, who take feminine attributes and engage in female behaviour. Sometimes known as the third sex, they are more widely known as effeminate homosexuals who are like women without being women. Both cultures have been significantly influenced by Western sex/gender dichotomies.

Concepts of gay identity have emerged in both the Philippines and Thailand, particularly in association with beauty and entertainment. In these societies, there is the view that such gender variant individuals cannot control their habits and therefore should not be ridiculed. Sexual behaviour has become central to the gender variant role in this culture since Western ideas have been introduced.

However, traditional values also prevail. In the Philippines, transformations of any kind are associated with power. In transvestite beauty contests, men remodel themselves in accordance with a highly valued, global and cosmopolitan image of glamour and style identified with the West, particularly America. The audiences include the transgendered and non-transgendered, men, women and children. This example shows how complex and dynamic the meanings of gender variants can be, particularly with the influence of Western ideas.

Intersexuality

According to Shaw and Ardener (2005), 'intersexuality' refers to a group of conditions where there is a difference between the external genitals and the internal genitals (the testes and ovaries). The older and now problematic term for this condition, hermaphroditism, came from joining the names of a Greek god and goddess, Hermes and Aphrodite. Hermes was a god of male sexuality (among other things) and Aphrodite a goddess of female sexuality, love and beauty. The term 'hermaphrodite' is now heavily criticized because it is regarded as misleading, confusing and insensitive. Intersexuality has been largely understood as a male phenomenon, partly because female-to-male surgery developed much later.

Shaw argues that the rigid male/female binary view of gender in Western society leads to intersexuality being regarded as problematic, as intersexuals are perceived to fit into neither category of male or female. In particular, ambiguous gender can be as challenging for the parents and medics as it is for those who are intersexual. Shaw also points to the medical, cultural and political pressures to classify a newborn whose sex is unclear.

Transgenderism

The transgender group of people consider that they are not limited to two genders, instead recognizing a continuum of options, from surgery to living one's life androgynously. Many trans-people lead part-time lives in both genders (Bolin 1996).

STOP & THINK

How does the idea of intersexuality challenge Western concepts of gender?
How is transgenderism different from intersexuality?

Globalization and Gender

Globalization has without doubt influenced individual and group ideas about gender in terms of roles, sexuality and power. It is also important to consider the way in which individuals respond to globalization through the creation of new or different forms of gendered identity. Below are two specific examples of the impact of globalization on gender.

'Women work, men sponge and everyone gossips' (Brennan 2004)

Despite advances towards gender equality, many women continue to face discrimination and other barriers to equal participation. Women in many regions of the world experience patriarchal ideology and violence against them in several forms. The statistics show that women are overwhelmingly represented among those living in poverty, being involved in low-paid work and informal sectors of the economy. Anthropologists have provided a number of empirical studies to try to raise awareness of the inequalities caused by the process of globalization. Denise Brennan conducted fieldwork in the Dominican Republic, focusing on marginalized women's use of the sex industry as a way of emigrating to Europe through marriages to European tourists. She shows how a globalized economy affects individuals within the sex-tourism market.

Since the 1990s, tourist towns on the coast of the Dominican Republic have been a major destination for European men seeking prostitutes. Women who are involved in sex work come from rural areas, and many are single mothers. With very few job opportunities, lack of education and no kinship support or any social network to help them, they find themselves under great financial pressure. Sex work provides them with the opportunity to survive and take care of their children.

Brennan argues that sex workers utilize their marginalized economic position to try to improve their life chances. One way in which they can do this is to marry a man from Europe and leave the island. However, the reality is that very few succeed, and the experiences of those who do are not usually successful or happy; most of them live in poverty and are continually exposed to danger.

We can see from this example how globalization can have negative effects on the lives of women in developing countries. The problems of massive economic inequalities on a global scale are exacerbated by more porous national boundaries and lead to increased migration flows, human trafficking and sex slavery.

Transgenderism and Beauty Pageants in Tonga (Besnier 2002)

Every year in Nuku'alofa, Tonga, 'men who act like women' organize the Miss Galaxy beauty pageant showcasing transgendered males, who form a small but visible minority in this society. Besnier explains that this ceremony, though superficially focused on gender, is actually an expression of identity, a response to globalization, and the Tongans' desire to retain and negotiate parts of their Tongan identity. Through the performance of an exotic ritual, these socially marginalized contestants claim to define what it means to be local. The pageant allows the participants an escape from their social exclusion and poverty and a reason to travel around the islands and reinforce what it means to be Tongan. Besnier claims that it provides for its participants and audience (many of whom are middle class and in positions of power) the opportunity to negotiate the meaning of their identity. In fact, it also reflects many of the tensions between tradition and modernity and the local and the global.

Activity

Explain some of the consequences of globalization on the construction of gender.

CONCLUSION

Recent studies have usefully pointed out that there is no single way of being male or female in any particular society. There is some debate over the degree to which individuals have control over their gendered identity; many women in particular experience structural repression. For example, we have seen how, for many women, to resist dominant models of gender can leave an individual vulnerable to persecution or marginalization. The same can be said of some male gender variants.

However, many individuals today can enjoy a considerable degree of agency, which can be used to create a gendered identity. In terms of anthropologists' understanding of gender, there has also been great progress. Increasingly, anthropologists study gender rather than just women, and recent ethnographic studies have also looked at the construction of masculinity.

END OF CHAPTER ASSESSMENT

Gender inequality is universal.' Assess this view

Teacher's guidance

Draw a table beneath this statement, with a 'yes' and a 'no' column. Decide which of the above examples provide evidence for or against equality between men and women. Take notes on the ethnographic examples above. Use Riegelhaupt and Canessa as evaluation studies.

Now you have a wide range of ethnographic evidence and data that you are able to incorporate in an essay. Make sure that your writing is discursive; remember that this is a debate and you need to present evidence for and against this view.

Begin by defining gender, stating that it is culturally constructed. Ensure that you use and explain a range of concepts. Show an awareness of changes within gender relations, the spread of Western feminism, and the shifting boundaries between men and women as a result of globalization (positive and negative effects). Point out that rules about gender are not always adhered to in reality. Consider the role of the anthropologist: is it possible for a male anthropologist to understand a female's world view? Refer to a named feminist theory in evaluating the claim that patriarchy is inevitable. In your conclusion, point to the complexity of this debate and avoid simple 'yes' or 'no' responses. Remember to mention that globalization often has a complex set of effects on gender.

KEY TERMS

Gender The socially constructed idea about what it means to be a man or a woman in a specific time and place

Gender relations The nature of relationships between men and women in terms of responsibilities, power and decision-making

Gendered identity The way we see ourselves and are seen by others in relation to culturally constructed ideas of what it means to be a man or woman

Patriarchy Male-dominated society

Personal investigation: construction of gender

Conduct a study on the construction of gender in two different cultural groups. Carry out interviews and observations on these different cultures, focusing on the following:

- How does a person become a gendered person?
- How are ideas about gender expressed?
- How is power distributed between men and women and how might roles, relationships and rituals reflect this particular construction of gender in these societies?

Consider how ideas about gender may have changed within these groups and the impact your own gender may have on your research.

SUGGESTED FURTHER READINGS AND FILMS

Books

Besnier, N. (2002) 'Transgenderism, locality and the Miss Galaxy beauty pageant in Tonga', *American Ethnologist* 29: 534–66.

Lewin, E. (ed.) (2005) *Feminist Anthropology: A Reader*. Wiley-Blackwell.

Nanda, S. ([1989] 1999) *Neither Man nor Woman: The Hijras of India*. Wadsworth.

Nanda, S. (2000) *Gender Diversity: Crosscultural Variations*. Waveland Press.

Roscoe, W., and S. O. Murray (eds) (2001) *Boy-Wives and Female Husbands: Studies of African Homosexuality*. St Martin's Press.

Simpson, A. (2005) 'Sons and fathers/boys to men in the time of AIDS: learning masculinity in Zambia', *Journal of Southern African Studies* 31(3): 569–86.

Ethnographic film

When four friends meet (2001), directed by Rahul Roy, Royal Anthropological Institute.

CHAPTER TEN

BOUNDARIES

CONTENTS

CHAPTER 10 Boundaries

KEY ISSUES AND DEBATES

This chapter considers:

- the extent to which boundaries are created or are imposed on individuals or groups by structural forces
- the extent to which boundaries between social groups lead to conflict
- the extent to which individuals negotiate boundaries; not every member of a social group accepts the socially expected boundaries
- the impact of globalization on boundaries – for example, are those between nations becoming less significant? Are other types of boundaries becoming more significant today?

> **Boundaries**
> The physical and imagined differences between groups and individuals; the furthest limit

In order to understand human diversity in any society, it is important to consider the way that humans classify and distinguish themselves from one another. The structuralist anthropologist Lévi-Strauss (1908–2009) argued that we understand the world around us through binary opposites such as man and woman, life and death. This process of **classification**, when applied to groups of people, leads to the creation of culturally constructed **boundaries**, which can exist on both a small and a large scale. The word 'boundary' is defined as 'something that marks the furthest limit'. In anthropology, boundary refers to both physical and imagined differences between individuals or groups. Imagined differences may not be physically visible but exist in the mind; such imagined boundaries can be expressed through rituals, ideas and beliefs.

As we will see later in the chapter, these boundaries have a huge array of consequences, including conflict or harmony. Boundaries exist at different levels, between individuals or social groups, as well as going beyond human realms – for example, between humans, animals and spirits. Recent advances in technology have led to the emergence of virtual entities, and these have begun to challenge the boundaries in terms of the furthest limits of being human.

STOP & THINK

Where are these boundaries?
Who are these boundaries between?
What might be the consequences of these boundaries?

BOUNDARIES AND BODIES

Small-Scale Boundaries: Personal Space

Personal space varies from culture to culture and according to individual experiences. For example, those living in densely populated places tend to have lower expectations of personal space. Residents of India or Japan tend to have smaller personal space than people in Western cultures. Personal space is also affected by a person's position in society, with richer and more powerful individuals expecting a larger personal space. In many parts of India, whole families sleep together on streets or station premises without being disturbed by other people around them.

Early morning in Pune railway station: most people value their personal space and feel uncomfortable if it is invaded. The closeness of the relationship between two people can be indicated by one permitting the other to enter their personal space. (© Karmen Mur)

Activity

Think about the boundaries around you. Carry out a small-scale study of a particular location – it could be a school, a café or an office. Consider the physical and imagined boundaries between people or groups of people.

How are boundaries expressed?

How are objects used to express these boundaries?

How do people uphold these boundaries in their behaviour?

Do people respect the boundaries or attempt to negotiate them?

BOUNDARIES OF THE BODY

In her book *Purity and Danger* (1966), Mary Douglas shows how the body can be used to express boundaries. For example, concerns over the body often reveal anxieties regarding wider social boundaries. Douglas also points out that the ways in which the body is used to express boundaries vary enormously between different societies.

One example of the ways in which the body is used to express social boundaries is through dying and death. Another example is the way in which menstruation is treated as polluting, which reflects ideas of boundaries between pure and polluted objects and people. In some societies menstruation is feared and there are complex rules and rituals associated with it.

> **Activity**
>
> What boundaries are being established and maintained in the two examples above? Why might there be concerns about both death and menstruation?

THE CASTE SYSTEM

Douglas uses the caste system to show how social boundaries are maintained through the body. She explains that excessive concerns with physical pollution and purity are linked to maintaining the differences between the various castes. Food entering the body is key to conserving the social boundaries between the various castes. A Brahmin (at the top of the caste system) should never eat food that has been touched by a member of a low caste; if he were to do so, he would consider himself polluted. This demonstrates how small-scale boundaries relate to social boundaries on a larger scale. In this case, boundary maintenance in the private sphere upholds boundary maintenance in wider society.

BOUNDARIES BETWEEN ETHNIC GROUPS

In order to grasp the significance of boundaries between ethnic groups and the effects these have on both individuals and groups, it is important to understand what ethnicity means. Every human is a member of a number of social groups. Belonging to these particular groups, whether chosen or given, can be part of a person's **ethnic identity.**

Ethnicity
The identification of a group based on a perceived shared cultural distinctiveness, expressed through language, music, values, art, literature, family life, religion, ritual, food, public life and material culture

- An ethnic group does not necessarily mean a minority; indeed, every person on the planet has an ethnic identity, and so ethnic groups can refer to a small group of people or the majority of a population.
- Ethnicity can be ascribed (given at birth) or chosen.
- People can belong to more than one ethnic group: there are no exclusive categories. For example, a person can feel Scottish and Asian at the same time.
- Ethnicity can be **situational** (change according to the situation) and **relational** (affected by who or what is around).
- Ethnicity does not necessarily have anything to do with physical appearance.

STOP & THINK
Give examples of the above points using specific ethnic groups.

Differences between ethnicities can be marked by outward signs such as choice of clothing or material culture, not just physical appearance. (© Adrian Mieras, Avebury Heart Centre)

Activity

What makes you who you are? Identify from the list below some of the factors that are important in making up your ethnic identity. Are there any factors missing? Place them in order of importance.

- Language
- Country of origin
- Cultural traditions
- Family values
- Religion

Next, consider if it is possible for one aspect of your ethnic identity to be more important in certain situations, places or times.

Is it possible that people can feel a conflict between different parts of their ethnic identity? Can you think of some examples of this?

How might differences in ethnicity lead to conflict on a larger scale?

Fredrik Barth: Ethnicity as Both Imposed and Negotiated

The concept of **ethnic identification** is a relatively recent one that appeared in anthropological work in the 1960s, particularly as a result of the work of Barth ([1969] 1998). In anthropological writings up to this point, ethnic identity was assumed to be linked simply to a person's culture. Barth showed that ethnicity is more complicated and dynamic than was originally thought.

Barth and several of his colleagues argued that differences *within* ethnic groups can be hard to detect or indeed greater than differences between groups. What is important, according to Barth, is the way that ethnicity is seen and how relationships are constructed between the groups. Therefore ethnic differences are not about fixed boundaries between people but about what differences are perceived to be important at a particular time.

Barth went on to argue that ethnicity can be simultaneously chosen and imposed (assigned to people). For example, it is very rare to be able to reject one's ethnic identity but, at the same time, a person can negotiate his or her identity depending on the situation: you cannot remove the fact that English is your first language, but you can choose to speak different languages in different situations.

Ethnicity as Situational and Relational

Situational identity
The idea that one's cultural group is a product of relations with others and depends on the social setting

Ethnicity can be a very complex concept for anthropologists to understand, as a person's ethnic group is rarely fixed and can change according to the social situation in which they find themselves. Therefore ethnicity can be **situational**.

Kathleen Hall's (2002) study of Sikh youth demonstrates this point very well. While the young Sikhs in her research are legally British, they encounter race as a barrier to becoming truly 'English'. Hall highlights the cultural dilemmas faced by this group in the different social settings through which they pass in their everyday life, such as school, the family, the arcade and nightclubs. As one Sikh youth explained, 'There's a time to act British and a time to act Indian.' This performance of identity shows how selective, fluid and negotiable ethnicity can be.

Young Sikhs, according to Hall, feel 'most Indian' in their place of worship, the *gurdwara*. Girls wear traditional dress, grow their hair long, apply little or no make-up, and never talk overtly to boys. This is mainly because the *gurdwara* has a separate seating area for men and women and is full of subtle messages about being Indian. Also, at home, Sikh youths speak Punjabi with their parents (although often not with their brothers and sisters) and are expected to 'behave Indian'.

In contrast, at school or in other Westernized cultural places, the young Sikhs feel 'less Indian' and describe themselves as acting 'more British'. Therefore ethnic identification (the process of developing and maintaining your identity) is shaped by the Sikh youths themselves. The way they dress and behave and the language they use changes according to the particular place in which they find themselves.

STOP & THINK

Can you think of a time or place where certain aspects of your ethnic identity become more or less important? Why is this the case?
What problems might this pose for an anthropologist trying to understand identity?

Activity

Explain what is meant by an 'ethnic group' and give an example.
London has a multicultural, multi-ethnic population of 8 million and claims to be one of the most ethnically diverse cities in the world. Over 300 languages are spoken by more than fifty different ethnic minority communities. According to the latest census (2011), 37 per cent of London's population were born outside the UK.
Is it possible to tell which ethnic group a person belongs to by their appearance?
What kinds of activities might people involve themselves in to express and maintain their ethnic identity?
Why might some people wish to 'play down' their ethnic origin?

Boundaries between Ethnic Groups Leading to Ethnic Conflict

This section of the chapter will explore the causes and consequences of boundaries between human social groups based on ethnic differences. In the past and present, classifying ethnic groups has been used as a powerful way of controlling, excluding or completely destroying people. In specific societies at specific points in history, and indeed today, it has been impossible for some groups to escape their ethnic identity. Prejudice and discrimination based on ethnic differences is found in almost every society in the world.

As we saw in chapter 1, race is now largely discredited as a concept, as it implies biological differences between people which have been used as a way of discriminating against particular groups. However, race continues to be important for anthropologists in understanding how and why people **racialize** differences between groups – that is, why race is culturally constructed at particular times and in particular places.

There is now widespread agreement that no single ethnic group is superior or has the right to be more dominant than any other. However, many conflicts in the twenty-first century are based on ethnic differences. Throughout history, there have been many atrocities carried in the name of ethnic differences. Some of the most recent conflicts in which ethnicity has played a part include those in the former Yugoslavia, Rwanda, Israel, India and Pakistan, Northern Ireland, Indonesia and South Africa.

It is important not to forget that ethnic struggles for recognition, power and autonomy often take a non-violent form; an example is the Quebecois independence

Since 1959, the Wagah ceremony – a unique military ritual in which the border security forces from Pakistan and India lower their flags – has been held every evening at the Wagah border post separating northern India from eastern Pakistan. Although the nightly gate-closing ceremony here may be grounded in a bloody history of partition conflict, for locals and the occasional tourist it remains a symbol of a peaceful back-and-forth between two neighbours who have fought each other in three wars. The ceremony involves elaborate choreography, and the armed soldiers on both sides of the border wear special clothing and sport facial hair. The happenings at this border post have been a barometer of India–Pakistan relations over the years. (Daniel Haupstein / Wikimedia Commons)

movement in Canada. Ethnic conflict can also take place on a small or large scale, and it is worth considering the role the individual has in negotiating, adapting and rejecting certain aspects of their ethnic identity and also which parts cannot be changed (indeed, one could expand this consideration to identity more generally). The degree of agency a person has can greatly affect their life chances.

Activity

Which of the following markers of ethnic identity can be negotiated and which are fixed?
- Nationality
- Religion
- Language
- Food preferences
- Dress
- Kinship practices

Give reasons for your answers.

KEY POINTS

- The boundaries of ethnic groups can be far from clear; boundaries can be blurred and shifting.
- In some cases, there are obvious markers of ethnic boundaries between groups, such as language or religion. More often, however, ethnic boundaries are imagined.
- Ethnic boundaries can also be expressed through nations and states (but this is not always the case).
- Ethnic differences and boundaries do not always lead to conflict; anthropologists are interested in why at particular times and in particular places the boundaries between ethnic groups leads to conflict.

We will examine two cases of ethnic conflict in more detail using ethnographic studies.

Genocide
The systematic killing of an ethnic group

Ethnic Conflict in Rwanda, 1994

Between April and June 1994, an estimated 800,000 Rwandans were killed in the space of 100 days. This deliberate attempt to eliminate the members of an ethnic category is known as **genocide**. The three ethnic groups occupying Rwanda were the Hutu majority, the Tutsi minority and the Twa (who made up only 3 per cent of the population at the time). These ethnic groups are in some ways actually very similar – they speak the same language, inhabit the same areas and follow the same traditions. There was much intermarriage between the Hutu and the Tutsi groups. So why, then, did the boundaries between them become so important and lead to such devastating violence?

Ethnic revitalization
A process of reaffirming and strengthening ethnic identity

THE CAUSES OF ETHNIC REVITALIZATION AND CONFLICT IN RWANDA

Colonialism
Exploitation by a stronger country of a weaker one; the use of the weaker country's resources to strengthen and enrich the stronger country

- **Political and economic instability** There was political unrest and economic instability in Rwanda before the genocide. When President Habyarimana's plane was shot down at the beginning of April 1994, it was the final straw. Exactly who killed the president – and with him the president of Burundi and many chief members of staff – has never been established. This lack of a clear political leader left Rwanda in a state of political and economic uncertainty.

- **Historical reasons** Tension between ethnic groups in Rwanda is nothing new. There have always been disagreements between the majority Hutus and minority Tutsis, but the animosity between them has grown substantially since the colonial period. These historical problems contributed to tension between the majority and minority ethnic groups and led to a **power asymmetry**. This meant that the Hutu majority had more power than the Tutsi or the Twa.

<aside>
Power asymmetry
An imbalance of power between a larger and a smaller group
</aside>

- **Racialization of Rwandans by colonialists** In order to strengthen their control, the Belgian and German colonists, who arrived in 1916, divided Rwanda's unified population into their three distinct groups by creating a strict system of racial classification. Both the Belgians and the Germans, influenced by racist ideas, thought that the Tutsi were a superior group because they were more 'white' looking. Because they believed that the Tutsi were natural rulers, they put only Tutsis into positions of authority and discriminated against Hutus and Twa. Identity cards were produced classifying people according to their ethnicity. For the next twenty years, the Tutsis enjoyed better jobs and educational opportunities than the Hutu and the Twa. When the colonizers gave up their power and granted Rwanda independence in 1962, the Hutus took their place, and thereafter the Tutsis were blamed for every crisis.

- **Lack of effective international intervention during the conflict** As the outside world looked in upon the situation in shock, there was little political will to stop the violence. The international community clearly had the capacity to do so, but failed to organize support and to stop the genocide.

Liisa Malkki's (1995) ethnographic research among displaced persons in Tanzania explores the ways in which political violence and exile may produce changes in the way people construct their past experiences and, as a result, reconstruct their national identity. Malkki argues that refugees occupy a **liminal** space (in other words, they are between places); as such they are very instructive for anthropologists, as they offer a unique insight into the development, reconstruction and maintenance of boundaries. Malkki concludes that, when people are forcibly removed from their homes as a result of ethnic conflict, they maintain their ethnic identity through **social memories** (for more on social memories, see chapter 7).

> **Activity**
> Explain how colonialism and the history of Rwanda contributed to the conflict there in the 1990s.

Ethnic Conflict in the Former Yugoslavia, 1992–1995

The complex and bloody conflict in this region dramatically demonstrates the ways in which ethnic identification is dynamic and changeable. While there have been outbreaks of rivalry between the ethnic groups in the region for hundreds of years, there have also been periods of peace. What is so shocking about the most recent conflict is that that the boundaries between the ethnic groups (Serbs, Croats, Montenegrins and Bosniaks) became divisive so quickly and in such a dramatic and violent way. In the decades before the war broke out, the different ethnic groups lived in the same communities and were neighbours and friends who would visit one another. The fact that different ethnic groups shared both private and public domains is significant and made

Ethnic cleansing
The planned or deliberate removal of a particular ethnic group from a specific territory

Ethnic conflict
War or conflict based on cultural groupings

During the Bosnian War the Serb nationalists, helped by neighbouring Serbia, laid siege to Sarajevo, the capital of Bosnia and Herzegovina; within a few months they occupied 70 per cent of Bosnia and expelled all non-Serbs from the territory they controlled. The siege of Sarajevo was the longest siege of a capital city in modern history, lasting from 5 April 1992 until 29 February 1996. Bosnian Serbs, whose goal was to create a new Bosnian Serb state called Republika Srpska that would include Bosnian territory, assaulted the city from the surrounding hills with a range of weapons – artillery, heavy machine guns, rocket launchers and sniper rifles – and fought government troops on the streets. They had almost complete control of the city. Thousands fled, but many people remained trapped. A deadly pattern evolved of random shelling and gun battles that caught out many who struggled to survive. More than 10,000 people were killed during the siege. (Michael Büker / Wikimedia Commons)

the violence even more difficult for those involved on all sides. It is also interesting that Serbs and Croats speak the same language. So why, then, did these ethnic boundaries become so lethally important in such a short space of time and result in the deaths of approximately 140,000 people?

Often described as Europe's deadliest encounters since the Second World War, these conflicts have become infamous for the war crimes they involved, including mass ethnic cleansing. **Ethnic cleansing** can be defined as the planned deliberate removal of a particular ethnic group from a specific territory by force or intimidation. Some of the specific methods are murder, torture, arbitrary arrest and detention, executions, rape and sexual assaults, confinement of the population in ghetto areas, forcible removal, displacement and deportation of the population, deliberate military attacks or threats of attacks on civilians and civilian areas, and destruction of property. These acts were the first in Europe since the Second World War to be formally judged genocidal in character, and many key participants were subsequently charged with war crimes.

THE CAUSES OF ETHNIC REVITALIZATION AND ETHNIC CONFLICT IN THE FORMER YUGOSLAVIA

- **History** Anthropologists attribute the extreme brutality of the war in large part to historic animosities and cultural divisions between different ethnic groups. For example, during the Second World War, Croatia became a Nazi satellite run by local fascists (right-wing nationalists) known as the Ustashe, who set up a notorious concentration camp at Jasenovac and began the systematic removal of minorities. Serbs, Muslims, Jews and Gypsies all suffered. It is also clear that the history of struggle between Christians and Muslims in the Balkans extends much further back, to the Ottoman Empire in the fourteenth century.

- **Religious conflict** Serbs are largely Orthodox Christian, while the majority of Bosnians are Muslim. Bosnian Croats, however, tend to be Roman Catholic. Despite this, according to Tone Bringa (1995), religion alone cannot explain the ethnic differences between these groups. Large numbers of the population are not religious due to the fact that they experienced sixty years of a communist system which rejected traditional organized religion.

- **Cultural, political and economic factors** The war was a product of not just religious differences but also of cultural factors, made worse by the following political and economic pressures. Until 1980 Yugoslavia had been ruled under a socialist system which bound various complex ethnic groups together as one nation. However, President Tito's death led to a series of complex and violent wars between the various ethnic groups. The loss of connection between ethnicity and national identity under Tito led to the resurgence of nationalism (where strong identification with the nation is seen as important). In basic terms, these conflicts were between Serbs on the one side and Croats and Bosnians on the other, although there was also conflict between Bosnians and Croats in Bosnia. The result of the warfare was the break-up of Yugoslavia into new nation-states.

- **Social memories** These are powerful accounts of the atrocities, past and present, that are passed down through both literature and the spoken word from generation to generation and that reflect and reinforce social boundaries. Such memories played an important role in maintaining boundaries between the ethnic groups in the former Yugoslavia in the most recent conflict. The consequence is that rival groups have long memories of both real and imagined injustices perpetrated throughout history, and each group as a result may seek revenge for past wrongs inflicted on them by one or more of the other groups. Individuals may use social memories as a way of warning against the atrocities occurring again.

- **The maintenance of ethnic segregation in the private sphere** Many were surprised at the brutality of the war, since all of the ethnic groups had lived in public harmony for a period of forty years. However, ethnic boundaries were, in fact, maintained throughout the interwar period. As mentioned earlier, cultural differences between ethnic groups in Bosnia before the war were not publicly noticeable. In public and private spaces, Croats, Serbs and Muslims shared the idea of Yugoslav socialism and an ideology of brotherhood and unity of all ethnic groups, which in some respects masked the other aspects of ethnic identity.

The key to the conflict lies in the fact that, in the **private sphere** (at home and in the family), especially in rural areas, ethnic groups maintained their boundaries. Although friendships occurred between different ethnic groups, marriage and close friendship tended to be within the same ethnic group. Through the process of **socialization** within the family, **social memories** were passed on through the generations. So, when the war started, **ethnic revitalization** occurred – that is to say, identification within each ethnic group was reignited and used in the process of **nationalism**, and the neighbours ceased to be regarded as real people with feelings, leading to the tragic events that followed.

Tone Bringa followed a Bosnian community for six years from 1988 to 1993 and continued to visit Bosnia during and after the war. Her deep immersion in Bosnian culture through participant observation allowed her to gain an insight into the ethnic conflict between the different groups, and her knowledge and expertise allowed her to play an active role in the development of new policies there. She served as an analyst for the UN in Bosnia and as a witness at the International Criminal Tribunal.

> **Nationalism**
> Identification of an ethnic identity with a state; it can include the belief that one's nation is of primary importance

> **Social memories**
> The collective retelling of past events which may shape identity in the present

---

Activity

In your own words, and using the concepts you have learnt about in this chapter, explain the meaning of the following quotation:

> The conflicts involving Serbs, Croats, Bosnian Muslims, Slovenes and Albanians were never conflicts over the right to assert one's ethnic or cultural identity, but were based on competing claims to rights such as employment, welfare and political influence. What needs to be explained is the fact that the conflicts over these resources were framed in ethnic terms rather than being seen as, say, regional, class-based, or even ideological. (Eriksen 2002)

Describe the boundaries that were drawn in the public and private sphere in the conflict in the former Yugoslavia.
How did the history of the former Yugoslavia contribute to the conflict in the early 1990s?
Summarize some of the key causes of the conflict.
Explain what ethnic revitalization means.
Write a paragraph summarizing the conflict using the following concepts:
- ethnic conflict
- ethnic revitalization
- social memories
- nationalism
- refugees
- ethnic cleansing.

Imagine you are an anthropologist giving a lecture to a group of secondary-school students on ethnicity. You need to use all of the ethnicity-related concepts from this section, but you know the students will not be able to understand them. Illustrate each concept in some student-accessible language so that it is easier to understand.

Reasons for Ethnic Conflict: Summary

As we have seen from these two case studies alone, there are many causes of ethnic conflict involving boundaries. Here is a summary of some of these causes.

Reason	*Explanation*	*Examples*
Competition for resources	Cohen (1969) argues that ethnicity must have a practical function to remain important. He claims that ethnicity can function to help people gain access to resources that are scarce.	Cohen studied the organization of the Hausa trade networks in the Yoruba city of Ibadan, Western Nigeria. The Hausa migrants succeeded in virtually dominating the cattle trade in the city by ethnic organization. Trade relationships were built through shared agreements based on ethnic groupings, thus reinforcing the Hausas' ethnic identity.
Territorial conflict	The most common form of ethnic conflict	The Canadian government decided to build a hydroelectric plant in an area where the Cree Indians carry out traditional hunting activities. The Indians protested against what they saw as an illegitimate use of force. This example highlights the fact that some groups do not have full membership of the state and as such may have fewer rights, leading among other things to conflict over territory.

Reason	Explanation	Examples
The role of the state	The government has the ability to employ violence, taxes and the law against particular ethnic groups or individuals. It also uses a chosen national language which is used in all official communications. Some governments deny linguistic minorities the right to use their language. Through policies and rhetoric, the state can favour a particular ethnic group. The government can try to encourage ethnic minorities to share the values of the wider social group. Policies such as these are known as assimilation policies. They may be non-violent but equally effective in causing an ethnic group to disappear.	Minorities can be perceived by the government as problematic. The most dramatic example of this response has been genocide and enforced displacement. The persecution of Jews and Gypsies by the Third Reich before and during the Second World War is one example. Another is ethnic cleansing in the former Yugoslavia. Segregation can be used, as in the Apartheid regime in South Africa.
Power asymmetry	An imbalance of power can exist between a larger group and a smaller group. A group becomes an ethnic minority when it is integrated (willingly or not) into a larger system. Minority–majority relationships may involve other agents – e.g., a minority group often appeals to members of the international community, such as anthropologists or NGOs, including Amnesty International.	The Yanomamö did not appear as a minority until they were labelled as one (Chagnon 1983). Indigenous people are often non-state people. Their rights and views have only recently begun to be politicized through the World Council for Indigenous Peoples.
Historical reasons	Eric Wolf (1982) claims that there were interconnections between societies from around 1400 AD. However, the intensity and range of contacts intensified after European colonialism began. Capitalism has often led to ethnic difference and conflict, and it has incorporated different ethnic groups into a ranking system within a political and economic structure.	The former Yugoslavia, where a history of violence dates back to the Ottoman Empire. Rwanda similarly has a history of violence which was exacerbated through colonial rule.
Economic exploitation (including colonialism)	It is a widely accepted view that colonialism exploited and compounded inter-ethnic relations. Colonial administrators applied the divide and conquer principle: divide ethnic groups and pit them against one another so that they focus their energies on fighting among themselves rather than overthrowing colonial governments.	Ethnic conflict appears across many parts of Africa, which was heavily influenced by colonial powers. In countries such as Nigeria, Burundi, Rwanda, Côte d'Ivoire, Ghana, Mauritania, Kenya, Tanzania, Zaire and Zimbabwe, colonial powers utilized the segmentation of ethnic groups to their advantage. 'Divide and conquer' was also the strategy employed by the Apartheid regime in South Africa.

Activity

Using the information above, undertake some research into the following cases to suggest some of the main causes for the conflicts. Using concepts and studies, write a paragraph on the causes and consequences of each one:

● the conflict between Mexico and the USA
● the conflict between Israel and Palestine
● the conflict over the status of Northern Ireland.

An estimated 4,000 to 5,000 ethnic nationalities exist in the world, but there are fewer than 200 states. This means that almost every nation-state is multi-ethnic. Much conflict today is between different ethnic groups. As we have seen, ethnic identity and boundaries arising from ethnic identification form a very complex field to research and understand. Ethnic boundaries are either created by people defining themselves or are imposed; they can remain dormant for many years and then become revitalized within a very short period of time. The consequences of such boundaries can be deadly.

Globalization: Location and Technology

It often used to be the case that markers of identification were obvious – through, for example, language, clothing, food or activities. But today, as a product of globalization, there has been a mass homogenization of world food, culture and technology. For instance, you can eat a McDonald's meal in almost every city in the world. It has therefore become increasingly difficult to deduce the ethnic identity of an individual.

Globalization has had significant impacts on ethnic conflict. In the past, ethnic conflict usually occurred in a particular region. With the increased movement of people, coupled with advances in technological forms of communication, societies are usually a mixture of different cultures, and ethnic groups are not simply located in specific geographic areas. Technological advances have also been used to create networks of terrorists that might not previously have existed to the same extent. For example, the growing tension between some Islamic fundamentalists and the Western world has resulted in a global network of individuals and groups who regard Western values and practices as a threat. Al-Qaeda's terrorist attacks on New York and Washington on 11 September 2001 resulted in the US-led invasion, first, of Afghanistan, where al-Qaeda was thought to be based, and then of Iraq. However, rather than resolving the ethnic conflict, this counter-attack fuelled the idea that the West is in opposition to the Islamic world.

The movement of large groups of people

Every war produces refugees. A **refugee** is a person who leaves their country of origin in search of protection, often in times of war, political oppression or religious persecution. There were over 2 million refugees as a result of the civil war in the former Yugoslavia, many of whom lived in camps or with relatives in Croatia. Large numbers of displaced persons also fled to Slovenia, Hungary, Austria, Germany, England and the rest of the world.

Refugees
Peoples who have been forcibly displaced

BOUNDARIES BETWEEN HUMANS AND CYBORGS

Humans have always used technology in order to shape the world around them and to create boundaries between themselves and other entities. We live in a fast-changing world where technology is developing at an increasing speed. The ability to develop and invent new technologies has not only helped humans survive, it has also helped to develop and shape human culture. Anthropologists are interested in exploring the ways in which new forms of technology have affected boundaries between humans and machines.

Cyborg
An organism that is part human and part machine; a person whose physiological functioning is aided or dependent on a mechanical or electronic device

What is a Cyborg?

A **cyborg** (cybernetic organism) is a fusion of human and machine. Humans have always developed technologies to help them survive and prosper, but in recent decades the rapid developments in human–technology interaction have exceeded anything known previously. From satellite communications to genetic engineering, high tech has affected all parts of human lives. People are changing their biological

産業技術記念館

おかげさまで 開館15周年

A trumpet-playing robot has been developed by the Japanese car manufacturer Toyota. Such robots are being developed to use tools. Able to move their artificial lips with the same finesse as humans, they demonstrate the agility of their arms, hands and fingers as they play the instrument. But the point of these humanoids is not really their musical competence: they are part of the larger Toyota Partner Robots project aimed at developing machines that can directly assist people by working in human environments. Intended applications could include care for the elderly (or general hospital/nursing home work), manufacturing, or work around the home. (© Gareth Evans)

and physical environment to such an extent that some anthropologists have even suggested that the proper object of anthropological study should be cyborgs rather than humans.

Cyborg Theory

Recently a group of anthropologists claimed that we are all cyborgs now. The American theorist Donna Haraway (1991) contends that we live in a 'cyborg culture'. Going to the gym is based on the idea of the body as a high-performance machine. For example, sports shoes are highly specialized for different activities. Running is no longer just about running. Rather, such an activity is characterized by a combination of diet, clothing, medicine, training, visualization and time-keeping. There are also 'apps' to help you run.

Cyborgs are very much a public issue. Donna Haraway is making the point that there is **no boundary** between what is artificial and what is real (cyborg theory). The cyborg encourages us to think about how we define 'the human body' and how it differs from technology. This can lead to **boundary paranoia** – what is the body and what might it turn into? The boundaries are not as stable as they once were, as can be seen in cosmetic surgery. What is 'natural'? Are we 'natural' any more? However, cyborgs can overcome or transcend traditional boundaries such as male/female, able/disabled, queer/straight. Initially Haraway, a feminist, used cyborgs as a way for women to transcend their gender. Creative possibilities and **boundary dissolution** (boundaries disappearing) may lead to potential political and social change.

Transhumanism
An international, intellectual and cultural movement supporting the use of science and technology to improve human intellectual and physical characteristics

TRANSHUMANISM

Transhumanism is an international, intellectual and cultural movement supporting the use of science and technology to improve human intellectual and physical characteristics. Those developing the technology have always striven to match the incredible sophistication of the human body. Now electronics and hi-tech materials are replacing whole limbs and organs in a fusion of machine and human. For example, a team of researchers have tried out the first bionic eye implant in the UK, allowing a blind patient see for the first time. Humans are constantly using technology in order to improve the quality of their lives and also to live longer. Anthropologists ask to what extent transhumanism challenges what it means to be human.

> **Activity**
>
> Think of ways in which humans use technology to improve or enhance themselves.
> Does transhumansim mean we are no longer human? Give reasons for your answer.

Cyborg Anthropology

A cyborg anthropologist looks at how humans and non-human objects interact with each other and how that changes culture. The best example for this is our mobile phones. We have these things in our pockets that make sounds, and we have to pick them up and respond. We have to charge them every day by plugging them into an electrical socket. And we are very dependent upon them. The idea of mobile technology and its effect on people's relationships is one of those studied by cyborg anthropologists. Another idea is that of extending into a second self online, through an avatar. So studying how people interact with one other through these engagements is another aspect of cyborg anthropology.

A traditional anthropologist visits another culture to examine what makes that culture unique, looking at how interaction occurs between different members of the society and examining ways of thinking, kinship, rituals, eating habits, social structure, and so forth. The anthropologist then writes an ethnography and presents it to their own society. Cyborg anthropology takes the theory and methodology of traditional anthropology and applies it to technology, non-human objects, and global cultural systems involving information and communication.

> **Activity**
>
> How much do you rely on your external brain (mobile phone and computers) in order to communicate with your friends?
> When was the last time you used or looked at your mobile phone?
> How often do you use it?
> Do you use your mobile as replacement for a watch or an alarm?
> Do you have a Facebook or Twitter account? How often do you use it?
> Imagine if someone took your mobile phone and computer for one week. Which would you miss the most?

AMBER CASE

Amber Case is a cyborg anthropologist who examines the way humans and technology interact. Like all anthropologists, she watches people, but her fieldwork involves observing how they participate in digital networks, analysing the various ways in which we project our personalities, communicate, work, play, share ideas and even form values. She suggests that the distance between individual and community will continue to decrease. Actions and devices will become lighter and lighter, and the 'social' will continue to become more and more mobile. Case (2010) concludes that the merging of various technologies will result in a rapidity of learning and communication never imagined before.

CYBER ETHNOGRAPHERS

Increasing numbers of anthropologists are applying anthropological research methods to virtual worlds. Denise Carter (2005) has conducted fieldwork in one particular virtual community known as Cybercity, which in June 2004 had 1,062,072 registered users. It includes many of the features of a normal city. Carter sees Cybercity not as a technological construct but as a cultural construct, mediated through experience rather than through technology. She spent three and a half years from September 1999 on her fieldwork.

Carter visited the community at least once every day. She used a predominantly Western sample and participant observation as a main research method, as well as questionnaires including open and closed questions and offline semi-structured interviews; she met four informants face-to-face. Her objective was to understand Cybercity culture and the performance and meaning of human relationships there. She asked three questions: What kinds of relationships are formed online? Do relationships formed online migrate to other social settings? How are real life and virtual life interwoven in terms of lived experiences? Carter was also interested in exploring friendship and to what extent online social relationships result in trustworthiness and authenticity.

Carter concluded that, for many people, cyberspace is just another place to meet. Interestingly, she suggests that people in Cybercity are investing as much effort in maintaining relationships in cyberspace as in other social spaces. She suggests that cyberspace results in the widening and strengthening of social networks of relationships rather than weakening them, and she found that friendship is a complex interaction between trust, intimacy, disclosure and time as deeper relationships develop. People move friendships offline. Carter discovered that relationships that begin online rarely stay there: cyberspace is becoming increasingly embedded in people's everyday lives.

The friendships developed online are very important to many inhabitants. Two-thirds of informants considered making new friends or meeting friends as their most important reason for living in Cybercity. Carter based her concept of friendship on traditional Western sociological and anthropological notions that it is chosen and voluntary, as opposed to kinship ties, which are imposed. Creating new friendships or maintaining friendships online have become daily activities for many individuals. Friends and family are now able to log into chat rooms, post blogs, or send instant messages to each other. Carter concludes that distance no longer extinguishes friendships, since friends are now able to communicate in the virtual world.

This study highlights the increasingly important role that technology has in mediating relationships and demonstrates how technology enables geographically remote individuals to transcend distance and establish or maintain relationships in ways never imagined before. In these ways, boundaries between different social actors are being broken down and reconstructed.

STOP & THINK

Who is most likely to gain access to virtual alternative identities in this culture and others? What are the implications of Carter's study for anthropologists wishing to understand boundaries and relationships?

Coming of Age in Second Life: An Anthropologist Explores the Virtually Human (Boellstorff 2008)

Millions of people around the world today spend large portions of their lives in online virtual worlds. Second Life is one of the largest of these virtual worlds. The residents of Second Life create communities, buy property and build homes, go to concerts, meet in bars, attend weddings and religious services, buy and sell virtual goods and services, find friendship, fall in love – and all of this is experienced through a computer screen.

Students taking part in a lecture in Second Life organized by the Academia Electronica-Instytut Filozofii UJ in Poland (DexEuromat / Wikimedia Commons)

Tom Boellstorff conducted more than two years of fieldwork (from June 2004 to January 2007) in Second Life, living among and observing its residents in exactly the same way anthropologists have traditionally done in order to learn about cultures and social groups in the so-called real world. His home and office in Second Life was called Ethnographia. His research was conducted as the **avatar** Tom Bukowski, and he applied the rigorous methods of anthropology to study many aspects of virtual life. Inside this virtual world he used participant observation and interviews to explore a range of issues, including gender, race, sex, money, conflict and antisocial behaviour, the construction of place and time, and identity. Boellstorff shows how virtual worlds can change ideas about identity and society.

However, there are some concerns about this virtual world. Belgian police have been 'patrolling' the virtual world of Second Life since 2007 after a user reported being raped in the game. The Brussels police who investigated this case gave a statement to the press: 'It is our intention to find out if a crime has been committed.' Following on from the recent news about prostitution and pornography on Second Life, again, thought

Avatar
A computer user's representation of himself/herself or an alter ego

needs to be given to how we understand a character being violated in a virtual world. The construction of virtual worlds seems to challenge the boundaries that usually exist between groups of people in non-digital reality.

> **STOP & THINK**
> What effect might the ability to create an alternative identity online have on people's concepts of personhood and identity?

Being a cyborg means we can negotiate our identity, and therefore it challenges traditional non-digital boundaries in many ways, such as what it means to be a person, including issues of life and death. Some anthropologists claim that boundaries between cyborgs and humans have become blurred and attempt to interpret this fast-changing interpersonal world of technology and humans.

CONCLUSION

Boundaries, both large and small scale, affect every individual's life in a number of ways. They are based on differences, and these differences can become more important at certain times than others, often according to a specific set of political, social and cultural circumstances – with devastating effect, as we have seen. Boundaries are often dynamic, and the influence of new forms of technology on the ways in which they are defined, redefined and negotiated have attracted increasing interest on the part of anthropologists.

END OF CHAPTER ASSESSMENT

'Boundaries between different ethnic groups inevitably lead to conflict.' Assess this view.

Teacher's guidance

Define the specific anthropological meaning of boundary. Explain that boundaries are situational and relational and can be both imposed and negotiated (Barth). Take two examples of ethnic conflict on a small scale and discuss them in detail, making sure that you use ethnographic sources, and then do the same with two examples of large-scale boundaries. Provide counter-evidence to show that boundaries do not necessarily lead to conflict. Conclude your argument and briefly discuss the impact of globalization on national boundaries.

KEY TERMS

Avatar A computer user's representation of himself/herself or an alter ego
Boundaries The physical and imagined differences between groups and individuals; the furthest limits
Colonialism Exploitation by a stronger country of a weaker one; the use of the weaker country's resources to strengthen and enrich the stronger country
Cultural group A group of people who share some cultural characteristics
Cyborg An organism that is part human and part machine; a person whose physiological functioning is aided or dependent on a mechanical or electronic device
Ethnic cleansing The planned or deliberate removal of a particular ethnic group from a specific territory

Ethnic conflict War or conflict based on cultural groupings

Ethnic revitalization A process of reaffirming and strengthening ethnic identity

Ethnicity The identification of a group based on a perceived shared cultural distinctiveness, expressed through language, music, values, art, literature, family life, religion, ritual, food, public life and material culture

Ethnocentrism Regarding one's own ethnicity as superior to others and/or viewing others only through one's own cultural categories; privileging one's own cultural world-view

Genocide The systematic killing of an ethnic group

Nationalism Identification of an ethnic identity with a state; it can include the belief that one's nation is of primary importance

Power asymmetry An imbalance of power between a larger and a smaller group

Racism Discrimination against an individual or group based on their perceived ethnicity and the idea that 'race' is a fixed and bounded reality

Refugees People who have been forcibly displaced

Situational identity The idea that one's cultural group is a product of relations with others and depends on the social setting

Social memories The collective retelling of past events which may shape identity in the present

Territorial conflict Conflict over land rights

Transhumanism An international, intellectual and cultural movement supporting the use of science and technology to improve human intellectual and physical characteristics

---

Personal investigation

Investigate the personal and group boundaries within a particular setting of your choice. This can be, for example, an office, a café or an educational setting. Using observational techniques, research the ways that people construct boundaries between themselves and others and explore the reasons for this. Consider both the extent to which these boundaries can be negotiated by the individual and the extent to which an individual has to accept the boundaries as given. Interview people about their perception of such boundaries if you can. Discuss how such boundaries are changing and what the functions of the existing boundaries might be.

SUGGESTED FURTHER READING AND FILMS

Books

Ashmore, R. D., L. Jussim and D. Wilder (eds) (2001) *Social Identity, Intergroup Conflict, and Conflict Reduction*. Oxford University Press.

Barth, F. ([1969] 1998) *Ethnic Groups and Boundaries: The Social Organization of Culture Difference*. Waveland Press.

Boellstorff, T. (2008) *Coming of Age in Second Life*. Princeton University Press.

Eriksen, T. H. (2002) *Ethnicity and Nationalism: Anthropological Perspectives*. Pluto Press.

Hall, K. (2002) *Lives in Translation: Sikh Youth as British Citizens*. University of Pennsylvania Press.

Malkki, L. (1995) *Purity and Exile: Violence, Memory, and National Cosmology among Hutu Refugees in Tanzania*. University of Chicago Press.

Ethnographic film

Disappearing World: *War: We are all Neighbours Now* (1993), directed by Debbie Christie, anthropologist: Tone Bringa

Website

For a range of resources and information on Cyborg Anthropology, go to http://cyborganthropology.com

CHAPTER ELEVEN

GLOBALIZATION

CONTENTS

CHAPTER
11 Globalization

KEY ISSUES AND DEBATES

- What is globalization?
- How do anthropologists study globalization?
- What are the key features or characteristics of transnational flows?
- What is the impact of globalization on different cultures?
- To what extent does globalization lead to homogenization or cultural diversity?

Globalization is a relatively new term used to describe a historical process that began with humans moving out of Africa to spread all over the world. As communication and transportation become faster and more extensive, connecting more and more people around the globe, the world seems to get smaller. It can be argued that globalization is really quite old but that global awareness is quite new; awareness of being part of an interconnected global system was basically impossible to most of the people traditionally studied by anthropologists. The key features in contemporary globalization are instantaneous communication and satellite television. As globalization makes the world smaller, cultures that were once relatively distant and insulated from one another are increasingly coming into contact. The results of these encounters are diverse and often unpredictable.

Activity

What is your connection to the rest of the world?
Look at the clothing that you are wearing today. Where was it produced? Empty your bag on the table. Where are the items in your bag produced? Where did you buy it? Who made your mobile phone? Why was it made there? What do you watch on TV or the Internet? Where are these programmes made? What is your favourite food? Where does it come from?

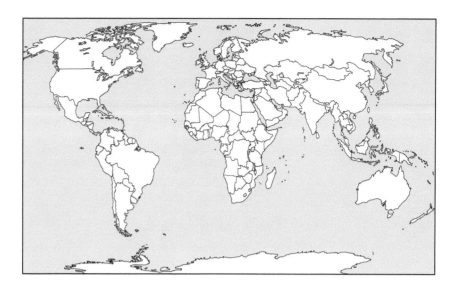

Activity

Look at the map above. How many countries can you name? How many connections can you make between yourself and other places? Have you got a friend whose family comes from Croatia? Are your jeans made in China? Do you have family or friends working abroad? Where have you travelled? Do you communicate through the social networks with people from other continents?

What are the reasons for our interconnectedness with the rest of the world? Explain your answer.

Globalization: Three Dimensions

Anthropologists recognize three dimensions of globalization – cultural, economic and demographic.

Cultural	*Economic*	*Demographic*
Changes include the spread of ideas across or between connecting societies and the spread of different cultural forms across the globe through music, film, food, clothing and other aspects of lifestyle.	Changes include the spread of capitalism around the world and the growth and strength of transnational corporations in promoting global consumerism. Globalization often refers to aspects of global economic integration, such as: • international banking, with money flowing around the world • the growing dominance of production by multinational or transnational corporations • the globalization of consumption – i.e., people all over the world buying similar products	Changes include the migration of people over national borders, leading to the complexities of cultural contact between migrants and the populations in the countries where they settle. Migration has facilitated the spread of political ideas around the world, such as the human rights movement, the global justice movement and fundamentalism.

Cultural	Economic	Demographic
	• the globalization of the world labour market, with people moving across borders to get work	
	• the existence of supranational bodies such as the World Bank and the International Monetary Fund, and economic policies being made by special summits of world leaders.	
	There are downsides to economic globalization, such as wars, increased poverty, exploited labourers and environmental pollution.	

Activity

Take a look at your evening meal. What do you see? Common foods are so much a part of daily sustenance that you would hardly suspect they originally came from another country. Most of the foods that people commonly eat today are the product of globalization.

Research the following products and explain how they are the result of globalization processes: spices, the tomato, the potato, coffee, tea, chilli, tobacco.

THE HISTORY OF GLOBALIZATION

Globalization is not a recent phenomenon. Interconnectedness between nations and cultures can be traced throughout history.

For the past 500 years, different representatives of Western civilization have occupied other continents, incorporating most non-Western people into a larger world system. The nineteenth century was an era of colonial expansion, scientific discovery and industrialization in the Global North. New technologies and innovations changed the perception of space and distance. Technological development in the two main forms of communication technology – that of transmitting messages and that transporting physical objects – continued in the twentieth century with the invention of the aeroplane, the radio, TV, satellites, and so on. All around the world, people are increasingly interconnected through economies, communication technologies, political interests and conflicts, tourism, immigration and other forces. Many people migrate between nations to study and work, which automatically affects their own countries and those to which they move. The Internet and mobile phones link people across national borders, facilitating the flow of information, ideas and messages. Twentieth-century innovations in communication and transportation have made it easier for people and things to move around the world. However, this process of globalization is an uneven one. Some people can afford to travel while others lack the means for transportation and communication. While the world is full of mobility and interconnectedness, there are still large numbers of people who are marginalized or excluded.

Globalization
The worldwide process of increasing economic, technological, political and cultural interactions, integration and interdependence of nations

Imperialism
A general term to describe the various ways in which one country may exploit and dominate another: in colonialism, one country takes over complete control of a country or region, whereas multinational companies take control of the resources of a country or exploit cheap labour in a form of economic domination

Mickey Mouse and American presidents are displayed alongside traditional Russian dolls on this stall in Latvia, highlighting the global spread of American culture. (© Ricardo Liberato / Flickr)

Origins of the Current Global System: Colonialism and Capitalism

Colonialism refers to a social system in which political conquest by one society of another leads to cultural domination with enforced social change. While some cultures embraced the colonialist trade patterns, politics and religion, many indigenous peoples rebelled and attempted to regain their cultural independence and economic autonomy. Despite their best efforts to resist the **economic imperialism** of the colonialists, indigenous peoples were often unable to fight against the Europeans and their guns, deception and disease. An example of this is the way in which Africa was colonized by Europeans. Many people believe that the worst aspect of colonialism is taking land that rightfully belongs to the indigenous inhabitants and then generally mistreating them.

Capitalism facilitates the belief that new wealth can be created through innovation and competition. By definition, capitalism is an economic system dominated by the supply and demand price mechanism called the market. Simply put, it is the idea that the world is a market and everything within it has, or should have, its price. In response to that market, and in service of it, an entire way of life grew and changed the face of Europe as well as many other regions. The new thought processes and practices were very different from the lifestyles common among indigenous peoples. Other cultures were forced into colonialism by European imperialism (acquisition of territories, or of economic or cultural power over the nations and territories, often by force). The Austrian economist Joseph Schumpeter (1928) famously characterized capitalism as a process of 'creative destruction'. While capitalism may help drive economic development, many people around the world are coming to question the impact that the worldwide expansion of the capitalist model is having on their identity. For many people, their own cultural values are too important to put a price tag on, and no destruction can be considered creative. On the other hand, globalization can also be a profoundly enriching process, opening minds to new ideas and experiences and strengthening the finest universal values of humanity. Many policy-makers have not yet considered how the protection of local or indigenous cultural values conflicts with the forces of globalization. The expansion of trade in cultural products such as food and clothing is increasing the exposure of all societies to foreign cultures and frequently brings about changes in local cultures, values and traditions. Although there is no consensus on the consequences of globalization for national cultures, many people believe that exposure to foreign cultures can undermine their own cultural identity.

Neocolonialism
The use of economic, political, cultural or other pressures to control or influence other countries, especially former dependencies

> **Activity**
>
> How has globalization changed over time?
> What is new about globalization over the last forty years?
> How has technology made a difference to the globalization of the world?
> How has the development of new media shaped the experience of globalization (for example, the Internet or the spread of Hollywood and, more recently, Bollywood)?
> Explain what imperialism is and illustrate with an example.
> Explain how transnational companies have replaced earlier forms of imperialism.

How Do Anthropologists Study Globalization?

Anthropological approaches are distinct from those of other disciplines studying globalization. They concentrate on a specific group of people and the meaning they give to what is happening in their lives and in the world around them. The global context has always been present in anthropological studies but, with the focus on in-depth studies of particular cultures and societies, it remained in the background. Over the past twenty years, the global context has become much more prominent. It is not just a question of being aware of the global dimension; rather, the global dimension has become for many a central feature of understanding the people studied. In other words, the global is not just contextual but is deeply part of people's lives. This means that, while maintaining the core methods and approaches of traditional anthropology, ethnographic studies may need to be different. The differences emerge because the 'field' is not necessarily located in one place.

Thomas Hylland Eriksen (2003) highlights some of the differences.

- Culture has become viewed as more of a process than a fixed 'thing'.
- Participant observation is supplemented by analysis of written sources, greater use of questionnaires and formal interviews, and online research.
- There is less intimate knowledge of the subjects of study because researchers are not in one locality for such a great length of time.
- There is now more multi-sited fieldwork or multi-level single-site fieldwork.

MULTI-SITED ETHNOGRAPHY

In the world of globalization there is a new trend in ethnographic research known as multi-sited ethnography – the investigation of cultures embedded in the larger structures of a globalizing world using a range of methods in various locations of time and space. Recently emerging techniques in multi-sited ethnography include more interdisciplinary approaches to fieldwork. Today the field has expanded to involve regional and national systems and the movement of people across national boundaries. Many anthropologists now follow the flow of people, information, finance and media to multiple sites. Such movement has been made possible by advances in transportation and communication. However, with so much time spent in motion, and with the need to adjust to various field sites and contexts, the richness of traditional ethnography may diminish.

Ulf Hannerz (1992) suggests that anthropologists now need to 'follow' the people, objects and goods. He says that anthropologists are now working with 'test sites of theory' where some inhabitants are creoles, cosmopolitans or cyborgs and where communities are diasporic and boundaries are more crossed than containing. Below is an example of how anthropologists study tourism as a truly global phenomenon – the movement of people and its impact on both hosts and guests.

> **Multi-sited ethnography**
> A method of data collection that follows a topic or social problem through different field sites geographically and/or socially

ANTHROPOLOGY OF TOURISM

Tourism is a great tool for exploring globalization. Think about how the remotest places have now been set up for tourists; islands in Melanesia where headhunting was common only a couple of generations ago now organize snorkelling trips for Australian visitors. There seems to be tourism everywhere – from the South African township (where the

In Thailand a Ronald McDonald statue greets customers with the *wai*, a traditional Thai greeting. (© Tin Cubacub / Flickr)

attractions are memories of Apartheid) to the Arab desert and the South American metropolis. This in itself indicates increased interconnectedness (people are able to travel much more easily than before) but also a yearning for difference. According to Valene Smith (1990), a tourist is 'a temporarily leisured person who voluntarily visits a place away from home for the purpose of experiencing a change'.

Tourism is the most important form of temporary migration in the world. It is a major global socio-economic industry and one of the driving forces of globalization. In many parts of the world it is a foundation of the economy. Tourism is now commonly seen as one of the exemplary manifestations of global flows that blur traditional territorial, social and cultural boundaries and create hybrid forms. Destinations worldwide are adapting themselves to rapidly changing global trends and markets while trying to maintain, or even increase, their local distinctiveness. This competitive struggle to obtain a piece of the tourist economy becomes a question of how 'the local' is (re)produced through the practices of 'touristified' representations. Global marketing companies and national as well as local authorities play a crucial role in manufacturing and selling images and imaginaries of destinations.

The history of tourism

Travel, for purposes such as religious pilgrimage, the seasonal movement of hunter-gatherer societies or warfare, has always been a feature of human societies. However, tourism is a particular form of travel. The origins of modern tourism might be traced to the 'Grand Tour', which started in the late sixteenth century after the 'Age of Discovery' had brought new riches to the wealthy classes of Europe. At first it was undertaken by young British aristocrats, accompanied by their tutors, to complete their education; by the nineteenth century it had spread to the upper middle classes. In the 1840s, Thomas Cook, a Methodist minister, arranged for the working classes of Northern England to visit the countryside. This became a business venture and marked the birth of tour operators and mass tourism. Tourism is also part of the 'democratization' of travel linked to ideas of personal freedom and freedom of movement. The arrival of the personal car led to tourist access to peripheral areas, especially in Europe, and enabled people to travel in couples or families rather than as part of a tour group. Tourism operates on a massive scale today and is a major global and globalized socio-economic activity. According to the United Nations World Tourism Organization, it was estimated that around a billion tourists, close to one-seventh of the world's total population, would travel abroad in 2013, while the travel and tourist industry was expected to generate about 9 per cent of total GDP and provide more than 250 million jobs worldwide.

Anthropological perspectives on tourism

Anthropologists look at tourism as a form of socio-cultural and socio-economic practice. Tourists leave their normal social settings and interact with 'natives' on their home grounds. Tourism is characterized by encounters between strangers who do not expect a long-lasting relationship and whose transactions are open to manipulation for short-term gain. As a result, the notions of 'hosts' and 'guests' are central to conceptualizing tourism (Smith 1990). This is the central social axis along which the tourist encounter takes place. Hosts and guests are culturally different, which is often the rationale for the guest's visit. Hence some tourism can be viewed as the search for the 'exotic' other. For some, tourism is even a form of amateur anthropology. Host–guest interactions are often characterized by inequalities of social class, leisure time and disposable income. But this also leaves tourists open to being exploited as sources of income – for example, by those better informed about local life, prices and services. Tourism is a form of cross-cultural communication in which misunderstanding and miscommunication may play a central role.

Tourism is contradictory. Many tourists seek authentic experiences, and contemporary tourism is a product of modernity. But the other, and the authentic, is frequently destroyed through tourism development. The tourist quest for authenticity also generates staged authenticity (the production of cultural artefacts and encounters which aim to provide the local experience of 'the other' which tourists seek). The extent to which tourists recognize this as staged or authentic – or even care either way – varies. Much tourist experience is **hybrid** and involves invented cultural productions

Tunisian folk artists perform for tourists visiting from a cruise ship. (© Magharebia / Flickr)

STOP & THINK

What is a tourist?
Are there different types of tourists?
What kind of tourist are you?
What kinds of questions might an anthropologist ask when studying tourism?
Why do people travel to other places on holiday?

(staged authenticity) that are mistaken for a 'real' way of life, past or experience which never actually existed.

Transnational Flows (Eriksen 2003)

Eriksen's concept of **transnational flows** is a useful way of understanding globalization. This term makes global processes seem less abstract and therefore more relevant for the empirical work of anthropology.

> These three dimensions of globalization – increased trade and transnational economic activity; faster and denser communication networks; increased tensions between (and within) cultural groups due to intensified mutual exposure – do not suggest that the world has been fundamentally transformed after the late 1980s, but that the driving forces of both economic, political and cultural dynamics are transnational. Whether it is ideas or substances that flow, or both, they have origins and destinations, and the flows are instigated by people. (Eriksen 2003: 4)

The globalizing processes of the late twentieth and early twenty-first century have a few significant characteristics in common. Eriksen (2007) identifies seven key features or characteristics of transnational flows: **disembedding**, **acceleration**, **standardization**, **interconnectedness**, **movement**, **mixing and vulnerability**.

Disembedding	Globalization means that distance is becoming irrelevant, relative or, at the very least, less important. Ideas, songs, books, investment, capital, labour and fashions travel faster than ever, and, even if they stay put, their location can be less important than it would have been formerly.
Acceleration	Speed is an important feature of globalization. The speed of transport and communication increased throughout the twentieth century, and this acceleration continues. It has been said that there are no delays any more in an era of instantaneous communication over mobile phones, Internet servers and television satellites. Distance no longer means separation.
Standardization	Continuing the processes of standardization begun by nationalism and national economies, globalization entails comparability and shared standards where formerly there were none. The rapid increase in the use of English as a foreign language is suggestive of this development, as is the worldwide spread of homogeneous institutions – for example, similar hotels and shopping centres, as well as the growing web of international agreements.
Interconnectedness	The networks connecting people across continents are becoming denser, faster and wider every year. Mutual dependence and transnational connections lead to a need for more international agreements and a refashioning of foreign policies, which create both fields of opportunities and constraints and forms of oppression.
Movement	Migration, business travel, international conferences and tourism have been growing steadily for decades, with various important implications for local communities, politics and economies.
Mixing	Although 'cultural crossroads' where people of different origins met are as ancient as urban life, their number, size and diversity is growing every day. Both frictions and mutual influence result. Additionally, at the level of culture, the instantaneous exchange of messages characteristic of the information era leads to more cultural mixing than ever before in human history.
Vulnerability	Globalization entails the weakening, and sometimes elimination, of boundaries. Flows of anything, from money to refugees, are intensified in this era. This means that territorial polities have difficulties protecting themselves against unwanted flows. Typical globalized risks include AIDS, transnational terrorism and climate change. None can effectively be combated by single nation-states, and it has often been pointed out that the planet as a whole lacks efficient political instruments able to deal with and govern the technology- and economy-driven processes of globalization.

Activity

According to Eriksen, what is a 'transnational flow'?

Give an example from your life for each of the main characteristics of transnational flows.

THE IMPACT OF GLOBALIZATION

Globalization, in all of its forms, brings us closer to each other, for better and for worse. Awareness of these interconnections gives a sense of both opportunities and vulnerability. The impact of globalization on all cultures around the world has long been a topic for discussion in anthropology. Anthropologists study the displacement of people as a result of globally driven economic deregulation. Many write about migration from a variety of perspectives. Others are concerned with the distribution of economic power in the global economy or the distribution of symbolic or definitional power in the global media world; some are interested in the standardization of goods and services as an outcome of the globalization of the economy, others in the spread of certain consumer preferences, and yet others in the global tourist industry, while others again study international law and human rights as a consequence of globalization.

Many of the societies that anthropologists have studied around the world are now in difficult situations. Indigenous societies have suffered as a consequence of the spread of Western culture over the last few centuries. Some of these peoples have died out, while most are in the process of rapid hybridization. This culture change is occurring today mostly in the Global South, whose countries usually provide cheap raw materials and labour (as in the example below of the Mumbai slum). Rich nations and transnational companies buy their natural resources and human labour cheaply. Small indigenous societies have not been the only ones experiencing rapid, dramatic culture shifts over the last century. People in all societies have faced rapid changes in their lives. There has been a globalization of economies so that a complex web of interdependence now ties the entire world together economically. The components of most manufactured items are produced in several countries on different continents. Fresh produce in supermarkets is often grown elsewhere. Corporations regularly outsource their technological support and other phone-based services to countries such as India. Manufacturing jobs are also progressively moving to China, Bangladesh, Sri Lanka, and other nations where labour is comparatively

Hybridization
The process by which an individual, group or people adopts cultural traits from another society; what happens to a culture when alien traits move in on a large scale and substantially replace traditional cultural patterns

One of the largest Mumbai slums, Dharavi, spreads over 525 acres (212 hectares) and is home to more than a million people. Dharavi has an active informal economy that employs the slum residents. It exports goods, among them leather, textiles and pottery products, around the world. The total annual turnover has been estimated to be more than US $500 million. (© Andreas Grosse-Halbuer, Reality Tours and Travel)

cheap. Distances no longer matter for communication and business. Economic wealth also has progressively shifted from nations to transnational corporations.

Dharavi is at the centre of small-scale industry in Mumbai. There are a wide range of activities: recycling, pottery-making, embroidery, baking, soap manufacture, leather tanning, poppadom-making, and many more. Old computers, parts and plastics come from all over the world to Dharavi to be recycled. According to various estimates, there are reportedly around 5,000 businesses and 15,000 single-room factories packed in the slum's narrow streets. It seems that all Mumbai's waste (in fact 80 per cent is recycled) arrives in Dharavi: bottle tops and aluminium for smelting in giant vats; plastic – not just bottles, but chairs and large items – is made into tiny beads and put in enormous sacks; paint tins are painstakingly stripped of labels and scrubbed; iron is put in cauldrons over a furnace and made into ingots. All of this carried out in dirty, airless rooms among toxic fumes and with no mind to health and safety.

The workers are peasant farmers from Uttar Pradesh who migrate to the slum for nine months of the year, returning home only during the monsoon season for planting. They work twelve hours a day and eat and sleep in these cells, leaving only to defecate, either in one of the disgusting public loos or in the mangrove swamps. Plastic workers earn $2 to $3 per day, the iron crushers $4. However, a $2 billion development project threatens the recycling district and part of Dharavi. The land upon which the slum is built is next to Mumbai's financial district, which makes it a prime target for redevelopment.

STOP & THINK

Using the example of Dharavi in Mumbai, how can we explain three dimensions of globalization?

GLOBALIZATION LEADING TO NEW FORMS OF CULTURAL DIVERSITY

As a result of increasing cultural contact, a number of traditional practices, whole ways of life and world-views may disappear – for example, the special fishing techniques of the Inuit have already been forgotten. It is estimated that just 10 per cent of the over 6,500 languages spoken today will survive. At the same time, globality leads to the emergence of new cultural forms – everywhere cultural traditions mix and create new practices and world-views. Ulf Hannerz (1992) uses the term 'creolization' to refer to cultural expressions which do not have historical roots but are the result of global interconnections. Across a number of academic disciplines, it is agreed that one of the most prominent and growing characteristics of the global age is cultural complexity. There have been many attempts to find new understandings of the diverse societies in which we now live. Some anthropological research and theory suggests that one way of understanding this diversity and complexity is through 'creolization' and 'hybridity' – by examining what it means to be Creole and how this informs our notions of mixed identities (Eriksen 2007).

> **Creolization**
> A complex process in which old beliefs and cultural practices survive alongside more recently acquired ones and mix with them to create new cultural forms

What is Creolization?

The term 'cultural creolization' is associated with the linguistic work carried out by Drummond (1980) and Hannerz (1992). Creolization is an analogy taken from linguistics. The term comes from a particular aspect of colonialism: the uprooting and displacement of large numbers of people in colonial plantation economies. Both in the Caribbean basin and the Indian Ocean, many groups who contributed to the slave-based economy were known as Creoles. Slaves also came from parts of West and East Africa. Creoles find it difficult to identify where their ancestors are from. Therefore, being creole means to be uprooted and to belong to a new world in contrast to a world that is old, deep and rooted. The term 'creolization' has often been applied to food, architecture, music and language. So, for instance, within creole cultures, aspects of traditional African religious beliefs continue to exist alongside Christianity, and the blending of the two has created new religious systems, such as Santeria in Brazil and Voodoo in Haiti.

Creoles as a National Symbol

Thomas Hylland Eriksen (2003) warns that, when studying creolization, anthropologists should be aware of the social inequalities that creole people experience while at the same time being used to promote national identity. He uses an example from his own study in Mauritius. In Mauritius, creole culture, the culture of the black population, has been elevated to the level of national culture. Most of the popular singers in Mauritius are Creoles. Because everything in Mauritius comes from somewhere else – there are Chinese, Indian and European influences, none of which is seen as truly Mauritian – creole music and culture is advertised by the national airline. Tourists can buy CDs with Séga music at the airport and watch Séga shows and performances at the big tourist hotels. However, Eriksen argues that, in reality, the Creoles are in a poor social and economic situation. They have been losing out in virtually every way since the economic transformation started in Mauritius in the mid-1980s, when it was turned into an industrial country almost overnight. Mauritius is such a small place that fairly minor changes can make a great difference, and so the country became industrialized very quickly. Most Creoles were hardly affected by this. They remained in the villages, which were undeveloped, often with no tap water or electricity, with no jobs or education. At the same time their culture was elevated to the level of national culture.

Examples of Creolization

Food can provide good examples of creolization. Mulligatawny soup, for example, is today served in many Indian restaurants in Britain as part of a 'traditional' or 'authentic' menu of Indian cuisine. But this mix of meats, spices and rice is in fact the product of Anglo-Indian creolization which took place during the period of British colonialism. It was invented to serve the tastes of the ruling whites but has, over the years, also been accepted as part of daily cuisine by some peoples of the Indian subcontinent.

The concept of creolization has also been applied to music. However, we should take into account that several types of music from the recent past can be referred to as a form of creolization. For instance, pop music has evolved over the years from a large number of different musical styles and genres – folk, blues, bluegrass, country, jazz, skiffle, early rock and roll, and many more. Most of these earlier styles and genres were already the products of a mixing of different cultural traditions. Blues and jazz, for example, combine Western and African musical sources. In the case of forms such as pop, blues, jazz and country, then, we can see that some forms of creolization create cultural forms which have a broad

In Hong Kong a fast-food meal can be made of a 'rice fun bowl' with Japanese *tonkatsu* (breaded pork) curry followed by a typical Western cheesecake dessert. (© Richard Allaway / Flickr)

STOP & THINK

Think of a meal or food that is hybrid or an example of creolization. Explain why you think it is so.

and popular appeal well beyond the groups from which they originate. Western pop music can now be found all over the world. Nevertheless, creolized music can continue to play an important role in the identity of some migrants while also appealing to a wider audience. Caribbean Reggae and North African Rai would be two examples of music with a wide international appeal which nevertheless continue to have deep importance for the cultural and political identities of peoples from the Caribbean and North Africa.

Activity

Conduct research on one form of music. Trace its roots and explore the types of music it is influenced by. Think about how and why this form of music emerged.

A Critique of Creolization

How may the concept of creolization be criticized? It may be applied to such a wide range of contexts that it lacks meaning. The term itself implies a response to a colonial history, yet it is currently being applied to a range of contexts that are not necessarily related to such a history. The concept does not provide any indication of the degree of influence of competing forms of hybridity – for example, one culture may dominate with a slight influence. This weakens its usefulness.

Activity

Investigate one of the following examples and explain how it is a global phenomenon: MTV, sex trafficking, McDonald's, transnational corporations, Disney theme parks, football, mobile phones.

DOES GLOBALIZATION LEAD TO HOMOGENEITY?

The McDonaldization of Society (Ritzer [1983] 2000)

McDonald's is certainly a very globalized institution, popular in over 100 countries, serving 30 million customers a day. The sociologist George Ritzer has named his **homogenization theory** after this fast food giant: the 'McDonaldization' of the world. Ritzer has argued that society is becoming increasingly 'McDonaldized', in that the principles of such a company are present in various elements of society and life. McDonaldization is characterized by efficiency, predictability, calculability and control through non-human technology. All McDonald's outlets, worldwide, share a similar look and layout. Customers are served by employees who are scripted in what they say and how they say it. There is an emphasis on numbers and quantity rather than quality – all elements of the food production are timed. Customers are even utilized in the drive for efficiency – they walk up to the counter, walk to their table and clear up after themselves. Ritzer sees these features spreading to other areas, such as theme parks, and even education. He believes that McDonaldization is leading to greater homogenization and less diversity. Overall he sees it as a threat to the customs of societie of as a whole. Perhaps, in addition to standardization, this theory also indicates the spread of the ideology of neoliberalism.

Criticism: Some of the ethnographic studies of McDonald's in East Asia or Russia suggest that the scenario of global homogenization can be questioned. Yes, some aspects of the rational, fast and standardized McDonald's system have been accepted in many societies, and the chain has effected small but influential changes in dietary patterns. But what comes out of the field research is that the meaning of McDonald's has been changed enormously by its various customers. Often the success of a global good has unexpected causes. One reason given by many people for eating at McDonald's was the clean and spacious toilets, which have since raised the general sanitary standards in East Asian restaurants.

> **Activity**
>
> Undertake research on the Kayapo of the Amazon using the Internet.
>
> To what extent do global processes alter local economies?
>
> Look at the global issues that have affected the Kayapo and other Amazonian indigenous peoples – e.g., the demand for gold, timber, land for crops such as soya, the influence of the global justice movement.
>
> Consider the effect these issues are having on the local culture – e.g., the conflict between different tribes within the Amazon.
>
> Think about the role the Kayapo have played in the global justice and environmental movement.
>
> Examine the use made of technology by the Kayapo and others in presenting their case to the world.

Globalization Case Studies

Globalization is a process that flows continuously in all directions and creates new cultural practices. The following three case studies show the varieties of impacts of globalization on people's lives at both the local and the global level.

Gangsters without Borders: An Ethnography of a Salvadoran Street Gang (Ward 2012)

Thomas Ward spent eight and half years on participant observation fieldwork in Los Angeles (see chapter 13, pp. 279–80). His is one of the rare ethnographies to explore the issues of globalization in relation to street gangs and how gang culture has spread from the streets of Los Angeles to El Salvador and other parts of Central America.

Globalization of street gang culture

According to Ward, street gang subculture was an American export to Central America. The Mara Salvatrucha street gang (MS-13), born during the bloody civil war in El Salvador, was formed in the 1980s in Los Angeles. Many of the refugee children who were illegally smuggled into the city during this period had been separated from their parents, did not speak English, and were traumatized from having seen the atrocities of warfare. To cope with this unfamiliar and sometimes hostile environment, these boys and girls formed Mara Salvatrucha, which roughly translates as 'Watch Out for Us Salvadorean Gangsters', to protect themselves from already established Los Angeles street gangs. While MS-13 started as a group for self-protection, it turned into a predatory gang involved in crime, drugs and violence and engaged in gaining territory and making money. In an effort to suppress an epidemic of gang violence, the USA began an aggressive policy of deporting undocumented gang members with felony records. When these youths returned to El Salvador, they discovered a country destroyed by war and facing a new wave of violence as the LA street gangs took root in their homeland. Many returned to a country they hardly knew. But in the chaos and desperation of post-war El Salvador, gangs found fresh ground, and their ranks increased. The MS-13 gangs are blamed for much of the violence that has plagued Central America, and particularly

Graffiti is used to mark out territory or to serve as a warning to rival gangs. MS-13 members often use gothic script for tattoos and graffiti. (Walking the Tracks / Wikimedia Commons)

El Salvador, for more than thirty years. From here the gangs spread, following the stream of immigrants northwards into neighbouring Honduras and Guatemala and into southern Mexico. Now they can also be found across thirty-three states of the USA.

Operating without borders does not mean that all of the gangs are connected and coordinated. Ward points out the cyclical nature of violence. The perceptions of those Salvadorean youths who had grown up during the civil war were distorted by the violence they had witnessed, which caused them to have a fatalistic view of the world and heavily influenced their decision to join a street gang in Los Angeles. While the creation of MS-13 in the United States was a byproduct of the civil war, the deportations of gang members resulted in a new form of violence.

> **Activity**
>
> What are the causes of the spread of the MS-13 street gangs?
> How did they become transnational gangs?

The Consequences of the Global Economy

The following ethnographic films provide examples of how economic global forces affect local communities.

Chain of Love (Marije Meerman, 2001)

Marije Meerman's study affords a comprehensive look at one of the consequences of the global economy and demonstrates how this phenomenon relates to the economic needs of each country involved. The consequence is migration, with increasing numbers of women in the Global South leaving their own children to take care of children in Europe. The demand for domestic help is increasing in the West because in so many families both parents work.

The film examines the phenomenon of women who emigrate from their home countries without their families in order to provide domestic services in other areas of the world. It explores how the economic needs of countries are tied to the economic responsibilities of the family and displays also how the global economy has succeeded in producing a long chain of care-giving, stretching around the world from wealthier individuals down to the most economically challenged.

Meerman shows that, in a world dominated by globalization, love and care have become raw materials that nations can export. The lack of time to provide care because of employment demands in the Global North is compensated by hiring care-givers from the Global South. *Chain of Love*, reveals how the demand for childcare in wealthy countries affects the lives of women from the Philippines. The need for reliable, cost-effective childcare has become very important for women who work outside the home. By using the services of a foreign domestic, families can get full-time care for four children for the price of placing one in daycare in an arrangement that allows parents both the flexibility to work outside the home and the freedom to have time to themselves while another woman cares for their children. Because tourism has decreased significantly in the Philippines since the 1980s, the domestic economy has come to rely primarily on foreign exchange. For this reason, from a governmental perspective, it is not cost-effective for whole families to emigrate, and women are encouraged to leave for the sake of the **remittances** (transfers of money by a foreign worker to his or her home country) they will send back. However, the women are reminded that the Philippines remains their true home and they should always long for the time when they can return. The government also likens this mass of emigrant women to soldiers sent by God to do battle for their country. This image of 'the soldier of God' is reinforced by the 'Women Overseas Workers' preparation classes that the women attend before they leave and the airport greetings and award ceremonies they receive upon their return.

Filipina maids enjoying a day off in Statue Square, Hong Kong (mcjerry / Wikimedia Commons)

The parental role that foreign domestic workers provide to the children of their employers has become a highly valued commodity. In effect, the women themselves are commodities and, as such, are described in generalized terms. The widely accepted view of Filipinas in the host communities is that they are hard workers and, because they are usually Catholic (and thus God-fearing), they are less likely to steal, go out drinking, or engage in other undesirable behaviour.

Government surveys show that most immigrant domestics are unmarried and travel abroad to earn money to support their parents (an image that blends well with the cultural ideal of caring for one's elders). However, independent surveys reveal that approximately 70 per cent of female immigrants are working to support their own children left behind in the Philippines. One consequence of this arrangement relates to the displacement of maternal affection from their own children to those of their employers. Meerman suggests that, as a direct result of being so far away from their own children, the domestics lavish a form of maternal love on the children or elderly of their hosts. The development of emotional bonds results in an additional benefit to the employer – the benefit of emotional labour. This is encouraged, since having a domestic as part of the family provides security to the employer. The great irony of this arrangement is that, because the domestics have to leave their children in the Philippines, they too must hire domestic help at home, thus creating 'the chain of love' referenced in the film's title. This chain connects groups of women, starting with the most privileged in the wealthiest nations and ending with the least privileged in the poorest. Here, money is used to quantify maternal love. The remittances sent home by the domestics are used to pay for their children's care and education and to provide them with opportunities they might not otherwise have. Frequently, when asked how they know their mothers love them, the children of the foreign domestics point out the items sent to them from overseas. This study shows one of the consequences of the global economy.

Calcutta Calling (André Hörmann, 2006)

Calcutta Calling shows how globalization affects the lives of people in India. 'Business Process Outsourcing' is the fastest growing industry in the world. In India, approximately 350,000 people are currently working in call centres to maintain contact between Western companies and their customers. Vikhee Uppal is one of them. From a busy office in Calcutta, he pretends to be a guy named Ethan Reed and calls Americans, Brits and Australians to try and sell them mobile phones and contracts. Vikhee hopes to make it in this sector. On the bulletin board, we see that he and his colleagues keep track of who sells the most. The Americans are the most impolite: they yell at the salespeople and hang up on them. The English, on the contrary, are the most willing to listen to their sales pitch. Even though Vikhee pretends to be a Westerner at work, Indian traditions remain very important for him. He wants to get married to a girl from Punjab, and, if he does not succeed, his family will find a bride for him. At work, he gets tutored in English. Each night he watches English soccer matches to see what the people on the other end of the line actually look like.

The City Beautiful (Rahul Roy, 2003)

Sunder Nagri (Beautiful City) is a small working-class colony on the margins of India's capital city, Delhi. Most families residing here come from a community of weavers. The last ten years have seen a gradual disintegration of the handloom tradition of this community under globalization, so the families have to reinvent themselves to eke out a living. *The City Beautiful* is a story of two families struggling to make sense of a world which keeps pushing them to the margins. In one family, Radha and Bal Krishan are at a critical point in their relationship. Bal Krishan is underemployed and constantly cheated. They are in disagreement about Radha going out to work. However, through all their ups and downs they retain the ability to laugh. In the other family, Shakuntla and Hira Lal hardly communicate. They live under one roof with their children but are locked in their own sense of personal tragedy.

Gods and Satans (Martine Journet and Gerard Nougarol, 2005)

Among the Wana people, semi-nomads from the Indonesian (Sulawesi) forest, Indo Pino is a shaman recognized by everybody. Her nephew, who is also a shaman's son, converted to Christianity some months ago and is now preaching about his visions. And, for him, if his visions come from God, the visions of the shamans inevitably must come from Satan. Through the Christian concepts of sin and original fault, notions of food and evil are revised, and the traditional healing practices of the shamans come under heavy attack. This film shows how a fight is taking place between two religious world-views.

Schooling the World: The White Man's Last Burden (Carol Black, 2010)

For the last 500 years, Christian missionaries have travelled to every corner of the world with Bibles in their hands, teaching Christianity to indigenous peoples. Today people travel around the world with computers and textbooks, teaching mathematics, science, history and English. Only 100 years ago, most Europeans and Americans of European descent truly believed that indigenous people were 'savages' and that the kindest thing they could do was to educate and civilize them away from their own cultures and assimilate them into white society. Black argues that the way people educate children lies at the heart of their culture, economy and ecology – their schools both mirror their society and reliably reproduce it into the future.

Many people believe that education is the key to solving the problem of poverty in the 'developing' world. *Schooling the World* is a documentary about the failure of institutional education to deliver on its promise as a way out of poverty in the Global North as well as in the so-called developing world. Black explores the world of education in Ladakh, in India, and compares it to the traditional ways of learning. She raises questions across a range of topics: the psychological impact of modern schooling on traditional children and families; the social consequences of disrupting the relationships between children and elders; the ecological consequences of replacing a deep relationship to the land with environmental education taught in a classroom; and the linguistic impact of the primacy of English education. Educational reformer and creativity expert Sir Ken Robinson argues that the current Western education system is based on the factory model, with children viewed in a mechanistic way as the raw materials for an industrial process. He maintains that this paradigm is outmoded and that our children need a more flexible, creative, open form of education to develop the traits they will require to meet the challenges of the twenty-first century. Black suggests with her film that standardized Western education has destroyed the connection of younger generations with their families and cultures, devalued the knowledge passed down within their cultures, and prepared children for life in an urban Western context, largely as workers and consumers.

> **Assimilation**
> The absorption of an individual or minority group of people into another society or group, achieved by learning and adopting the cultural traditions of the society in which assimilation occurs; it is also often hastened by intermarriage and by de-emphasizing cultural and or biological differences

---

Activity

Globalization can be both an opportunity and a threat. Assess this view.

Utilizing Internet research, include examples of the following propositions in your answer.

- Globalization promotes education and literacy; democracy and human rights; protection of the environment; economic development and cultural understanding.
- Globalization causes exploitative labour conditions; loss of language; ethnic and social conflict; threats to land and territory; the spread of contagious diseases.

CONCLUSION

Globalization is an inevitable phenomenon in human history that has for centuries been increasing interconnectedness between nations and societies through the exchange of goods and products, information, knowledge and culture. But, over the last few decades, the pace of this global integration has become much faster because of unprecedented advancements in technology, communications, science, transport and industry. While globalization is a vehicle for, and a consequence of, human progress, it is also a process that requires adjustment and creates significant challenges and problems. The rapid pace of change can be unsettling, and most societies want to control or manage it. Climate change, food insecurity, water scarcities, natural disasters, war, ethnic fighting and violence, terrorism, tourism, migration and population displacement are phenomena of concern that need to be addressed from a global perspective. Anthropologists examine globalization's relationship to culture, power and resistance, language and communication, social networks, socio-political movements, ecological change, livelihood strategies and more, and emphasize the need to interact with and learn from particular places and people in order to understand how global processes operate on a local level.

END OF CHAPTER ASSESSMENT

Assess the view that globalization is destroying cultural diversity.

Teacher's guidance

This assessment involves an examination of the impact of globalization on local cultures. To what extent does globalization lead to the homogenization of societies? Start by defining globalization and summarize its history. Outline the main features of globalization (Eriksen). Explore the impact of cultural colonialism on local cultures (*Schooling the World*). Discuss how globalization is a two-way flow, pointing out how it can lead to new forms of cultural practice (creolization and hybridity). Show an understanding of concepts of heterogeneity and homogenization (Ritzer, Hannerz) and explain how commoditization of the culture can lead to McDonaldization. Explain the role of anthropology in understanding globalization. Examine new ways of conducting anthropological research through multi-sited ethnography. Evaluate the impact of globalization on local communities and come to a clear conclusion about its impact on local cultures.

KEY TERMS

Assimilation The absorption of an individual or minority group of people into another society or group, achieved by learning and adopting the cultural traditions of the society in which assimilation occurs; it is also often hastened by intermarriage and by de-emphasizing cultural and or biological differences

Creolization A complex process in which old beliefs and cultural practices survive alongside more recently acquired ones and mix with them to create new cultural forms

Diffusion The movement of cultural traits and ideas from one society or ethnic group to another: while the form of a trait may be transmitted to another society, the original meaning may not be

Glonbalization The worldwide process of increasing economic, technological, political and cultural interactions, integration and interdependence of nations

Hybridization The process by which an individual, group or people adopts cultural traits from another society; what happens to a culture when alien traits move in on a large scale and substantially replace traditional cultural patterns

Large-scale society A society with cities, industry, intensive agriculture and a complex international economy

Multi-sited ethnography A method of data collection that follows a topic or social problem through different field sites

Small-scale society A society of a few dozen to several thousand people who live by foraging wild foods, herding domesticated animals, or non-intensive agriculture on the land or village level

Transnational corporation (TNC) A corporate business that has outgrown its national roots and identity and is multinational, with facilities in many countries, but has no overriding feeling of obligation or loyalty to any one of them; such companies typically move their production facilities from nation to nation in response to labour costs and tax advantages. As a result, they are generally independent and beyond the control of any one national political system. TNCs have had a major impact on previously isolated indigenous societies in the late twentieth century.

Personal investigation: the impact (or lack) of tourism in the area where you live

Your task is to observe the dynamics and impact of intercultural contact between tourists and locals in your area (in the absence of tourism you can undertake a research study from literature on a famous tourist destination). In your research, observation and interviews, focus on the following questions.

- How is culture represented in tourist settings and how is it perceived?
- How are cultural traditions changed or reinvented over time to match tourist expectations?
- How and why are ethnic stereotypes constructed and manipulated for tourism purposes?
- How do indigenous societies change as they become incorporated into a tourism market?
- How do cultural values change once they are commodified?
- How can conserving natural areas and cultural traditions for tourism lead to benefits for local communities?
- What are the power relations in the context of tourism that determine who wins and who loses in the tourist trade?
- How significant is tourism as a global industry?

SUGGESTED FURTHER READING AND FILMS

Books

Bruner, E. (2004) *Culture on Tour: Ethnographies of Travel.* University of Chicago Press.

Burns, P. (1999) *An Introduction to Tourism and Anthropology.* Routledge.

Chambers, E. (2009) *Native Tours: The Anthropology of Travel and Tourism.* 2nd edn, Waveland Press.

Eriksen, T. H. (2003) *Globalization: Studies in Anthropology.* Pluto Press.

Eriksen, T. H. (2007) *Globalization: The Key Concepts.* Berg.

Inda, J. X., and R. Rosaldo (eds) (2008) *The Anthropology of Globalization: A Reader.* 2nd edn, Blackwell.

Ward, T. W. (2012) *Gangsters without Borders: An Ethnography of a Salvadoran Street Gang.* Oxford University Press.

Ethnographic films

Chain of Love (2001), directed by Marije Meerman, Icarus films
Schooling the World: The White Man's Last Burden (2010), directed by Carol Black, Lost People Films
The following can be found in RAI film collection; see www.discoveranthropology.org.uk/home.html
Calcutta Calling (2006), directed by André Hörmann
The City Beautiful (2003), directed by Rahul Roy
Gods and Satans (2005), directed by Martine Journet and Gerard Nougarol

CHAPTER TWELVE

THE ROLE OF
MATERIAL CULTURE

CONTENTS

CHAPTER 12

The Role of Material Culture

One significant characteristic of humans is that they use material objects in a variety of ways, as tools, symbols and aesthetic objects, to express ideas, identity and belonging, and as a medium through which to express social relationships. Material objects are also key vehicles within exchange systems, where they may well carry economic value. This chapter begins by exploring what **material culture** is, including a discussion about the extent to which digital things can be considered to be material. Ethnographic examples will be used to illustrate the complex and varied ways in which material culture shapes and is shaped by individuals in a range of different contexts. The final part of the chapter examines the representation of material objects.

Material culture
The physical objects, resources and spaces that people use to define their culture

> **Activity**
>
> In small groups, try to define material culture. Discuss as a group and then research some definitions online.
>
> Think of three examples of objects in your own life which you use to communicate your own identity.
>
> Think of as many specific examples as you can of symbolic objects used to express identity in the ethnographic studies you have read or films you have watched.
>
> Consider theoretical explanations of the meanings of material objects – for example, Marxist or feminist views on the role of material culture in expressing identity.
>
> Imagine you were putting a time capsule together. Pick four objects to put into the time capsule which represent this era. Explain why you chose these objects.

The study of the material world has recently gained great prominence in anthropology, perhaps because there is a growing awareness of the ways in which objects shape social relations and help construct individual and group identities.

WHAT IS MATERIAL CULTURE?

Artefact
Any object made by a human

'Material objects'are items with a physical substance. One possible definition of material culture in this context is 'the objects through which we live our lives'. Objects that have been made are sometimes known as **artefacts**, and such objects can tell us a great deal about the lives and culture of people. Archaeologists use artefacts to understand past cultures and groups about which not much is known by other means.

Figure 12.1 Why objects are of interest to anthropologists

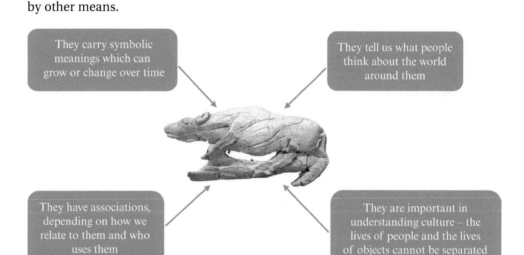

They carry symbolic meanings which can grow or change over time

They tell us what people think about the world around them

They have associations, depending on how we relate to them and who uses them

They are important in understanding culture – the lives of people and the lives of objects cannot be separated

STOP & THINK
For each caption in figure 12.1, give an example of an object that relates to that particular point.

Are Digital Objects Material?

Anthropologists have recently begun to ask if digital worlds are material. Horst and Miller (2012: 4) acknowledge the materiality of digital worlds, claiming that they are an extension of what it means to be human and therefore no more or less material than the worlds that preceded them. They suggest that there are three types of material digital culture. The first is the infrastructure. In basic terms, the digital world requires some infrastructure – computers and cables, for example. Horst and Miller suggest that those who work with such infrastructure are known as 'geeks', who are seen as antisocial, and this ensures that knowledge about the working of such technology is kept at a distance from everyday life.

The second area of material digital culture is the content. Horst and Miller point out that content is inevitably shaped by the ideas of those who design software, which shapes people's language, social lives and much more. The content can give power to some and take it from others. Disadvantaged groups may feel either more or less empowered online. Finally, Horst and Miller state that the context – in other words, space and place – is created in digital worlds. Boellstorff (2008), who carried out an ethnographical study on Second Life, claims that such digital worlds are not placeless; rather, they are a different kind of place (see earlier discussion, pp. 223–4).

STOP & THINK

In your view, are digital worlds material? Provide arguments for and against.

When Did Humans Develop a Relationship with Material Culture?

Material objects are shaped or produced by human action, though objects by nature can also play an important role in the history of human societies. For example, a tool is the product of human action. An animal horn is not, but it takes on meaning if used as a drinking cup or a decorative or ritual object. Historical texts or images – for example, a legal charter on a piece of parchment or a religious painting – are also material objects, perhaps significant symbolically. The physical existence of a religious image in a cave as a work of art provides evidence of early forms of religion.

Through part of the time that humans were evolving biologically, they were also developing cultural technologies that allowed them to become increasingly successful at acquiring food and surviving predators. These early forms of technology included tools.

Hand axes are one of the first types of flint tool made by early hominids. (Discott / Wikimedia Commons)

TOOL-MAKING

Some primates such as chimpanzees are known to use stone and wood as hammers to crack nuts and as crude ineffective weapons in hunting small animals, including monkeys. However, they rarely shape their tools in a systematic way to increase efficiency in the way that early humans did. The first clearly recognizable stone tools were made and used by early hominids, and possibly by *Australopithecus afarensis*, in East Africa about 2.5 million years ago.

In addition to stone tools, *Homo habilis* probably made simple implements out of wood and other substances that have not survived. *Homo habilis* made and used stone tools in the Oldowan tradition for nearly a million years but with gradual improvements over time. Throughout most of the geographic range of *Homo erectus* there is clear evidence of progressive improvements in tool-making: the late *Homo erectus* had more complex techniques. Inevitably, human reliance on tools increased as they became more useful. By half a million years ago, the sites which *Homo erectus* inhabited commonly reveal thousands of discarded stone tools.

Such tools provide evidence for anthropologists which is key to understanding the way humans spread to different parts of the world. One of the earliest indicators of human activity in North America, for example, was the type of spearhead known as the Clovis point. These were used to hunt large game such as mammoths, giant sloth, camels and giant bison. North America was one of the last continents in the world to be inhabited by humans, after about 15,000 BC.

During the last ice age, water, which previously flowed off the land into the sea, was frozen in vast ice sheets and glaciers, so sea levels dropped. This exposed a land bridge that enabled humans to migrate through Siberia to Alaska. These early Americans were highly adaptable, and Clovis spear points have been found throughout the continent. Material objects from our past therefore provide important clues about evolution, not just in terms of the kinds of skills possessed by early humans but also in providing evidence of patterns of human migration and settlement.

It is interesting to note that important new technologies and material objects were often developed for non-utilitarian purposes (Brumfiel and Fox 2003) and only later became used for utilitarian ones. For example, clay firing was used originally to make clay figurines, not ceramic vessels. It was copper bells that were made first in Mesoamerica, then, later, copper axes. Brumfiel suggests that what often drives human creativity is not in fact necessity but play or the need for competitive prestige.

MATERIAL CULTURE AND THE SENSES

It is often observed by anthropologists and archaeologists that academics and those who use the objects themselves do not actually 'see' the objects in the same way (Latour 2000). Edwards et al. (2006: 25) argue that it is crucially important not only to see objects but to sense them. They claim that thinking through objects with the senses also re-engages with objects at a very profound level: it moves them to the centre of our consideration and brings them back to the world of people. This view suggests that, in order to understand the true role of material objects, one must not simply look at them as a 'text' to be read. Rather, it is best to understand them through all the senses and also explore their sensual biographies.

The Process of Making Material Objects

Many anthropologists are interested in the ways in which humans engage with materials, not just in terms of their skills or techniques, but also in the actions themselves – working *with* materials rather than doing something to them. Stephanie Bunn (1999) suggests that, as many anthropologists are not personally involved with working with materials, they simply observe others making things, and because of this they often overlook the action of creation. According to Bunn, observing the process of making an object is inadequate for understanding the way people engage with objects, given that 'making' is often such a multisensory experience. She points to the documentation of Inuit carving by Carpenter (ibid.:17), who claims that 'a carving, like a song, is not a thing, it is an action'. Tim Ingold (2007) suggests that it is better to avoid widening the gap between mind and matter. Rather, he suggests that it is important to think about the nature of the process by which individuals engage with the material world in a practical as well as an abstract way. In this respect, the process of producing material culture is all-important. An object can provide significant information about the person who made it.

> **STOP & THINK**
>
> Why is it that looking at objects alone is not enough truly to understand them?
> Why might it be important for anthropologists to observe the making of objects?

Aesthetics: The Culturally Constructed Nature of Beauty

One of the many ways of understanding people through the material world is to consider what makes an object beautiful or desirable. **Aesthetics** is a branch of philosophy concerned with beauty and the ability to recognize it. Although it appears that there is

Aesthetics
A branch of philosophy concerned with beauty and the ability to recognize it

An immense mausoleum of white marble, built in Agra between 1631 and 1648 by order of the Mughal emperor Shah Jahan in memory of his favourite wife, the Taj Mahal is the jewel of Muslim art in India and one of the universally admired masterpieces of the world's heritage. (© Arain Zwegers / Flickr)

a degree of difference among individuals in terms of desire and taste, each social group has culturally constructed ideas about what it considers beauty to be. It may be that, owing to the development of religious and spiritual ideas in the past, material objects took on new meanings and enabled individuals to communicate and express deeper concerns and appreciation.

> **Activity**
>
> Think of three objects considered beautiful or desirable in your culture.
> Think of three objects considered beautiful in a culture different to your own.
> Suggest some reasons why ideas about what is considered to be beautiful change over time and from place to place.

Dirt, Unseen Objects and Immateriality

In *Purity and Danger* (1966), the anthropologist Mary Douglas famously explains dirt as 'matter out of place'. Dirt, she explains is not something absolute; rather, it is a cultural construct which makes clear the categories of any given culture. Any material which falls outside the boundaries of the classification system of a specific culture is dirt or dirty, thereby reaffirming the validity, naturalness and purity of that which remains within the boundary.

Miller (2005) considers the role of objects that are not discussed or recognized: for example, objects that might be lost or forgotten. Interestingly, where a lack of objects (immateriality) is seen as the ultimate goal in belief systems such as Hinduism, these ideas are still expressed through material forms and practices such as particular architecture in temples or yogic control over bodies.

> **Activity**
>
> What is dirt, according to Douglas?
> Do you agree? Think about what you consider to be matter out of place and compare your answer with that of someone else; are your answers the same?
> What is the meaning of dirt?

ARCHAEOLOGY, ANTHROPOLOGY AND THE ROLE OF MATERIAL CULTURE

Archaeology is the study of human activity in the past, primarily through the recovery and analysis of material culture and environmental data. Its main focus is on artefacts, which means any objects made by human beings. In an article which examines the relationship between anthropology and archaeology, Brumfiel (Brumfiel and Fox 2003) argues that the present is intrinsically linked to the past through material conditions. The past determines the quality of articles in the present as well as influencing and constraining human action today. Brumfiel explains how archaeology as an academic discipline controls the material remains of the past, and how these remains play an important role in human history. For instance, material objects provide historical information about times and places that are not recorded in oral histories or written accounts.

Material remains provide information about the actions and interactions of daily life, and, as Brumfiel explains, such interactions often go unrecorded in history. In fact, such information can correct unconscious bias or deliberate misinformation in historical texts. Furthermore, material objects can enable us to understand the ways that the material world has constrained human choices, actions and labour.

As a result of the potentially complex, rich and varied information that can be produced from objects, artefacts are also a source of power to those who interpret them. Since documents do not extend very far into the history of human culture, there is a tendency to focus on the West as a source of cultural change and as the dynamic and forceful presence, in contrast to those who, when it comes to material culture, may be seen as passive, exotic indigenous populations. Brumfiel is critical of this tendency, claiming that it can lead to a very limited view of the past. It is not just the distant past to which material objects speak: they can in fact be used by anthropologists to evoke the telling of oral histories, allowing people to describe their experiences in a collaborative way.

Activity

What is the difference between archaeology and anthropology?
Why are material objects so important for understanding the past?
What problems might there be with anthropologists' and archaeologists' interpretations of the meanings of material objects?

How Do Material Objects Symbolize Relationships?

Both public and private symbols exist, and both can play a significant role in the way people express their relationships with others. In conflicts, symbols are very important; for instance, weapons and flags help present a group as having specific qualities or characteristics. Totem poles are an example of how some First Nation Americans were able to identify themselves with their ancestors. In Britain today, the royal family have distinctive regalia.

Coffins such as this are designed by relatives of a deceased family member in Ghana to reflect the trade or ambition of the deceased. For example, for a fisherman, a coffin might be made in the shape of a fish, while the one pictured here is of the kind that could be made for a shopkeeper. Known worldwide as 'fantasy coffins', these works are now bought and sold on the international art market and are sought after by galleries and collectors. This coffin was purchased by the Pitt Rivers Museum and is exhibited as a part of a collection on material culture. (© Tomislav Marić)

Symbols in Rituals

Symbolic material objects are used in the majority of rituals. Consider, for example, the study by Victor Turner (1967) of the Ndembu puberty ritual for girls. Here a young initiant is wrapped up in a blanket and made to lie under a tree for a whole day. It is not just any tree that is used, but a particular tree, the *mudyi* tree, which is symbolic of the transformation of the girl into a woman because, when the bark is scratched, a white milky substance is secreted, said to represent breast milk. Thus the tree represents not just the fact that the girl is ready for puberty but that she will at some point produce breast milk. This affirms the matrilineal society and strengthens mother–child relationships (more on rituals in chapter 8).

RELIGIOUS OBJECTS AND SYMBOLS

Religious symbols are often highly visible, and so decisions about where they are displayed and by whom have become complex political debates concerning individual rights and freedoms. In 2011, the European Court of Human Rights made a ruling that ran counter to the current trends in European courts and legislatures. This ruling came at a time when the French government had banned headscarves from classrooms and *burquas* and *niqabs* from being worn on the streets, and when a referendum altered the Swiss constitution to forbid the construction of minarets throughout the country. Elaine Oliphant (2012) explains why the European Court, on this particular occasion, affirmed the right of the Italian state to display crucifixes on the walls of its public classrooms. She claims that those in support of the move argued that the crucifix was a cultural and historical sign that could not be considered only in religious terms. In particular, they claimed, the cross is a symbol of 'tolerance' and therefore a secular symbol. For others, Oliphant argues, the cross symbolizes a religion which is anything but tolerant – for example, the Inquisition, anti-Semitism and the Crusades that are part of the history of Christianity. So, in some respects, the Italian case both drew attention to and denied the legitimacy of the history that the crucifix symbolizes for some people.

Similar decisions about Islamic symbols tend to indicate that these are considered 'purely' religious. Oliphant is critical of the freedom given to Christian symbols, as it stands in sharp contrast to the excessive legislation surrounding similar Islamic religious symbols. This example highlights the significance of particular religious symbols. It is clear that such a decision reflects the importance of such symbols as a site for the contestation and negotiation of beliefs and identity.

STOP & THINK

What insights might anthropologists gain from religious symbols?
Why is the ability to display religious symbols felt to be so important?

Theory of Material Culture

Anthropologists since Mauss ([1954] 1970) and Malinowski ([1922] 2014) have argued that, in certain contexts, persons can seem to take on the attributes of things and things can seem to act almost as persons. Studies of traditional exchange systems have elaborated on this idea by explaining how objects can be given a gender, name, history and ritual function. Some objects can be so closely associated with persons as to seem inseparable (Weiner 1992).

Some persons – slaves, dependants – can have their own humanity devalued so that they acquire the status of mere possessions. Conversely, material objects can be said to have 'biographies' or 'social lives' (Appadurai 1986), as they go through a series of transformations – at some points being gifts, at other times being commodities or possessions – and a person can also invest aspects of their own biography in things.

Marx's philosophy rests upon how people relate to the material world. His basic tenet is that the way humans engage in the exchange of objects shapes their ideas and attitudes. Marx often sees objects assigned monetary or exchange value as commodities. Objects are part of the shaping of ideas to maintain the capitalist system. Capitalism, for Marx, is to be criticized for corrupting the way in which people create objects, a process through which individuals should be able to understand themselves.

The concept of **objectification** is central to feminism. Seeing and/or treating a person, usually a woman, as an object has been strongly criticized by many feminist writers (Dworkin and MacKinnon 1988). Others, such as Strathern (1988), claim that objects can express complex messages about gender and gender relations, as the latter found in her research in Melanesia.

> **Objectification**
> The process of treating another person or persons as if they are objects or instruments, sometimes for personal gain

Bourdieu (1977) combines a range of influences, including structuralism with an understanding of what objects mean to people and how they shape the way that people see the world. He draws attention to the ways that objects implicitly condition human actors, which also becomes the means by which people become socialized.

Bourdieu develops Lévi-Strauss's ideas and argues that we are brought up with the expectations of particular social groups and the relationships found between everyday objects. He draws attention to the categories, orders and placement of objects – for example, where spaces and objects are found within the home – and claims that the order of objects reflects the social order – for instance, social hierarchies or gender. These relationships between objects and individuals become habitual ways of being in the world and become almost second nature, or, as Bourdieu puts it, habitus.

ARJUN APPADURAI (1986)

Appadurai takes an interpretivist approach and focuses on the circulation of objects, not just in the sense of exchange but as objects in motion. The meaning that people attribute to things necessarily derives from human transactions and motivations, particularly from how those things are used and circulated. Appadurai treats objects as if they are actual beings living 'social lives', acquiring and losing value (Ferguson 1998). Objects, then, have lives, which can be understood by using the anthropological technique of taking a life history. Appadurai illuminates the ways in which people find value in things and things give value to social relations. He asks how objects circulate and under what circumstances and at what points they become exchangeable, and he argues that, beneath the seemingly infinite human wants and the apparent multiplicity of material forms, there in fact lie complex, but specific, social and political mechanisms that regulate taste, trade and desire.

Activity

Apply each of these theoretical perspectives to an object of your choice. How might each perspective be applied to understanding the role of material objects?

Daniel Miller

For Daniel Miller (2005), humans need to be understood through their relationship with materiality, as this is very important for appreciating how people see the world. According to Miller, some anthropologists see the study of material culture as unimportant, something with which he strongly disagrees.

Miller has carried out a number of ethnographic studies of material culture and shows how people can be understood through the objects they choose – for example, in their homes or the clothes they choose to wear. In *The Comfort of Things* (2008) he researches the inhabitants of one London Street. Miller's choice of location is unsurprising; the diversity of contemporary London is extraordinary, and people from very different backgrounds live in close proximity to one another. This study leads the reader behind closed doors to encounter thirty people who live on the same street, showing their intimate lives, their aspirations and frustrations, their tragedies and accomplishments. Miller focuses on the things that really matter to the people he meets, which quite often turn out to be material things: the house, the dog, the music, the Christmas decorations. He creates a gallery of portraits, some comic, some tragic, and finds that a random street in modern London contains the most extraordinary stories. By studying the people by means of their objects, Miller uncovers the orders and forms through which people make sense of their lives today.

Another interesting ethnographic study carried out by Miller, entitled *Stuff* (2009), also focuses on material objects, and is based on more than thirty years of research in the Caribbean, India, London and elsewhere. Miller claims that things make us just as

A Nepalese child playing with a camera: taking photos and showing them to friends and others via social media is one way in which our social relations, aspirations and character are demonstrated and created. (© Peter Smith)

much as we make things, and yet very little academic attention is given to the study of material objects. The book opens with a critique of the idea that clothing is superficial. It presents the theories describing the way we are created by material as well as social relations and takes us inside the private world of people's homes, exploring their possessions. It examines issues of materiality in relation to the media and also poverty. Finally, the study considers objects which we use to define what it means to be alive and how we use objects to cope with death.

Biographical Objects: How Things Tell the Stories of People's Lives (Hoskins 1998)

Janet Hoskins's findings in this study are based on six women and men from Eastern Indonesia who narrate their own lives by talking about their possessions, particularly domestic objects that are used to construct and negotiate their identity. Hoskins explores how objects are given biographical significance, entangled in sexual politics and expressed in metaphors where the familiar distinctions between person and object and female and male are drawn in unfamiliar ways.

Through telling stories, people not only provide information about themselves but also construct their identities in a particular way, creating a 'self' for public consumption. But Hoskins found that, in Kodi, at the western tip of the Eastern Indonesian island of Sumba, the notion of telling one's life directly to another person did not exist. What she discovered, to her surprise, was that people communicated through metaphors based on objects. This is perhaps not astonishing when one understands that Kodi is a society in which the origins and circulation of valuables are crucial to a sense of time and history. Hoskins focuses on everyday objects that are given an extraordinary significance by becoming entangled in the events of a person's life and are used as a vehicle for a sense of selfhood. Objects, therefore, provide a way both through which to discuss complex issues such as gender and sexuality and for individuals to reflect on the meaning of life.

Hoskins draws on Strathern's study of Melanesia, in which Strathern (1988) claims that objects can be complexly gendered. Strathern also argues that personhood is made and unmade by the circulation of objects. Hoskins focuses in particular on objects and their relationships to individuals. For example, she shows how, in Kodi, love is often expressed through an image of a possession, a desire to possess another person totally, and that, when frustrated, the feeling may be deflected onto the possession. Interestingly, Hoskins found that few people were willing to talk about sexual politics, but through the language of metaphors and objects it was possible to access such sensitive topics.

The Betel Bag: A Sack for Souls and Stories

The betel bag, containing a supply of betel leaves and areca nuts, is widely carried by Kodi people. It is a very personal object but also intensely social, being thought to contain secrets and wisdom from the ancestors. The nuts are ground, crushed and chewed with the betel and a small amount of lime. The effect of this combination is concentration, reduction of hunger pangs, and an increase in memory so that stories can be told for a long time, in full. One notable Kodi storyteller, Maru Daku, told some of his most personal and meaningful narratives through the betel bag: 'You see this bag?

This is how I became a storyteller; this is where my words come from. My grandfather put them in here many years ago.'

The bag plays a significant role in death rituals, as one can only become an ancestor once the betel bag is placed on a spirit ladder during a death ritual and then in a stone tomb, marking the final resting place of the soul and the transformation of the dead person. The betel bag is also a medium through which to transfer stories down the generations and is used as a way to discuss relationships between men and women, particularly relating to the practice of polygyny, which is common in Kodi. There are stories of neglected wives who come back again and again to the empty betel bag, symbolizing the man who could not be shared between two women.

Activity

How are objects important to Kodi culture?

How did Hoskins use objects as a way to find out about Kodi life?

How are objects used in the stories that people tell?

What role does the betel bag play in creating an identity?

How is identity negotiated in Kodi society through material culture?

Can you think of any objects used in your own culture to tell stories about relatives or important people in your life?

Material Objects being Used to Communicate and Negotiate Identity – 'Clothing and innovation: a Pacific perspective' (Küchler and Were 2003)

Clothing has always played an important role in anthropological theory. There has been a strong interest in clothing in the Pacific region, and there is a wealth of archives, collections and photographs that document clothing as an instrument of colonial and missionary interventions. Küchler and Were (2003) suggest that clothing is a material resource through which we can focus on ways of *being* and *thinking*. Research into clothing helps us gain insight into how Pacific Islanders have dealt with change.

Clothing, missionaries and conversion

Clothing was a central concern for missionaries. It makes visible the transformations that swept the South Pacific in the second half of the nineteenth century, as it demonstrated the importation of new ideas into the region. The Christian values attached to the wearing of clothes led missionaries to see the Pacific Islanders' willingness to adopt them as a sign of religious conversion. One Methodist missionary, George Brown, recorded with some enthusiasm in 1908: 'I was glad to see Le Bera [the chief] clothed in a shirt and a waistcloth, and his wife and daughters each wearing a handkerchief or a small piece of cloth.'

What did clothing mean to the missionaries?

Missionaries believed that clothing brought with it a new moral economy of the body and mind, and they recognized its potential power. The Pacific Islanders' fervent attachment to clothing was also inspired by its material quality, a quality that demanded immediate action in the form of cutting, sewing and folding, in order to harness the power contained within the fabric.

Clothing was either directly worn or ripped to shreds to be remade anew. In some places, clothes were stored in houses, hidden away from sight, and only revealed in ceremonial exchanges, as though reserved for ancestral presence. Records show that patterns, texture and colour were vital qualities to the Pacific Islanders. In fact, clothing provoked such a strong reaction that missionaries carried bags of cloth as gifts when attempting to settle, to avoid conflict, or to placate local people. Anthropologists working in the South Pacific also argue that Western clothing brought with it innovations in social relations, domesticity, behaviour and manners.

Clothing, for the islanders, offered agency, which meant that they were able to negotiate or communicate values through cloth. Imported patterned cloth held a particular value – indeed, patterned cloth could be seen as enhancing status in ritual politics in South Pacific societies. So cloth came to be seen both as an agent of change and as a form of social and economic reward.

Traditional cloth (barkcloth) continued to be produced in some areas (such as

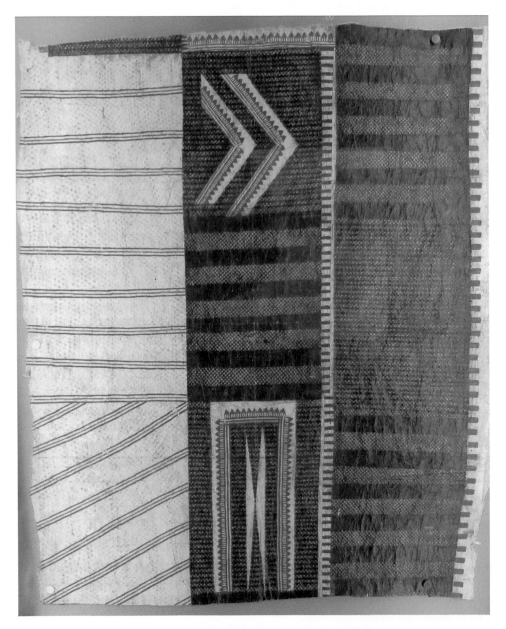

Barkcloth from Fiji showing traditional patterns (Hiart / Wikimedia Commons)

Polynesia). However, in other areas, such as Nuie, the *hiapo* – a hand-painted barkcloth – underwent major changes in pattern from the 1860s to the late 1880s as a response to the introduction of European fabrics.

In conclusion, cloth and clothing have contributed to new ways of thinking and being for the Pacific Islanders. Cloth is a powerful material which can be used in a number of different ways. Cloth and clothing can be a way to negotiate meanings or signify change. Clothing represents an important way in which the body is made symbolic.

Activity

How did missionaries use cloth and clothing?

What did the islanders feel about clothing and cloth?

How did European cloth and clothing transform social relations?

What does this study show us about the power of material objects?

Think about the way you use clothing to communicate who you are. Which clothes do you consider to be important (or, conversely, which clothing is not important and why)?

Why might clothing be important to people in the UK?

Is this related to age? If so, why?

Identify seven anthropological concepts that relate to clothing.

In and Out of Africa (Ilisa Barbash and Lucien Taylor, 1993)

In this film, a Nigerian, Gabai Baare, is followed from the Ivory Coast to Long Island, New York, as he conducts his job in the transnational trade in African art. Through commercial exchange, the commoditization of these art objects is revealed, as is the negotiation of cultural values between European and American collectors and African artists and traders. This study shows how objects carry different values according to the specific cultural context in which they are found.

Fatmawati's Wedding: The Weddings of Two Sisters, the Preparations (Fiona Kerlogue, 1998)

This film records the preparations for the wedding of two sisters in eastern Sumatra in December 1996. There is an emphasis on the importance of the role of women in the village. Ritual exchanges of textiles and cakes and a series of purification rituals are shown, highlighting the importance of material objects in an exchange system within a ritual.

THE REPRESENTATION OF MATERIAL CULTURE

A contested issue in contemporary anthropology is how best to represent another culture. Increasingly, museums face similar challenges about the use of objects to represent culture, particularly when artefacts displayed in exhibits convey conflicting symbolic messages to different audiences. Museums are both overtly and covertly involved in the preserving, representing and contextualizing of objects, cultures and histories over space and time. Museum professionals act as memory-shapers and have an influential role in shaping and reshaping popular perceptions of the past.

During the nineteenth century, at the height of **colonialism**, the collection of diverse objects was highly fashionable. The popularity of the natural sciences led museums to exhibit collections of human remains and other biological specimens. Imperialist and nationalist values led to the development of museums to house imperial memories. During the formative years of modern anthropology, Euro-American museums were devoted to collecting ethnographic materials as a way of guarding national identity and promoting ethnocentric cultural values. Since the late twentieth century, museums have been at the centre of complex, often contentious debates around colonial representations, the impact of scientific studies, and the ownership and repatriation (return) of human remains and cultural property. Museum staff members have been increasingly challenged to include the diverse perspectives of different ethnic groups, women, and underrepresented minorities.

Museums have occupied an ambiguous role in anthropology. The anthropologist Franz Boas resigned from the American Museum of Natural History in 1905, convinced that it was impossible to represent culture adequately through such a restricted part of heritage as physical objects. Museums were further marginalized in anthropology once they became identified as a material manifestation of colonial encounters, from which many anthropologists now sought distance (Trigger 2006).

Stewart (1984) suggests that, in contemporary Western society, museums continue to focus the mind on the visual at the expense of a more complex, rich and sensual experience of objects, thus limiting the viewer's understanding. This is because, in its original cultural context, the visual appearance of the object may play only a small role in understanding its significance and meaning. What might be much more interesting to the anthropologist than the object itself is the cultural significance placed on it. It may be the case that, in order to understand and engage with an object, it may need to be touched, smelled and felt, as well as looked at.

Since the 1980s, however, much has changed, and today many museums work closely with the groups that they represent to ensure that they participate in deciding how they might be represented. There is a growing interest in the performance (Bauman 1992) of culture in museums, which are becoming centres for often highly interactive cultural performance of indigenous music, dance and political statement, attracting wide audiences. They are also increasingly holding events where visitors can get close to and handle articles.

Activity

Who has the power in a museum to handle or touch collections? Why?

What kinds of information might be gained by handling an object rather than by simply looking at it behind glass?

What are the problems with looking at objects outside their original setting?

Should indigenous groups be able to claim back the human remains of their ancestors kept in museums (a process known as repatriation)?

Perceptions of Representation through Objects

Horst and Miller (2012) talk about how objects are displayed in museums – in particular, how material, visible objects may be used to control invisible worlds (social worlds that cannot necessarily be seen). They suggest that this view helps us understand why objects may have been presented in ways which may be exaggerated and extreme.

The Pitt Rivers Archaeological Museum in Oxford: following the original designs from the nineteenth century, the museum floor is packed with glass display cases. (© Chris McGeehan / Flickr)

It has been suggested that Western museums, with their glass cases, spotlights and obscure labels, are not liked by non-Western people. For example, in the National Museum in Bamako, Mali, the word 'museum' is taken out of marketing literature, as it would deter the local people from visiting. This may well be an obstacle in other Western and non-Western cultures, and many museum curators and education officers work hard to ensure that local people participate in museums which represent them.

Michael Rowlands uses the example of West Africa, where in the 1950s museums were inherited as a colonial legacy and seen by some as an 'alien space'. They were largely visited only by local elites, tourists and school parties. However, today such museums use outreach and education programmes to work with local people, and this emphasizes the fact that such 'new' museums appeal to more diverse groups and enjoy a much wider range of visitors.

STOP & THINK

How might local people feel about museums?
What can be done to improve local people's perceptions about museums?

Activity

Match the words below to the appropriate definition.

Concept	Definition
	Sites for the representation of cultures, historically controlled by colonial groups
	To restore or return to the country of origin
	The performance of cultural identity in a museum
	Professionals who work in museums
	European nations explored, conquered, settled and exploited large areas of the world
	Unseen aspects of cultural groups
	Physical aspects of cultural groups
	The relations between groups and individuals
	The ability to impose your will over others
	Studied invisible worlds of groups and argued that leaving out important information about certain groups leads to distortion and exaggeration
	The idea that museums are unfamiliar to those they are meant to represent
	A recent attempt to create a more authentic museum experience

Museums	**Invisible worlds**	**Material worlds**
Power	**Alien space**	**'New' museums**
Colonialism	**Social worlds**	**Curators**
Artefacts	**Repatriation**	**Exhibition and display**

Ownership of Material Culture

There have been many debates over who owns the objects in museums and who controls the representation of those objects, known as **repatriation** issues. Since the 1980s, representatives of cultural groups and individuals have requested that certain material objects be returned to their places of origin. An early and important effort in North America was the struggle of the Zuni Pueblo in New Mexico to return the sacred Ahayuda figures to their traditional resting places in tribal shrines. Figures representing the twin war gods Uyuyemi and Maia'sewi are placed in shrines to harness their potentially destructive powers. The Zuni believe that, when Spanish

> **Repatriation**
> The process of returning an object or person to their place of origin

and US agents stole the communally owned figures from their designated resting places, it caused the spiritual imbalance that the world is suffering in this century. The return of the figures to their shrines is regarded as necessary to restore harmony and protect the Zuni community (more on the role of anthropologists in repatriation in chapter 13).

Globalization: Ethnomusicology the Movement of People and Material Culture

As suggested earlier, objects are sometimes considered to have social lives and stories of their own, revealing interesting information about those who made them. The creation of new musical genres and new musical instruments can often be traced by following human migration and trading routes. For example, the African diaspora – the enforced journey of African people to enslavement in the Americas – had a profound influence on the history of music. The traditional instruments of South America and the Caribbean reflect African and Hispano-Portuguese heritage as well as the music cultures of the native peoples.

One example of this is to be seen in the African and European heritage in Venezuelan music, shown in an ensemble of instruments made by Cruz Quinal, 'the Bandolin King'. Quinal was a musician and instrument-maker working in a village near Cumanacoa in Venezuela. The adoption of musical instruments previously used by groups dominant in a region's society has had different interpretations; some scholars see this as related to a struggle for power and the construction of new identities.

Another example of Western musical influences selectively reformulated by other cultures is to be found in the West African lamellaphone (a set of tuned tongues fitted to a resonator), a large number of which were made and collected in the 1950s from peoples whose enslaved ancestors brought their musical traditions to the West, forming the roots of jazz.

Ethnomusicology
The study of music in its cultural context

Activity

Why were these instruments developed?
Why are instruments similar to this found all around the world?
Can you think of other objects which change as they have moved?

CONCLUSION

Material culture is important to various theoretical ideas, provides anthropologists with a methodological approach, and is a way of describing objects that have meanings. It plays a significant role in shaping and changing identity. New technologies have recently begun to play a key role in expressing identity. There are different perspectives on the nature and role of material culture, which is dynamic and ever changing. Museums play a key role in representing other cultures through material objects. Generalizations cannot be made about the role of such objects 'in the West' or beyond. An individual can also use one and the same object to express different aspects of identity.

END OF CHAPTER ASSESSMENT

Assess the role of material culture in understanding different societies.

Teacher's guidance

Explain what is meant by material culture – as a concept, a theory and a means of understanding an individual or group. Use examples of ethnographic studies, such as that of Hoskins (1998), which use material culture as a way of understanding different societies. Discuss theoretical approaches to interpreting material culture and some of the problems with using and interpreting artefacts. Enumerate some potential benefits and problems of using museums to understand other cultures.

KEY TERMS

Aesthetics A branch of philosophy concerned with beauty and the ability to recognize it
Archaeology The study of human history and prehistory through the excavation of sites and the analysis of artefacts
Artefact Any object made by a human
Commodity Anything that can be bought or sold
Ethnomusicology The study of music in its cultural context
Immaterial Lacking substance
Material culture The physical objects, resources and spaces that people use to define their culture
Objectification The process of treating another person or persons as if they are objects or instruments, sometimes for personal gain
Repatriation The process of returning an object or person to their place of origin

Personal investigation 1

Visit your local museum if you can (or, if not, their website) and consider the way that it portrays other cultures, both historically and in the present. Look at the ways material objects are displayed and how they are explained. Arrange a meeting with curators in the museum and ask them what factors they take into consideration in their presentation of objects. Construct a list of all the benefits of and problems with the accurate portrayal of other cultures through material objects. Also ask about the repatriation process and how the museum might manage the return of important objects to those they seek to represent. Investigate what activities are offered within the museum and explore their intended outcomes.

Personal investigation 2

Visit the house of someone you know and take notes on the types of objects they have. Discuss with them what they feel are their most important objects and why. Consider the functions of material objects in their house and what meanings these might express about the person's identity. Discuss with them why certain objects have become more or less significant over time.

SUGGESTED FURTHER READING AND FILMS

Books

Horst, H. A., and D. Miller (eds) (2012) *Digital Anthropology*. Berg.
Hoskins, J. (1998) *Biographical Objects: How Things Tell the Stories of People's Lives*. Routledge.
Miller, D. (2008) *The Comfort of Things*. Polity.

Ethnographic films

Fatmawati's Wedding: The Weddings of Two Sisters, the Preparations (1998), directed by Fiona Kerlogue
In and Out of Africa (1993), directed by Ilisa Barbash and Lucien Taylor

Websites

British Museum: www.britishmuseum.org
Horniman Museum: www.horniman.ac.uk
Museum of Anthropology and Archaeology: http://maa.cam.ac.uk/maa/
Pitt Rivers Museum: www.prm.ox.ac.uk

CHAPTER THIRTEEN

RESEARCH METHODS

CONTENTS

13 Research Methods

Fieldwork
The first-hand observation of human societies

Anthropology as a discipline is unique in its commitment to explore human cultures. This chapter discusses only the research methods of social/cultural anthropology. Social anthropologists learn about the culture of another society most distinctively through **fieldwork** and first-hand observation in that society, although other methods are used as well. Anthropological research involves a range of methods, such as informal (unstructured) interviews, direct observation, participation in the life of the group, collective discussions, analyses of personal documents produced within the group, self-analysis, results from activities undertaken off- or online, and life histories over a prolonged period of time. These kinds of data are rich, detailed and **qualitative**, offering deep insight into the culture studied. This chapter looks at some of these research methods and at the practical, ethical and theoretical issues that are associated with them. It concludes with reflections by two anthropologists (Brian Morris and Garry Marvin) on their fieldwork and the techniques that they used in gathering their knowledge of particular cultures.

ETHNOGRAPHY

Probably the best explanation of what ethnography entails in terms of data collection is given by Hammersley and Atkinson (2007: 3):

> ethnography usually involves the ethnographer participating, overtly or covertly, in people's daily lives for an extended period of time, watching what happens, listening to what is said, and/or asking questions through informal and formal interviews, collecting documents and artefacts – in fact, gathering whatever data are available to throw light on the issues that are the emerging focus of inquiry.

Ethnography usually involves a researcher studying a whole community of people, sometimes in a small town or village, or possibly part of a larger town. The method involves the researcher going to live among the people being studied and becoming involved in community life as a participant observer. The best way to understand people is to observe them by interacting with them over an extended period, sometimes years. Anthropologists have to share the lives of the people as much as they can. This experience is sometimes romanticized (seen as exciting or wondrous); however, in reality, most anthropologists work alone and experience loneliness, especially in the early stages of fieldwork. While fieldwork can be a challenging experience, almost all anthropologists find themselves **assimilating** to the culture of their host communities to a greater or lesser degree.

There are a number of advantages and limitations in ethnographic research methods. People can be studied when acting in ways they consider normal to them and may not be completely aware that they are being watched.

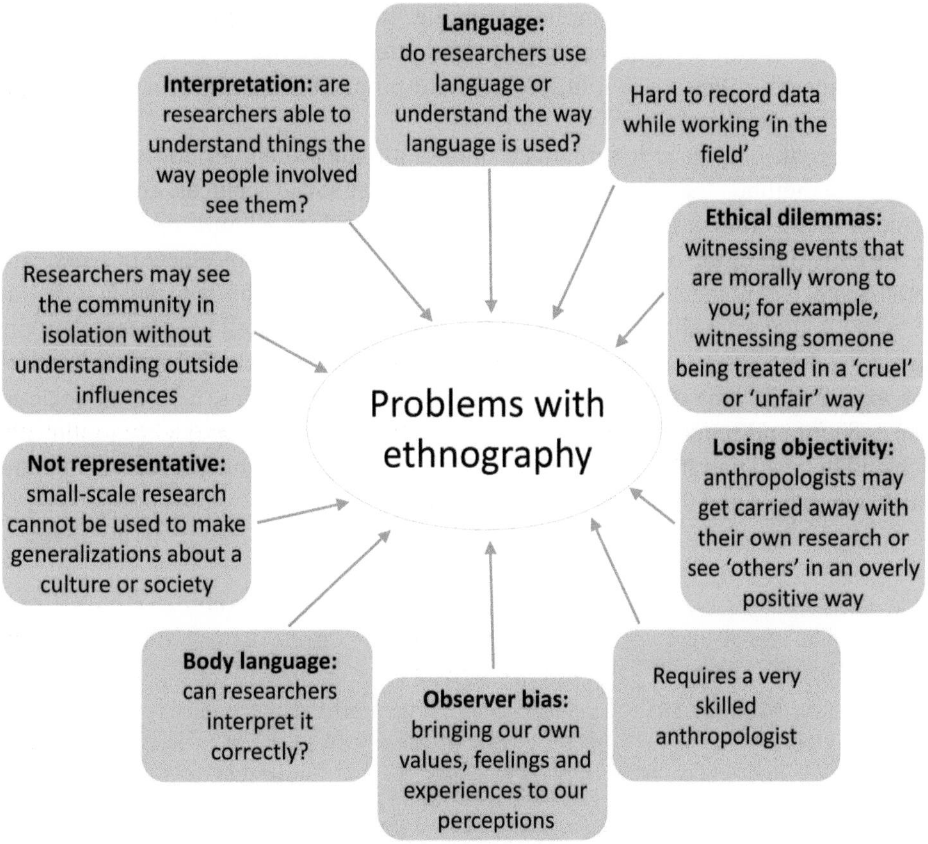

Assimilation
The absorption of an individual or minority group of people into another society or group, achieved by learning and adopting the cultural traditions of the society in which assimilation occurs; it is also often hastened by intermarriage and by de-emphasizing cultural and or biological differences

Interpretation: are researchers able to understand things the way people involved see them?

Language: do researchers use language or understand the way language is used?

Hard to record data while working 'in the field'

Researchers may see the community in isolation without understanding outside influences

Ethical dilemmas: witnessing events that are morally wrong to you; for example, witnessing someone being treated in a 'cruel' or 'unfair' way

Not representative: small-scale research cannot be used to make generalizations about a culture or society

Problems with ethnography

Losing objectivity: anthropologists may get carried away with their own research or see 'others' in an overly positive way

Body language: can researchers interpret it correctly?

Observer bias: bringing our own values, feelings and experiences to our perceptions

Requires a very skilled anthropologist

Figure 13.1 Problems with ethnography

Activity

Define ethnography.
What is assimilation?
What role do you think the anthropologist should play when researching, and why?
Read the list of problems in figure 13.1. Can you think of any others?
Put the problems in order of importance; be ready to justify your reasons.
What are the strengths of ethnographic research?

The History of Anthropological Research Methods

Anthropology – the study of 'humanity' – grew from the intersection of European discovery, colonialism and natural science. In the early nineteenth century, anthropologists were interested in reconstructing the stages of social and cultural evolution. Early anthropologists such as Edward Burnett Tylor and Lewis Henry Morgan published influential works tracing everything from writing systems to marriage practices, from their primitive beginnings to the more complex modern state. Originally anthropology was thought of as a science studying the 'savage'. This meant that anthropologists researched societies that had either already or would soon become dominated territories within the European empires. By the beginning of the twentieth century, anthropologists were no longer content to rely on the accounts of other non-specialists, such as colonial officials, missionaries and travellers, for their primary data, and they began to go into 'the field' as ethnographers to gather their own information at first-hand. Observations made during the colonial era were later seen as flawed, as they had at their heart the idea that Western civilization was at the pinnacle of human evolution and that all other ways of life were inferior.

Although anthropology has changed quite a bit since then, ethnography remains one of the methods that distinguish it from the other social sciences, and the importance of doing ethnography is perhaps one thing on which all anthropologists agree. In the early part of the twentieth century, anthropology was typically concerned with small-scale, technologically simple societies. The purpose of this was partly to record ways of life that were changing under colonialism (they may well have been changing anyway – don't assume that colonialism was the only reason). Today anthropology has extended its area of interest into more developed societies, taking all societies into account and treating them all as equally significant. Anthropologists retain their rich and detailed narrative approach (including storytelling), which reveals a lot about particular people and places.

A Founder of Ethnographic Fieldwork

Bronislaw Malinowski (1884–1942) is often called the father of ethnography. The role of ethnography for him was to grasp the 'native's' point of view. He worked among the Trobriand Islanders, studying kinship, trade, and the practical purposes of ritual and religion, as well as the connection between cultural ideals and actual daily behaviour. There he developed his style of fieldwork, which came to be called participant observation: speaking the language, living in and becoming part of the community, making a detailed record of all aspects of 'native' life. Malinowski's close experience with Trobriand society generated a growing awareness of the various links that hold society together. Participant observation emerged as the primary approach to ethnographic research and relied on the development of personal relationships with local **informants** as a way of learning about a culture, involving both observing and participating in the social life of a group. By living with the cultures they studied, these researchers were able to formulate first-hand accounts of their lives and gain new insights.

Informant
A person who provides information about his or her culture to the ethnographic fieldworker

Factors Influencing Choice of Research Method

There are a number of methods of data collection and associated issues that anthropologists commonly need to consider in their preparation for fieldwork and during the data-gathering phase of their work. When choosing their research topic and research methods, they are influenced by a number of practical, ethical and theoretical issues.

PRACTICAL ISSUES

Time and cost	Observation is time consuming and expensive in comparison with a postal questionnaire. All methods cost some money, but some, such as questionnaires or secondary data, are cheaper than others. It may take time and skill to gain acceptance into the group to undertake participant observation.
Access	Some cultural situations are far easier to gain access to than others. Market researchers can freely stand in the street to talk to members of the general public, whereas some 'closed' research settings, such as schools or prisons, pose more difficulties. Often 'closed' settings will only be accessible if entry is approved by a **gatekeeper** (such as a head teacher in a school).
Researcher characteristics and skills	Some topics are difficult for certain researchers: for example, it would be very difficult for a female researcher to conduct participant observation in a monastery, or, indeed, for a man to do so in a convent. Also, some individuals are better at mixing with people and building relationships than others.
Subject matter	Some methods suit certain topics and subject matters better than others.
Research opportunity	Sometimes the chance to conduct research will happen spontaneously and not allow time to plan questions for a questionnaire or structured interview. For example, Thomas Ward was offered the chance to study a gang's culture in Los Angeles and used participant observation (see his case study in this chapter, pp. 279–80).

ETHICAL ISSUES

Ethics refers to moral issues of right and wrong. Ethnographers are obliged to follow ethical principles before, during and after their fieldwork. There are several major anthropological associations that have created codes of ethics. In short, ethnographers have to respect the dignity of people they study as well as take responsibility for how they use their findings after the research is completed.

The Association of Social Anthropologists of the UK and Commonwealth and the American Anthropological Association have set out guidelines for the conduct of research, including the following principles.

Informed consent	Research participants should be offered the right to refuse to take part. The researcher should tell them about all relevant aspects of the research so that they can make an informed decision. Consent should be obtained before research begins.
Confidentiality and privacy	Researchers should keep the identity and personal details of participants confidential in order to help prevent possible negative effects on them.
Effects on research participants	Researchers need to be aware of the possible negative effects on participants, such as police intervention, harm to education or employment, social exclusion and psychological damage. If someone is asked to talk about a sensitive event in their life, such as abuse or rape, they may also find this upsetting.
Covert research	This is when the researcher's identity and purpose are hidden from the people being studied. It can create serious ethical problems, such as deceiving or lying to people in order to win their trust or obtain information. It is impossible to gain informed consent while at the same time keeping the research or its purpose secret. Anthropology does not use **covert observation** during research. However, some anthropologists argue that the use of covert methods may be justified in certain circumstances (see chapter 14).
Involvement in illegal acts/danger	If the researcher is investigating a deviant gang or group, for example, they may have to take part in or be seen to condone illegal behaviour. They may also be in danger, particularly if the gang members think that they might be deceived (see Thomas Ward's study, pp. 279–80).

THEORETICAL ISSUES

Theoretical issues cover questions concerning what anthropologists think culture is like and whether they can obtain an accurate, truthful picture of it. The way in which an anthropologist studies the social world can be influenced by their theoretical beliefs about society.

Validity	A valid method is one that produces a true or genuine picture of what something is really like. It allows the researcher to get close to the truth. Many anthropologists argue that qualitative methods such as participant observation provide a more valid or truthful account of what it is like to be a member of a group than quantitative methods such as a questionnaire.
Reliability	A reliable method is one which, when repeated by another researcher, gives the same results. Quantitative methods, such as written questionnaires, tend to produce more easily comparable results than qualitative methods such as observation, but many anthropologists argue that qualitative methods yield a deeper and more complex form of knowledge.
Representativeness	A representative method is one where the people studied form a typical cross-section of the group in which the researcher is interested. If the sample selected is representative or typical of the wider population, the findings can be used to make generalizations (for example, statements about the whole group can be made).
Choice of topic	Theoretical issues will impact not only on the choice of method but also on the choice of topic in the first place. Anthropologists may well be influenced in their choice of research topic by their theoretical position.

> ### Activity
>
> Your school is funding you to travel to South America and conduct anthropological fieldwork. You are going to visit a people called the Yanomamö who live in the rainforest of Venezuela. Their village has no electricity, no mobile phones or any modern technology. The nearest town with a hospital, shops and electricity is 200 miles away. The only way you can reach this community is by boat, and the journey takes five days from the nearest town. You are travelling on your own. You have to stay in the village for a period of three months and conduct a participant study to find out 'What is the Yanomamö relationship with nature?'
>
> Plan your journey and explain the issues that you might encounter before, during and after your fieldwork. Consider the practical, ethical and theoretical issues
>
> - before the journey: What do I need to take with me? Food? Medicine? Money? How to get there? Planning the journey?
> - during the stay at this village: How do I communicate? How do I find relevant information? What if I make a mistake? How do I record the information?
> - after the journey: How do I leave the community? How do I write the report? What about my own views and beliefs? How do I represent this community?

Gangsters without Borders: An Ethnography of a Salvadoran Street Gang (Ward 2012)

Thomas Ward spent eight and a half years of participant observation fieldwork in Los Angeles (see chapter 11, pp. 242–3). His is one of the rare ethnographies to explore the issues of globalization and street gangs and how gang culture has spread from the streets of Los Angeles to El Salvador and other parts of Central America. Ward spent the better part of sixteen years inside what is considered to be one of the world's largest gangs, the Mara Salvatrucha (MS-13). Ward drank with gang members at parties, celebrated the birthdays of hard-core members, and met their children and parents. He visited them in hospitals after they were shot or stabbed and in prison after they were convicted. He also attended their funerals. Ward became close to a dozen hard-core gangsters as he interviewed more than 150 gang members from eight different cliques during the course of his fieldwork – in Los Angeles, California state prisons, Salvadorean prisons, and the homes of retired members in El Salvador. He provides an insight into the world of street gangs and their spread throughout Central America and the USA.

According to Ward, his goal was to understand the motives for the Salvadorean immigrants' behaviour and to document the complexity of gangsters' lives. He began his research in 1993 by meeting with five active members of the gang in Los Angeles. Two of these subsequently died from gang violence, one recovered from crack addiction, another is serving life in prison, and the last one is free and has survived to old age. Those first connections led Ward into the hard, fast life of gangsters. Over the years he had many open conversations with gang members, from the time of their initiations until long after, when they were thinking about leaving the gang. He discovered that they were often allowed to retire after a few years of service with the gang and move on to a full-time job and family responsibilities. While Ward was invited to sell drugs, commit robberies, participate in drive-by shootings, and even become an honorary member of the gang, he always declined to participate in illegal activities. Before immersing himself in the street gang subculture, he had spent fourteen years researching the Salvadorean immigrant community and homeless people living on skid row in downtown Los Angeles.

Ward first started working with the Salvadorean community in 1981 while volunteering with a social service agency that provided food, shelter and legal services for Central American refugees fleeing their war-ravaged country. The experience would prove valuable: he learnt about Salvadorean history and culture, including their slang, which helped him earn trust among the MS-13 members. But this background provided only minimal protection when Ward had a gun put to his head and a knife held against his throat, with the warning that he would be killed if he was an undercover policeman. The gang members did not take Ward's word for it – they did a background investigation by calling his employer and checking out his references in Los Angeles. Despite the death threats, Ward saw a human side to these MS-13 members – people who had lived difficult lives and were searching for something better. In their own way, they were looking for family security, status and self-respect.

G-Strings and Sympathy (Frank 2002)

In order to conduct research in six different strip clubs in a southern city in the United States, Katherine Frank had herself to become a stripper. Her ethnographic work offers an insight into the public performance of (all-male) sexual desire and the importance of observation as a primary element of these experiences for the men who frequent strip clubs. In discussing her experience, Frank describes her role as 'observing the observers'. Feminist understandings inspire her research strategies, and the choice to conduct participant observation as a stripper allows her to analyse male erotic desire. Because she is a female ethnographer studying male customers of strip clubs, she raises a variety of perspectives and issues regarding power and gender.

> **Activity**
>
> Using the two case studies above, assess practical, ethical and theoretical issues that Thomas Ward and Katherine Frank might have experienced in their research.

Participant Observation

There are many issues that anthropologists have to think about and deal with before, during and after the participant observation in their fieldwork.

> **Participant observation**
> When a researcher takes part in the everyday life of the group while observing it

- **Getting in** To do their study, anthropologists must first gain entry to the group in question. Some groups are easier to enter than others – a football crowd? No problem. A criminal gang? Not so easy. Observed populations may alter their behaviour around the researcher because they know that they are being studied, an effect that has been exhaustively documented and studied in psychological research. Thus, while this research method allows for a deeper immersion and understanding of the culture, it faces a very real set of challenges.
  - *Making contact* This depends on a range of factors – e.g., the researcher's personal skills, having the right connections and maybe even luck.
  - *Acceptance* To gain entry to the group, it is necessary to win their trust and acceptance. Making friends with a key individual could help.
  - *Observer's Role* It is essential to adopt a role within the group – one that doesn't

disrupt their normal patterns but one that allows the researcher to make observations.

- **Staying in** Once the researcher has been accepted into the group, they need to be able to stay in to complete their study. A problem arises if the researcher becomes overinvolved. If they overidentify with the group, they become biased and cease to be an objective observer. However, if they preserve their detachment to avoid bias, they risk not understanding the events they are observing.
- **Getting out** Getting out is less problematic than getting in or staying in – if the worst comes to the worst, the researcher can just call a stop to their observations and leave. They may also find that loyalty to the group they have been studying makes it difficult to disclose everything they have learnt for fear of harming members of the group (e.g., exposure of the activities of criminal groups could lead to prosecution or reprisals against the researcher), but such omissions will reduce the validity of the data.

The anthropologist Peggy Froerer with her research assistant, Shantilal, a young man from the Kolga village in the state of Chhattisgarh, central India. He assisted her in transcribing her field notes from Chetriboli or Kurukh into Hindi. (© Peggy Froerer)

An Evaluation of Participant Observation (PO)

Strengths	Weaknesses
Validity: Observing people (rather than asking questions) results in qualitative data and a true picture of how they really live. PO studies often take a long time, and the research provides a rich, detailed, thorough picture of culture.	Practicality: PO can be time consuming, stressful and demanding. The researcher needs good observational and interpersonal skills and it is difficult to write up notes. The personal characteristics of the researcher may limit who can be studied.
Insight: By sharing experiences and seeing life through the group's eyes (*verstehen*), the researcher can understand their world as they themselves understand it.	Bias and lack of objectivity: The researcher may get too involved with the group being studied (going native).
Flexibility: The researcher starts with an open mind – PO can therefore provide new insights and ideas.	Representativeness and reliability: The group may be too small to make generalizations and the study cannot be replicated, so it is difficult to make comparisons with other studies.
Practicality: PO is a means of researching groups who could or would not complete a survey.	Ethics: The researcher may have to deceive people and participate in immoral or illegal activities and so become subject to personal dangers.
Presentation of self: Interpretivists are very interested in how people present a different image in different circumstances to different audiences.	Validity: Observations may be subjective or provide only a selective view of the group (the researcher cannot be in all places at all times), and the group's behaviour may be affected by the presence of a researcher.

Strengths	Weaknesses
PO avoids ethical (moral) problems (not deceiving people).	The group may refuse the researcher permission to observe them.
The researcher can ask questions openly.	The group may prevent the researcher from seeing everything.
The researcher can take notes openly. The researcher can interview people to check on their observation data.	The group may behave differently because they know they are being observed (this could undermine the validity of the data).

Activity

For each evaluation above, link the strengths and weaknesses to the anthropological case studies that you know. You can use the examples of the studies from this and other chapters.
What is participant observation?
Is it ever possible for anthropologists to be accepted by the people they study?
What are the practical issues that you have to consider in living with a community?
What reduces the cultural barriers between the fieldworker and people studied?
Who is a gatekeeper?
What are the ethical issues that fieldworkers need to consider?
What is ethnography?

Interviews

Although the main method of ethnography is participant observation, the fieldworker has to conduct interviews as well. This can take the form of one-to-one in-depth interviews, group interviews, or simply general talking and asking questions. It is difficult to describe how to conduct an interview as this depends on the skills of the fieldworker, but it is more like everyday conversation, which is informal and free flowing. The researcher is unlikely to have a set of questions, although they are likely to have certain topics they wish to cover. An unstructured interview offers greater opportunity for respondents to take control of the situation, providing them with an opportunity to express their own views. This will increase the validity of the data obtained, since there is a greater chance that the views expressed by the interviewee will present a true, accurate description of what is being studied. The researcher is also able to probe with further questions or to ask the interviewee to expand or clarify a point that has been made. This, again, provides more depth to the data. Despite these advantages, unstructured interviews have their limitations. For example, the researcher might 'probe' a little too far, directing the research and so steering the conversation away from what the interviewee wants to discuss. This influence is called **interviewer bias**. A similar problem occurs when the researcher is able freely to interpret what the interviewee is saying. Misleading and inaccurate interpretations will reduce the validity of the research. Generally, people like to present themselves in a favourable light. This can result in interviewees emphasizing **socially desirable** aspects of their behaviour and attitudes in the presence of the researcher. Consequently, interviewees might exaggerate or lie.

If you came upon this group of people would you be able to figure out what was going on? What cultural patterns could you identify and understand? For instance, what is the significance of the colours and styles of clothing? Why are all the girls together? What are they waiting for? Where are they? Is the arrangement of people in this photo random? What questions would you ask them to find out what they are doing? (© Maria Salak)

Unstructured Interviews

Advantages	Disadvantages
Can gain an in-depth understanding (especially via rapport)	Interviewer bias
Interviewees can develop their answers and interviewers can probe deeper	Social desirability effect – people like to make themselves look good (may lie)
Can change direction of interview if new ideas emerge	Time consuming and costly
Can compare observation of the respondent with replies given (e.g., body language)	Difficult to compare interviews – each is unique
Good for sensitive groups and/or topics	Fewer interviews conducted affects representativeness and means it is more difficult to make generalizations

> **STOP & THINK**
> What are open-ended questionnaires?
> How do you conduct an interview?
> What are the advantages and disadvantages of using questionnaires in anthropological research?

Life Histories

The life history, or personal narrative of one's life, is an important research method in anthropology for learning about how culture is experienced and created by individuals. It involves collecting and recording individuals' experiences, and can be done either by the individual writing down their own life story or by using semi-structured or unstructured interviewing, often tape-recorded, which the researcher then writes up.

Life histories are a rich source of insight both into a person's individual experiences, presented from their own point of view, and into the wider social forces that affect their lives. For example, they can provide an insight into how war affects those who live through it. This approach, like other kinds of ethnography, places most importance on the person's own interpretations and explanations of their experiences.

However, life histories obtained through interviews require the ability to empathize with the subject and demand good listening skills. They are also very time consuming and labour intensive. They rely upon the person's memory recall, and sometimes memories can be distorted, unclear or lacking altogether. They are also unrepresentative of the population as a whole. So, even though they may give us an insight into one person's experience, that might not be representative of other people's experiences at that time.

Activity

Effects of Globalization on Individual Identity

Conduct a life history project in which you have to carry out an extended series of interviews with a chosen informant. Transcribe the interviews and write up a life history, including themes such as childhood, education, career and family.

You should choose someone who is older so they have experienced changes throughout their lives.

Interview with Brian Morris

Describe your ethnographic research.

I have carried out four major pieces of fieldwork. The first was for my PhD, studying the Hill Pandaram people, who are hunters and gatherers in South India. I also carried out my research in Malawi on the relationship people have with their environment. I later returned to Malawi to study people's relationship with animals, small mammals.

How did you gain access to the group you studied?

I never actually had a problem gaining access in Malawi, as I lived and worked there for seven years on a tea plantation before I began my fieldwork. Very few people spoke English there at that time, so I had to learn the local language, Chichewa. So, when I began my research, I already knew the context and language well.

What research method(s) have you used in your fieldwork?

The main research method I use is to participate and join in activities and to observe. The best way to join in is by chatting with people. If you ask me what my research method is, it is chatting! In Malawi the word they use for chatting is *kucheza'*. It is very important in Malawi culture. To chat or discuss means to be sociable, so it is seen as important to chat to people. I would also go with local Malawi people to do what they were doing, and I constantly asked questions. When I studied mammals in Malawi I joined in rituals, which allowed me to be part of the group. I would often just listen to people's conversations. I learnt a lot about Malawi culture this way.

What was the most difficult part of your fieldwork?

The main difficulty I faced in my research in India was living in the forest. I decided to walk barefoot in the same way as the Hill Pandaram people, which was not easy. Sleeping was another problem. I am only an average height, but the Hill Pandaram are small, on average around 5 foot tall. They don't have houses; instead they make small conical shelters with palm leaves to cover themselves and to protect them from the rain. I found it very difficult sleeping in these because it rains most of the time and there is always a dog trying to hog the warmth of the fire (dogs are very important to them for hunting), and it was really a problem. I would have to sleep either in the foetal position or put my legs straight, with my legs outside the sleeping bed. I got wet with the rain and I did not have any blankets. The Hill Pandaram people are nomadic and move continually between camps, approximately every ten days, so I became nomadic too. I would spend three days with the Hill Pandaram in the jungle and then return to the village, where I lived with my family. I was there with my wife and three young daughters. It was very difficult for my family, but having children actually was not a handicap for my research at all. It opened to us many things as Indians love children. So we were accepted very quickly in the village.

How did you learn what to look for?
I go around like a hunter-gatherer but I gather knowledge, and I gather anything that relates to my topic of research. So I would go and chat with people, stay at cheap rest houses, sitting there and drinking beer, and then I would turn the conversation towards insects, for example, to see how people might relate to them. I would cut out all of the local newspapers reports on insects. I would look at archives for locust swarms and dig up information on everything. I would then gather this data and put it into my field book.

How did you record your data?
The only thing I would have is my notebook. So everything I did, learnt, would go into my journal. I call my notebooks 'journals'. Fifteen to twenty journals would be the basis of my book. I have a camera and a pair of binoculars, which is all of my equipment.

Who were your main informants?
All my informants are people that I get along with. For example, there were some people in Malawi who knew what I was after straight away and there were some others who were not very informative at all. You naturally gravitate towards people that you get on with and with the people that will help you with your research. I got close to certain individuals that I worked and shared food with.

What was the impact on your research process and findings of individual differences (age, gender, ethnicity, class, nationality) between you and your informants?
There are certain behaviours in Malawi that you have to observe. You have to conform to local customs. Malawians have always related to Europeans throughout history in one way or another. When you are an anthropologist you are always ambiguous. You are part of the culture but you are always an outsider.

What were the practical issues that you encountered before, during and after your fieldwork?
In Malawi I always had a motorbike, as you can get everywhere, especially during the rainy seasons. There are lots of dirt roads and they get very muddy, so buses and lorries get stuck and nothing can get past. However, on a motorbike you can go any-where. Unfortunately I always had accidents on my motorbike and suffered a lot in my research – falling off the motorbike!

What were the ethical issues that you experienced in your fieldwork?
Ethics are a part of everyday life for everyone. Doing fieldwork is no different than my going around here and talking to people here in my town in England. There are certain

things that I should do as a human being and those that I should not. Anthropology is always ethical. I don't see the difference between how I treat people here and how I treat people in Malawi. You can't just barge into people's houses and ask questions; you have to have tact. All my informants became my friends. It starts off with being an informant but then it turns into friendship, so there is no distinction between informant and friend. I always tell my informants that I am there because I am interested in understanding their way of life.

What were the theoretical issues that you considered in the process of writing your ethnography?
I was always aware of the theories regarding hunters and gatherers, about the movements of these people, and all my books are theoretical in a way. But I don't have a high theory in my head when I do research. My research is more in the way of a broad interest. I am not going there to prove Mary Douglas's thesis or Tim Ingold's theory.

What were your findings?
I argue that there are many ways to understand the world around us. When I studied insects it was basically my view that there are these insects called termites and they are *real*, rather than being socially constructed. Malawi people look at the context of these creatures in their world in different ways. So there are many different ways of looking at the world or insects or mammals. Sometimes they are important in terms of the way they see animals in an empirical way; animals are important in terms of eating, in terms of hunting, medicines, for example. In local rituals, animals are important as well as in folklore and myths. Malawians have multiple ways of relating to animals and understanding them. We always see the world from a certain perspective, a particular way of looking at it, and some of these ways are contradictory. Termites, for instance. In Malawi, in some contexts, termites are the most blessed things on the Earth; for Malawians the termites are real food, absolutely wonderful. Then in another context termites are horrible, because they destroy your crops. Termites are also used as symbols. The termite mounds are of real symbolic significance in relation to the matrilineal society. If you look at the termite colony, it has a queen that is 100 times bigger than other small termite workers. And she continually produces. So in different contexts the termite means different things.

What impact (if any) did this research have on your own life?
Doing research fieldwork, they say, is like a doing a vision quest, an ordeal. I have never seen research as an ordeal. I always enjoyed it. I am a perpetual student. In a way my research and my life are intertwined. I never had a problem with my identity. I have always seen myself as a working-class lad from the Black Country [English West Midlands]. And, added to that, I have always seen myself as a teacher and as a kind of anthropologist doing research, so my life in a way and my research are completely intertwined. It is not like my research is there and my life is here. They complement each other. Doing fieldwork is an experiential thing as well as being intellectual. The move from being experiential to intellectual is the process of conveying the experience into a kind of knowledge.

Garry Marvin's Testimony

My ethnographic research has focused on events in which humans engage with animals and in which the death of animals is the usual outcome. My first research project was a study of the bullfight in southern Spain. Here I also explored the cultural significance of cockfighting. Since then, I have conducted fieldwork in the world of English fox-hunting and with European big-game hunters.

Observing the
corrales in Spain
(© Garry Marvin)

For many people, these are disturbing events because they apparently involve people enjoying witnessing or actually bringing about the deaths of animals. But through my research I have attempted to show that, while the events do generate pleasures for the human participants, such pleasures are complex and these complexities cannot be understood by mere outside observation. Matadors spoke to me about their love of bulls, game hunters expressed great respect for their quarry, and fox-hunters spoke with me of their admiration for the hunted fox. Such attitudes might seem odd when all of these people are involved with the deaths of these animals. My task was to listen attentively, to ask carefully and to observe attentively in order to generate understanding. In all these events, animals are killed, but I slowly came to understand that what was of cultural significance, and therefore of anthropological interest, was *how* these deaths are brought about. My work, as an anthropologist, has been to reveal and to interpret the cultural significance of performances with, and killing of, animals in these events. Here, what is important is that, as an anthropologist, I had to enter the worlds of bullfighting and hunting in order to understand them from within rather than to impose meaning on them from outside.

All of these events generate considerable criticism from many people who are not part of them; and those people who are part of them are often suspicious of the motives of outsiders who come asking questions. In a crude sense, they are concerned that such outsiders might have a political animal rights/animal welfare agenda and are seeking access and information in order to criticize, to condemn and to discredit the event and its people in various ways. Such concerns caused some difficulties for me when I sought access to conduct ethnographic, participant observation research. The difficulties centred on people querying who I was, what I wanted to find out, what my motives were, what exactly this sort of research would involve and what I would do with the information I gained.

At the outset of my research in Spain, I had no contacts and had on one occasion to turn to a supporter or a sponsor. However, a chance meeting with someone whose father was a member of a bullfight aficionado's social club offered me an initial step forward. I was introduced to the club, where the members were initially suspicious of someone coming from a country where it was thought that people were fiercely critical of bullfighting. However, they seemed to accept my claim that I was not there to gather evidence against a supposedly barbaric practice. Their main concerns then became about testing my seriousness, my commitment, to understanding the bullfight world. Was it worth bothering spending time with me, talking to me and helping me? My genuine interest was accepted, and I spent several hours a day, almost every day of the week, in the club. This generated the conversations I wanted and the contacts I needed to go to bullfights with knowledgeable people, to meet matadors, to spend time on bull ranches. It was my willingness to immerse myself in their world that allowed me to generate the ethnographic material I needed for the project.

Seeking entry into the world of fox-hunting was far more difficult because of the political context and because people opposed to the event had, through deception, been able to gain access in order to obtain information for their political campaigns. Was I such an 'anti' in disguise? Could I be trusted? After a complex process of checking and vetting, I was gradually permitted to take part in fox-hunts as a foot follower, to jump into Land Rovers to keep up with hunts, to help with tasks on a hunting day, invited to social events and to ask what I wanted of anybody. This was as fine and as complete an access as I could have hoped for as an anthropologist. I could never prove that I was not an anti in disguise, and I think it is only when I was able to give members of the hunt world my academic publications that they could begin to see what it was that I was interested in accomplishing as an anthropologist.

In all of this research I have had the great privilege to enter the worlds of others, and people there have given me the opportunity, and taken the time, to help me with my anthropological interests. My responsibility as an anthropologist has always been to respect the trust and the help of those I have been able to spend time with – without them I would have had no project. This responsibility has also been, in my publications, to reveal, represent and interpret these complex social and cultural practices and worlds in ways that capture the significances they have for those who inhabit them. They have opened their worlds to me, and I, as an anthropologist, must attempt to open these worlds for others.

Activity

List all of the practical, ethical and theoretical issues that Marvin and Morris have encountered in their fieldwork.

How did they gain entry into the cultures they studied?

CONCLUSION

Anthropology is defined by its research method: fieldwork. This method allows the researcher to gain valuable information without disturbing and intruding on the privacy of the people being studied. The researcher participates in all daily activities of the community, observes the group or individuals, records their findings and then reflects on those findings. The body of data collected is often substantial and is used selectively in analysis and in writing up the results. Fieldwork data is usually supplemented by other data collected in libraries and museums. Nowadays fieldwork is used in many other disciplines outside anthropology and is recognized as a valuable way of gathering rich and valid data.

END OF CHAPTER ASSESSMENT

Assess different practical, ethical and theoretical issues that anthropologists have to consider in their fieldwork.

Teacher's guidance

Begin your answer with definitions of fieldwork. Explain the main practical, ethical and theoretical issues arising before, during and after fieldwork. Show your awareness of how these issues can affect anthropologists' choices of topic as well as their research method. Don't just list different problems but use different ethnographic examples from this book or your own readings to illustrate all of the issues.

KEY TERMS

Assimilation The absorption of an individual or minority group of people into another society or group, achieved by learning and adopting the cultural traditions of the society in which assimilation occurs; it is also often hastened by intermarriage and by de-emphasizing cultural and or biological differences

Cross-cultural research A method that uses a global sample of societies in order to test hypotheses

Cultural relativism The ability to view the beliefs and customs of other peoples within the context of their culture rather than one's own

Cultural universal A general cultural trait found in all societies of the world

Culture shock The feeling of confusion, distress and, sometimes, depression that can result from psychological stress during the first weeks or months of a total cultural immersion in an alien society

Emic A perspective in ethnography that uses the concepts and categories that are relevant and meaningful to the culture under analysis

Empirical Verifiable through the senses (sight, touch, smell, hearing, taste), either directly or through extensions (reliance on observable and quantifiable data)

Fieldwork The first-hand observation of human societies

Holistic approach An approach to the study of a society which looks at the whole/totality (a comprehensive approach)

Informal interview An unstructured question-and-answer session in which the informant is encouraged to follow his or her own train of thought, wherever it may lead

Informant A person who provides information about his or her culture to the ethnographic fieldworker

Overt observation When the identity of the researcher and purpose of the research is made clear to those being studied

Participant observation When a researcher takes part in the everyday life of the group while observing it

Reflexivity A turning back on oneself, a process of self-reference

Personal investigation: participant observation – places of worship

Conduct a mini-fieldwork project on places of worship within your own religious or other community. Religion often guides human behaviour and regulates interactions between human beings and their environment. Because religion is a complex mix of behaviours, material items, beliefs and people, studying places of worship can be an ideal setting for the study of the total integration of culture, a setting in which you can bring your own knowledge and background into observation.

In order to gain an idea of regular practices at the place of worship you have chosen, you should attend for at least three services and also conduct an interview with a religious leader. It is essential to ask consent of this leader before attending services and clearly explain your role as a student observer rather than as a potential member.

Guidelines for Observation

Record the following information:

- the physical layout and material culture of the service:
  * If allowed, take photos of the place of worship and any rituals observed.
- the human dimension of the service:
  * What ethnicity are the people attending?
  * Are there more male or more female participants? Are they young/old?
  * Are there any majority or minority groups?
  * Are people clustered in groups by age or sex?
- the service itself:
  * What kind of music is used, if any?
  * Who was leading the ceremony?
  * What was the time of day?
  * What was the style of audience participation?

The following are some questions to ask the leader of the place of worship:

- What are his/her reasons for becoming a minister/imam/priest?
- What is her/his education and training for this position?
- What is her/his experience of being the leader of the particular place of worship?

Using your field data, write a descriptive narrative essay on both the place of worship and the community of which it was a part. Include some ideas of your methodology. How did you get the information you needed? How did you start making connections with people? How did you portray your research to them? Did you use questionnaires, open interviews, etc.? What sorts of questions did you ask?

SUGGESTED FURTHER READING

Books

Aull, D. C. (2008) *Reflexive Ethnography: A Guide to Researching Selves and Others.* 2nd edn, Routledge.
Hammersley, M., and P. Atkinson ([1990] 2007) *Ethnography: Principles in Practice.* 3rd edn, Routledge.
Jeffrey, S. A., and A. Robben (eds) (2007) *Ethnographic Fieldwork: An Anthropological Reader.* Blackwell.
Kutsche, P. (1998) *Field Ethnography: A Manual for Doing Cultural Anthropology.* Prentice-Hall.
Marvin, G. ([1988] 1994) *Bullfight.* University of Illinois Press.
Morris, B. (2000) *The Power of Animals: An Ethnography.* Berg.
Murakami, H. (2003) *Underground: The Tokyo Gas Attack and the Japanese Psyche.* Vintage.

Websites

American Anthropological Association: *Handbook on Ethical Issues in Anthropology:* www.aaanet.org/committees/ethics/toc.htm
Association of Social Anthropologists of the UK and Commonwealth: *Ethical Guidelines for Good Research Practice:* www.theasa.org/ethics/guidelines.shtml
Luis Devin: Anthropological and ethnomusicological fieldwork among hunters and gatherers (Pygmies) and other peoples of Central Africa: www.luisdevin.com/home.php
Alan Macfarlane: Anthropological fieldwork – a personal account: www.alanmacfarlane.com/FILES/films.html

CHAPTER FOURTEEN

APPLIED ANTHROPOLOGY

CONTENTS

Applied Anthropology

Applied anthropology
'Anthropology put to use', or the application of anthropological skills and knowledge

Studying anthropology opens doors to many fields of work and equips students with the skills and knowledge that are required in the twenty-first century. Organizations such as the World Bank employ anthropologists on all their development projects. Organizational anthropology saves businesses money and increases productivity, and UK firms have found that, given the cultural diversity of those who use their services, healthcare providers benefit from staff with anthropological training. The previous chapter was about the way anthropologists conduct their research and possible issues that arise from doing fieldwork. This chapter will explore what anthropologists do with their knowledge and experience of fieldwork and how they use their skills in many fields beyond anthropology. While the first part looks at the theoretical aspects of **applied anthropology**, the second part consists of voices from different anthropologists around the world who apply their anthropological training and knowledge in different fields. All of the interviews were conducted by the authors.

WHAT IS APPLIED ANTHROPOLOGY?

Applied anthropology uses the theories, methods and ethnographic research of anthropology to explore and solve human problems. It focuses on practising anthropology in areas such as communities, organizations and businesses, health and education. In these fields, the anthropologist applies anthropological perspectives, theory and cultural knowledge to assess the main issues for the benefit of users.

WHAT DO ANTHROPOLOGISTS DO IN THE TWENTY-FIRST CENTURY?

Anthropologists study past and present cultures, language, human evolution and biological variation. Unlike other sciences, anthropology attempts to study the entire human condition over all time and space. Anthropologists work in many settings. Here are some of the examples (adapted from the RAI website) of where anthropologists are involved and how they use their broad knowledge of the world and a range of skills that are increasingly sought after by local and international organizations.

> **Academic anthropology**
> Teaching anthropology in schools/colleges and universities; academic anthropologists do research, often with the general objective of contributing to human knowledge

Academic anthropology	Academic anthropologists give lectures and seminars, publish articles and books, undertake administrative tasks and pursue ongoing research.
Business	Anthropologists working in business may be involved in market research, looking at product design, social trends and intercultural marketing, analysing consumer behaviour, researching purchasing trends, and identifying cultural responses to advertising in organizations such as Intel, IBM, General Motors, Hewlett Packard, Saatchi & Saatchi, and a growing number of manufacturing and service companies around the world.
Cultural organizations – museums	Museum work can encompass a wide variety of different roles: as a curator, researching and presenting artefacts in displays; as an education officer, working on educational materials and ongoing learning projects; or, as an independent researcher, doing contract work for a particular exhibition.
Developmental/ international aid	The development and international aid sectors involve complex interactions between academics, NGOs, charities, local communities, public and private agencies, donors and government bodies. Anthropologists may be actively involved in planning a development project or working as a cultural mediator between a particular community and a development organization. In other circumstances they may be brought in when a development project has not achieved its aims and be asked either to help bridge communication difficulties or to find alternative solutions requiring an intimate knowledge of the local language and community dynamics. Development anthropologists can also be found working as activists or advocates, helping indigenous communities with human rights claims, land disputes, or conservation of cultural heritage.
Government	Anthropologists can be found working at various levels of government. They may be directly involved in planning and policy-making activities, obtaining jobs in government funding bodies, or taking on senior administrative roles.
Media	Visual anthropologists may work as independent film-makers, set up their own businesses, or serve as consultants for major TV and film productions. They may also find work as curators in museums, art galleries or cultural institutions that have visual collections, or in businesses working on marketing strategies that incorporate visual elements.
Health	Biological anthropologists work in medical schools or departments of physiology, nutrition and pathology, conducting research on evolutionary origins, lifestyles and dietary changes that may shed light on contemporary health issues. They also find posts as researchers looking at human genetic development or, if they have undergone specialized forensic training, as medical/legal consultants identifying skeletal remains.
Teaching	A number of teachers with degrees in anthropology currently teach subjects such as anthropology, religious education, sociology, geography, citizenship, psychology or biology.
Tourism	Many anthropologists work as researchers alongside other social scientists on government-funded projects dealing with heritage, cross-cultural exchange and communication. Others find jobs as private consultants or analysts working on policy issues or as educators informing tour operators and tourists about cultural and environmental sensitivities. Anthropologists may also work alongside media companies producing films about tourism in particular regions.

Activity

Conduct research online and find a case study to illustrate each of the professions above. You can start by exploring the Royal Anthropological Institute website: www. discoveranthropology.org.uk.

ADVOCACY IN ANTHROPOLOGY

One of the most debated issues in anthropology is advocacy. It is understood that anthropology mainly involves understanding the world. Advocacy may be an emerging area of anthropology, but it has already raised much controversy. Is it the role of an anthropologist to try and change the world, or does their role end in understanding it? Should anthropologists work as advocates for the rights of minority groups they try to study, and does this compromise their objectivity?

Advocates such as Michael Jackson (1995), who has fought for land rights of Aboriginal Australians, would suggest we assess both positive and negative aspects of engagement and do our best to minimize any harmful elements.

Advocate
In this role, an applied anthropologist actively supports a cause or a group of people

The Object of Advocacy

Advocacy in anthropology looks beyond our understanding of the world to the role that anthropologists can play in changing the way things currently are for communities – the same communities that anthropologists have tried to understand over the years. However, while advocacy appears to have become more acceptable in recent years, there are issues regarding the extent to which anthropologists should take part in

Anthropologist Andrew Canessa and agroarchaeologist Alejandra Korrstanje using Andean foot ploughs in tilling land on steep slopes where oxen cannot plough (© Andrew Canessa)

changing things. Some argue that it is one thing to understand some of the communities and the problems they face and quite another to be actively involved in political matters: it is not their role to campaign for the causes of such communities.

By researching and communicating the perspective of their informants to others, anthropologists have always played a kind of advocacy role. Therefore it could be argued that *all* anthropology involves advocacy, as it has the goal of presenting a view of a given people to the rest of the world. The difference drawn between academic anthropology and advocacy is that the former ends with collecting and documenting information about communities, which may end up in the library, while the latter goes beyond acquiring this information to communicate it to the world and call for action.

That anthropologists have a moral duty to the communities they are involved with is beyond question (as illustrated in the ethical issues discussed in chapter 13). But should their role be more than just collecting and documenting everything they witness in a community and then maybe letting it gather dust in a university or library? Those supporting advocacy would say it has to be. Currently, advocacy in anthropology is redefining the discipline. This could be due to the huge increase in numbers of professional anthropologists and the lack of academic jobs. But it could also be due to the increase in awareness of problems facing the communities that anthropologists study, causing more of them to want to make a difference.

STOP & THINK

How does advocacy in anthropology challenge academic anthropology?
What are the main criticisms of advocacy in anthropology?
Can anthropology be objective? And should it *aim* to be objective?

Applied Anthropology and Public Health – A World Cut in Two: Global Justice and the Traffic in Humans for Organs

In various lectures Nancy Scheper-Hughes has suggested that anthropological knowledge and understanding should be put to service as a tool for human liberation. For her, public anthropology stands for change within the discipline and within humanity. Scheper-Hughes looks at the medical issues surrounding different societies, and through her ethnographic research and collaborations with journalists and politicians she attempts to raise awareness of matters such as illegal organ trafficking and women's health rights. She spent more than ten years tracking the illegal sale of human organs across the globe, posing as a medical doctor in some places and as a would-be kidney buyer in others, and linked gangsters and surgeons in a trail that led from South Africa, Brazil and other nations from the Global South all the way back to some of the USA's best medical facilities. She believed surgeons had been transplanting black-market kidneys from residents of the world's most deprived slums into the bodies of wealthy dialysis patients from Israel, Europe and the United States.

According to Scheper-Hughes, the kidney transplant arrangements were being arranged and organized by a network of criminals who kept most of the money themselves. The exchange of human organs for cash is illegal in every country except Iran. Nonetheless, international organ trafficking, mostly of kidneys but also of half-livers, eyes, skin and blood, is thriving.

The World Health Organization estimates that one-fifth of the 70,000 kidneys transplanted worldwide every year come from the black market. In America, the number of people in need of a transplant has nearly tripled during the past decade, topping 100,000 for the first time. Scheper-Hughes claims that organ selling has become a global problem. This example shows how anthropological skills and knowledge are employed in raising awareness of health issues in the public domain.

Activity

Scheper-Hughes conducted a research project exploring the illegal and covert activities surrounding the traffic in humans and their body parts by outlaw surgeons, kidney hunters and transplant tourists engaged in 'back-door' transplants in the global economy. Her work involved a combination of ethnography, documentation, surveillance and human rights work.

How does one investigate covert and criminal behaviour anthropologically?

When, if ever (and on what grounds), is it permissible to conduct research 'under cover'?

When crimes are being committed, to whom does one owe one's divided loyalties?

Is Scheper-Hughes's work a form of anthropology or not? Justify your answer. Think about whether an anthropologist should be impartial and whether this directs the research and determines its outcomes.

Where does power lie in public health? With the surgeon? Maybe with an anthropologist? Or perhaps with the gang members involved in illegal trafficking?

Ethics and Applied Anthropology

Practising applied anthropologists have ethical concerns about the programmes in which they are engaged in seeking to help others. Some of these have to do with whom the projects benefit and their long-term consequences. The box below explores some examples.

NANCY SCHEPER-HUGHES (1995)

Scheper-Hughes argues for a radical approach which is politically committed and morally engaged. She believes that anthropology must be ethically grounded and that cultural relativism, which she equates with moral relativism, is no longer appropriate. She is critical of the anthropologist as a 'neutral, dispassionate, cool and rational, objective observer of the human condition' (Scheper-Hughes 1995: 410).

KIRSTEN HASTRUP AND PETER ELSASS (1990)

We cannot separate ourselves from the material world within which we act: 'subject and object merge in a world of betweenness', and 'fieldwork is now openly recognized as a personal encounter and ethnography as an inter-subjective reality' (Hastrup and Elsass 1990: 302). These authors argue that advocacy and ethnography cannot work together and that the main role of an anthropologist should be academic: they should let other people advocate for their cause based upon the anthropologists' findings. However, most people, especially indigenous communities, lack the skills to advance their cause alone.

MELISSA DEMIAN (2003) – ANTHROPOLOGY AND LAW

Melissa Demian's experience with the community in the Ok Tedi copper and gold mine in Papua New Guinea shows that it is difficult for the local community to advocate for their causes because of a power imbalance. The members of the community have been complaining for a long time about environmental pollution downstream of the mine and have carried out legal and political campaigns, but they have not been successful because of the influence of large corporations. Demian – a lecturer in the anthropology of law at the University of Kent, who has strong knowledge of Papua New Guinea law to aid her – argues that anthropologists should not just collect and document the struggles of such communities but need to take an active role in fighting to ensure that their problems are addressed.

THE SFAA – THE SOCIETY FOR APPLIED ANTHROPOLOGY

The SFAA lists its mission as 'promoting interdisciplinary scientific investigation of the principles controlling the relations of human beings to one another, and the encouragement of the wide application of these principles to practical problems'. Essentially, this means applying what anthropologists have learnt about human culture at large, and the culture in question specifically, to policy statements and implementation.

THE AMERICAN ANTHROPOLOGICAL ASSOCIATION AND APPLIED ANTHROPOLOGY

American Anthropological Association
The major professional association for anthropologists in the United States

The two principal professional organizations for applied and practising anthropologists are the Society for Applied Anthropology and the National Association for the Practice of Anthropology, which is a section of the American Anthropological Association (AAA). Below is an interview with Dr Edward Liebow, the executive director of the AAA, in which he explains the purpose and aims of the largest anthropological association in 2013 and the future.

What is the role and history of the AAA?
The association was established in 1902 and today is the world's largest scholarly society of anthropologists. We have about 11,000 members, 20 per cent of whom are based outside the USA, including 244 from the UK. We publish a set of twenty-two journals, covering cultural, biological, linguistic and archaeological issues across the broad sweep of cultures throughout human history. As our bylaws state, 'the purposes of the Association shall be to advance anthropology as the science that studies humankind in all its aspects, through archaeological, biological, ethnological and linguistic research; and to further the professional interests of American anthropologists, including the dissemination of anthropological knowledge and its use to solve human problems.'

How does the AAA operate and can you describe some of the work it does?
Our main activities are to promote scholarly exchange through our publications and conferences, to promote excellence in training through professional development workshops, student internships and fellowships, and to increase public awareness of the work that anthropologists do through such initiatives as the association's project on race (www.understandingrace.org). We have a full-time staff of twenty-two and countless hundreds of volunteers who guide our publishing, meetings and various committee-led activities.

How can anthropology contribute to the world in which we live?
The training that anthropologists receive is of enormous value in a wide variety of settings. This training is essential in a world of global connections. While a large segment of our membership is involved in pushing the frontiers of knowledge about the human condition through research and training, a growing segment is involved in such endeavours as improving healthcare and educational systems, working towards

environmental sustainability, cultural heritage protection, reducing global inequalities, and increasing awareness of the many forms of households and families that raise our children and take care of our elderly. An anthropologist runs the World Bank. The prince of Wales, next in line to become the king of England, is an anthropologist. And an anthropologist raised the president of the United States. But we are also working in storefront NGOs in Nairobi, advising on marine protected areas in Southeast Asia, and working to restore traditional cultural properties in Mongolia after decades of attempts by outsiders to eradicate all vestiges of a rich and long-standing heritage.

What are the benefits of studying anthropology?
Students of anthropology become familiar with the broad sweep of human variation across cultures and throughout history. They learn about what people have in common the world over and also about the endless variations in language and local knowledge that make up the cultures of the world. These lessons help us appreciate one of the central tenets of anthropology, that no culture is 'better' than any other, just different. These lessons also help us appreciate that what we take to be 'common sense' is really the result of our upbringing, and that we must not assume that everyone else sees the world the same way we do. The benefit of such lessons can be applied in any situation where one must get along with others to accomplish something together, whether that is in school, community or workplace.

In 2008 the anthropologist Katarina Fritzsche conducted a combination of fieldwork and volunteering for the charity organization African Impact in the Western Cape Province, near Cape Town, where she studied childhood in a squatter camp and a township. Her daily activities included teaching, helping educators with their daily schedule at the pre-schools, sports, helping students with their homework, and renovating the school. (© Katarina Fritzsche)

What are the kinds of jobs that anthropologists do?
Many anthropologists work in higher education as lecturers, professors and researchers. However, the range of professions that employ anthropologists is breathtaking. Anthropologists are found at technology organizations such as Microsoft and Intel doing user experience research. We are found at the National Health Service and private healthcare delivery organizations understanding disease prevention and health

promotion, evaluating what works in improving healthcare outcomes, and training healthcare providers to be more sensitive to the needs of their patients. We are found in educational systems, contributing to culturally appropriate curricula, improving teachers' performance, and strengthening ties between school and community. We are helping to protect important historical properties, curating museum collections, and making documentary films. We do forensic work to help criminal investigations, and we help improve food security among the drought- and famine-stricken regions of the world.

Why is anthropological knowledge important in the twenty-first century?
The world today is connected in ways we have never seen before, with movements of people and information across great distances at lightning speeds. Differences among people who are inevitably brought together under these circumstances can lead both to conflict and to productive cross-pollination. A key lesson from anthropological knowledge is to help people resist the temptation to substitute introspection for observation – that is, to refrain from assuming that everyone thinks the same way you do and, similarly, to refrain from assuming that, just because someone you encounter may look different from you, that you have nothing in common.

What is the future of anthropology?
This is a great time to be an anthropologist. Our work continues to advance understanding of the human condition and is highly applicable to helping tackle some of the larger challenges we face, including the reduction of global inequalities and problems of environmental sustainability.

Should anthropological knowledge and research methods be used for helping others?
Absolutely. Our research cannot be undertaken without the trust, confidence and collaboration of the communities with whom we work, and we have a key responsibility to assure that our work is of benefit to our collaborators.

Is fieldwork an objective research method?
Certainly. Ethnographic research is systematic, hypothesis-driven, and focused on achieving the same standards of reliability and validity as any other form of social science research.

Should anthropology use scientific research methods?
We like to say that anthropology is the most humanistic of sciences and the most scientific of the humanistic disciplines. By that, we mean that, as with all scientific disciplines, our inquiry involves a cycle of 'prediction – systematic observation – revised prediction'. But our work involves more than that – we breathe life into the numbers and put a human face on the dry statistics in order to illuminate the arc of change and illustrate the specific circumstances that contribute to general understanding. At the same time, we recognize that 'science' is sometimes used to cloak bigotry and prejudice. At various times, racism has been justified by pseudo-scientific claims, as have arguments against evolutionary biology and global environmental change. The use of science is not free from social hierarchies, and it must be acknowledged that the uses of science create burdens and benefits, winners and losers. To have this awareness is not 'anti-science'. Indeed, anthropology offers the sort of tough love of science that all responsible scientists ought to share.

ANTHROPOLOGISTS' TESTIMONIES

The best way to understand what anthropologists do is to ask them to explain it to us. Although this is by no any means the most representative sample, it is a glimpse at what some anthropologists do and what they think about applied anthropology in the twenty-first century. It is impossible to cover all of the involvement of anthropology in the wider world; however, the following interviews provide good examples of how anthropologists use their skills and knowledge to help raise awareness of different issues in the world, as well as how their findings can be used in many different ways. All those interviewed answer the same sort of questions and show how they applied their skills and knowledge in different fields.

The Forensic Anthropologist

Forensic anthropology is the application of the science of physical anthropology to the legal process. The identification of skeletal remains which are badly decomposed, or otherwise unidentified human remains, is important for both legal and humanitarian reasons. Forensic anthropologists apply standard scientific techniques developed in physical anthropology to identify human remains and to assist in the detection of crime. In addition they work to suggest the age, sex, ancestry, stature and unique features of a descendant from the skeleton. When skeletalized remains are discovered, one needs to establish first if the bones are human. If so, the sex, race, age, stature, weight, and any pathology of the newly acquired skeleton must be established in order to make an identification of the remains, determine manner and cause of death and, if homicide, identify the murderer. It is the job of the forensic anthropologist to pursue these matters, make a report and possibly testify in court.

INTERVIEW WITH FORENSIC PATHOLOGIST HEATHER BONNEY, NATURAL HISTORY MUSEUM, LONDON

What is your role?
I have two roles; I am the human remains data collection project manager for the Natural History Museum. I also carry out forensic work for the police, to assist their investigations, and I am called upon when bones are discovered in building sites or people's gardens. It is my job to determine if these bones are recent or historic. Also I assist searches for human remains, for example, by differentiating human bones from animal bones. I am sometimes called to the mortuary to identify bones and to create a biological profile of the person to match them against the missing person register, also using DNA evidence.

The information I might investigate for the police includes cut marks, any type of injury, X-ray images for previous bones broken or diseases the person might have had, and information to help identify a person. I might also get called upon to identify remains in a mass disaster – for example, a large terrorist incident. Forensic anthropologists focus on bones whereas coroners tend to focus more on soft tissues.

What qualifications and experience did you have to work in this role?
I took a degree in forensic science, followed by an MA in human osteology and funerary archaeology, and then a PhD in forensic anthropology. I was also mentored by a forensic anthropologist.

Can you explain what forensic work goes on at the Natural History Museum?
There are around 20,000 sets of human remains held at the museum, covering a wide geographical area and a time period of up to 10,000 years. Some of these collections are heavily used and handled by researchers, and some sets of remains have been at the museum for 120 years. The handling of these remains can lead to their deterioration. To avoid this, the Natural History Museum is trying to produce data on the remains so that researchers can access them virtually.

Another important part of my role is to collect data on human remains so that they can be prepared to be returned to their place of origin at the request of representatives of their community. This process of **repatriation** is important to those communities, as it is felt that the remains can be properly laid to rest. There have been requests for repatriation from a range of different places, among them New Zealand, Northern America, Australia, the Torres Straits and Papua New Guinea. This process will often involve collaboration with representatives from the communities from which the remains originated. These representatives will visit the museum, and information will be exchanged to help us understand more about the culture from which the remains came. As well as this, it is important that the representatives are able to see the work that we do and particularly how careful we are with the remains. We work very hard to make sure the data collected is accurate and thorough so that the correct remains are returned to their place of origin.

Repatriation
The process of returning an object or person to their place of origin

What sort of information can be discovered about human remains?
The kinds of information that can be discovered about remains include age, sex, how someone lived, and their health (if, for example, they were malnourished, diseased or experienced starvation). Remains can also provide information about where the person came from. The two bones which provide a lot of this important information are the skull and the pelvis. The male skull has larger features because muscle attachments are larger. The female pelvis is larger than the male pelvis and is adapted for childbirth. Teeth remains can also indicate information about the age of the individual through signs of wear and tear.

The place in which the remains are found can provide important information. For example, the direction in which the body is lying can indicate a particular type of burial: bodies that lie east to west are likely to indicate an authorized Christian burial. The soil type is important, as it can help explain the rate of decomposition of the bones. It can be hard to identify older bones as they get soft and crumbly, depending on the age and health of the individual.

An examination is carried out on each of the remains and digital photographs are taken. A micro CT scan is taken so that the information about the remains can be stored

The forensic anthropologist
Heather Bonney examines a skull.
(© Natural History Museum, London)

digitally. This is a very detailed and time-consuming process. From each set of remains several hundred sets of data are collected. This includes the age and sex, and information about the measurement of the skull. Computer software is then used to suggest the geographic origin of the skull. We also use laser scanners that provide a 3D surface scan of the remains as well as a digital microscope.

What do you enjoy about your work? What do you find challenging?
Every day is different! Being a forensic anthropologist is a fascinating job which is very varied. The challenges: a lot of TV shows make forensic work look very glamorous, but it is not! I spend a lot of time in isolated spots, working sometimes outdoors in poor conditions, at any time of the night or day, and sometimes in bad weather conditions. Working with remains is a very time-consuming job and the process of identification and repatriation is lengthy. I really enjoy my job, however, and the different roles that I play.

The Applied Anthropologist

Anthropologists provide real insight from different cultures on perceptions of basic human rights; consequently they may be able to prevent human rights abuses in the future. Below is the testimony of an anthropologist from Italy, who conducted research on illegal migration in the Balkans.

> **STOP & THINK**
> What is forensic anthropology?
> What are the roles and responsibilities that Bonney has?
> What is repatriation?

INTERVIEW WITH DESIRÉE PANGERC – ANTHROPOLOGY OF HUMAN TRAFFICKING, ITALY

What is your role?
I teach applied anthropology as a contract professor in a private university. I am a consultant for some NGOs and for some public authorities involved in decentralized cooperation, and I am an external civil instructor at some military bases.

What are your main interests in anthropology?

My main interest is applied and action anthropology, but I also specialize in illegal and forced migrations, so my work is connected to the anthropology of security, too.

What was your main fieldwork? How were your findings used in other disciplines/policies, etc.?

My main fieldwork was researching in the Balkans, especially in Bosnia and Herzegovina, where I spent two years of my life. The book I wrote about that experience, *The Traffic of the Invisibles: Illegal migration along the Balkan routes* (2012) is used mainly by social and judicial operators. In order to understand the phenomenon, I investigated with a comprehensive approach and was prepared to assist the victims and to work with them during the trials against the perpetrators – and during the rehabilitation phase, too. At the same time, my book is considered a good tool for politicians, because it underlines the weaknesses of counter-trafficking activities by explaining what Alain Bauer calls *crime perception* in the Balkans.

Can you give us a brief summary of your work on applied anthropology?

In 2008, I was employed by the Italian Ministry of Foreign Affairs in Bosnia and Herzegovina as a programme officer. My role was to evaluate and monitor all Italian cooperation projects regarding legal and social issues, also projects on human trafficking. Human trafficking is a new form of slavery: criminal groups sell and buy especially women and minors – but also men – to exploit them sexually, to oblige them to work in terrible conditions for free, and to commit thefts and other types of crime. Linked to human trafficking are also illegal adoptions, organ trade and money laundering. As an applied anthropologist, I followed the projects involved in the assistance of the victims, and I started to gain information from the people I met by dividing them into three levels: an institutional one (ministries, embassies); an operative one (policemen, social operators); and, finally, an informal one (civil society, victims, perpetrators). And I can assure you that my informal network was very important during my fieldwork: they gave me direct evidence, suggestions and, sometimes, protection.

Should anthropologists get involved? What about objectivity?

I think that anthropologists must be involved. For instance, in the Balkans the statistics show us that human trafficking is no longer a social evil. However, the anthropologists in the field can observe facts and can confirm that the phenomenon has decreased in the last years but that it is still there; and, worse, it is increasing again now. In this sense, facts are 'objective' – if we are obliged to use this term, not data, because data on human trafficking are scarce, not comparable and unreliable. What the civil society tells you, what the victims, the operators and also the criminals tell you, what you observe every day, all this gives you the true dimension of the crime.

How can anthropology help solve human problems?

Anthropology provides a **holistic** view of the problems in a society. In my experience, I discovered that human trafficking in the Balkan countries was not considered a crime *tout court*, but only as a business – even for the victim who wants to escape from the country or to have more money for her/his family or for a better life, because they are convinced that their 'slavery' can be only temporary. So, if an anthropologist discovers this misperception of a very serious problem, he/she can easily identify where the gaps in the system are. I mean, there are a lot of conventions against human trafficking, a lot of local penal rules, a lot of international cooperation projects, a lot of police operations to combat the criminal organizations involved in this traffic. All these efforts were not able to stop human trafficking. Why? Because they haven't considered the **emic** perception; so, the challenge now is to raise awareness in the civil society and to change the wrong idea that a crime can be a business.

Have you collaborated with other disciplines?
I have. And I am still collaborating with a lot of experts from other disciplines. I firmly agreed with Gillian Tett from the *Financial Times* when she said at the Anthropology in the World conference that anthropology 'is to connect the dots'. To carry on my research, I used to have long conversations with legal experts, social operators, psychologists and other specialists. So I mixed my anthropological vocational training with law, sociology, economics, criminology, psychology and epistemology.

Refugees from North Africa in a boat off the coast of Italy (© Vito Manzari / Flickr)

What do you think the role of anthropology in the twenty-first century should be?
This is a very difficult question; there is a huge debate on this topic also here in Italy. I hope that anthropology has a stronger impact in the decision process at every level and in every part of the world. In my country, for instance, anthropology has still to overcome the division between academic anthropologists and applied ones. If we are not able to combine our efforts, I fear that our discipline will not have the expansion and the consideration it deserves.

STOP & THINK

What are the ethical and practical issues that Desirée Pangerc might have encountered in her work?

Anthropological Research

Some applied and practising anthropologists go back and forth between academic and non-academic settings. In the following two interviews anthropologists Pat Caplan and Sarah Pink explain how their research has been used in different fields outside anthropology academia.

INTERVIEW WITH PAT CAPLAN, EMERITUS PROFESSOR, DEPARTMENT OF ANTHROPOLOGY, GOLDSMITHS, UNIVERSITY OF LONDON

What are your main interests in anthropology?

I have worked on many issues over my long career in the discipline, but currently I am working around the following: biography (I am just publishing the biography of a Tanzanian); activism and the state (I have just been involved in campaigns around my local library in North London); the effects of animal disease on rural communities in the UK (currently bovine TB and badger culling); communicating with an audience outside of anthropology; and the politics and ethics of archiving.

What was your main fieldwork?

I have worked on Mafia Island, Tanzania, since 1965, with a most recent visit in 2010. I have published on kinship and descent; gender relations, including marriage, sexuality, the household, and the division of labour; food, health and fertility, including food security and gendered entitlements to food; personal narratives; and local concepts of modernities – to name only some. My second area is India, and I have worked in Chennai (Madras) since 1974. My most recent visit was in 2011. The topics have included the role of social welfare in class formation; the lives of middle-class women; women's voluntary organizations; and changes in food practices. In more recent years I have also focused on the UK, with research in the 1990s on the relationship between food and health in Southeast London and Southwest Wales. This led to work on risk and on disease in farm animals and its social consequences in South Wales.

How were your findings used in other disciplines or policies?

In Tanzania, UNICEF used some of my work on gendered entitlements to food in campaigns. And much of my work has been read, cited and used for teaching outside the discipline. In India, my work on gender was effectively interdisciplinary, as has been the work on food. Some of it was read by members of the Indian women's movement as this was developing in the 1980s. In the UK, my work on the effects of BSE and of TB have been widely read and used by people outside the discipline.

Should anthropologists get involved? What about objectivity?

Anthropologists need to be involved with their research participants, and this may lead in various directions, including advocacy. I am not sure I believe any longer that objectivity exists (or if I ever did).

In your view, how has anthropology changed in its application?

The classic view of 'applied' anthropology is in terms of development studies. But today it is also involved in medicine, policy-making and analysis, visual and other forms of media, to name a few.

How can anthropology help solve human problems?

By showing the connections between things which appear disconnected and by emphasizing social relations.

Have you collaborated with other disciplines?

Yes, frequently: with gender studies, development studies, 'history', risk analysis (itself an interdisciplinary concept), media studies, cultural studies, sociology, psychology, medicine and 'hard' science (such as physics).

What do you think the role of anthropology in the twenty-first century should be?

To continue to do what it does best – analysis of micro processes – but within a wider framework of time and space: historical, globalized. To share its insights with as wide an audience as possible by using a wide variety of means of dissemination, including websites and films. It's particularly important for anthropologists to make the strange familiar.

INTERVIEW WITH ANTHROPOLOGIST SARAH PINK, APPLIED VISUAL ANTHROPOLOGY, AUSTRALIA

What is your role?

I am currently professor of design (media ethnography) at RMIT University in Melbourne. I also have a part-time professorship in social sciences at Loughborough University in the UK. I have a BA in social anthropology (Kent University), an MA in visual anthropology (Manchester University) and a PhD in social anthropology (Kent University), but I have never worked in an anthropology department.

What was your main fieldwork? How were your findings used in other disciplines and policies?

While it was more conventional when I trained for anthropologists to have one context where they did their fieldwork and to maintain this focus throughout their career, this has not been the case for me. My PhD research was in Southern Spain, looking at women and bullfighting. I have continued to do research in Spain since, looking at domestic life and the slow city movement there. However, this has been comparative in relation to my work in the UK, where my fieldwork has covered these two areas, along with digital media and energy consumption in the home and the construction industry. I am now doing research in Australia. I would also note that, as my career has developed, I have been doing less actual fieldwork myself but, instead, often working with research associates with whom I collaborate in the analysis.

Can you give a brief summary of your work in applied anthropology?

My work in applied anthropology has focused on everyday life in the home and organizations. It has been funded or developed with a range of different types of sponsor from both the corporate and the public sector. My current work in applied anthropology includes projects looking at energy demand reduction and occupational safety and health. I have also been active in promoting applied anthropology through a publications series, Studies in Public and Applied Anthropology, which I co-edit for Berghahn Books. One of the ideas behind this series is to ensure that work in theoretical, scholarly and applied scholarship in anthropology is brought together in publications so as to create a bridge between the two areas.

Should anthropologists get involved? What about objectivity?
Yes, anthropologists should definitely get involved; they have much to contribute to debates and issues in applied research contexts. Anthropology can bring unique insights that do not emerge from other approaches. Anthropology and the types of anthropological knowledge that can be produced through ethnography often challenge, and turn upside down, existing assumptions, and this is important for advancing knowledge and producing innovations. For me it is not a question of objectivity; I do not believe it is possible to achieve true objectivity in research. However, we do need to be able to convince people from other disciplines that the subjectivity of qualitative knowledge such as that produced in anthropology is valid.

How can visual anthropology help solve human problems?
One of the key possibilities that visual anthropology offers is a route to creating empathetic understandings between people from different disciplines or who have different subjectivities.

Have you collaborated with other disciplines?
I have worked with people from across a wide range of disciplines, including photographers, engineers, designers and sociologists.

CONCLUSION

The world in the twenty-first century is becoming more complex. The globalized world is coming closer than ever before to small-scale indigenous communities, threatening their existence. Applied anthropology could be the next step to understanding people's cultures better. There is no sharp division between 'pure research' and applied anthropology. Depending on the skills and interests of the researcher, a lot of innovative insights and theoretical ideas can come out of applied research. The anthropologist's goal is to help ensure that societies are not negatively affected by the continuing advancement of the modern world as it expands through less developed countries. The testimonies from anthropologists in this chapter suggest that no anthropologist can escape involvement. Anthropologists realize that their subject matter always implies a degree of involvement, which, in itself, contributes to change.

As a director of the AAA, Edward Liebow suggests that anthropological study provides training particularly well suited to the twenty-first century. The economy will be increasingly international; workforces and markets increasingly diverse; participatory management and decision-making increasingly important; communication skills increasingly in demand. Anthropology is the only contemporary discipline that approaches human questions from historical, biological, linguistic and cultural perspectives. As a discipline it has evolved and changed since its beginnings. Applied anthropology as a product of academic anthropology has an important role to play in solving human problems.

END OF CHAPTER ASSESSMENT

The role of anthropology is to try to change the world. Assess this view.

Teacher's guidance

Using both information from this chapter and independent research, evaluate the above statement. Show different points of view and answer the following questions. Is the role of the anthropologist to try to change the world or only to understand it? Can (and should) anthropologists act as advocates for the rights of people they study, or does this compromise their objectivity? This inevitably engages with fundamental questions about the role of anthropology. What is anthropology for? Who is it for? Why should anthropologists strive for objectivity? Should the anthropologist act to try to improve the circumstances of local people? Should the anthropologist act as an intermediary and voice on behalf of local people, particularly when requested to do so? Should anthropologists engage as active agents of change? Illustrate your arguments with ethnographic case studies.

KEY TERMS

Academic anthropology Teaching anthropology in schools/colleges and universities; academic anthropologists do research, often with the general objective of contributing to human knowledge

Advocate In this role, an applied anthropologist actively supports a cause or a group of people

American Anthropological Association The major professional association for anthropologists in the United States

Applied anthropology 'Anthropology put to use', or the application of anthropological skills and knowledge

Cultural relativity Suspending one's ethnocentric judgement in order to understand and appreciate another culture. Anthropologists try to learn about and interpret the various aspects of the culture they are studying in its own terms rather than in terms of their own

Holistic No dimension of culture can be understood in isolation; cultures are integrated wholes

Humanism Concern for human welfare, dignity and values

Multidisciplinarity Independent research on the same issues and problems from different disciplines

Repatriation The process of returning an object or person to their place of origin

SUGGESTED FURTHER READING

Books

Eriksen, T. H. (2006) *Engaging Anthropology: The Case for Public Presence*. Berg.

McDonald, J. H. (ed.) (2001) *The Applied Anthropology Reader*. Pearson.

Pink, S. (2006) *Applications of Anthropology: Professional Anthropology in the Twenty-First Century*. Berghahn.

Scheper-Hughes, N., and L. Wacquant (2002) *Commodifying Bodies*. Sage.

Websites

American Anthropological Association: www.aaanet.org

Applied Anthropology in the Corporate World: www.youtube.com/watch?v=94fdBg0HBT0

Applied Anthropology videos: www.ovguide.com/applied-anthropology-9202a8c04000641f80000000 002eda79

National Association for the Practice of Anthropology (NAPA): www.practicinganthropology.org
Royal Anthropological Institute: www.therai.org.uk
Royal Anthropological Institute, Anthropology in the World conference, 8–10 June 2012: www.youtube.
  com/watch?v=V6mLr5st-ac
Society for Applied Anthropology: www.sfaa.net

Glossary

Academic anthropology   Researching and teaching anthropology at schools/colleges and universities; academic anthropologists do research, often with the general objective of contributing to human knowledge

Achieved identity   Parts of a person's identity which are chosen

Achieved status   A position that is earned

Advocate   In this role, an applied anthropologist actively supports a cause or a group of people

Aesthetics   A branch of philosophy concerned with beauty and the ability to recognize it

Affine   Kin created through marriage

Age grades   Levels of seniority through which age sets pass collectively as they grow older

Age set   A group of individuals of a similar age, often sharing special social links with one another

Agency   The capacity for human beings to make choices, create their own world, have their own ideas, etc.

Altruism   The ability to put the needs of others before your own

American Anthropological Association   The major professional association for anthropologists in the United States

Animism   A belief that natural phenomena such as rocks, trees, thunder, or celestial bodies have life or divinity; giving souls or a spiritual existence to animals, plants and other natural objects, meaning that non-humans are given the identity of a 'person' in some form

Anthropocentric   The tendency for human beings to regard themselves as the central and most significant entities in the universe, or the assessment of reality through an exclusively human perspective

Anthropomorphism   To attribute human characteristics to animals

Applied anthropology   'Anthropology put to use', or the application of anthropological skills and knowledge

Archaeology   The study of human history and prehistory through the excavation of sites and the analysis of artefacts

Artefact   Any object made by a human

Ascribed identity   Parts of a person's identity which are given

Ascribed status   A position that is given, usually at birth

Assimilation   The absorption of an individual or minority group of people into another society or group, achieved by learning and adopting the cultural traditions of the society to which assimilation occurs; it is also often hastened by intermarriage and by de-emphasizing cultural and or biological differences

Autonomy   Freedom and independence, the right to self-governance

Avatar   A computer user's representation of himself/herself or an alter ego

Biocentric   A view that nature does not exist simply to be used or consumed by humans, but that humans are simply one species among many

Bipedalism   Walking upright on two feet for the majority of time

Body modification   The deliberate altering of the human anatomy

Boundaries   The physical and imagined differences between groups and individuals; the furthest limits

Bounded   The idea that a person is restricted to his or her physical body and is not permeable or transferable to others

Bridewealth   Payment by a groom's kin to a bride's kin in return for his rights to her labour and reproductive powers

Capitalism   Society based on the ownership of private property and individual rights

Catastrophism   The theory that the Earth has been affected in the past by sudden, short-lived, violent events, possibly worldwide in scope, which have led to the contemporary world with its current variety of animals and plants

Code-switching   Where a person uses two or more different languages within one conversation

Colonialism   Exploitation by a stronger country of a weaker one; the use of the weaker country's resources to strengthen and enrich the stronger country

Colonialization   The forming of a settlement or colony by a group of people who seek to take control of territories or countries, usually involving large-scale immigration of people to a 'new' location and the expansion of their culture into this area

Commodity   Anything that can be bought or sold

Communitas   Group solidarity

Consanguineous relatives   Kin related by blood

Consumption   The desire to have more material objects than is necessary for survival

Covert observation   When a study is carried out 'under cover': the researcher's identity and purpose of research are concealed from the group

Creationism   The belief that all life was created by the actions of God

Creolization   A complex process in which old beliefs and cultural practices survive alongside more recently acquired ones and mix with them to create new cultural forms

Cross-cultural research   A method that uses a global sample of societies in order to test hypotheses

Cultural ecology   The study of the adaptation of human societies or populations to their environments; the emphasis is on the arrangements of technique, economy and social organization through which cultures mediate the experience of the natural world

Cultural evolution   The ways in which humans have evolved beyond their biology

Cultural group   A group of people who share some cultural characteristics

Cultural materialism   A view that says that the best way to understand human culture is to examine material conditions – climate, food supply, geography, etc.

Cultural relativity   Suspending one's ethnocentric judgement in order to understand and appreciate another culture; interpreting the various aspects of a culture in references to that culture rather than one's own

Cultural universal   Those general cultural traits found in all societies of the world

Culturally constructed   Something which is created by society

Culture shock   A feeling of confusion, distress and, sometimes, depression that can result from psychological stress during the first weeks or months of a total cultural immersion in an alien society

Cyborg   An organism that is part human and part machine; a person whose physiological functioning is aided or dependent on a mechanical or electronic device

Diaspora   The movement, migration or scattering of people away from their established or ancestral homeland or people dispersed, by whatever cause, to more than one location

Diffusion   The movement of cultural traits and ideas from one society or ethnic group to another; while the form of a trait may be transmitted to another society, the original meaning may not be

Dividual   A being who is incomplete and continuously involved in the process of being made up of the relations that define him or her

Dowry   Gifts that a bride brings from her family into the marriage

Ecocide   The extensive damage to or destruction or loss of ecosystem(s) of a given territory, whether by human agency or by other causes, to such an extent that peaceful enjoyment by the inhabitants of that territory has been or will be severely diminished

Ecology   The study of the interaction between living and non-living components of the environment

Embodiment   A tangible or visible form of an idea, quality or feeling

Emic   A perspective in ethnography that uses the concepts and categories that are relevant and meaningful to the culture under analysis

Empirical   Verifiable through the senses (sight, touch, smell, hearing, taste), either directly or through extensions (reliance on observable and quantifiable data)

Endogamy   Marriage takes place only within a group

Environmental determinism   A deterministic approach assigns one factor as the dominant influence in explanations; environmental determinism is based on the assumption that cultural and natural areas are interconnected, because culture represents an adaptation to the particular environment

Environmentalism   A social movement to protect the natural environment

Ethnic cleansing   The planned or deliberate removal of a particular ethnic group from a specific territory

Ethnic conflict   War or conflict based on cultural groupings

Ethnic revitalization   A process of reaffirming and strengthening ethnic identity

Ethnicity   The identification of a group based on a perceived shared cultural distinctiveness, expressed through language, music, values, art, literature, family life, religion, ritual, food, public life and material culture

Ethno ecology   Any society's traditional set of environmental perceptions – that is to say, a cultural model of the environment and its relation to people and society

Ethnocentrism   Regarding one's own ethnicity as superior to others and/or viewing others only through one's own cultural categories; privileging one's own cultural world-view

Ethnomusicology   The study of music in its cultural context

Etic   An approach centred on how an outsider might think about things

Evolution   Any change across successive generations in the inherited characteristics of biological populations

Exogamy   Marriage is practised only with people outside a group

Fictive kinship   Forms of kinship or social ties that are based on neither consanguinal (blood) nor affinal ('by marriage') ties

Fieldwork   The first-hand observation of human societies

Fossils   The preserved remains or traces of animals, plants and other organisms from the remote past

Gatekeepers   People who control access to a research site

Gender   Culturally constructed notions of what it means to be male or female, depending on the social context

Gender relations   The nature of relationships between men and women in terms of responsibilities, power and decision-making

Gendered identity   The way we see ourselves and are seen by others in relation to culturally constructed ideas of what it means to be a man or woman

Genealogy   The study of kinship and descent patterns

Genocide   The systematic killing of an ethnic group

Gift exchange   The giving and receiving of objects, usually reciprocal

Globalization   The worldwide process of increasing economic, technological, political and cultural interactions, integration and interdependence of nations

Greenpeace   An international organization that works for environmental conservation and the preservation of endangered species

Habitus   The lifestyle, values, dispositions and expectations of particular social groups that are acquired through the activities and experiences of everyday life

Handedness   A preference for using one hand as opposed to the other

Hierarchy   A form of social organization where some individuals or groups have greater power, social status or ranking than others

Holistic   No dimension of culture can be understood in isolation; cultures are integrated wholes

Holistic approach   An approach to the study of humanity which looks at the whole/totality (a comprehensive approach)

Hybrid identity   The mixture of two different identities leading to the emergence of a new form of identity that is different from its constituent parts

Hybridization   The process by which an individual, group or people adopts cultural traits from another society; what happens to a culture when alien traits move in on a large scale and substantially replace traditional cultural patterns

Identification   The ongoing process that describes the way in which individuals and groups see themselves and the way that others see them

Immaterial   Lacking substance

Imperialism   A general term to describe the various ways in which one country may exploit and dominate another

Informal interview   An unstructured question-and-answer session in which the informant is encouraged to follow his or her own train of thought, wherever it may lead

Informant   A person who provides information about his or her culture to the ethnographic fieldworker

Intelligent design   Also known as neo-creationism, the belief that the current state of life on Earth has come about through the actions of an intelligent designer; this designer need not be God, but most proponents of intelligent design seem to have God in mind

Kinning   The social process where adopted/non-biologically related children become kin

Kinship   Sets of relationships considered primary in any society, also called family and relations, in practice demonstrating huge variety in different societies

Large-scale society   A society with cities, industry, intensive agriculture, and a complex international economy

Liminal   Relating to a transitional stage between states or categories

Mammal   Any warm-blooded vertebrate animal, including humans, characterized by a covering of hair on the skin and, in the female, milk-producing mammary glands for feeding the young

Material culture   The physical objects, resources and spaces that people use within their culture

Matrilineal   Descent through the female

Matrilocal   Where a married couple lives near or with the family of the wife or mother

Means of production   The factories, machines and other resources that help produce goods and services and result in profit for those who own them

Mode of production   The dominant way in which people make a living in a particular culture

Multidisciplinarity   Independent research on the same issues and problems from different disciplines

Multi-sited ethnography   A method of data collection that follows a topic or social problem through different field sites

Myth   A story, which is not necessarily accurate, often told about a people and their origins, sometimes involving supernatural beings

Nationalism   Identification of an ethnic identity with a state; it can include the belief that one's nation is of primary importance

Natural selection   The process in nature by which, according to Darwin's theory of evolution, only the organisms best adapted to their environment tend to survive and transmit their genetic characteristics in increasing numbers to succeeding generations, while those less adapted tend to be eliminated

Objectification   The process of treating another person or persons as if they are objects or instruments, sometimes for personal gain

Opposable thumb   A thumb that is sufficiently separate from the other fingers of the hand to allow for precision grip

Overt observation   When the identity of the researcher and purpose of the research is made clear to those being studied

Partible   The idea that persons are permeable and that personhood can be transferred, in part, to others through the exchange of bodily fluids or auras

Participant observation   When a researcher takes part in the everyday life of the group while observing it

Patriarchy   Male-dominated society

Patrilineal   Descent through the male

Patrilocal   Where a married couple lives near or with the family of the husband or father

Personhood   A social status granted in various ways to those who meet certain criteria; all societies have criteria concerning who can become a person

Potlatch   An important ritual practised by some Native Americans involving competitive gift giving, which plays an important part of the economy

Power asymmetry   An imbalance of power between a larger and a smaller group

Primate   A mammal of the order Primates, characterized, for example, by refined development of the hands and feet and a large brain

Racism   Discrimination against an individual or group based on their perceived ethnicity and the idea that 'race' is a fixed and bounded reality

Reciprocity   Informal systems of exchange

Reflexivity   The ability to stand back and assess aspects of one's own behaviour, society, culture, etc.

Refugees   People who have been forcibly displaced

Reincarnation   The rebirth of a soul in a new body

Repatriation   The process of returning an object or person to their place of origin

Reproductive technology   Technology, including IVF and other forms of fertility treatment, that creates new forms of kinship relations

Rites of passage   A series of rites that mark the transformation from one stage of life, season or event to another

Ritual   Behaviour prescribed by society in which individuals have little choice about their actions; sometimes having reference to beliefs in mystical powers or beings

Sacred   Pertaining to or connected with religious or spiritual matters

Secular   Relating to worldly matters

Situational identity   The idea that one's cultural group is a product of others and depends on the social setting

Small-scale society   A society of a few dozen to several thousand people on the band or village level who live by foraging wild foods, herding domesticated animals or practising non-intensive agriculture

Social class   A socio-economic group found within capitalist society, usually based on the occupation and attitudes of the individual

Social construction   The view that the phenomena of the social and cultural world and their meanings are created in human social interaction

Social kinship   Relationships created through social interaction rather than biologically based relations

Social memories   The collective retelling of past events which may shape identity in the present

Sociobiological view of kinship   The view that biology plays a central role in explaining kinship relationships

Sociobiology   The study of the biological determinants of social behaviour

Sociocentric concept of personhood   Where a person is defined by the relationships he or she has with others

Subsistence patterns   The sources and methods a society uses to obtain its food and other necessities

Symbol   Something which is used to represent an idea or object

Taboo   A custom prohibiting or restricting a particular practice or forbidding association with a particular person, place or thing

Tattoo   A permanent mark or design made on the skin by a process of pricking and ingraining an indelible pigment or by raising scars

Taxonomy   The classification of organisms in an ordered system that indicates natural relationships

Territorial conflict   Conflict over land rights

Totem   A natural object, plant or animal that is believed by a particular society to have spiritual significance and that is adopted as a symbol of the characteristics of that group

Transhumanism   An international, intellectual and cultural movement supporting the use of science and technology to improve human intellectual and physical characteristics

Transnational corporation (TNC)   A corporate business that has outgrown its national roots and identity and is multinational, with facilities in many countries, but no overriding feeling of obligation or loyalty to any one of them; such companies typically move their production facilities from nation to nation in response to labour costs and tax advantages. As a result, they are generally independent and beyond the control of any one national political system. TNCs have had a major impact on previously isolated indigenous societies in the late twentieth century

UNESCO   The United Nations Educational, Scientific and Cultural Organization works to create the conditions for dialogue among civilizations, cultures and peoples, based upon respect for commonly shared values; it is through this dialogue that the world can achieve global visions of sustainable development encompassing observance of human rights, mutual respect and the alleviation of poverty, all of which are at the heart of UNESCO'S mission and activities

Western philosophical individualism   The idea that a person is a distinct entity, based on the view that personhood is derived from the biological separation of one person from another, each possessing individual autonomy; social relations are regarded as less important

References

Books and Articles

Ahearn, L. (2001) 'Language and agency', *Annual Review of Anthropology* 30: 109–37.

Anderson, B. ([1983] 2006) *Imagined Communities: Reflections on the Origin and Spread of Nationalism*. Rev. edn, Verso.

Appadurai, A. (ed.) (1986) *The Social Life of Things: Commodities in Cultural Perspective*. Cambridge University Press.

Archetti, E. (1997) *Guinea-Pigs*. Oxford: Berg.

Archetti, E. (1999) *Masculinities*. Berg.

Ardener, S. (1975) *Perceiving Women*. Malaby Press.

Ashmore, R. D., L. Jussim and D. Wilder (eds) (2001) *Social Identity, Intergroup Conflict, and Conflict Reduction*. Oxford University Press.

Aull, D. C. (2008) *Reflexive Ethnography: A Guide to Researching Selves and Others*. 2nd edn, Routledge.

Barnard, A. (2011) *Social Anthropology and Human Origins*. Cambridge University Press.

Barth, F. ([1969] 1998) *Ethnic Groups and Boundaries: The Social Organization of Culture Difference*. Waveland Press.

Barthes, R. (1974) *S/Z: An Essay*. Cape.

Bateson, G., and M. Mead ([1942] 1962) *Balinese Character: A Photographic Analysis*. New York Academy of Sciences.

Bauman, R. (1992) *Folklore, Cultural Performances, and Popular Entertainments*. Oxford University Press.

Beauvoir, S. de ([1952] 1989) *The Second Sex*. Vintage.

Becker, A. E. (1995) *Body, Self, and Society: The View from Fiji*. University of Pennsylvania Press.

Bell, C. (2010) *Ritual Theory, Ritual Practice*. 2nd edn, Oxford University Press.

Benedict, R. (1989) *Patterns of Culture*. Houghton Miffin.

Bennett, R. L., A. G. Motulsky, A. Bittles, S. Hudgins, S. Uhrich, D. L. Doyle, K. Silvey, C. R. Scott, E. Cheng, B. McGillivray, R. D. Steiner and D. Olson (2002) 'Genetic counseling and screening of consanguineous couples and their offspring: recommendations of the National Society of Genetic Counselors', *Journal of Genetic Counseling* 11(2): 97–119.

Besnier, N. (2002) 'Transgenderism, locality and the Miss Galaxy beauty pageant in Tonga', *American Ethnologist* 29: 534–66.

Bickerton, D. (2000) *Lingua ex machina: Reconciling Darwin and Chomsky with the Human Brain*. Bradford Books.

Bloch, M. (1998) *How We Think They Think: Anthropological Studies in Cognition, Memory and Literacy*. Westview Press.

Boas, F. (1974) *The Shaping of American Anthropology, 1883–1911: A Franz Boas Reader*, ed. G. W. Stocking. University of Chicago Press.

Boddy, J. (1998) 'Remembering Amal: on birth and the British in northern Sudan', in M. Lock and P. A. Kaufert (eds), *Pragmatic Women and Body Politics*. Cambridge University Press.

Boellstorff, T. (2008) *Coming of Age in Second Life*. Princeton University Press.

Bohannan, P., and L. Bohannan (1968) *Tiv Economy*. Northwestern University Press.

Bolin, A. (1996) 'Transcending and transgendering: male to female transsexuals, dichotomy and diversity', in G. Herdt (ed.), *Third Sex, Third Gender: Beyond Sexual Dimorphism in Culture and History*. Zone Books.

Bourdieu, P. (1977) *Outline of a Theory of Practice*. Cambridge University Press.

Bourque, N. (2001) 'Eating your words: communicating with food in the Ecuadorian Andes', in J. Hendry and C. W. Watson (eds), *An Anthropology of Indirect Communication*. Routledge.

Bowie, F. (2006) *The Anthropology of Religion: An Introduction*. 2nd edn, Blackwell.

Brennan, D. (2004) 'Women work, men sponge and everyone gossips: macho men and stigmatized/ing women in a sex tourist town', *Anthropological Quarterly* 77(4): 705–33.

Bringa, T. (1995) *Being Muslim the Bosnian Way: Identity and Community in a Central Bosnian Village*. Princeton University Press.

Bromberger, C. (1995) 'Football as world-view and as ritual', *French Cultural Studies* 6(3): 293–311.

Brumfiel, E., and J. W. Fox (2003) *Factional Competition and Political Development in the New World*. Cambridge University Press.

Bucholtz, M., and K. Hall (2005) 'Identity and interaction: a sociocultural linguistic approach', *Discourse Studies* 7: 585–614.

Bunn, S. (1999) *Working with Living Willow*. Woodland Craft Supplies.

Butler, J. (1990) *Gender Trouble: Feminism and the Subversion of Identity*. Routledge.

Canessa, A. (2005) *Natives Making Nation: Gender, Indigeneity and the State in the Andes*. University of Arizona Press.

Canessa, A. (2012) *Intimate Indigeneities: Race, Sex, and History in the Small Spaces of Andean Life*. Duke University Press.

Carsten, J. (2004) *After Kinship*. Cambridge University Press.

Carter, D. M. (2005) 'Living in virtual communities: an ethnography of human relationships in cyberspace', *Journal of Information, Communication and Society* 8(2): 148–67.

Case, A. (2010) 'We are all cyborgs now', www.ted.com/talks/amber_case_we_are_all_cyborgs_now?language=en.

Chagnon, N. A. ([1968] 1983) *Yanomamö: The Fierce People*. 3rd edn, Holt McDougal.

Charlton, N. G. (2008) *Understanding Gregory Bateson: Mind, Beauty, and the Sacred Earth*. State University of New York Press.

Cohen, A. (1969) *Custom and Politics in Urban Africa: A Study of Hausa Migrants in Yoruba Towns*. Routledge & Kegan Paul.

Cohen, A. (1985) *The Symbolic Construction of Community*. Routledge.

Comaroff, J. L., and J. Comaroff (eds) (1993) *Modernity and its Malcontents: Ritual and Power in Postcolonial Africa*. University of Chicago Press.

Condry, I. (2001) 'Japanese hip-hop and the globalization of popular culture', in G. Gmelch and W. Zenner (eds), *Urban Life: Readings in the Anthropology of the City*. Waveland Press.

Condry, I. (2006) *Hip-Hop Japan: Rap and the Paths of Cultural Globalization*. Duke University Press.

Conklin, B., and L. Morgan (1996) 'Babies, bodies, and the production of personhood in North America and a native Amazonian society', *Ethos* 24(4): 657–94.

Csordas, T. J. (1999) 'The body's career in anthropology', in H. L. Moore (ed.), *Anthropological Theory Today*. Polity.

Cushing, F. ([1901] 2007) *Zuni Folk Tales*. Kessinger.

DeMello, M. (2000) *Bodies of Inscription: A Cultural History of the Modern Tattoo Community*. Duke University Press.

Demian, M. (2003) 'Custom in the courtroom, law in the village: legal transformations in Papua New Guinea', *Journal of the Royal Anthropological Institute* 9(1): 97–115.

Dirks, N. (1992) *Colonialism and Culture*. University of Michigan Press.

Douglas, M. (1966) *Purity and Danger: An Analysis of Concepts of Pollution and Taboo*. Routledge.

Douglas, M. ([1970] 2003) *Natural Symbols: Explorations in Cosmology*. 3rd edn, Routledge.

Douglas, M. ([1975] 1999) *Implicit Meanings: Selected Essays in Anthropology*. 2nd edn, Routledge.

Dove, R. M., and C. Carpenter (2007) *Environmental Anthropology: A Historical Reader*. Wiley-Blackwell.

Drummond, L. (1980) 'The cultural continuum: a theory of intersystems', *Man*, 15(2): 352–74.

Du Gay, P., J. Evans and P. Redman (2000) *Identity: A Reader*. Open University Press.

Dumont, L. (1980) *Homo Hierarchicus: The Caste System and its Implications*. University of Chicago Press.

Dunbar, R. (2004) *Grooming, Gossip and the Evolution of Language*. Faber & Faber.

Dupré, J. (1998) 'Normal people', *Social Research* 65: 221–48.

Durkheim, E., and M. Mauss ([1903] 1963) *Primitive Classification*. Routledge.

Dworkin, A., and C. A. MacKinnon (1988) *Pornography and Civil Rights: A New Day for Women's Equality*. Organizing Against Pornography.

Edwards, E., C. Gosden and R. Phillips (2006) *Sensible Objects: Colonialism, Museums and Material Culture*. Berg.

Eriksen, T. H. (2001) *Small Places, Large Issues: An Introduction to Social and Cultural Anthropology*. Pluto Press.

Eriksen, T. H. (2002) *Ethnicity and Nationalism: Anthropological Perspectives*. Pluto Press.

Eriksen, T. H. (2003) *Globalization: Studies in Anthropology*. Pluto Press.

Eriksen, T. H. (2006) *Engaging Anthropology: The Case for Public Presence*. Berg.

Eriksen, T. H. (2007) *Globalization: The Key Concepts*. Berg.

Eriksen, T. H. (2010) *Small Places, Large Issues: An Introduction to Social and Cultural Anthropology*. 3rd edn, Pluto Press.

Evans-Pritchard, E. E. (1937) *Witchcraft, Oracles and Magic among the Azande*. Oxford University Press.

Evans-Pritchard, E. E. ([1940] 1987) *The Nuer: A Description of the Modes of Livelihood and Political Institutions of a Nilotic People*. 3rd edn, Oxford University Press.

Farace, D., E. Durkheim and M. Eliade (1982) *The Sacred-Profane Dichotomy*. Rijksuniversiteit Utrecht.

Ferguson, J. (1998) 'Cultural exchange: new developments in anthropology of commodities', *Cultural Anthropology* 3(4): 488–513.

Firth, R. (1973) *Symbols: Public and Private*. Cornell University Press.

Firth, R. (1981) 'Bronislaw Malinowski', in S. Silverman (ed.), *Totems and Teachers: Perspectives on the History of Anthropology*. Columbia University Press.

Firth, R. (1988) 'Malinowski in the history of social anthropology', in R. F. Ellen, E. Gellner, G. Kubica and J. Mucha (eds), *Malinowski Between Two Worlds: The Polish Roots of an Anthropological Tradition*. Cambridge University Press.

Foucault, M. ([1973] 1994) *The Birth of the Clinic: An Archaeology of Medical Perception*. Vintage.

Frank, K. (2002) *G-Strings and Sympathy: Strip Club Regulars and Male Desire*. Duke University Press.

Frayer, D., and M. Wolpoff (1985) 'Sexual dimorphism', *Annual Review of Anthropology* 14: 429–73.

Frazer, J. ([1890] 1993) *The Golden Bough: A Study in Magic and Religion*. Wordsworth.

Geertz, C. (1973) *The Interpretation of Cultures*. Basic Books.

Gellner, P. L., and M. K. Stockett (eds) (2006) *Feminist Anthropology: Past, Present, and Future*. University of Pennsylvania Press.

Gluckman, M. (1955) *Custom and Conflict in Africa*. Free Press.

Gordillo, G. (2002) 'The breath of the devils: memories and places of an experience of terror', *American Ethnologist* 29(1): 33–57.

Haenn, N., and R. R. Wilk (eds) (2006) *The Environment in Anthropology: A Reader in Ecology, Culture and Sustainable Living*. York University Press.

Hall, K. (2002) *Lives in Translation: Sikh Youth as British Citizens*. University of Pennsylvania Press.

Hallowell, A. ([1955] 2009) *Memories, Myths, and Dreams of an Ojibwe Leader*. Queens University Press.

Hammersley, M., and P. Atkinson ([1990] 2007) *Ethnography: Principles in Practice*. 3rd edn, Routledge.

Hannerz, U. (1992) *Cultural Complexity: Studies in the Social Organization of Meaning*. Columbia University Press.

Haraway, D. J. (1991) *Simians, Cyborgs, and Women: The Reinvention of Nature*. Routledge.

Harris, M. (1992) 'The cultural ecology of India's sacred cattle', *Current Anthropology* 33(1): 261–76.

Harris, M. (1998) *Theories of Culture in Postmodern Times*. AltaMira Press.

Hastrup, K., and P. Elsass (1990) *Anthropological Advocacy*. University of Chicago Press.

Hendry, J. (2008) *An Introduction to Social Anthropology: Sharing our Worlds*. 2nd edn, Palgrave Macmillan.

Herdt, G. H. (1982) *Rituals of Manhood: Male Initiation in Papua New Guinea*. University of California Press.

Hertz, R. ([1909] 2008) *Death and the Right Hand*. Routledge.

Holy, L. (1996) *Anthropological Perspectives on Kinship*. Pluto Press.

Horst, H. A., and D. Miller (eds) (2012) *Digital Anthropology*. Berg.

Hoskins, J. (1998) *Biographical Objects: How Things Tell the Stories of People's Lives*. Routledge.

Howell, S. (1989) *Society and Cosmos: Chewong of Peninsular Malaysia*. University of Chicago Press.

Howell, S. (2006) *Kinning of Foreigners: Transnational Adoption in a Global Perspective*. Berghahn Books.

Hua, C. (2008) *A Society without Fathers or Husbands: The Na of China*. MIT Press.

Inda, J. X., and R. Rosaldo (eds) (2008) *The Anthropology of Globalization: A Reader*. 2nd edn, Blackwell.

Ingold, T. (1986) *Evolution and Social Life*. Cambridge University Press.

Ingold, T. (2007) *Lines: A Brief History*. Routledge.

Jackson, M. (1995) *At Home in the World*. Duke University Press.

Jeffrey, S. A., and A. Robben (eds) (2007) *Ethnographic Fieldwork: An Anthropological Reader*. Blackwell.

Kapadia, K. (1995) *Siva and her Sisters: Gender, Caste, and Class in Rural South India*. Perseus.

Kelly, R. L. (1995) *The Foraging Spectrum: Diversity in Hunter-Gatherer Lifeways*. Smithsonian Institution Press.

Kippenberg, H. G., Y. B. Kuiper and A. F. Sanders (eds) (1990) *Concepts of Person in Religion and Thought*. De Gruyter.

Knight, J. (2006) 'Monkey mountain as a megazoo: analyzing the naturalistic claim of "wild monkey parks" in Japan', *Society and Animals* 14(3): 245–64.

Krishtalka, L. R., K. Stucky and K. C. Beard (1990) 'The earliest fossil evidence for sexual dimorphism in primates', *Proceedings of the National Academy of Sciences* 87: 5223–6.

Küchler, S., and G. Were (2003) 'Clothing and innovation: a Pacific perspective', *Anthropology Today* 19(2): 3–5.

Kuper, A. ([1977] 2010) *The Social Anthropology of Radcliffe-Brown*. Routledge & Kegan Paul.

Kutsche, P. (1998) *Field Ethnography: A Manual for Doing Cultural Anthropology*. Prentice-Hall.

Kuwahara, M. (2005) *Tattoo: An Anthropology*. Berg.

La Fontaine, J. S. (ed.) (1972) *The Interpretation of Ritual: Essays in Honour of A. I. Richards*. Tavistock.

Lambert, H. (2001) 'Not talking about sex in India: indirection and the communication of bodily intention', in J. Hendry and B. Watson (eds), *An Anthropology of Indirect Communication*. Routledge.

Latour, B. (2000) 'When things strike back: a possible contribution of "science studies" to the social sciences', *British Journal of Sociology* 51: 107–23.

Leach, E. (1954) *Political Systems of Highland Burma*. Harvard University Press.

Leacock, E. (1978) 'Women's status in egalitarian society: implications for social evolution', *Current Anthropology*, 19(2): 247–75.

Lee, R. (1979) *The !Kung San: Men, Women and Work in a Foraging Society*. Cambridge University Press.

Lepowsky M. (1994) *Fruit of the Motherland: Gender in an Egalitarian Society*. University of Wisconsin Press.

Levine, N. E. (1988) *The Dynamics of Polyandry: Kinship, Domesticity, and Population on the Tibetan Border*. University of Chicago Press.

Lévi-Strauss, C. (1964) *Totemism*, trans. Rodney Needham. Merlin Press.

Lévi-Strauss C (1966) *The Savage Mind*. University of Chicago Press.

Lévi-Strauss, C. (1983) *Mythologiques*. University of Chicago Press.

Lévy-Bruhl, L. ([1910] 1985) *How Natives Think*. Princeton University Press.

Lewin, E. (ed.) (2005) *Feminist Anthropology: A Reader*. Wiley-Blackwell.

Lincoln, B. (1991) *Emerging from the Chrysalis: Rituals of Women's Initiation*. Oxford University Press.

Lock, M., and J. Farquhar (2007) *Beyond the Body Proper: Reading the Anthropology of Material Life*. Duke University Press.

McDonald, J. H. (ed.) (2001) *The Applied Anthropology Reader*. Pearson.

Mageo, J. M. (1994) 'Hairdo's and don't's: hair symbolism and sexual history in Samoa', *Man* 29: 407–32.

Malinowski, B. ([1922] 2014) *Argonauts of the Western Pacific*. Routledge.

Malinowski, B. (1939) 'The group and the individual in functional analysis', *American Journal of Sociology* 44: 938–64.

Malkki, L. (1995) *Purity and Exile: Violence, Memory, and National Cosmology among Hutu Refugees in Tanzania*. University of Chicago Press.

Marchand, T. H. J., and K. Kresse (eds) (2009) *Knowledge in Practice: Expertise and the Transmission of Knowledge*. Edinburgh University Press.

Marvin, G. ([1988] 1994) *Bullfight: A Study of Human and Animal Nature in Andalusia*. University of Illinois Press.

Mauss, M. ([1954] 1970) *The Gift: Forms and Functions of Exchange in Archaic Societies*. Rev. edn, Routledge & Kegan Paul.

Mauss, M. ([1934] 2007) 'Techniques of the body', in M. Lock and J. Farquhar (eds), *Beyond the Body Proper: Reading the Anthropology of Material Life*. Duke University Press.

Mauss, M. ([1979] 2013) *Seasonal Variations of the Eskimo: A Study in Social Morphology*. Routledge.

Mead, M. ([1949] 2001) *Coming of Age in Samoa: A Psychological Study of Primitive Youth for Western Civilisation*. HarperCollins.

Merleau-Ponty, M. ([1962] 2014) *Phenomenology of Perception*. Routledge.

Miller, D. (ed.) (2005) *Materiality*. Duke University Press.

Miller, D. (2008) *The Comfort of Things*. Polity.

Miller, D. (2009) *Stuff*. Polity.

Miller, D. (2011) *Tales from Facebook*. Polity.

Miller, G. (2000) *The Mating Mind: How Sexual Choice Shaped the Evolution of Human Nature*. Heinemann.

Milton, K. (1996) *Environmentalism: The View from Anthropology*. Routledge.

Mithen, S. (2005) *The Singing Neanderthals: The Origins of Music, Language, Mind and Body*. Phoenix Press.

Moore, H. (1988) *Feminism and Anthropology*. Polity.

Morris, B. (1982) *Forest Traders: A Socio-Economic Study of the Hill Pandaram*. Humanities Press.

Morris, B. (1987) *Anthropological Studies of Religion*. Cambridge University Press.

Morris, B. (1995) *Anthropology of the Self: The Individual in Cultural Perspective*. Pluto Press.

Morris, B. (1999) *Being Human Does Not Make You a Person: Animals, Humans and Personhood in Malawi*. Goldsmiths, University of London.

Morris, B. (2000) *The Power of Animals: An Ethnography*. Berg.

Mullan, B., and G. Marvin (1999) *Zoo Culture*. University of Illinois Press.

Murakami, H. (2003) *Underground: The Tokyo Gas Attack and the Japanese Psyche*. Vintage.

Murphy, Y., and R. Murphy (1985) *Women of the Forest*. Columbia University Press.

Nanda, S. ([1989] 1999) *Neither Man nor Woman: The Hijras of India*. 2nd edn, Wadsworth.

Nanda, S. (2000) *Gender Diversity: Crosscultural Variations*. Waveland Press.

Needham, R. (1963) 'The Wikmunkan mother's brother: inference and evidence', *Journal of the Polynesian Society* 72(2): 139–51.

Niehaus, I. (2002) 'Bodies, heat and taboos: conceptualizing modern personhood in the South African lowveld', *Ethnology* 41(3): 189–207.

Noske, B. (1997) *Beyond Boundaries: Humans and Animals*. Black Rose Books.

Nowak, B., and P. Laird (2010) *Cultural Anthropology*. Bridgepoint Education.

Oliphant, E. (2012) 'The crucifix as a symbol of secular Europe: the surprising semiotics of the European Court of Human Rights', *Anthropology Today* 28(2): 10–12.

O'Neil, D. (2009) 'Anthropology of religion: an introduction to folk religion and magic', http://anthro.palomar.edu/tutorials.

Ortner, S. B. (1974) 'Is female to male as nature is to culture?', in M. Z. Rosaldo and L. Lamphere (eds), *Woman, Culture, and Society*. Stanford University Press.

Ortner, S. B. (1984) 'Theory in anthropology since the sixties', *Comparative Studies in Society and History* 26(1):126–66.

Pallier, C. (2007) 'Critical periods in language acquisition and language attrition', in B. Köpke, M. S. Schmid, M. Keijzer and S. Dostert (eds), *Language Attrition: Theoretical Perspectives*. John Benjamins.

Pink, S. (2006) *Applications of Anthropology: Professional Anthropology in the Twenty-First Century*. Berghahn Books.

Rankoana, S. A. (2001) 'Plant-based medicines of the Dikgale of the northern province', *South African Journal of Ethnology* 24(3): 99–104.

Rappaport, R. A. (1968) *Pigs for the Ancestors: Ritual in the Ecology of a New Guinea People*. Yale University Press.

Rappaport, R. A. (1999) *Ritual and Religion in the Making of Humanity*. Cambridge University Press.

Richards, A. (1956) *Chisungu*. Faber & Faber.

Riegelhaupt, J. (1967) 'Saloio women: an analysis of informal and formal political and economic roles of Portuguese peasant women', *Anthropological Quarterly* 40(3): 109–26.

Ritzer, G. ([1983] 2000) *The McDonaldization of Society*. Pine Forge Press.

Rivers, W. H. R. ([1926] 1999) 'The peopling of Polynesia', in Rivers, *Psychology and Ethnology*. Routledge.

Rosaldo, M. (ed.) (1974) *Women, Culture, Society*. Stanford University Press.

Roscoe, W. (1991) *The Zuni Man-Woman*. University of New Mexico Press.

Roscoe, W., and S. O. Murray (eds) (2001) *Boy-Wives and Female Husbands: Studies of African Homosexuality*. St Martin's Press.

Rubin, A. (1988) *Marks of Civilization*. Los Angeles Museum of Cultural History.

Sahlins, M. (1972) *Stone Age Economics*. Transaction.

Sahlins, M. (1976) *Culture and Practical Reason*. University of Chicago Press.

Sanders, T. (2003) 'Reconsidering witchcraft: postcolonial Africa and analytic (un)certainties', *American Anthropologist* 105(2): 338–52.

Scheper-Hughes, N. (1995) 'The primacy of the ethical: propositions for a militant anthropology', *Current Anthropologist*, 36(3): 409–40.

Scheper-Hughes, N., and L. Wacquant (2002) *Commodifying Bodies*. Sage.

Schlegel, A. (1977) *Sexual Stratification: A Cross-Cultural View*. Columbia University Press.

Schneider, D. M. (1984) *A Critique of the Study of Kinship*. University of Michigan Press.

Schumpeter, J. (1928) 'The instability of capitalism', *Economic Journal*, 38(151): 361–86.

Shaw, A., and S. Ardener (2005) *Changing Sex and Bending Gender*. Berghahn Books.

Simpson, A. (2005) 'Sons and fathers/boys to men in the time of AIDS: learning masculinity in Zambia', *Journal of Southern African Studies* 31(3): 569–86.

Smith, V. (1990) *Hosts and Guests*. University of Pennsylvania Press.

Song, H. (2010) *Pigeon Trouble: Bestiary Biopolitics in a Deindustrialized America*. University of Pennsylvania Press.

Spiro, M. E. (1993) 'Is the Western conception of the self "peculiar" within the context of the world cultures?', *Ethos* 21: 107–53.

Spitulnik, D. (1998) 'The language of the city: Town Bemba as urban hybridity', *Journal of Linguistic Anthropology* 8(1): 30–59.

Staples, J. (2010) 'Body', in A. Barnard and J. Spencer (eds), *Encyclopedia of Social and Cultural Anthropology*. 2nd edn, Routledge.

Steward, J. H. ([1955] 1972) *Theory of Culture Change: The Methodology of Multilinear Evolution*. University of Illinois Press.

Stewart, S. (1984) *On Longing: Narratives of the Miniature, the Gigantic, the Souvenir, the Collection*. Johns Hopkins University Press.

Strathern, A. (1971) *The Rope of Moka*. Cambridge University Press.

Strathern, M. (1988) *The Gender of the Gift: Problems with Women and Problems with Society in Melanesia*. University of California Press.

Tambiah, S. J. (1990) *Magic, Science and Religion and the Scope of Rationality*. Cambridge University Press.

Trawick, M. (1990) *Notes on Love in a Tamil Family*. University of California Press.

Trigger, B. (2006) *A History of Archaeological Thought*. Cambridge University Press.

Turnbull, C. M. ([1961] 1987) *The Forest People*. Touchstone.

Turner, T. (1995) 'Social body and embodied subject: bodiliness, subjectivity, and sociality among the Kayapo', *Cultural Anthropology* 10(2): 143–70.

Turner, V. (1967) 'Betwixt and between: the liminal period in *rites de passage*', in Turner, *The Forest of Symbols: Aspects of Ndembu Ritual*. Cornell University Press.

Turner, V. (1969) *The Ritual Process*. Aldine.

Van Gennep, A. ([1909] 1960) *The Rites of Passage*. University of Chicago Press.

Van Meijl, T. (2008) 'Culture and identity in anthropology: reflections on "unity" and "uncertainty" in the dialogical self', *International Journal for Dialogical Science* 3(1): 165–90.

Vansina, J. (1985) *Oral Tradition as History*. James Currey.

Wacquant, L. (2004) *Body & Soul: Notebooks of an Apprentice Boxer*. Oxford University Press.

Ward, T. W. (2012) *Gangsters without Borders: An Ethnography of a Salvadoran Street Gang*. Oxford University Press.

Weiner, A. B. (1992) *Inalienable Possessions: The Paradox of Keeping-While-Giving*. University of California Press.

Westermarck, E. ([1891] 1922) *History of Human Marriage*, Vol. 3. 5th edn, Kessinger.

White, L. A. (1943) 'Energy and evolution of culture', *American Anthropologist* 45(3): 335–56.

Wilson, E. O. (1978) *On Human Nature*. Harvard University Press.

Winslow, D. (1980) 'Rituals of first menstruation in Sri Lanka', *Man: The Journal of the Royal Anthropological Institute* 15(4): 603–25.

Wolf, E. R. (1982) *Europe and People without History*. University of California Press.

Wrangham, R. (2009) *Catching Fire: How Cooking Made Us Human*. Profile Books.

Wrangham, R., and D. Peterson (1997) *Demonic Males: Apes and the Origins of Human Violence*. Mariner Books.

Young, R. W. (2003) 'Evolution of the human hand: the role of throwing and clubbing', *Journal of Anatomy* 202(1): 165–74.

Younghusband, P., and N. Myers (1986) 'Playing God with nature', *International Wildlife* 16(4): 4–13.

Yu, D. and G. Shepard (1998) 'Is beauty in the eye of the beholder?', *Nature*, *396*, 321–2.

Ethnographic films

BBC, *The Incredible Human Journey* (2009), presented by Alice Roberts

BBC, *Origins of Us* (2009), presented by Alice Roberts

BBC, *Prehistoric Autopsy* (2012), presented by Alice Roberts

BBC, *Racism: A History* (2007)

Breeding Cells (2009), directed by Anna Straube, Gregor Gaida, Miren Artola and Saskia Warzecha, Royal Anthropological Institute

Calcutta Calling (2006), directed by André Hörmann

Chain of Love (2001), directed by Marije Meerman, Icarus Films

The City Beautiful (2003), directed by Rahul Roy, Royal Anthropological Institute

Disappearing World series (Granada TV): *The Kayapo* (1987) directed by Michael Beckham, anthropologist Terence Turner

Disappearing World series: *Masai Manhood* (1975), directed by Chris Curling, anthropologist Melissa Llewelyn-Davies

Disappearing World series: *Masai Women* (1974), directed by Chris Curling, anthropologist Melissa Llewelyn-Davies

Disappearing World series: *Ongka's Big Moka: The Kawelka of Papua New Guinea* (1974), directed by Charlie Nairn, anthropologist Andrew Strathern

Disappearing World series: *War: We Are All Neighbours* (1993), directed by Debbie Christie, anthropologist Tone Bringa

Duka's Dilemma (2001), directed by Jean Lydall [in Hamar with English subtitles]

Every Good Marriage Begins with Tears (2006), directed by Simon Chambers

Fatmawati's Wedding: The Weddings of Two Sisters, the Preparations (1998), directed by Fiona Kerlogue, Royal Anthropological Institute

Gods and Satans (2005), directed by Martine Journet and Gerard Nougarol, Royal Anthropological Institute

In and Out of Africa (1993), directed by Ilisa Barbash and Lucien Taylor

The Internet Bride (2004), directed by Eleanor Ford, Royal Anthropological Institute

The Land on which We Stand (2007), directed by Rebecca Payne, Royal Anthropological Institute

Ngat is Dead – Studying Mortuary Traditions (2007), directed by Christian Suhr Nielsen and Ton Otto, Royal Anthropological Institute

Raised by Humans (2010), directed by Karlia Campbell

Schooling the World: The White Man's Last Burden (2010), directed by Carol Black, Lost People Films

Since the Company Came (2001), directed by Russell Hawkins, Icarus Films

Singing Pictures: Women Painters of Naya (2005), directed by Lina Fruzzetti and Ákos Östör, Royal Anthropological Institute

Strange Beliefs: Sir Edward Evans-Pritchard (1902–1973) (1985), directed by André Singer
Temporary Sanity: The Skerrit Bwoy Story (2006), directed by Dan Bruun, Royal Anthropological Institute
Tiempo de Vals (2006), directed by Rebecca Savage, Granada Centre for Visual Anthropology series
Tighten the Drums: Self-Decoration among the Enga (1983), directed by Chris Owen
When Four Friends Meet (2001), directed by Rahul Roy, Royal Anthropological Institute
Without Fathers or Husbands (1995), directed by Hua Cai

Websites

American Anthropological Association: www.aaanet.org
American Anthropological Association: *Handbook on Ethical Issues in Anthropology*. www.aaanet.org/committees/ethics/toc.htm
American Anthropological Association, Statement on Race (17 May 1998): www.aaanet.org/stmts/racepp.htm
Applied Anthropology in the Corporate World: www.youtube.com/watch?v=94fdBg0HBT0
Applied Anthropology videos: www.ovguide.com/applied-anthropology9202a8c04000641f80000000002eda79
Association of Social Anthropologists of the UK and Commonwealth: *Ethical Guidelines for Good Research Practice*. www.theasa.org/ethics/guidelines.shtml
British Museum: www.britishmuseum.org
Ian Condry: http://web.mit.edu/condry/www/Cultural Survival: www.culturalsurvival.org.[non-governmental organization which partners with indigenous communities around the world to defend their lands, languages, and cultures]
Cyborg anthropology: http://cyborganthropology.com [a range of resources and information]
Luis Devin: Anthropological and ethnomusicological fieldwork among hunters and gatherers (Pygmies) and other peoples of Central Africa: www.luisdevin.com/home.php
Horniman Museum www.horniman.ac.uk
Alan Macfarlane: Anthropological fieldwork – a personal account: www.alanmacfarlane.com/FILES/films.html
Museum of Anthropology and Archaeology: http://maa.cam.ac.uk/maa/
National Association for the Practice of Anthropology (NAPA): www.practicinganthropology.org
Patterns of subsistence: http://anthro.palomar.edu/subsistence/default.htm [classification of cultures based on the sources and techniques of acquiring food and other necessities]
Pitt Rivers Museum: www.prm.ox.ac.uk
Pitt Rivers Museum, Body Arts, Virtual Collections: http://web.prm.ox.ac.uk/bodyarts
Race: www.understandingrace.org [Put together by the American Anthropological Association, a great website for understanding the concept of race and all the problems associated with it]
Royal Anthropological Institute www.therai.org.uk
Royal Anthropological Institute, Anthropology in the World conference, 8–10 June 2012: www.youtube.com/watch?v=V6mLr5st-ac
Smithsonian Institution: http://humanorigins.si.edu [gives an excellent interactive overview of human evolution]
Society for Applied anthropology www.sfaa.net

Index